THE ISGAP PAPERS
ANTISEMITISM IN COMPARATIVE PERSPECTIVE
VOLUME TWO

THE ISGAP PAPERS

ANTISEMITISM IN COMPARATIVE PERSPECTIVE

VOLUME TWO

Charles Asher Small

Editor

ISGAP © 2016

New York · Montreal · Kyiv · Tel Aviv · Paris · Rome · Oxford · Vienna

ISGAP
165 East 56th Street, 2nd Floor
New York, New York 10022
Phone: 212-230-1840
Fax: 212-230-1842
www.isgap.org

Cover design and layout by AETS
Cover image by TrotzOlga / Shutterstock

ISBN 978 1 537032 93 1

In memory of Elie Wiesel (ז״ל)

Holocaust survivor, Nobel laureate, champion of the oppressed, and honorary president of ISGAP

An unwavering voice for justice and humanity

Table of Contents

Introduction

Charles Asher Small*

Antisemitism is a highly complex and, at times, perplexing form of hatred. It spans history and has infected many societies, religious and philosophical movements, and even civilizations. In the aftermath of the Holocaust, some contend that antisemitism illustrates the limitations of humanity itself. Manifestations of antisemitism emerge in numerous ideologically-based narratives and in the constructed identities of belonging and otherness such as race and ethnicity, nationalisms, and anti-nationalisms. The investigation of antisemitism has a long and impressive intellectual and research history. It remains a topic of ongoing political importance and scholarly engagement. However, when it comes to the formal study of antisemitism, especially in its contemporary manifestations, such as extreme anti-Israel practice and sentiment and the growth of Islamist antisemitism in the West and the Middle East, there is an unwillingness within the academy to address the topic in accordance with its traditions of serious and unfettered intellectual inquiry. In fact, some might argue that, in this politically correct, postmodern moment, the academy in general has actually been guilty of antisemitism as a result of its refusal to engage with these important issues in an open and honest manner and its attempts to silence those who seek to challenge the new status quo. In other words, the academy itself has become a purveyor of antisemitism in contemporary society.

History teaches that antisemitism affects all of society. It is not just a Jewish parochial issue. As Elie Wiesel warned, antisemitism may begin with the Jews, but it never ends with Jews. Once unleashed, the forces of antisemitism also affect other vulnerable groups in society, including women, religious minorities, gay people, those with unconventional political ideals, and members of the mainstream who are deemed to be impure by these reactionary forces. The rise of political Islam, which incorporates antisemitism at the core of its ideology, has been largely met with acquiescence in the West. As a result, this reactionary social movement has wreaked havoc across the Middle East and beyond, including the ongoing genocide in Syria and a refugee crisis that has spilled over from the Middle East into Europe. In spite of this, the West's response to criticism of its tolerance of political Islam is itself becoming increasingly intolerant, with the emergence of nationalist and xenophobic tendencies becoming more mainstream, as the vacuum created by denial and inaction is filled.

---

* Founder and Executive Director, Institute for the Study of Global Antisemitism and Policy (ISGAP); Visiting Professor, Moshe Dayan Center for Middle Eastern and African Studies, Tel Aviv University.

In 2004, the Institute for the Study of Global Antisemitism and Policy (ISGAP) was established with the aim of promoting the interdisciplinary study of antisemitism—with a focus on the contemporary context—and publishing high-caliber academic research in this area. ISGAP's mission encompasses the study of such subjects as the changing historical phases of antisemitism, regional variations, and how hatred of the Jewish people relates to other forms of hate. From the outset, the aims and objectives of ISGAP have been supported by scholars from many disciplines and countries and by a group of dedicated philanthropists initially led by the great humanitarian William (Bill) Prusoff. ISGAP is committed to countering efforts to sweep antisemitism under the carpet by providing scholarly research, academic programming, curriculum development, and publications of unassailable quality. It is also the only interdisciplinary research organization that is seeking to confront and combat antisemitism within the academy on a practical and ideological level. ISGAP aims to ensure that future generations of scholars and professionals are both aware of the destructive nature of antisemitism and determined to eradicate it from society.

Between 2006 and 2011, ISGAP sponsored the Yale Initiative for the Interdisciplinary Study of Antisemitism (YIISA), the first academic research center dedicated to the study of antisemitism based at a North American university. During this period, YIISA hosted a successful graduate and post-graduate fellowship program, research projects, conferences, and a high-level interdisciplinary seminar series at Yale University. A selection of the papers presented in the framework of this seminar series, as well as several other working papers, conference papers, and lectures commissioned by or submitted to YIISA by eminent scholars and researchers from around the world, was published in 2015 in *The Yale Papers: Antisemitism in Comparative Perspective*. In addition to providing a fascinating overview and scholarly analysis of some of the many facets of historical and contemporary antisemitism around the globe, this substantial volume stands as a solid and incontrovertible testament to the abundant—and, above all, productive—academic activity that characterized YIISA's truncated tenure at Yale.

Since parting ways with Yale, ISGAP has continued to flourish as an independent academic institute that works closely with leading scholars and top tier universities in the United States and around the world. Among its many activities, ISGAP continues to host its "Antisemitism in Comparative Perspective" seminar series at Harvard University, McGill University, and Columbia University Law School. As part of its international efforts, moreover, ISGAP has established seminar series at Rome's Sapienza University (2013), at the Sorbonne University and the Centre National de la Recherche Scientifique (CNRS) in Paris (2014), at the National University of Kyiv-Mohyla Academy in Kiev (2015), and at the American College of Greece in Athens (2016). In June 2016, ISGAP also cosponsored a conference at Sapienza University on the Dynamics and Policies of Prejudice from the Eighteenth to the Twenty-First Century.

Another major ISGAP project is the Summer Institute for Curriculum Development in Critical Antisemitism Studies, a two-week workshop-based program aimed primarily at professors with full-time college or university positions. Under the guidance of leading international scholars, participants in the program design a course syllabus and curriculum for the interdisciplinary study of contemporary antisemitism, which they subsequently implement at their home universities by teaching courses for credit. The first Summer Institute, which took place at the University of Oxford's Hertford College in July 2015, was a resounding success. The second Summer Institute will take place at St Anthony's College, Oxford, in July 2016. This is just one of the many ways in which ISGAP is encouraging and supporting the study of antisemitism within academia.

ISGAP has an active publishing program that includes published collections of conference and seminar papers as well as co-publications with leading international academic publishers. Recent titles include *Global Antisemitism: A Crisis of Modernity* (2013), *The Yale Papers: Antisemitism in Comparative Perspective* (2015), and *The First Shall Be The Last: Rethinking Antisemitism* (2015). In addition to providing information and updates about its various activities, ISGAP's website provides access to a database of academic papers, a large video library of seminar and conference presentations, and the new *Flashpoint* series (2015), which disseminates up-to-date comments and articles on antisemitism, extremism, and global politics. A printed collection of *Flashpoint* articles is scheduled to appear in the near future.

As mentioned above, ISGAP's "Antisemitism in Comparative Perspective" seminar series is still going strong and continues to generate a steady flow of interesting presentations and papers on a wide range of topics relating to antisemitism. Between 2012 and 2014, ISGAP hosted seminars at Harvard University, McGill University, Columbia University Law School, Fordham University's Lincoln Center Campus in New York, the Hoover Institution at Stanford University, the University of Miami, Sapienza University (Rome), and other academic institutions. The present volume contains a selection of papers presented during this period. Like the seminars on which they are based, these papers cover a range of topics that have profound implications for our understanding of historical and contemporary antisemitism, its impact on Jews and non-Jews, and our efforts to combat this irrational yet enduring prejudice. Although originally presented at different times and without an underlying thematical connection, the papers in this volume can be divided into two broad categories.

The papers in the first category examine antisemitism and extremism in the Arab and Muslim world from several different perspectives. The first three papers analyze the roots, current manifestations, and consequences of antisemitism in Turkey, Iran, and the discourse of Hezbollah.

Rıfat Bali presents a detailed overview of the roots, history, and current state of Turkish antisemitism. This issue is often overlooked as a result of the country's location on the outskirts of the Middle East, as well as its status as a secular Muslim state and its supposed history of good relations with the Jews from Ottoman times until the recent crisis in relations with Israel. Contrary to common belief, however, Bali shows that antisemitism was not only clearly evident in the Ottoman period but that it continued following the break-up of the Ottoman Empire, the establishment of the Turkish Republic, and Ataturk's policy of secularization, which have all been blamed on Jewish influence. In practice, an unlikely alliance has developed between Turkish nationalists and Islamists, who accuse the Jews of undermining the state and seeking to overthrow Islam, and left-wing liberals, who are nominally opposed to antisemitism but refuse to condemn it for various reasons, including their heavily pro-Palestinian stance and the Jewish leadership's reluctant position on the Armenian genocide. In the current climate, Bali concludes, Turkey's Jews are obliged to keep a low profile and publicly disavow Zionism in order to stay out of trouble.

In a similar vein, Matthias Küntzel examines the roots and implications of Iranian antisemitism. Despite suggestions to the contrary, this is still a relevant topic in the post-Ahmadinejad era. While Iran appears to have abandoned the virulent antisemitism of its former president, whose claims to be an anti-Zionist were clearly belied by his frequent use of anti-Jewish stereotypes, Holocaust denial and calls for the destruction of Israel, antisemitism is actually deeply rooted in the country's religious, cultural, and political identity in the form of traditional Islamic anti-Judaism, imported Nazi propaganda, and Ayatollah Khomeini's revival of antisemitism, which has formed a key part of the regime's ideology since 1979. In today's Iran, therefore, the Holocaust is still denied, "international Zionism" is still held responsible for all the evils of the world, and Israel's annihilation continues to be propagated—though in a less radical form. The West cherishes the hope that Iran has undergone a fundamental change in this respect—or that such change is genuinely possible—under President Hassan Rouhani. As demonstrated in Küntzel's paper, however, this is clearly not the case.

Matthew Levitt and Kelsey Segawa examine the supposed decline of antisemitism in the public and private discourse of Hezbollah since the late 1990s. Thanks to the organization's strong media presence, they are able to analyze its antisemitic lexicon, the various expressions of its antisemitic ideology, and the impact of this change of direction—if any—on its followers. Hezbollah's antisemitism can be broken down into three familiar categories: insults against the Jewish character, including the classic stereotype of the greedy, power-hungry Jew, abuse of Judaism as a religion, including a revival of the Jewish blood libel, and the propagation of modern-day conspiracy theories, such as Holocaust denial and the idea that the Jews are trying to overthrow Islam. The authors report that there has in fact been little decline in the Hezbollah's use of antisemitic rhetoric in recent years. This is because it continues to play a useful role in fundraising and in drawing attention away from the organization's criminal activities, which include drug trafficking. More importantly, however, antisemitism continues to serve as a moral justification for Hezbollah's terror and political violence, especially at a time when the organization is facing substantial challenges as a result of its involvement in the murder of former Lebanese prime minister Rafiq Hariri and, more recently, its active participation in the war in Syria on the side of the Assad regime.

The next two papers in this category examine the circumstances and conditions that give rise to Muslim extremism and antisemitism. In the process, they try to unravel the religious, social, and cultural connections between these phenomena from a historical and contemporary perspective.

According to Salim Mansur, the key question with regard to Muslim antisemitism is in finding to what extent it is traceable to or rooted in the Qur'an and in the life of Muhammad, and to what extent it is a modern phenomenon that is in part imported from the West and in part a symptom of the deep-seated civilizational crisis within the Muslim world. Mansur argues that Arab and Muslim antisemitism is a modern phenomenon and that attempts by Muslims to give legitimacy to this politics and culture of hate by citing the Qur'an or the traditions of the Prophet as references are not merely misguided but constitute an abuse of Islam and its sacred texts. To successfully confront Muslim hate-mongers and antisemites, it is vital to deny and delegitimize their abusive reading of Islam's sacred texts. According to Mansur, the quelling of Muslim hate-mongers is inseparable from advancing modernist reform of Islam, and this is why non-Muslims are mistaken when they make allowances for Arab and Muslim antisemites cultural, religious, or political grounds.

Meir Litvak examines the causes and outcomes of the so-called Arab Spring, which initially saw Islamists succeed and secular opposition forces fail. As Litvak explains, however, the Muslim Brotherhood soon suffered setbacks in Tunisia and Egypt, where it was side-lined fairly quickly. This contrasts with the fortunes of radical Salafist organizations, which scored violent successes in Iraq, Syria, Yemen, and Libya. Litvak provides a brief but illuminating history of the recent conflict in Syria and the rise of the self-proclaimed Islamic State. In terms of the developments set in motion by the popular uprisings of 2011-2012, both groups of Sunni Islamists have failed in their own ways to bring renewal to the Arab world. The Muslim Brotherhood was not fit (or arguably inclined) to govern, and ISIS has entirely different goals, which have left a trail of death and destruction across the Middle East and beyond. Finally, for two movements with such extreme anti-Jewish and anti-Israel ideologies, there has so far been surprisingly little focus on Israel and the Jews. According to Litvak, this may be explained by the exigencies of their rivalry with Shi'a Islam and their rejection of (Palestinian) nationalism.

The next two papers look at the rise of Muslim antisemitism—particularly in Europe—and the West's mixed response to this alarming development.

Günther Jikeli presents a detailed statistical study and analysis of Muslim antisemitism in Europe, with a focus on Germany, France, and the United Kingdom, which shows that many young Muslims in Europe exhibit antisemitic attitudes, with some resorting to violence and posing a serious threat to Jewish communities in Europe. While polls reveal that fewer European Muslims endorse antisemitic views than Muslims in Islamic countries, they also show that the level of antisemitism is significantly higher among Muslims than among non-Muslims. A study of young male Muslims from Berlin, Paris, and London provides some insights into the sources of and reasoning behind negative views of Jews among young Muslims. The genesis of these views cannot be reduced to a single factor. Ethnic or religious identity and interpretations of Islam are a factor for many. In this sense, use of the term Muslim antisemitism is apt and meaningful. Others relate their hostility toward Jews to their hatred of the State of Israel. At the same time, many use classic antisemitic attitudes that are also widespread in mainstream European society. Jikeli concludes that, while discrimination and exclusion of Muslims in Europe is still a reality, this does not seem to be a relevant factor influencing antisemitic attitudes.

Neil Kressel contends that the West has a dangerous blind spot concerning Muslim antisemitism. Despite recent efforts to raise consciousness, most mainstream political leaders, journalists, scholars, and human rights activists continue to ignore, misunderstand, or downplay the significance of anti-Jewish hostility in the Islamic world. This mentality has its roots in a mixture of apathy, ignorance, confusion, bigotry, ideology, supposed pragmatism, and misguided multiculturalism. On some occasions, the need to avoid engaging the challenge of antisemitism in the Islamic world becomes an all-out effort to sweep this hatred under the carpet. As a result, those who call attention to this prejudice may occasionally find themselves under attack. Shockingly, all these misconceptions and dysfunctional tendencies regarding Muslim antisemitism feature prominently in the works of Western Middle Eastern studies scholars. In other words, the experts who might guide us out of this impasse have—with a few exceptions—become part of the problem. Kressel concludes that those who value human rights ignore antisemitism at their peril. In fact, he argues, the current wave of Muslim antisemitism provides a litmus test to determine whether the West is serious about defending its own values.

The next paper, by Michael Widlanski, examines the impact of similar attitudes on US foreign policy in the Middle East. Specifically, he tracks the effects of various prejudicial ideas—and the role of the media and academia in promoting them—at the highest levels of government and the intelligence community. Widlanski argues that the failure or refusal of the so-called thinking class to hold Arab and Muslim countries to account can be attributed to the twin tendencies of Arabism and Islamophilia, which have been deeply entrenched in the academic and political establishment for decades. In this context, for example, he cites the continued refusal of President Obama and other senior officials to use the terms Islamic extremism and Islamist terror, even in the face of the atrocities perpetrated by al-Qaeda and the self-proclaimed Islamic State. According to Widlanski, these attitudes have also muted the response of successive US administrations to Iran's belligerent policies and antisemitic rhetoric. In addition, he argues that US foreign policy itself has at times been influenced by a strain of bias against Israel and the Jews, ranging from personal antipathy to charges of dual loyalty and far-fetched accusations concerning Israel's influence over US policy.

The second group of papers looks at antisemitism in the context of the enforcement of national and international law against hate speech and incitement, as well as various issues relating to the definition of antisemitism. The first paper focuses on the differences between the US and European approaches to antisemitism and free speech, while the second and third papers focus on the implications of some recent judicial responses to antisemitism in the United States and Poland. The fourth paper assesses the relationship between hate speech and incitement by returning to legal precedents established during the Nuremberg trials. The fifth paper, finally, seeks to explain how and why the unique nature of Nazi antisemitism has been misunderstood in recent Holocaust scholarship.

Alexander Tsesis discusses the fact that the US approach to antisemitic propaganda differs substantially from that of other democracies around the world. Despite the historical differences that inform this discrepancy, he demonstrates that there is as much reason to regulate antisemitic speech in the United States as there is abroad. On the whole, the value accorded to free speech in the United States is no different than the importance of free expression in other countries. What is different is the much more limited regulation of hate speech in the United States. The US Supreme Court's jurisprudence has established doctrinal barriers against the creation of robust laws against hateful incitement. In practice, this means that a variety of expressive conducts, such as Holocaust revisionism and outright denial, are protected under current First Amendment doctrine even though other democratic countries outlaw them. According to Tsesis, it is therefore high time to look for ways to bring the United States into line with other democracies in this regard. Options include expanding existing restrictions on hate symbols, bringing group defamation suits, and acknowledging that the Supreme Court has long recognized that it is outside the scope of the First Amendment to expose citizens of any race, color, creed, or religion to "contempt, derision, or obloquy."

Kenneth Marcus examines the legal response to campus antisemitism in the United States. He starts by recalling that on one day in 2013 the US Department of Education's Office for Civil Rights (OCR) dismissed four cases in which the complainants argued that university administrators at three campuses of the University of California had tolerated direct harassment of Jewish students and the creation of a hostile environment. In all four cases, the OCR rejected claims that the students' rights had been violated. Marcus argues that the failure to pursue these (and other) cases of campus antisemitism to their proper conclusion can be boiled down to three key factors: a reluctance to grant Jews protection under Title VI of the Civil Rights Act, which prohibits certain discrimination on the basis of race, color, or national origin but not on the basis of religion, an unwillingness to classify certain types of criticism of Israel as antisemitic, and concerns that the suppression or punishment of antisemitic speech would violate the First Amendment or at the very least create a public backlash. Marcus shows how these obstacles can be overcome while protecting freedom of speech and ensuring greater civility on campus.

Aleksandra Gliszczyńska-Grabias notes that great strides have been made in combating antisemitism in Poland in recent years, but cites three antisemitism cases that were dismissed on questionable grounds as proof that much still remains to be done in this area. These cases are significant, she notes, because the law plays such an important role in the fight against antisemitism. When the state uses its authority to punish hate speech and hate crimes, it sends a clear signal as to what it considers an unacceptable abuse of rights and freedoms. However, three conditions must be fulfilled simultaneously. First, the law must be implemented in an effective way and without any exceptions. Second, public authorities and officials must openly speak out against racist and xenophobic hatred every time it appears in the public sphere. Finally, legal actions must be accompanied by responsible and honest efforts to educate. Fortunately, responsible judges and prosecutors are increasingly willing to call racism and antisemitism by their true names. Other positive developments include the launch of a series of training courses on hate speech and hate crimes for police officers, prosecutors, and judges by the Polish ombudsman and the prosecutor general, as well as the ongoing projects of the "Open Republic" Association against Anti-Semitism and Xenophobia.

Gregory Gordon takes a fresh look at the relationship between hate speech and incitement. The conventional wisdom is that atrocity speech law sprang fully formed from two judgments issued by the International Military Tribunal at Nuremberg (IMT): the conviction of Nazi newspaper editor Julius Streicher of crimes against humanity and the acquittal on the same charge of Third Reich Radio Division Chief Hans Fritzsche. Gordon argues that this exclusive focus on the IMT judgments is misplaced. Not long after, the United States Nuremberg Military Tribunal (NMT) issued an equally significant judgment against Reich Press Chief Otto Dietrich, who was found guilty of persecution as a crime against humanity for his inflammatory language in support of the Hitler regime, despite the fact that the language at issue did not directly call for violence. This judgment is significant today because the latest generation of atrocity speech decisions is still at loggerheads over the relationship between hate speech and persecution as a crime against humanity: the International Criminal Tribunal for Rwanda (ICTR) has found that such speech, standing alone, can form the basis of a charge of crimes against humanity, while the International Criminal Tribunal for the former Yugoslavia (ICTY) has reached the opposite conclusion. Like much of the academic discourse, these judicial decisions completely ignore the *Dietrich* judgment. Gordon remedies this omission by historically situating the case, elucidating its holding and its relationship to the IMT and ICTR/ICTY decisions, describing its significance for current and future hate speech cases, and explaining why it has lain in obscurity for over six decades.

In the final paper in this collection, Dan Michman examines how the unique nature of Nazi antisemitism has been misrepresented in some recent studies on the Holocaust. Attempts to properly understand the Holocaust have given rise to decades of research. Explanations focus on a variety of issues, but it is commonly accepted that the Final Solution was a central feature of the entire Nazi project and that its ultimate purpose was to wipe out the Jewish people. Recently, however, some scholars have reinterpreted and recontextualized the Holocaust as a simple murder campaign by claiming that it had no special or extraordinary characteristics or dimensions. In doing so, they turn antisemitism in general and Nazi antisemitism in particular into just another ethnic or social hatred like so many others. Michman argues that this failure to understand or acknowledge the unique scope and nature of the Holocaust is sometimes the result of insufficient knowledge of the relevant sources but that efforts to downplay the true motivations behind the Holocaust may also result from non-scholarly considerations, such as competing victimhoods, political correctness, anti-Israelism, and perhaps even a covert form of new antisemitism. He rightly concludes that a detailed analysis of the reasons for this omission is undoubtedly deserving of further study.

* * *

ISGAP's core mission is to encourage high-caliber academic research that seeks to map, decode, and combat antisemitism. As well as serving an important purpose in its own right, we believe that such scholarship will spur the academy to accept and encourage the study of this unique and timeless hatred. It is the hope of all those connected with ISGAP that the papers in this volume will stimulate and inspire readers, help them understand the changing realities of contemporary antisemitism, and encourage them to develop policies and strategies to combat and defeat this and other destructive hatreds. With the publication of this latest volume, as well as all its other academic efforts, ISGAP continues to fight antisemitism on the battlefield of ideas.

The Roots and Themes of Turkish Antisemitism

Rıfat Bali*

Although a great number of words of foreign origin have established themselves within the Turkish language, and the term "antisemitism" is even found in the official dictionary of the *Türk Dil Kurumu*, or Turkish Language Association, neither the Turkish cultural sphere nor the Turkish "man in the street" can be said to know the meaning of the term "antisemitism," and the general preference is for the term *yahudi düşmanlığı*—literally, "hostility toward Jews." This statement is likewise valid for the adjectival form "antisemitic," with the country's media and intelligentsia using the strange neologism "antisemitist" in its place. How did such a word, which, although of Western origin, has no equivalent in European languages, come to take root in Turkish? The answer is very simple. The word "antisemitist" was actually inspired by and created as a sort of linguistic equivalent of the term "communist." But what at first glance seems to be a simple observation about the Turkish language shows us just how alien the subject of antisemitism is to much of the Turkish intellectual world.

I. "Antisemitism Does Not Exist in Turkey"

A widespread opinion in Turkey, one repeated ad nauseum et ad infinitum by politicians and social commentators and almost reactively mouthed by a broad swath of the Turkish public is that antisemitism is an ideology that was created within the Christian world but is not encountered within Turkey. One of the classic arguments frequently repeated by Islamist intellectuals and columnists is that antisemitism is a sin from the Islamist point of view. Of course, for an Islamist a "good Jew" is not a Zionist, whereas a "bad Jew" is one by definition. And this assessment is valid for all Jews, whether living in the State of Israel or the Diaspora.[1] Thus, in such circles, one can publish all manner of insult and calumny against "bad Jews" and not consider oneself an antisemite, nor be considered such by others.

Another argument that is often tacked onto the previous one is that antisemitism is a phenomenon and ideology foreign to Turkey, since both the Ottoman Empire and its successor the Turkish Republic have historically shown great tolerance

* Research Fellow, Alberto Benveniste Center for Sephardic Studies and Culture, Religious Studies Department, École Pratique des Hautes Études, Sorbonne; Member, Ottoman-Turkish Sephardic Culture Research Center.

[1] Ali Bulaç, "İsrail, dinî mi?," *Zaman*, January 10, 2009.

toward their Jewish citizens. The three pieces of evidence usually appealed to in order to bolster this claim are: (a) Sultan Beyazıd II's acceptance of Jewish refugees from Spain after their expulsion in 1492;[2] (b) the rescue of "hundreds" of former Turkish Jews from the Nazi death camps by several Turkish diplomats during the Second World War;[3] and (c) the acceptance and university employment of dozens of dismissed Jewish scholars and scientists fleeing Nazi Germany in the early 1930s.[4]

For these reasons, there is a readily observable phenomenon in Turkey whereby all manner of writers, intellectuals, and opinion makers from all ends of the political spectrum, including Islamists, neo-nationalists, mainstream nationalists, Kemalists, and others—an assembly of diverse persons who would never agree on anything else—all seem to agree on this topic and readily parrot the claim of "continued Ottoman and Turkish tolerance and humane treatment toward the Jews." Nevertheless, scholarly research has appeared in recent years that would belie this notion of "continued tolerance," showing it to be largely a myth constructed for the purpose of public relations in countering claims concerning the so-called "Armenian genocide" originating from the United States and Europe.[5] Although this may change in time, at present this historical "revision" has barely made a ripple outside of academic circles, and both the Turkish public and officialdom continue to mouth—and, by all appearances, believe—the official line of Turkish tolerance and the non-existence of antisemitism.

More troubling than the fact that revisionist arguments are not being accepted is the fact that the claim of continued tolerance is simply untrue. Antisemitism has manifested itself in various forms within the Turkish polity and ruling classes ever since the very beginning of the Turkish Republic. Between its establishment in 1923

---

2 For an unpublished work on this subject, see Erkan Erçal, "Desiring Jews: The Fantasy of Ottoman Tolerance" (master's thesis, York University, Toronto, 2005).

3 For works heavily stressing the "official" Turkish line on the rescue of Turkish Jews during the Holocaust, see Stanford J. Shaw, *Turkey and the Holocaust: Turkey's Role in Rescuing Turkish and European Jewry From Nazi Persecution, 1933-1945* (New York University Press, 1993); Arnold Reisman, *Shoah: Turkey, the US and the UK* (Charlestone: Booksurge, 2009); Arnold Reisman, *An Ambassador and a Mensch: The Story of a Turkish Diplomat in Vichy France* (Lexington: CreateSpace Independent Publishing Platform, 2010).

4 On the experience of the Jewish refugees, see Arnold Reisman, *Turkey's Modernization: Refugees from Nazism and Atatürk's Vision* (Washington D.C.: New Academia Publishing, 2006); Fritz Neumark, *Zuflucht am Bosphorus: Deutsche Gelehrte, Politiker und Kulnster in der Emigration: 1933-1953* (Frankfurt am Main: Knecht, 1980); Horst Widmann, *Exil und Bildungshilfe. Die Deutschsprachige Akademische Emigration in die Türkei nach 1933, Mit einer Bio-Bibliographie der emigrierten Hochschullehrer im Anhang* (Bern/Frankfurt am Main: Peter Lang, 1973); Murat Ergin, "Cultural Encounters in the Social Sciences and Humanities: Western Émigré Scholars in Turkey," *History of the Human Sciences* 22, no. 1 (February 2009): 105-30; Kemal Bozay, *Exil Türkei: Ein Forschungsbeitrag zur Deutschsprachigen Emigration in der Türkei (1933-1945)* (Lit-Verlag, 2001).

5 On the use of this argument as "counter-propaganda," see Rıfat N. Bali, *Model Citizens of the State: The Jews of Turkey During the Multi-Party Period* (Langham: Rowman and Littlefield, 2012). For a recent work dismantling the "official" Turkish version of events, whereby Turkish diplomats in Nazi-occupied Europe went out of their way to rescue former Turkish Jews from the camps, see Corry Guttstadt, *Turkey, the Jews, and the Holocaust* (Cambridge University Press, 2013).

and the end of one-party rule in 1946, antisemitism was repeatedly—if intermittently—expressed within the Turkish press and among the intelligentsia through various campaigns, ranging from accusations that the country's Jews were resisting assimilation into Turkish society, including a refusal to even learn Turkish or speak it in public, to claims that they were controlling or exploiting the Turkish economy.[6] During this period, the various humor magazines were full of caricatures of Jews straight out of Nazi iconography. The recurring archetypes of Salomon, a hook-nosed, bearded Jew, and his wife Rebeka can be found throughout these years. The couple are depicted as dirty—afraid of water, even—miserly, capable of all manner of intrigue and subterfuge if it brings them monetary advantage, and always speaking with a ridiculous and easily identifiable Jewish accent.

II. Cevat Rifat Atilhan: State-Sponsored Antisemitism?

One of the leading figures most closely identified with antisemitism during this period is the retired colonel and veteran of the Turkish War of Independence, Cevat Rıfat Atilhan. He published numerous works of antisemitism and remained active in this field until his death in 1967, in the process profoundly influencing generations of intellectuals, journalists, and politicians on Turkey's Islamic and ultra-nationalist right.[7] In general, the question whether antisemitism is very widespread in Turkey and what role Atilhan played in its spread are not very often discussed. Nevertheless, a recent event provides some evidence of an affirmative answer to both questions. In a lengthy interview given shortly after the Israel Defense Forces boarded the "Gaza flotilla" ship *Mavi Marmara* in 2010,[8] Hüseyin Çelik, Deputy Chairman in charge of Publicity and Media in the Justice and Development Party (JDP) government, made the following reference to Atilhan in regard to antisemitism:

Q: You conducted research on Turkish politics, you're someone at the very center of political life. What do you see? When Israel makes a mistake, do suppressed antisemitic feelings tend to come to the surface? Does every one of those offenses awaken those previously dormant feelings?

---

[6] On this subject, see Rıfat N. Bali, *Cumhuriyet Yıllarında Türkiye Yahudileri—Bir Türkleştirme Serüveni (1923-1945)* (Istanbul: İletişim Yayınları, 1999); Rıfat N. Bali, "Politics of Turkification During the Single Party Period," in *Turkey Beyond Nationalism: Towards Post-Nationalist Identities*, ed. Hans-Lukas Kieser (I.B. Tauris, 2006).

[7] For a biography of Atilhan, see Celil Bozkurt, *Yahudilik ve Masonluğa Karşı Cevat Rıfat Atilhan* (Istanbul: Doğu Kütüphanesi, 2012); Rıfat N. Bali, *Musa'nın Evlâtları Cumhuriyet'in Yurttaşları* (Istanbul: İletişim Yayınları, 2001), 211-56; Özen Karaca, "The Theme of Jewish Conspiracy in Turkish Nationalism: The Case of Cevat Rıfat Atilhan" (master's thesis, Middle East Technical University, Ankara, 2008).

[8] On May 31, 2010, the Israel Defense Forces boarded various ships sailing to the Gaza Strip as part of the so-called "Gaza Freedom Flotilla," which claimed its mission was to break the Israeli naval boycott on the Hamas-ruled territory and deliver humanitarian supplies. After attempting to board the ship *Mavi Marmara*, which was sent by the Turkish Islamic Foundation for Human Rights and Freedoms and Humanitarian Relief or IHH, the forces met resistance and at first aborted the boarding, only to return later in greater force, during the course of which one Turkish American and eight Turkish nationals were killed. Source: "Gaza Flotilla raid," https://en.wikipedia.org/wiki/Gaza_flotilla_raid.

A: I actually think that it's the opposite situation. For example, you know that Cevat Rıfat Atilhan's antisemitist book was purchased by the Turkish Army in the 1940s and some 50,000 copies were distributed among the army.[9] And this was performed by the hand of the state. These books had antisemitism as their basis. From Cevat Rıfat Atilhan's time until now a great number of antisemitists have appeared in Turkey. And there is a history of antisemitism in Turkey. But with us there's no antisemitism and such. Look at the other side; if it weren't for our Prime Minister's reactions [to Israel's actions], antisemitism in Turkey would be far greater.

Q: In other words, it's only because of this that it's being held in check and not bursting out openly?

A: Absolutely! The public thinks in the manner of: "My country responds the way that it needs to respond."

Q: And it's calming down, isn't it?

A: Yes, it is calming down, because [the Turkish public feels that] "Tayyip Erdoğan is speaking in my name." With his famous "one minute" statement at Davos,[10] he embodied and gave voice to a number of feelings that people had suppressed for many long years. The Prime Minister is trying to be the voice of the Turkish nation and, in this sense, also that of humanity's conscience.

---

9 The aforementioned book is *Suzi Liberman, Yahudi Casusu* (Suzy Liberman, Jewish spy), which was published in 1935. The book's introduction (and in subsequent printings its cover) mentions that upon its review by the Office of the Turkish Chief of Staff an order (#43782) was issued on May 26, 1935 purchasing 40,000 copies of the work and offering it to Turkish army officers.

10 "At the 2009 World Economic Forum in Davos, Switzerland, [David] Ignatius moderated a discussion including Turkish Prime Minister Recep Tayyip Erdoğan, Israeli President Shimon Peres, UN Secretary-General Ban Ki-moon, and Arab League Secretary-General Amr Moussa. As the December 2008-January 2009 conflict in Gaza was still fresh in memory, the tone of the discussion was lively. Ignatius gave Erdoğan 12 minutes to speak, and gave the Israeli President the final 25 minutes to respond. Erdoğan objected to Peres' tone and raised voice during the Israeli President's impassioned defense of his nation's actions. Ignatius gave Erdoğan a minute to respond, and when Erdoğan went over his allocated minute, Ignatius repeatedly cut the Turkish Prime Minister off, telling him and the audience that they were out of time and that they had to get to a dinner. Erdoğan seemed visibly frustrated as he said to the President of Israel, 'When it comes to killing, you know well how to kill.' Ignatius put his arm on Erdoğan's shoulder and kept telling him that his time was up. Erdoğan then gathered his papers and said, 'I do not think I will be coming back to Davos after this because you do not let me speak.' Erdoğan then got up from his chair and walked off the stage while the other discussion panelists were still seated, but Amr Moussa stood up to shake his hand as he left. At that point the discussion ended. Five minutes after the discussion ended, Peres called Erdoğan to apologize for any misunderstanding. Erdoğan later told reporters that he was not upset with Peres, rather he was upset with Ignatius for failing to moderate the discussion impartially, by giving Peres 25 minutes to speak while earlier giving Erdoğan only 12 minutes and then just another minute to respond to Peres. Erdoğan returned to Istanbul a day later to a hero's welcome at the airport." Source: https://en.wikipedia.org/wiki/David_Ignatius. Erdoğan's demand to the moderator David Ignatius for "one minute" more to continue talking has become known to the Turkish public as the "one minute" speech. For Ignatius' take on the event, see David Ignatius, "Caught in the Middle," *Foreign Policy*, April 15, 2009.

Q: What would you say in regard to the Prime Minister's use of the Star of David, which is the symbol of the Jewish faith, and the swastika in the same sentence?[11]

A: I would say to you the following: the attitude of our government is clear. In the final analysis, the actions we have taken have not given rise to antisemitism and such, on the contrary. Indeed, antisemitism was long animated and allowed to flourish by the hand of the state in Turkey.

I'm telling you, 50,000 copies of an antisemitist work written by a former officer were ordered by the Turkish Army and distributed [within its ranks]. But we say to this "No. All 73 million citizens, regardless of their religion, ethnicity, color, or denomination are full, equal citizens of the Turkish Republic."

The fact is, if today there was any other party than the JDP in power and such events were to take place, if this had not been the JDP's attitude and there wasn't this effective and influential foreign policy [on the part of the JDP], believe me, antisemitism would have increased much more. What I am saying here is very important; don't ignore it.[12]

It is true that, in the early years of the Republic, one of Atilhan's books was indeed endorsed and offered to members of the Turkish armed forces by the country's Chief of Staff. But the more fundamental truth that Hüseyin Çelik failed to state is that it was not the Kemalists and members of the military who were most influenced by Atilhan's ideas but the "older generation" of Islamists and nationalists. It should be pointed out that Hüseyin Çelik is not simply a run-of-the mill politician. Rather, he is a former faculty member with a PhD in sociology and the author of some twelve books.[13] Thus, when Çelik speaks of Atilhan and those affected by him, he does so from a place of familiarity and knowledge. Even so, Hüseyin Çelik prefers to place the blame for antisemitism in Turkey solely at the feet of the Kemalists. But it is Çelik's own words about how the JDP's effective foreign policy is responsible for reducing the amount of antisemitism in Turkey that unwittingly stand as the clearest admission of just how widespread antisemitism is—not among the Kemalists, but among the Islamists and conservatives that form the bulk of his party's constituency.

The phrase "older generation of Islamists" refers to those politicians associated with the "National View" (*Millî Görüş*) ideology[14] of the founder of Turkish political

---

11 The event in question is a speech that Erdoğan gave in Konya on June 4, 2010, in which the prime minister criticized Israel, saying that "Israel has put both its government and its people into difficulty with its belligerent policies, it has isolated itself and damaged its image in the eyes of the world," further adding that "the [Israeli] government is the reason that world opinion now tends to equate the Star of David with the swastika, and I believe that this bothers the Israeli public." Source: Sedat Ergin, "Nazizmle Yahudiliğin sembolleri bir tutulabilir mi?," *Hürriyet*, June 16, 2010.

12 Devrim Sevimay, "Başbakan bu tavrı koymazsa antisemitizm daha çok artar," *Milliyet*, June 14, 2010.

13 For Çelik's biography, see his website at http://www.huseyincelik.net.

14 Ahmet Yıldız, "Politico-Religious Discourse of Political Islam in Turkey: The Parties of National Outlook," *The Muslim World* 93, no. 2 (April 2003): 187-209; Necmettin Erbakan, *Millî Görüş* (Istanbul: Dergâh Yayınları, 1975); "Millî Görüş," https://en.wikipedia.org/wiki/Milli_Gorus. For some studies on the National View movement and its principal organization in the Federal Republic of Germany, the Islamische Gemeinschaft Millî Görüş (IGMG), see Daniel

Islam Necmettin Erbakan,[15] as well as the journalists and writers who have adopted it. This movement began in tandem with Erbakan's establishment in 1970 of the short-lived National Order Party (*Millî Nizam Partisi*) (January 26, 1970-May 20, 1971). Although Turkey's Constitutional Court ultimately ordered the party shut down for actions "contrary to the principles of the secular nature of the state and the defense of Atatürk's revolutionaryism," Erbakan and his followers quickly established another Islamist party, the National Salvation Party (*Millî Selamet Partisi*) (October 11, 1972-October 16, 1981), which in the wake of the September 1980 military coup would eventually meet the same fate as its predecessor.[16] With the return to multi-party democracy after the military coup of September 1980, further attempts to create an Islamist party were made through the Welfare Party (*Refah Partisi*) (July 19, 1983-January 16, 1998),[17] the Virtue Party (*Fazilet Partisi*) (December 17, 1997-June 22, 2001),[18] and the current Felicity Party (*Saadet Partisi*) (July 20, 2001-).[19] After the banning of the Virtue Party following a "soft coup" against its coalition government, the Islamist movement met with a major schism, with many of the party's young guard, including Prime Minister Recep Tayyip Erdoğan and President Abdullah Gül, publicly declaring a break with the National View ideology and reforming as the Justice and Development Party (*Adalet ve Kalkınma Partisi*). While unthinkable in the past, in this party the "new generation of Islamists" sat side-by-side with conservatives, nationalists, and liberals.[20]

Timm, *Politischer Islam: Millî Görüş in Deutschland* (Munich: Grin Verlag, 2010); Göksel Yılmaz, *Millî Görüş: Vertreterin des Politische Islam in der Türkei: Eine Historische Analyse: 1970-2000* (Munich: Grin Verlag, 2003); Ahmet Yükleyen, "State Policies and Islam in Europe: Millî Görüş in Germany and the Netherlands," *Journal of Ethnic and Migration Studies* 36, no. 3 (2010): 445-63; Werner Schiffauer, *Nach dem Islamismus. Die Islamische Gemeinschaft Millî Görüş—Eine Ethnographie* (After Islamism. An ethnographic study of the Islamic movement Millî Görüş) (Frankfurt am Main: Suhrkamp Verlag, 2010); David Vielhaber, "The Mili Görüş of Germany," *Current Trends in Islamist Ideology* 13 (June 2012), http://www.currenttrends.org/research/detail/the-milli-gorus-of-germany.

15 For a short biography on Necmettin Erbakan, see "Who is Erbakan," http://www.gencsaadet.com/2011/03/who-is-erbakan and "Necmettin Erbakan," https://en.wikipedia.org/wiki/Necmettin_Erbakan.

16 Jacob M. Landau, *Politics and Islam: The National Salvation Party in Turkey* (Salt Lake City, Utah: Middle East Center, University of Utah, 1976); Türker Alkan, "The National Salvation Party in Turkey," in *Islam and Politics in the Modern Middle East*, ed. Metin Heper and Raphael Israeli (New York: St. Martin's Press, 1984), 79-102; Binnaz Toprak, "Politicisation of Islam in a Secular State: The National Salvation Party in Turkey," in *From Nationalism to Revolutionary Islam*, ed. Said Amir Arjomand (Albany: State University of New York Press, 1984), 119-33.

17 For more information on the establishment and closing of the Welfare Party, see Haldun Gülalp, "Political Islam in Turkey: The Rise and Fall of the Refah Party," *The Muslim World* 89, no. 1 (January 1999): 22-41.

18 For more information on the Welfare Party's successor, the Virtue Party, see Birol A. Yeşilada, "The Virtue Party," *Turkish Studies* 3, no. 1 (Spring 2002): 62-81.

19 "Felicity Party," https://en.wikipedia.org/wiki/Felicity_Party.

20 On the JDP, see M. Hakan Yavuz, ed., *The Emergence of a New Turkey: Democracy and the AK Parti* (Salt Lake City: Utah University Press, 2006); Ümit Cizre, ed., *Secular and Islamic Politics in Turkey: The Making of the Justice and Development Party* (London/New York: Routledge, 2008); Arda Can Kumbaracıbaşı, *Turkish Politics and the Rise of the AKP* (London/New York: Routledge, 2009); William Hale and Ergun Özbudun, *Islamism, Democracy and Liberalism in*

Now that we have established the widespread nature of antisemitism in Turkey, the next step is to examine the main themes that are encountered in Turkish antisemitism and analyze the reasons for its emergence.

III. Is there such a thing as Turkish antisemitism?

At this point we should take a few moments to consider the concept of Turkish antisemitism. When the question is broached about whether antisemitism exists in Turkey, those arguing against its existence tend to claim that: (1) if there is antisemitism in Turkey, it tends to be marginal; and (2) in any case it is a foreign strain, introduced from the West, that has never really been accepted in Turkish society. Although this claim is partially correct, as a whole it is simply wrong. It is correct that a great many aspects of Turkish antisemitism are "imports," but it is equally true that there is no lack of "local" themes, and it is due to these local themes—not foreign elements—that antisemitism exists in Turkey and is so widespread, especially among Islamists and ultra-nationalists.

1. Foreign themes

The most significant of the "foreign imports" that have influenced Turkish antisemitism are, without doubt, the various translations of *The Protocols of the Elders of Zion.*[21] In addition to the *Protocols,* the theme of "Jewish world domination" is prevalent in other antisemitic publications.[22] Variations on this theme include claims:

– that the ultimate goal of Zionism is a "Greater Israel" that stretches "from the Nile to the Euphrates;"[23]

Turkey: The Case of the AKP (London/New York: Routledge, 2009); Hasan Turunc, "Islamicist or Democratic? The AKP's Search for Identity in Turkish Politics," *Journal of Contemporary European Studies* 15, no. 1 (2007): 79-91; Şebnem Gümüşçü and Deniz Sert, "The Power of the Devout Bourgeoisie: The Case of the Justice and Development Party in Turkey," *Middle Eastern Studies* 45, no. 6 (2009): 953-68; Fulya Atacan, "Explaining Religious Politics at the Crossroad: AKP-SP," *Turkish Studies* 6, no. 2 (2005): 187-99.

[21] For a report—albeit not up-to-date at this point—on antisemitic publications in Turkey, see "The hate industry: in recent years, anti-Semitic publications are becoming increasingly widespread in Turkey. The Islamic government of Turkey does not do enough to prevent the distribution of the anti-Semitic publications, even though some of them are aimed against it and its policy" (Intelligence and Terrorism Information Center at the Israel Intelligence Heritage and Commemoration Center (IICC), January 17, 2008), http://www.terrorism-info.org.il/data/pdf/PDF_08_013_2.pdf.

[22] On this subject, see Jacob M. Landau, "Muslim Attitudes Towards Jews, Zionism and Israel," in *Jews, Arabs, Turks: Selected Essays,* ed. Jacob M. Landau (Jerusalem: The Magnes Press, 1993), 77-86.

[23] For a discussion of the historical roots of the term "Greater Israel," see the web article: "Greater Israel," https://en.wikipedia.org/wiki/Greater_Israel. For more on the "Nile to the Euphrates" calumny, see Daniel Pipes, "Imperial Israel: The Nile-to-Euphrates Calumny," *Middle East Quarterly* (March 1994). For a study of the Palestine Liberation Organization's repeated use of this accusation, see Itamar Marcus and Barbara Crook, "From the Nile to the Euphrates—PA Continuous Libel (1997-2007) about Secret Plan to Conquer Arab Nation" (United Jerusalem Foundation, June 12, 2007), http://www.unitedjerusalem.org/index2.asp?id=930949&Date=5/10/2012.

- that Freemasonry is simply a tool used by Zionism and Jewry to achieve their goal of "world domination;"[24]
- that the Lions, Rotary, and the Bilderberg Group are all organizations that are under the control of the Jews;[25]
- that both communism and capitalism are Jewish ideologies;[26]
- that Wall Street, Hollywood, and the American media are all in the hands of the Jews;[27] and
- that the father of Marxism, Karl Marx, was a Jew and that the Jews played a major role in the Bolshevik revolution, proving that communism is a Jewish ideology.[28]

Among the aforementioned themes, the recurring figures of the "Freemasons," the "Communists," and the "Jews" served during the 1960s and 1970s as the three principle "enemies" of the Islamists and nationalists. A play entitled *Mas-Kom-Yah,* staged in the 1970s, best explains the powerful symbolic value of these three groups. The play, whose title is an abbreviated amalgamation of the Turkish words for "Mason," "Communist," and "Yahudi" (Jew), was written and staged in 1977 by Turkey's current Prime Minister [now President—*Ed.*] Recep Tayyip Erdoğan, who

[24] On this claim's spread in the West, see https://en.wikipedia.org/wiki/Masonic_conspiracy_theories.

[25] For the various Turkish publications making this claim, see Ali Uğur, *Görünmeyen Önderler Rotary ve Lions Kulüpleri,* 2nd ed. (Istanbul: Burak Yayınları, 1989); Cenkhan Yılmaz, *Rotary ve Rotarienler* (Ankara: Türk Kültür Yayınevi, 1979) (Cenkhan Yılmaz was actually the nom de plume of Ali Uğur, see Mehmet Cemal Çiftçigüzeli, http://www.sanatalemi.net/kose_yazi.asp?ID=1021); Selahaddin Eş, *Kavşak Noktasında Türkiye'nin Siyasi Görüşü* (Bir Düşünce Yayınları, 1977), 168-69; Halil İbrahim Çelik, "Lions ve Rotaryenler Yahudi Kontrolünde," *Cuma,* July 24, 1992, 105; "Siyonizmin Görünmeyen Gizli Örgütleri gibi tanıtılan Lions, Rotary ve Mason Örgütleridir," *İslam* (August 1988): 7-19; I.H. Pirzade, *Türkiye ve Yahudiler* (Istanbul: Ark Matbaacılık, 1968), 28-34. For more on the Bilderberg conspiracy, see "Bilderberg mystery: Why do people believe in cabals?," *BBC News Magazine,* June 8, 2011, http://www.bbc.co.uk/news/magazine-13682082.

[26] The allusion here is to the Rothschild family and other wealthy Jewish-American businessmen. Such names are frequently mentioned in stressing that the "fathers of large-scale capital" were Jewish and that the very system itself is of Jewish origin. The seemingly contradictory idea is widespread that both opposing systems were created by the Jews as a means of controlling the world.

[27] Regarding the claims of "Jewish control" of the American media, see Mark Crispin Miller, "The Jewish Media: The Lie That Won't Die," *Extra!* (September-October 1996), http://www.fair.org/index.php?page=1365; "Allegations of Jewish control of the media" (work in progress), https://en.wikipedia.org/wiki/User:Pseudo-Richard/Allegations_of_Jewish_control_of_the_media. On conspiracy theories about Jewish control of the American financial system, see Anti-Defamation League, "Jewish 'Control' of the Federal Reserve: A Classic Anti-Semitic Myth" (special report, July 1995), http://www.adl.org/special_reports/control_of_fed/print.asp. On the theory of Jewish control of Hollywood, see Anti-Defamation League, "Alleged Jewish 'Control' of the American Motion Picture Industry" (special report, September 1999), http://www.adl.org/special_reports/movie_industry/print.asp.

[28] For more on the claim of Jewish control of the Bolshevik Revolution, see "Jewish Bolshevism," https://en.wikipedia.org/wiki/Jewish_Bolshevism; Andre Gerrets, *The Myth of Jewish Communism* (Frankfurt am Main: Peter Lang, 2009).

at the time was the 23-year-old president of the youth branch of the National View–oriented National Salvation Party.[29]

With the fall of the Soviet Union in 1991, the persistent theme of "communism as a Jewish invention" began to disappear from the discussion within Turkish rightist circles. Nevertheless, talk of Freemasonry as a Jewish tool and of "Jewish control" of Wall Street, Hollywood, and the American media have continued apace, along with other variations on the "Jewish world domination" theme. For example, during the presidency of George W. Bush, the claim that Jewish so-called "neo-cons" had taken control of the White House and were actually attempting to steer US foreign policy in the direction of Israel's interests was repeated ad nauseum in the Turkish press (and elsewhere).[30] Other related themes that one continues to hear are that Zionism is a satanic, expansionist, and imperialist ideology, that Israel is a colonial state that must be eliminated from the Middle East, and that the Holocaust is actually a lie—or, at the very least, a gross exaggeration created by Jewish media manipulation in order to depict Jews as perennial "victims," engender sympathy for the Jewish state, and forestall criticism of Zionism and its deeds.

2. Local themes in Turkish antisemitism

When we speak about "local" themes, we are referring to those themes that are unique to the Turkish experience. Almost all of these themes tend to use as their starting point the widespread but—needless to say—erroneous convictions concerning the role of Jewish individuals in three major "hinge events" in Turkey's recent history: the fall and breaking up of the Ottoman Empire, the establishment of the Republic of Turkey, and Atatürk's large-scale, radical social engineering project within the new republic he established, including its aggressive secularization.

A. "The deposition of Abdulhamid II was a Jewish plot"

This widespread conviction is based on a conspiracy theory that can be summarized thus: Zionist leader Theodor Herzl paid a visit to Sultan Abdulhamid II in order to request from him property in Ottoman Palestine for Jewish settlement in exchange for arranging for wealthy European Jews to pay off the Ottoman Empire's public debt. When the Sultan refused, the Zionists, Dönmes (crypto-Jews), and International Jewry in general conspired to take their revenge, doing so by means of the revolutionary Committee of Union and Progress (CUP) in which they held great influence.[31] For

---

29 Ömer Karslı and Kenan Butakın, "Ve Erdoğan sahnede!," *Vatan*, May 1, 2012.

30 For some examples that reflect the content of these themes, see Erhan Başyurt, *Kabal/ABD Başkanları ve Neocon Çetesi* (Istanbul: Karakutu, 2008); Ömer Özkaya, "Amerika kaybetti, Kabalistler kazandı," *Karizma* 6, no. 21 (January-March 2005): 107-10. See also Baskın Oran, "Habeas Corpus" (speech, Ankara Free University, February 12, 2005), http://www.baskinoran.com/konferans/OzgurUniversiteBOP(12-02-05).rtf.

31 In fact, most Western scholars who have examined this issue have concluded that neither Ottoman nor foreign Jewry strongly influenced or played a significant role within the Young Turk movement. See Elie Kedourie, "Young Turks, Freemasons and Jews," *Middle Eastern Studies* 7 (1971): 89-104; Jacob M. Landau, "The Young Turks and Zionism: Some Comments," in *Jews, Arabs, Turks: Selected Essays*, ed. Jacob M. Landau (Jerusalem: The Magnes Press, 1993), 169-77; Robert Olson, "The Young Turks and the Jews: A Historiographical Revision," *Turcica* 18 (1986): 219-35. For a study in Turkish of the existence of this conspiracy

proof of this claim, adherents point to the presence of the CUP member and parliamentary deputy for Salonica Emmanuel Carasso[32] within the four-person delegation sent to inform the Sultan of his deposition and to the fact that the Sultan was exiled to house arrest in the villa of the Jewish banking family Allatini in the predominantly Jewish city of Salonica. But according to this conspiracy theory, "Herzl's revenge" did not end there. Islamist circles are also generally convinced that Mustafa Kemal Atatürk was a Dönme himself and that behind his abolition of the Ottoman Caliphate, separation of "mosque and state," and transformation of the new Turkish Republic into a secular state—thereby detaching the Turks from the Muslim heritage and Turkey from other Islamic countries—lay his desire to take revenge on the Turks for Herzl's slight. According to this view, Turkey is weaker as a result of these actions and under the control of Jews. As a result, they often disparagingly refer to the Republic of Turkey as a "second Jewish state" in the Middle East.[33]

According to Islamist popular belief, apart from Atatürk, two other Ottoman/Turkish Jews are regarded as having played an influential role in the establishment of the Republic of Turkey as a secular state. The first of these is Rabbi Haim Nahum Efendi (1873-1960), the last Chief Rabbi of the Ottoman period, and the other is Moise Kohen (1883-1961), a Turkish Jew who Turkified his name to "Tekinalp" and was a central figure in the ideological formation and propagation of the Kemalist policy toward the country's Muslim and non-Turkish minorities. Through his theoretical works and other writings, he encouraged the Jews in particular to adhere to the country's assimilationist policies.

B. Haim Nahum Efendi and Moise Kohen "Tekinalp"

Let us first take a look at Haim Nahum. In Islamist circles there is a widespread belief that Haim Nahum, who served on the Turkish delegation to the Lausanne Peace Conference in the capacity of advisor, was the one who originally convinced the delegation head Ismet Inönü to abolish the Caliphate.[34] The same public that

---

theory in Turkish historiography, see Haluk Hepkon, *Jön Türkler ve Komplo Teorileri* (Istanbul: Kırmızı Kedi, 2012).

32 For a biography of Carasso, see "Emmanuel Carasso," https://en.wikipedia.org/wiki/Emmanuel_Carasso; Hüseyin Cahit Yalçın, "Tanıdıklarım—Karasu Efendi," *Yedigün*, no. 154 (1936): 5 (this article was later republished in the author's book *Tanıdıklarım* (Istanbul: Yapı Kredi Yayınları, 2001)); Roni Margulies, "Karasu Efendinin Biyografisine Bir Başlangıç," *Toplumsal Tarih*, no. 21 (September 1995): 24-29; Edhem Eldem, "Emanuel Karasu Biyografisine Bir Devam (?)," *Toplumsal Tarih*, no. 23 (November 1995): 43-45; Necmettin Alkan, "Emanuel Karasu Biyografisine Katkı (I) Karasu ve II. Abdülhamid ile İlişkisi," *Toplumsal Tarih*, no. 170 (February 2008): 64-68; Necmettin Alkan, "Emanuel Karasu Biyografisine Katkı (II) II. Abdülhamid'in Tahttan İndirilmesi," *Toplumsal Tarih*, no. 172 (April 2008): 22-28.

33 Mehmed Şevket Eygi, "İki Yahudi Devleti," *Millî Gazete*, November 27, 2010.

34 For a sample of such articles, see M. Latif Salihoğlu, "Lozan'ın Gizli Mimarı Haim Nahum (I)," *Yeni Asya*, August 25, 2007; M. Latif Salihoğlu, "Lozan'ın Gizli Mimarı Haim Nahum (II)," *Yeni Asya*, August 27, 2007; Kadir Mısıroğlu, *Lozan Zafer mi? Hezimet mi?*, vol. 1 (Istanbul: Sebil Yayınevi, 1975), 272-73; Abdurrahman Dilipak, *Cumhuriyete Giden Yol* (Istanbul: Beyan Yayınları, 1991), 330-35; Mehmet Şevket Eygi, "Eyvah! ... Lozan'ın Gizli Protokolleri Tehlikede," *Millî Gazete*, August 23, 2007. Dedektif X Bir, "İşte!," *Büyük Doğu*, no. 2 (October 21, 1949) and no. 3 (October 28, 1949); Necip Fazıl Kısakürek, "Yahudi ve Menderes," *Başmakalelerim 1* (Istanbul: Büyük Doğu Yayınları, 1999), 69-71; Hasan Hüseyin Ceylan, "Halifeliğin kaldırıl-

holds to this view tends to hold Tekinalp up as an object of loathing, both because of his general Kemalist orientation and because he titled one chapter of his 1936 work *Kemalizm*, "To Hell with the Shari'a." Even though he was an ardent Turkish nationalist, Turkish nationalist circles largely reject his credentials as a "true Turk" due to his Jewish origins, while the Islamists regard him as a Jew who, by hiding behind a Turkish name, spread the seeds of nationalism into the Turkish intellectual world and thus opened the way for the destruction of the Ottoman state.[35]

C. "The Hat Law was created for the Jews"

Another aspect of the early Kemalist reforms that elicits a strong reaction in Islamist circles and is generally seen as a "Jewish subterfuge" is the so-called "Hat Law."[36] The law itself, one of a series of radical social reforms proposed by Atatürk and passed by the Turkish Grand National Assembly (*Türkiye Büyük Millet Meclisi*, TBMM) in 1925, obliged all adult males to don brimmed headgear, effectively prohibiting the traditional Turkish fez and turban in an attempt to "Westernize" the country's population and social mores. Since a Jewish entrepreneur from Istanbul, Vitali Hakko (1913-2007),[37] grew very wealthy in the exploding hat market generated by this law, the conviction has taken root within the minds of many Islamists that a "Jewish hand" was behind the proposal and passing of this law.[38]

D. "Mustafa Kemal was a Dönme"

There are a number of reasons that the Islamist public in Turkey believes that Mustafa Kemal was a Dönme, the first of which being that he was born in Salonica, the Jewish-majority "Jerusalem of the Balkans," and that he received much of his early education at Dönme schools and under Dönme teachers.[39] Another factor that has gone some way toward strengthening this conviction is the appearance of a 1994 article in the leading Jewish-American daily *Forward*. In the piece, which the reporter Hillel Halkin

---

masında İsmet İnönü-Yahudi Hahambaşısı Haim Nahum İşbirliği," *Yörünge*, December 23, 1990, 35-36: Mustafa Kaplan, "Yolumuz Açıldı mı?," *Akit*, April 4, 1996; Mustafa Akgün, *Yahudinin Tahta Kılıcı* (Istanbul, 1992), 180.

35 Rıfat N. Bali, *Bir Günah Keçisi: Munis Tekinalp*, vol. 1 (Istanbul: Libra Kitap, 2012), 229-334. Although the works for which he is most famous/notorious among the Islamists, *Kemalizm* (1936) and *Türkleştirme* (1928) were both published long after the establishment of the Republic, Tekinalp's works on Turkish Turkic and Turkish nationalism stretch back to his contributions to *Turk Yurdu* in the first decade of the twentieth century.

36 Law No. 671, "The Law Regarding the Wearing of Hats," was passed by the Turkish Parliament on November 28, 1925.

37 For the story of Vitali Hakko, see Vitali Hakko, *Vakko: My Life*, trans. Michael McGaha (Istanbul: Libra Kitap, 2012).

38 After Vitali Hakko's death, two of Turkey's more radical Islamist dailies, *Anadolu'da Vakit* and the National View–affiliated *Millî Gazete*, ran pieces emphasizing that the Jewish businessman became rich from the Hat Law. See Hasan Karakaya, "Şapka ve Eşarptan Zengin Olan Adam," *Anadolu'da Vakit*, December 12, 2007; Emre Öztürk, "Kartelin Musevi Aşkı," *Anadolu'da Vakit*, December 13, 2007; Hasan Karakaya, "Kartel 'Görev'ini yapıyor ya Müslüman," *Anadolu'da Vakit*, December 14, 2007; "İslamcı Basında Vakko Kırılması," *Milliyet*, December 16, 2007.

39 On this subject, see Rıfat N. Bali, "Mustafa Kemal and the Claim of His Dönme Roots," *A Scapegoat For All Seasons: The Dönmes or Crypto-Jews of Turkey* (Istanbul: Isis Press, 2008), 229-56.

penned before the state visit of then-President of Israel Ezer Weizman to Turkey,[40] he makes reference to the recollections (published in 1961) of the Israeli journalist Itamar Ben-Avi (1882-1943), the son of the "father of modern Hebrew" Eliezer Ben-Yehuda (1858-1922), who claims that he had met Mustafa Kemal twice, the first time in a Jerusalem hotel during the period of the Turco-Italian war of 1911-1912, and that the latter had admitted to him that he was of Jewish origin.[41] After calling President Weizman's office, Halkin reminded him with this article of the ethno-religious origins of the founder and first president of the Turkish Republic that he would soon visit. These recollections, written in Hebrew, were largely consigned to obscurity for the first thirty-three years after their publication, but following the appearance of Halkin's English-language article they were soon translated into Turkish. They thus finally came to the attention of the Turkish public and were quickly embraced by the Islamists as "positive proof that Atatürk was a Dönme."

For these reasons, among others, Turkey's Islamists and ultra-nationalists tend to hold up both Jews and Dönmes as the central objects of their hatred, seeing them as enemies of Shari'a law and, due to their role in the destruction of the Ottoman Empire and the forcible, top-down imposition of the country's secular order, as the founders of the "Jewish Republic" of Turkey. One Islamist writer has characterized the arrival of Sephardic Jewry in Ottoman lands as "the introduction of the termite [literally: worm] into the trunk of the Ottoman tree."[42]

E. Other themes

From the Islamist viewpoint, the Dönmes have traditionally occupied the most sensitive positions in Turkish society and thus are the only remaining obstacle to transforming the current Republic of Turkey into a Turkish Islamic Republic. For them, "the Jew" represents so much more than just a small religious minority; instead their power and evil intentions assume mythic proportions. They are seen as a type of deadly virus, possessing near demonic qualities and capabilities. And this human pestilence, whether in its open "Jewish" form or disguised as Muslims in the case of the Dönmes, works to gain the trust of Muslims, so that it may more easily infiltrate Islam and Turkish society in order to corrupt it and weaken the Turkish state. For the Islamists, the Jew was not simply the planner and agent of all manner of calamity and conspiracy to weaken and destroy the Ottoman Empire but the true source of all evil that befell it over the long centuries of its existence. In their mind, it was a Jewish convert, the court physician Yakup Pasha, who poisoned Mehmed II, the Conqueror of Constantinople,[43] it was Jewish moneychangers who exploited the

40 Hillel Halkin, "When Atatürk Recited Shema Yisrael 'It's my Secret Prayer Too' He Confessed," *Forward*, January 28, 1994. Halkin wrote a subsequent article on this subject several years later: Hillel Halkin, "Atatürk's Turkey Overturned," *New York Sun*, July 24, 2007.

41 Itamar Ben Avi, *Im Shahar Atzmautenu: Zichronoto Shel HaYeled Ha'Ivri HaRishon* (At the dawn of our independence: the memoirs of the first Hebrew child) (Public Committee for the Publication of Itamar Ben-Avi's Writings, 1961), 213-18.

42 Ahmet Varol, "Türkiye'de Yahudi Lobiciliği," http://www.vahdet.info.tr/filistin/dosya2/0399.html.

43 This claim is utterly without basis in reality. For a discussion and refutation, see Yaşar Demir, "Venedik Krallığının Fatih Sultan Mehmet ve Bosna Sancakbeyi Ömer Bey'i Zehirleme Projesi," *Mustafa Kemal Üniversitesi Sosyal Bilimler Enstitüsü Dergisi* 6, no. 11 (2009): 316-27.

Ottomans,[44] and the peak of these treacheries was reached during the First World War, both through the NILI espionage network that gathered information on the Ottoman army in Palestine[45] and the participation of the Zionist Mule Corps, made up of Jewish volunteers, in the British cause at the 1915 Gallipoli landing.[46]

There are two other themes that are worth mentioning here, both of which were referred to repeatedly in the 1970s by the Islamist leader Necmettin Erbakan but have largely been forgotten in our day. These are the slogans that the European common market was a "Zionist ploy," and that "Zionism is the source of anarchy." The reason for the disappearance of this first accusation is the fact that, unlike earlier manifestations of political Islam, the ruling JDP is not opposed becoming a member of the European Union. Additionally, during the time that these slogans were more frequently voiced, Turkey was the scene of protracted and bloody clashes between ultra-right and left-wing paramilitary forces in both urban and rural areas. These clashes have long since receded into the past. Thus, since neither of these themes retain any further political use for their proponents, they have faded into disuse. However, other claims have been invented to take their place, accusations and theories more in line with the issues and problems now current in the international arena. As a result, there are a great number of antisemitic themes, once only mouthed by Islamists, that are now frequently heard emanating from the mouths of the opposition nationalist and neo-nationalist circles.[47] On the basis of the biblical verse "In the same day the Lord made a covenant with Abram, saying, Unto your

---

44 What is generally referred to here is Joseph "Nasi," Duke of Naxos, who was an influential personality during the period of Suleiman the Magnificent and his son, Selim II. For the most comprehensive biography on Joseph Nasi, see Cecil Roth, *The Duke of Naxos of the House of Nasi* (Philadelphia: The Jewish Publication Society of America, 1948).

45 "Nili," https://en.wikipedia.org/wiki/Nili.

46 On this subject, see J.H. Patterson, *With the Zionists in Gallipoli* (New York: George H. Doran Company, 1916); Martin Sugarmann, "The Zion Muleteers of Gallipoli (March 1915-May 1916)," *Jewish Virtual Library*, http://www.jewishvirtuallibrary.org/source/History/gallipoli.html. For some recent examples from the Islamist press, see Osman Toprak, "Sion Katır Birliği," *Millî Gazete*, July 23, 2007; Ramazan Yücel, "Çanakkale'de Müslüman Türklere Karşı Siyon-Yahudi Katır Bölüğü," *Millî Çözüm* (November 2010); Ekrem Şama, "Ey Yahudi! Unuttun mu?!," *Millî Gazete*, January 6, 2009. The theme is oft-repeated by Yalçın Küçük, a Marxist professor of economics who has gained some credence on Turkey's right through his numerous books on Dönme conspiracies in Turkey. In the face of the frequent and widespread accusations, a writer for Istanbul's Jewish newspaper *Şalom* felt compelled to pen an article reminding his readers that the Jewish population was actually the only religious minority *not* to work against the Ottoman Empire and refuting the error-filled and spurious claims of their detractors. See Denis Ojalvo, "Siyon Katır Birliği nedir, ne değildir?," *Şalom*, September 27, 2012.

47 An interesting example of this can be seen in the best-selling works of the nationalist-leaning journalist Soner Yalçın and Marxist economics professor Yalçın Küçük, both of whom have met great success with hefty tomes claiming the pervasive influence within or outright control of the Turkish Republic by the Dönmes and/or the "Israel Lobby." For a study on the neo-nationalist movement *ulusalcılık*, see Emrullah Uslu, "Ulusalcılık: The Neo-nationalist Resurgence in Turkey," *Turkish Studies* 9, no. 1 (March 2008): 73-97; Doğan Gürpınar, *Ulusalcılık, İdeolojik Önderlik ve Takipçileri* (Istanbul: Kitap Yayınevi, 2011); Gün Zileli, *Ulusalcılık / Bir İdeolojinin Krizi* (Istanbul: Özgür Üniversite, 2007); Ioannis N. Grigoriadis and Irmak Özer, "Mutations of Turkish Nationalism: From Neo-Nationalism to the Ergenekon Affair," *Middle East Policy* 17, no. 4 (Winter 2010): 101-13.

descendants have I given this land, from the river of Egypt unto the great river, the river Euphrates" (Genesis 15:18),[48] it is believed in much of Turkey that the modern state of Israel continues to nourish expansionist intentions on Turkish soil[49] and supports the PKK, the independence movement among Turkey's Kurdish population. Rumors and reports abound in the Turkish press of Israelis secretly purchasing lands in Turkey's southeastern provinces with the eventual goal of "Israelizing" them.[50]

IV. THE SITUATION SINCE THE ASCENT OF THE JDP

During the period of the so-called *Refahyol* ruling coalition (June 28, 1996-June 30, 1997),[51] Welfare Party leader Necmettin Erbakan became Turkey's prime minister—the first time the post was held by an Islamist politician.[52] Although significant in its own right, it did not yet represent a "turning point" in Turkish politics, as the short-lived government mostly distinguished itself by its Janus-faced declarations, foreign policy embarrassments, and provocative domestic policies. Turkey's traditionally secular and military-dominated National Security Council (*Millî Güvenlik Kurulu*), which acts as the overseer and effective arbiter of Turkish politics, delivered an ultimatum to the head of the governing coalition on February 28, 1997, stating that, in light of the worrisome recent increase in Islamist activity within the country and the tepid and irresolute response of the current government, Erbakan's coalition was hereby handed a laundry list of "recommendations" to be implemented in order to stem this trend. After a couple months of ineffective maneuvering to save the coalition, the prime minister was ultimately forced to announce its dissolution and

---

48 "On that day the Lord made a covenant with Abram and said, To your descendants I give this land, from the river of Egypt to the great river, the Euphrates—the land of the Kenites, Kenizzites, Kadmonites, Hittites, Perizzites, Rephaites, Amorites, Canaanites, Girgashites and Jebusites." (Genesis 15:18-21).

49 Harun Yahya, *İsrail'in Kürt Kartı—İsrail'in Ortadoğu Stratejisi ve "Kürt Devleti" Senaryoları* (Istanbul: Araştırma Yayınları, 2000).

50 There is abundant literature on this subject in Turkey. For only a few of the examples, see Hasan Taşkın, *İstihbarat Raporlarında İsrail'in GAP Senaryosu* (Istanbul: Ozan Yayıncılık, 2004); Fedai Erdoğ, *Anadolu'da İsrail'in GAP'ı* (Istanbul: Ara Kitap, 2008); Fedai Erdoğ and Atilla Akdemir, *GAP ve İsrail* (Istanbul: Kitap Kağıdı, 2005). It should also be mentioned that this claim has also found some traction both on al-Jazeera and—perhaps less surprisingly—within the Iranian press. See "Latest myth: 'Israelis to establish settlement in Turkey,'" *Tom Gross Mideast Media Analysis*, January 13, 2005, http://www.tomgrossmedia.com/mideastdispatches/archives/000030.html.

51 The coalition was formed through an alliance of expedience between the secular center-right True Path Party (*Doğru Yol Partisi*, from which the "yol" part of the name derives) of Tansu Çiller and Necmettin Erbakan's Islamist Welfare Party (*Refah Partisi*), in which Çiller would first serve as foreign minister under Erbakan with an agreement to trade positions after two years. However, the coalition was forced from power by an ultimatum from Turkey's National Security Council (*Millî Güvenlik Kurulu*) after just one year.

52 During the short-lived 37th Turkish government (February-November 1974), Erbakan, then heading the National Salvation Party (*Millî Selamet Partisi*), assumed the role of deputy prime minister in the coalition led by Bülent Ecevit's Republican People's Party (*Cumhuriyet Halk Partisi*).

watch his place be taken by a new center-right/liberal coalition.[53] The process started by the February 28 decision and ending with the government's fall at the end of June has come to be known as Turkey's first "post-modern coup."[54] Nevertheless, this "restoration" of the secular and Kemalist order proved to be short-lived, as only five years later the Justice and Development Party (*Adalet ve Kalkınma Partisi*), touting a new, more moderate brand of political Islam, swept into power by a great majority in Turkey's 2002 national elections. This victory would ultimately prove to be just the beginning of a tectonic shift in Turkish political life. Unlike any of its predecessors, the JDP was the first "Islamist" party in Turkey's history to enjoy significant support from libertarian leftists and social/economic liberals, both of whom had long resented the repressive and authoritarian behavior of the old-guard Kemalists and the military brass. Even more significant than this electoral victory was the new regime's claim to have uncovered a widespread coup plot among Kemalist officers and journalists, known by their code names "Ergenokon" and "Sledgehammer," that included the planting of bombs to be used as a pretext for another intervention by the armed forces. In what has been described by critics both at home and abroad as a pretext for rounding up all its political opponents, the JDP government has nevertheless arrested hundreds of high ranking military officers, journalists, and others and brought them to trial.[55]

Surprisingly, perhaps, this "settling of accounts" by the JDP regime has also given rise to a number of antisemitic themes. Turkey's Islamist media blamed Israel and the Jewish "neo-cons," who were regarded as holding sway over White House policy, for the "post-modern coup." Lying behind this claim is the belief that the top brass of the Turkish armed forces, who are one of the principle lynchpins in Turkey's

---

53 The new centrist government, dubbed the *ANASOL-D* coalition by commentators, consisted of a coalition of the Motherland Party (*Anavatan Partisi*), Democratic Left Party (*Demokratik Sol Partisi*) and Democratic Turkey Party (*Demokratik Türkiye Partisi*) under Motherland Party leader Mesut Yılmaz.

54 "1997 military memorandum (Turkey)," https://en.wikipedia.org/wiki/1997_military_memorandum_(Turkey); Ümit Cizre-Sakallıoğlu and Menderes Çınar, "Turkey 2002: Kemalism, Islamism, and Politics in the Light of the February 28 Process," *South Atlantic Quarterly* 102, nos. 2-3 (Spring-Summer 2003): 309-32.

55 For a further explanation of the alleged plot, see "Sledgehammer (Coup Plan)," https://en.wikipedia.org/wiki/Sledgehammer_(coup_plan); Gareth Jenkins, "Ergenekon, Sledgehammer and the Politics of Turkish Justice: Conspiracies and Coincidences," *MERIA* 15, no. 2 (June 2011), http://www.rubincenter.org/2011/08/ergenekon-sledgehammer-and-the-politics-of-turkish-justice-conspiracies-and-coincidences. Among those arrested, convicted, and sentenced were [Full] General Çetin Doğan. A Turkish language blog started by his daughter Pınar and her husband Professor Dani Rodrik discusses the arrests and the trials and analyzes the evidence against the defendants: http://www.balyozdavasivegercekler.com. This critical view of the affair is repeated in their book and in a series of articles. See Pınar Doğan and Dani Rodrik, *Balyoz Bir Darbe Kurgusunun Belgeleri ve Gerçekler* (Istanbul: Destek Yayınları, 2010); Pınar Doğan and Dani Rodrik, "How Turkey Manufactured a Coup Plot," *Foreign Policy*, April 6, 2010; Pınar Doğan and Dani Rodrik, "A Turkish Tragedy," *The National Interest*, September 27, 2010; Dani Rodrik, "A Sledgehammer Blow for Turkish Democracy," *Financial Times* (London), March 3, 2011; Dani Rodrik, "Ergenekon and Sledgehammer: Building or Undermining the Rule of Law?," *Turkish Policy Quarterly* 10, no. 1 (Spring 2011): 99-109; Dani Rodrik, "Turkey's miscarriage of justice," *Washington Post*, September 22, 2012.

Kemalist order, and—until recently—the chief defenders and guarantors of the secular Turkish Republic, are all either Dönmes or "friends" and supporters of Israel. In many ways, this is simply the most recent expression of the conviction that Mustafa Kemal's abolition of the Caliphate and subsequent secular reforms derived from the fact that he was a Dönme.

A number of circumstances and events have been picked up by the Islamist press as "evidence" of collusion between the Turkish high command, the State of Israel, and the Jewish neo-cons in Washington,[56] including (1) that the son-in-law of the most high-ranking defendant in the "Sledgehammer" case, First Army Commander General Çetin Doğan, is Harvard Professor Dani Rodrik, an Istanbul-born Turkish Jew;[57] (2) that immediately before General Yaşar Büyükanıt was elevated to the post of Commander of the Turkish armed forces, a post in which he served from 2006 to 2008, there were reports in the press that he was actually of Dönme extraction;[58] (3) that a photograph of Büyükanıt's eventual successor, General İlker Başbuğ (also arrested and in prison) praying at the Wailing Wall in Jerusalem was published in the radical Islamist daily *Vakit*;[59] and (4) that the hard-line secularist General and Deputy Chief of Staff Çevik Bir, who displayed an uncompromising attitude toward the Islamists during the February 28 "post-modern coup" process, was an ardent and outspoken proponent of closer economic and military ties between Turkey and Israel.[60] More interesting, perhaps, is the fact that certain leading liberal and leftist

---

56 "Asiltürk: 28 Şubat, ABD-İsrail ve işbirlikçilerin işi," *Anadolu'da Vakit*, March 2, 2009; Aslan Değirmenci, "İsrail'e hizmet ettiler," *Anadolu'da Vakit*, March 2, 2009; "Erbakan: 28 Şubat'ı Makovsky planladı," *Milliyet*, February 28, 2007; Hasan Karakaya, "31 Mart Vak'ası, 28 Şubat Darbesi ve Masonlar!," *Anadolu'da Vakit*, June 17, 2008; Furkan Atılgan, "28 Şubatçı Paşalar Yahudi şeref defterinde," *Anadolu'da Vakit*, December 31, 2008.

57 For an article stressing the Jewishness of the general's son-in-law, see Kemal Gümüş, "Generallerin Yahudi damatları," *Anadolu'da Vakit*, June 29, 2010. For a critique of this article, see Roni Margulies, "Generallerin Yahudi damatları," *Taraf*, June 30, 2010. This "Jewish son-in-law" theme would be repeated in 2011 by the Islamist daily *Vakit*. See Abdurrahman Dilipak, "Ulusalcı—darbeci paşaya Yahudi damat," *Yeni Akit*, January 4, 2011; Murat Alan, "Yahudi damat da kurtaramadı," *Yeni Akit*, January 15, 2011; Murat Alan, "Yahudi damat şimdi de 1. Ordu'yu mu suçlayacak," *Yeni Akit*, January 22, 2011.

58 Rıfat N. Bali, *A Scapegoat For All Seasons: The Dönmes or Crypto-Jews of Turkey* (Istanbul: Isis Press, 2008), 63-65.

59 "Ağlama Duvarı'nda Bir Bürokrat," *Anadolu'da Vakit*, June 12, 2008. Başbuğ was arrested on January 6, 2012 on the charge of "establishing or leading an armed terror organization" (*silahlı terör örgütü kurmak veya yönetmek*). For an analysis of the case, see Gareth H. Jenkins, "The Changing Objects of Fear: The Arrest of İlker Başbuğ," *Turkey Analyst* 5, no. 1, January 9, 2011, http://www.turkeyanalyst.org/publications/turkey-analyst-articles/item/290-the-changing-objects-of-fear-the-arrest-of-ilker-basbug.html.

60 A biography of the former Deputy Chief of Staff can be found at "Çevik Bir," https://en.wikipedia.org/wiki/cevik_bir. In 1999, the Jewish Institute for National Security Affairs (JINSA) awarded Bir its "International Leadership Award." See Harun Kazaz, "US Jewish group bestows leadership award on Bir," *Hürriyet Daily News*, October 27, 1999. Along with Tel Aviv University political scientist Martin Sherman, Çevik Bir would co-publish an article "Formula for Stability: Turkey Plus Israel," *Middle East Quarterly* (Fall 2002): 23-32, which contains the following statement: "Under the provisions of Turkey's constitutional system, the military is charged with protecting the secular republican legacy of Kemal Atatürk, the founder of modern Turkey. The army made it clear to Erbakan that it would not sit idly by and watch

intellectuals have also embraced these views. Cengiz Çandar, for instance, a liberal columnist for the center-left daily *Radikal* has claimed that Israel and its Washington lobby were behind the "post-modern coup" of February 28.[61] For his part, Halil Berktay, a professor at Istanbul's Sabancı University and columnist for the center-left daily *Taraf*, has confirmed Çandar's claims by speculating that "the belligerence of the Israel lobby is so great that it engages in efforts to destroy the most esteemed professional institutions," and that "Bernard Lewis and his allies" established the academic forum on the Middle East ASMEA as an alternative to MESA,"[62] while reminding his readers that the aforementioned secular firebrand Turkish General Çevik Bir was one of the founders of this new organization. In addition, Berktay has referred to Bernard Lewis as an "unbending Atatürkist" and "a thoroughgoing ally of the Turkish nationalist-militarist nation-state" and has stated that Çandar's declaration "was a story showing the type of attire in which the collaboration between Turkey's Atatürkist coup planners, on one hand, and the State of Israel and the Israeli lobby, on the other, would wrap itself, all in the name of preserving secularism in the Middle East."[63]

V. The Position of Turkey's Intelligentsia

1. *The Kemalists, neo-nationalists, nationalists, and Islamists*

Turkey's intelligentsia can be divided into six main currents across the political spectrum: libertarian leftists, liberals, Kemalists, neo-nationalists, nationalists, and Islamists. The Kemalist intellectuals have over recent decades been most exercised by what they perceive as the continued erosion of secularism in Turkish society and the constant weakening of Atatürkist principles. As such, the question of Turkish antisemitism is not an issue that overly excites or interests them. The other three sectors mentioned, the Islamists, neo-nationalists, and nationalists, are where antisemitism is most widespread and, ironically, where the question of antisemitism in Turkey is most frequently rejected out of hand and certainly never brought up for discussion. It suffices to provide just one example of this phenomenon. Necip Fazıl

Turkey turn toward Islam or allow Israeli-Turkish relations to be jeopardized." This statement, along with the aforementioned JINSA award have been used against the general, both by Turkey's Islamists and liberals. Bir was arrested on April 16, 2012 and questioned in connection with the JDP government's investigation of the events of February 28. See http://bianet.org/english/human-rights/137650-cevik-bir-arrested and http://www.thenational.ae/news/world/europe/turkey-settles-score-with-military-with-general-cevik-bir-arrest.

61 See Neşe Düzel's interview with Cengiz Çandar: "28 Şubat darbesinde İsrail var," *Taraf*, April 16, 2012; "US, Israel behind Feb. 28 coup d'état, Claims Çandar," *Today's Zaman*, April 16, 2012. Lehigh University Professor Henri Barkey, who is an Istanbul-born Turkish Jew, countered Çandar's views. See Aslı Aydıntaşbaş, "28 Şubat'ta dahlimiz yok," *Milliyet*, April 23, 2012. For Cengiz Çandar's counter-response, see "28 Şubat'taki Washington ve İsrail," *Radikal*, April 25, 2012.

62 The Association for the Study of the Middle East and Africa (ASMEA) was founded by Professor Bernard Lewis and Professor Fouad Ajami on October 24, 2007 in response to what Lewis would term a MESA "dominated by academics who have been critical of Israel and of America's role in the Middle East." See "Association for the Study of the Middle East and Africa," https://en.wikipedia.org/wiki/Association_for_the_Study_of_the_Middle_East_and_Africa.

63 Halil Berktay, "Bernard Lewis, Çevik Bir ve ASMEA," *Taraf*, April 19, 2012.

Kısakürek (1904-1983), the Islamist and nationalist poet and writer known to his many admirers as "The Master," is one of the central figures in the spread of antisemitism in Turkey, having for decades been the publisher of the Islamic-nationalist journal *Büyük Doğu* and the producer of numerous antisemitic works himself.[64] He is still mentioned today with great fondness and respect by many in rightist and Islamist circles, including the JDP Prime Minister Recep Tayyip Erdoğan and President Abdullah Gül. The Turkish daily *Star*, which is a supporter of the current JDP government, currently distributes facsimile prints of Kısakürek's *Büyük Doğu* journal with its Saturday edition, a practice that has been praised by government officials as an important cultural service.[65]

2. *The libertarian left and the liberals*

Due to its predilection for human rights and individual freedom, this sector tends to be the most sensitive toward hate speech in the media and prejudices toward the country's minorities. But even this sensitivity is a relatively recent development and has arisen in reaction to a series of high profile murders—religiously and politically motivated assassinations, actually—that took place in Turkey in the past decade. The first of these was the murder of the Roman Catholic priest Andrea Santoro, who was serving as a member of the Catholic Church's *Fidei donum* missionary program, in the Santa Maria Church in Trabzon on February 5, 2006.[66] Following this killing, the editor of the Turkish-Armenian daily *Agos*, the journalist Hrant Dink, was gunned down in Istanbul's Osmanbey district on January 19, 2007.[67] Three months later, two Turkish converts to Protestant Christianity and a German national, all employees of Zirve, a Bible publishing house, were killed in Malatya.[68] In all of these cases, the assailants turned out to be young men who were closely aligned with nationalist circles. As a result of this series of shocking murders, the leftist and liberal circles began issuing public condemnations of "racism" and "hate speech" against minorities, gays, and Kurds in the media and declaring their own sensitivity on these issues.

These same circles have also recently begun to include antisemitism under the heading of "hate speech" and "racism" and condemn it as such.[69] Yet, even while

64 For a brief compilation of Kısakürek's antisemitic writings in *Büyük Doğu*, see Suat Ak, ed., *Necip Fazıl Kısakürek, Yahudilik-Masonluk-Dönmelik* (Istanbul: Büyük Doğu Yayınları, 2006).

65 The newspaper *Star* began this practice of including copies of *Büyük Doğu* as a supplement in its Saturday editions on March 24, 2012. Among the various Islamist politicians offering praise for this "cultural service" are Deputy Prime Minister and Government Spokesperson Bülent Arınç, Deputy Prime Minister Beşir Atalay, former Minister of Culture İsmail Kahraman, and economics professor and former Turkish radio and television Director-General Nevzat Yalçıntaş.

66 "Andrea Santoro," https://en.wikipedia.org/wiki/Andrea_Santoro.

67 "Hrant Dink," https://en.wikipedia.org/wiki/Hrant_Dink.

68 "Zirve Publishing House Massacre," https://en.wikipedia.org/wiki/Zirve_Publishing_House_massacre.

69 The number of works and organizations devoted to this topic has increased greatly in recent years. See, for instance, Yasemin İnceoğlu, *Nefret Söylemi Nefret Suçları* (Istanbul: Ayrıntı Yayınları, 2012); Esen Aygül, Günseli Bayraktutan Sütçü, İlden Dirim, Mutlu Binark and Tuğrul Çomu, *Yeni Medyada Nefret Söylemi* (Istanbul: Kalkedon Yayınları, 2010). The website of a project by the Hrant Dink Foundation tracking hate speech in the media can be found at http://www.nefretsoylemi.org. See also the websites of the Legal Campaign against Hate Crimes

doing this, these groups have preferred to target the old-guard Kemalists, chauvinists, and ultranationalists, in the process largely giving the Islamists a pass, despite the fact that Islamist intellectuals and politicians and the Islamist press—most significantly the JDP-affiliated dailies *Akit* and the National View mouthpiece *Millî Gazete*—have for decades been the leading propagators of antisemitic speech. And this statement remains equally true today. In the fall of 2012, liberal and leftist intellectuals and journalists took the radical Islamist daily *Akit* to task for its smear campaign against three liberal columnists from other papers. The *Akit* newspaper and its website www.habervaktim.com came under harsh criticism from the left-liberal press[70] for accusing liberal-minded columnist Ali Bayramoğlu of the Islamist daily *Yeni Şafak* of having Armenian roots,[71] accusing *Radikal* columnist Cengiz Çandar of being a supporter of the PKK,[72] and criticizing *Milliyet* columnist Hasan Cemal for writing a book in which he admitted that the mass murder of the Ottoman Armenians in 1915 was a genocide.[73] Nevertheless, none of these critiques mentioned the starkly antisemitic nature of *Akit*.

In fact, while leftist and liberal intellectuals and columnists have no qualms about accusing Kemalists and the nationalist right of hate speech and antisemitism, they have repeatedly shown themselves to be averse to confronting the Islamists with similar charges.

Liberals and libertarian leftists have been quite vocal about a series of events affecting Jews that occurred in the early years of the Turkish Republic, such as the 1934 Jewish boycott and expulsion from Thrace[74] and the arbitrary and discriminatory implementation of the 1942 Capital Tax Law. Yet, when a Jewish dentist was murdered by Islamic militants in his Istanbul office in August 2003[75] and two synagogues were attacked by suicide bombers a few months later by al-Qaeda–affiliated Islamic militants,[76] these circles by-and-large remained silent. No investigation was made into

---

(*Nefret Suçları Yasa Kampanyası*) at http://nefretme.net; Say "Stop!" to Racism and Nationalism (*Irkçılığa ve Milliyetçiliğe Darbe Girişimi*) at http://www.durde.org; and the Association for Social Change (*Sosyal Değişim Derneği*), established in 2009, at http://www.sosyaldegisim.org. See also Murat Onur, "Hate Speech and Turkey's Islamist Media Problem," *Foreign Policy Association Blogs*, February 5, 2012, http://foreignpolicyblogs.com/2012/02/05/hate-speech-turkeys-islamist-media-problem.

70 Özgür Mumcu, " Vakit'i sorgulama vakti," *Radikal*, September 13, 2012.

71 "Cemaatten rötarlı destek," *Taraf*, June 29, 2012.

72 Cengiz Çandar, "Yazıklar olsun size…," *Radikal*, August 11, 2012.

73 "Akit'in yazdığı aynen çıktı," *Yeni Akit*, September 9, 2012.

74 On this subject, see Rıfat N. Bali, *1934 Trakya Olayları* (Istanbul: Libra Kitap, 2012); Hatice Bayraktar, *"Zweideutige Individuen in schlechter Absicht"—Die antisemtischen Ausschreitungen in Thrakien 1934 und ihre Hintergründe* (Berlin: Klaus Schwarz Verlag, 2011); Berna Pekesen, *Nationalismus, Türkisierung und das Ende der Jüdischen Gemeinden in Thrakien, 1918-1942* (Münich: R. Oldenbourg Verlag, 2012).

75 The Jewish dentist Yasef Yahya was murdered by Islamist militants trained in Kashmir on August 21, 2003. The assailants were arrested several months later while attempting to carry out a suicide attack on a Masonic lodge. While in detention they admitted to having murdered Yahya for being Jewish.

76 On November 15, 2003, Islamist terrorists associated with al-Qaeda carried out suicide attacks against the Neve Shalom Synagogue in Galata and the Beth Israel Synagogue in Osmanbey, as a result of which twenty-four members of Istanbul's Jewish community were

the reasons for the attacks or their perpetrators, which received only summary mention in the left and liberal press. Furthermore, there has been little or no mention of the long-running phenomenon of antisemitism in the Islamist press.

3. The reasons for this attitude

A. The shared enemy of the "New Left" and the Islamists: Kemalism and the Turkish armed forces

This unconcerned, even apathetic attitude toward antisemitism on the part of the libertarian left and liberal circles derives from several different sources. The first is that these circles both arose at least in part in opposition to the anti-democratic and dictatorial aspects to the Kemalist regime and its principle defender, the Turkish armed forces. Especially riling for them were the military interventions that seemed to appear like clockwork every decade between 1960 and 2000, toppling Turkish civilian rule and reorganizing Turkish political and social life (the coups d'état of 1960 and 1980, the "coup-by-memorandum" of 1971, and the "post-modern coup" of February 28, 1997). These groups have come out strongly against the ultra-rightist Nationalist Action Party and its adherents, as well as against the Kemalists and other Turkish chauvinists, for their belligerent nationalism and extreme hostility toward non-Turkish ethnic groups.

Many of the older liberal columnists and intellectuals in Turkey today were arrested as part of the large-scale "round-ups" performed by the military regime after the military intervention of September 1980, while others experienced similar pressures during the "post-modern coup" of February 28, 1997.[77] For this reason, many of them have a certain amount of sympathy with their Islamist counterparts, who before the electoral victory of the JDP in 2002 also suffered greatly under the Kemalist order and at the hands of the Turkish armed forces. Likewise, they tend to view the state's traditional hostility toward the Islamist political parties and the laws preventing devout Muslim girls with headscarves from taking part in higher education at state universities as issues of human rights. In these struggles against what is seen as the anti-democratic regime, the Islamists could be portrayed as "brothers-in-arms." The irony, however, is that these same secular, libertarian think-

killed. Five days later, other suicide attacks were carried out against the British Consulate in Istanbul and the General Directorate of HSBC Bank. A brief account of these events can be found at: "2003 Istanbul Bombings," https://en.wikipedia.org/wiki/2003_Istanbul_bombings.

77 After the 1998 capture of leading PKK figure Şemdin Sakık, a fabricated version of the minutes of his interrogation was "leaked" to the press. In this version, which has become known in Turkey as the "Andıç Scandal" and was sent to the press by the then-serving Armed Forces Deputy Chief of General Staff Çevik Bir and the Secretary-General of the Chief of Staff Major General Erol Özkasnak, Sakık is "recorded" as having claimed that a number of Turkish journalists had given their support to the PKK in exchange for payment. In response to the report, a number of media barons fired some of the country's preeminent center and center-left journalists, such as Cengiz Çandar, Ahmet Altan, Mehmet Altan, Mehmet Barlas, and Mehmet Ali Birand. After eleven years, it became clear that the minutes were fabricated. For more on the affair, see "Andıç Skandalı," https://tr.wikipedia.org/wiki/And%C4%B1%C3%A7_skandal %C4%B1; E. Barış Altıntaş and Ercan Yavuz, "New military media scandal exposed," *Today's Zaman*, March 9, 2007.

ers who argue that Islamist politics are reconcilable with a democratic and liberal order see no contradiction in making cause with the same Islamist writers and journalists who for decades have been publishing a steady stream of ferocious anti-Jewish conspiracy theories and antisemitic sentiments.[78]

Nor is this a situation peculiar only to those on the liberal or libertarian left. It is now regarded as politically correct and proof of "coexistence, democracy and pluralism" to either invite Islamist columnists and intellectuals to mainstream television debate programs or include their names among the columnists of mainstream newspapers.[79] As a result of all these developments, we have today arrived at the point where some of the Islamist columnists who have for years poisoned the minds of their readers with antisemitic writings and conspiracy theories about Israel and "World Jewry" are now held in high esteem within Turkish society as respectable public intellectuals.

B. The position of Turkey's Jewish leadership on the Armenian genocide

The second reason for this phenomenon is the attitude of the leadership of Turkey's small Jewish community. For the past four decades, Turkey's Jewish communal leaders have allied themselves closely to successive Turkish governments, particularly in regard to lending their support to the Turkish regime's long-standing policy of denying that the Armenian genocide ever happened. On the other hand, the liberal and left-leaning media have largely allied with the late Hrant Dink's paper *Agos* and various young Turkish-Armenian activists and journalists[80] in opposing the establishment, entering into dialogue with Kurdish groups and human rights activists, and demanding a restitution for the wrongs perpetrated against the Armenians in the past.[81] As a result of these activities, a very close alliance has emerged between the Armenian activists and public intellectuals and these groups. For its part, the Jewish community has neither public figures nor a newspaper that are willing or able to oppose the establishment or make demands upon it. Moreover, those members representing the community to the Turkish public have consistently adopted a stance supportive of the current regime and have tended to shy away from engaging in discussions with opposition activists. Even as the Turkish political order has increasingly passed into the hands of Islamists and social conservatives, these "new patrons"

[78] For example: Fehmi Koru (who writes another column under the pen name of Taha Kıvanç) (*Star*), Abdurrahman Dilipak (*Yeni Akit*), Mehmed Şevket Eygi (*Millî Gazete*), Salih Tuna (*Yeni Şafak*), and Hakan Albayrak (a former *Millî Gazete* and *Yeni Şafak* columnist).

[79] Such as Nihal Bengisu Karaca at the centrist daily *Habertürk*, Sibel Eraslan at the pro-government *Star*, and Cihan Aktaş and Hidayet Şefkatli Tuksal at the leftist-liberal *Taraf*. Hilal Kaplan also used to be a columnist at *Taraf*.

[80] For instance, *Radikal İki* writer Karin Karakaşlı, *Taraf* former publishing coordinator Markar Esayan, *Agos* editor-in-chief Rober Koptaş, Yeşilköy Armenian school principal Garo Paylan, activist Hayko Bağdat, *Zaman* columnist and advisor to the TESEV Democratization Program Etyen Mahçupyan, and *Evrensel* columnist Mıgırdiç Margosyan.

[81] Including the discriminatory and arbitrary implementation of the 1942 Capital Tax Law (*Varlık Vergisi Kanunu*), the discriminatory imposition of the Law on Pious Foundations (*Vakıflar Kanunu*) against the country's religious minorities, and the acceptance of the historicity of the state-sponsored large-scale massacre of Armenians during the 1915 Deportations.

of the establishment have not followed markedly different policies than their Kemalist predecessors in regard to the Armenian genocide question, and the leadership of Turkey's Jewish community is therefore obliged to continue its support of the JDP government's denialist policy. In this situation, Turkey's Jews now find themselves between a rock and a hard place. Having previously been actively excluded by the country's liberal left and its media for their close relations with the former regime, their complaints about widespread antisemitism within the current regime and among its adherents continue to fall on deaf ears, being largely ignored by those who might otherwise be expected to show concern.

C. The liberals, the left, and Israel

The third reason for the lack of enthusiasm among Turkey's libertarian leftists and liberals for confronting antisemitism is their problematic relationship to the State of Israel and to Zionism in general. Historically, Turkey's leftists have been pro-Palestinian and anti-Israel in their stance. Since the rise of radical left student groups in Turkey in the second half of the 1960s, a good number of Turkish student leaders began to travel to PLO camps in Lebanon and elsewhere to receive "education" and training, some even losing their lives in attacks or Israeli counter-attacks.[82] In fact, on the subjects of Israel and Zionism, there is a great deal of overlap between the views of the liberal left and the Islamists. With few exceptions, all of these groups tend to see the State of Israel as a colonialist, expansionist state occupying Palestinian lands.[83] They also believe that Israel and its supporters consistently use the accusation of "antisemitism" to stifle its critics and any criticism of Israel.[84]

---

82 Soner Yalçın, "İsrail saldırısı'nda sekiz Türk devrimci can verdi," *Hürriyet*, January 4, 2009. On the Turkish leftist youth and their training in Palestine, see Turhan Feyizoğlu, *Denizler ve Filistin* (Istanbul: Alfa Kitap, 2011).

83 On this subject, see Laurent Mallet, "La Crise Libanaise vue de Turquie," *Hérodote* 2, no. 124 (2007): 51-68. Additionally, the cover of the October 2004 issue (no. 186) of the self-proclaimed "socialist culture journal" *Birikim* bore the headline "Two sides of the same coin: Antisemitism and Zionism" and contained articles representing the liberal left view of Zionism and Israel. See, for example, Ömer Laçiner, "Siyonizmin ikizi veya karşıtı," *Birikim*, no. 186 (October 2004): 18-24; Murat Paker, "Bir ırkçılık madalyonunun iki yüzü: Siyonizm ve anti-semitizm," *Birikim*, no. 186 (October 2004): 25-30; Ümit Kıvanç, "Politik doğruluk hakikate karşı," *Birikim*, no. 186 (October 2004): 31-43; Roni Margulies, "Yahudi düşmanlığı ve İslam-Arap düşmanlığı," *Birikim*, no. 186 (October 2004): 44-48. For responses to the report, from the same issue, see "Antisemitizme sıfır tahammül," *Birikim*, no. 186 (October 2004): 58-59, and in subsequent issues, Murat Paker, "Anti-semitizme karşı bildiri üzerine," *Birikim*, no. 187 (November 2004) and Roni Margulies, "Evet 'sıfır tahammül' ama nasıl?," *Birikim*, no. 188 (December 2004): 65-68. For replies to Ümit Kıvanç's aforementioned *Birikim* article, see Doğan Tarkan, "Politik doğruluk hakikate dayanır…," *Birikim*, no. 188 (December 2004): 72-75 and Rıfat N. Bali, *Ümit Kıvanç'a Cevap—Birikim Dergisinin Yayınlamayı Reddettiği Makalenin Öyküsü* (Istanbul, 2005). For a reply to *Birikim*'s headline, see Nora Şeni, "Antisemitizm," *Radikal İki*, November 21, 2004. Fore a reply to Şeni's article, see Murat Paker, "Anti-semitizm—Siyonizm: Nora Şeni'ye cevap," *Radikal İki*, December 5, 2004.

84 For example, when Yunus Emre Kocabaşoğlu published an article recalling the document of the European Union Agency for Fundamental Rights entitled "Working Definition of Antisemitism" ("Ne antisemitizmdir?," *Taraf*, June 16, 2010), he was criticized by Sabancı University faculty member Y. Hakan Erdem ("Ne antisemitizm değildir?," *Taraf*, June 23, 2010).

In light of these three factors, it is easier to understand why the issue of antisemitism in Turkey has found so little resonance among the country's liberals and leftists.

VI. Conclusion

Given this persistent apathy in the face of relentless antisemitism, the first question that comes to mind for many is how Turkey's Jewish community can continue to live securely in its own country. Turkey's Jewish leadership often feels obliged to make public declarations to the effect that they are "Turks," and, while they may admit to an "emotional connection" with Israel, one will never hear the word "Zionism" spoken in public. In parallel, the various youth-oriented cultural activities within Turkey's Jewish community include subjects such as "Zionism" and "The History of the State of Israel." Despite the term's highly negative associations among the general public, in whose midst the tiny community must live, the Jewish leadership still labors to instill a "Zionist identity" among the community's young, albeit with the proviso that this identity is not intended for public consumption. If we recall to what extent the terms "Israel" and "Zionism" are demonized within Turkish society, we can more easily understand the narrow and difficult choices faced by the community's leaders. Were they to behave differently—in other words, if they were to publicly express "pro-Israel" or "Zionist" opinions—they would undoubtedly subject themselves to the open hostility and rage of the Islamists as individuals, as an institution, and as a community in general. Judging from recent history, this would constitute a very real threat to the community's continued existence. The following example puts this in more concrete terms. After one of the plotters of the November 2003 synagogue attack was arrested, he gave the following statement under interrogation:

> Tell me, while we Muslims of Turkey condemn and curse the cruelties that Israel inflicts upon the Palestinians, have you ever heard a similar statement and criticism from a Jew born and raised in these [i.e. Turkish] lands?
>
> After the events of September 11 and November 15-20, [2003,] even after the suicide attacks in Palestine, which many Islamic institutions and religions personalities described as "terror," did you even hear one statement from the [Turkish] Jewish community and its leader condemning and naming the attacks that Israel had inflicted upon Palestine and that the world also condemned, as terror? ... We thus concluded that the synagogues in Turkey were actually places that served the Jewish State of Israel. The fact that Israeli statesmen who come to Turkey visited these places and have lectured there has strengthened our opinion. We saw such a target as a suitable payback for Israel's actions, as a way of calling [these actions] into question. We have shown that as long as World Jewry continues to support Israel's policies, they are vulnerable to attack. If on the other hand they are in favor of peace and opposed to Zionist policies as they have said, then we should expect them to make declarations clarifying their own stance and position on the matter, and we can present to them these actions [suicide attacks] as an opportunity for them to move in this direction.[85]

[85] Rıfat N. Bali, *Cumhuriyet Yıllarında Türkiye Yahudileri Devlet'in Örnek Yurttaşları (1950-2003)* (Istanbul: Kitabevi, 2009), 475-76.

What can be distilled from this statement is that a "good Jew" is one who is publicly opposed to Israel and Zionism. A "bad Jew" is one who does not take this stance, which means that he silently supports Israel and Zionism. The key to the Turkish Jewish community's security and its ability to continue living in Turkey is to be "good Jews."

The Roots and Current Implications of Iranian Antisemitism

Matthias Küntzel*

I. Introduction

The topic of this paper is controversial in two respects. Some will say that this is a topic of the past, connected to former Iranian president Mahmoud Ahmadinejad but not to his successor. Hassan Rouhani, the new Iranian president, seems to be quite friendly toward the Jews and less hostile to Israel. I will return to this objection later.

Others might say that there is and was no Iranian antisemitism in the first place. Why? Because even former president Mahmoud Ahmadinejad sent Rosh Hashanah greetings to the Jews every year and stated: "We are friends with the Jewish people." His self-image is that of an ardent anti-Zionist, not that of an antisemite. In addition, Jews have lived in Iran for more than 2,000 years, and even today the 10,000 or so Jews in Iran represent the largest Jewish community in any Muslim country. Against this background, does "Iranian antisemitism" actually exist?

My answer to this question is "yes." Ahmadinejad's worldview was in fact steeped in uncompromising antisemitism.

First, he invested the word "Zionist" with exactly the same meaning Hitler poured into "Jew": the incarnation of evil. And so, instead of saying the "Jews" are conspiring to rule the world, he said "two thousand Zionists want to rule the world,"[1] or "the Zionists have for the last sixty years blackmailed all Western governments,"[2] or "the Zionists fund Western election propaganda [and thus] control their affairs."[3] In addition, he claimed that the Zionists were behind the 2011 Norway attacks, 9/11, the Danish Muhammad cartoons, the destruction of Iraq's Golden Mosque, and many other calamities. Anyone who makes Jews responsible for all the ills of the world—whether as "Judas" or as "Zionist"—is obviously driven by antisemitism.

Second, Ahmadinejad proudly engaged in Holocaust denial, which is an extreme form of antisemitism. Whoever declares Auschwitz to be a "myth" implicitly portrays the Jews as fraudsters and enemies of humanity who have been duping the rest

---

* Author and political scientist; research associate, Vidal Sassoon International Center for the Study of Antisemitism (SICSA), Hebrew University of Jerusalem.

1 Hooman Majd, "Mahmoud and Me," *New York Observer*, October 2, 2006.

2 "Iranian President Ahmadinejad on the 'Myth of the Holocaust'...," MEMRI, Special Dispatch Series, no. 1091, February 14, 2006.

3 "Antisemitic Statements, Publications by Iranian Regime," MEMRI, Special Dispatch Series, no. 4445, January 25, 2012.

of the world for the past seventy years for financial gain. Whoever talks of the "so-called" Holocaust suggests that the Jews control over 90 percent of the world's media and university professorships, which are thereby cut off from the "real" truth. This incites precisely the same sort of genocidal hatred that helped pave the way for the Shoah. Every denial of the Holocaust thus tacitly contains an appeal to repeat it.

Ahmadinejad's portrayal of the Shoah was neither a new nor a personal obsession but rather an intensification of themes long prominent in the Islamic Republic's ideological discourse. From the 1990s onward, Iran has gone further than any Arab country in hosting and officially endorsing Western Holocaust deniers who have been shunned in their home countries, including Jürgen Graf, Wolfgang Fröhlich, and Fredrick Töben. In 1998, President Mohammad Khatami bemoaned the prosecution of French Holocaust denier Roger Garaudy. Iran's Supreme Leader Ali Khamenei even met Garaudy in person. Ali Akbar Hashemi Rafsanjani has also voiced moral support for Holocaust deniers. As early as 2001, the *Tehran Times* called the findings of the Nuremberg trials about Auschwitz "the biggest lie in history."[4]

Ahmadinejad became president of Iran in the summer of 2005. From the end of that year, he placed Holocaust denial at the center of his rabble-rousing. Now, the Iranian regime established the "exposure" of the "Holocaust myth" as the new historiographical paradigm. The "lie about the Holocaust" became a regular topic of the regime's televised Friday sermons. Talk shows on public television featured a parade of historians mocking the "fairy tale about the gas chambers." The Iranian state press agency turned into a platform for Holocaust deniers from all over the world.[5]

In December 2006, Iran's foreign minister Manouchehr Mottaki opened the regime's infamous Holocaust denial conference. This conference was particularly noteworthy because of its purpose. Previously, Holocaust deniers had wanted to revise the past. With this conference, however, Iran also wanted to shape the future. If "the official version of the Holocaust is called into question," declared Mottaki in his opening speech, then "the nature and identity of Israel" must also be called into question.[6] In his closing speech, Ahmadinejad promised the audience that "the life-curve of the Zionist regime has begun its descent, and it is now on a downward slope toward its fall. ... The Zionist regime will be wiped out, and humanity will be liberated."[7]

This sentiment—liberation through destruction—is the one for which Holocaust historian Saul Friedländer coined the term "redemptive antisemitism." It is not so far removed from the ideas expressed in a Nazi directive from 1943: "This war will end with antisemitic world revolution and with the extermination of Jewry throughout the world, both of which are the precondition for an enduring peace."[8] Ahmadinejad's hatred of Jews resembles Hitler's ideology in that they both contain this utopian

---

[4] David Menashri, "Iran, the Jews and the Holocaust" (research paper, Stephen Roth Institute for the Study of Contemporary Antisemitism and Racism, Tel Aviv, 1997), 8.

[5] "Iranian Leader: Statements and Positions (Part I)," MEMRI Special Report, no. 39, January 5, 2006.

[6] Boris Kalnoky, "Iran versammelt die Holocaust-Leugner," *Die Welt*, December 12, 2006.

[7] Yigal Carmon, "The Role of Holocaust Denial in the Ideology and Strategy of the Iranian Regime," MEMRI Inquiry and Analysis Series, no. 307, December 15, 2006.

[8] Jeffrey Herf, *The Jewish Enemy: Nazi Propaganda During World War II and the Holocaust* (Cambridge, MA; Harvard University Press, 2006), 209.

element. Just as Hitler's "German peace" required the extermination of the Jews, so the Iranian leadership's "Islamic peace" depends on the elimination of Israel.

I have so far mentioned three aspects of Iranian antisemitism: Holocaust denial, demonization of Zionists/Jews, and the desire to eliminate Israel. All three of them are interwoven and belong together. They form what I call an ideological triangle.

Anyone who accepts the reality of the Holocaust cannot simultaneously believe that the Jews are the rulers of the world. Anyone who accepts the Jews as they are, instead of demonizing them, cannot call into question the facts of the Holocaust. Anyone who accepts Israel's right to a secure existence must repudiate antisemitism. Elimination of Israel, demonization of Jews, and Holocaust denial—if any one of the three sides of this ideological triangle is absent, the whole structure collapses.

The Iranian regime pretends to struggle against Zionism, not against the Jews. However, this anti-Zionism is just a Trojan horse that the Islamic Republic uses to make its redemptive antisemitism respectable. It is the Iranian leadership's special sense of mission—to "liberate" the world—that propels it to propagate its toxic blend of antisemitism and Holocaust denial all over the world via the United Nations, satellite TV channels, and the Internet.

II. The Roots of Iranian Antisemitism

Many believe that Iranian antisemitism is caused by the Middle East conflict, but this is not true. There is no doubt that it is whipped up by events in the Middle East, but some of its roots are much older than the Jewish state.

1. Islamic anti-Judaism

The first root of Iranian antisemitism is of a religious nature and takes the form of Islamic anti-Judaism.

Jews and non-Jews share a history that goes back some 2,700 years in the area now known as Iran. However, this does not mean that Jews enjoyed equality under Shi'ite rule, which began in 1501. On the contrary, in no other Islamic country were Jews so poorly treated and so brutally persecuted as in Persia. In 1830, 400 Jews in Tabriz had their throats slashed. In 1839, all the Jews in Mashhad were forced to convert to Islam. In 1910, following rumors of a ritual murder, 6,000 Jews in Shiraz were robbed of all their possessions. In addition, twelve were killed and another fifty wounded.[9] "I do not know any more miserable, helpless, and pitiful individual on God's earth than the Jahudi in those countries," the Orientalist and voyager Arminius Vámbéry wrote in 1905 following his return from Persia: "The poor Jew is despised, belabored and tortured ... he is the poorest of the poor."[10]

This inhuman treatment was the result of a particular aspect of the Shi'ite image of the Jew, which has no counterpart in Sunni Islam. Only the Shi'ite branch of Islam established a system of "ritual purity" that bears similarities to the attitude of Hindus toward the Dalits or "untouchables." According to this system, anyone who

---

[9] David Littmann, "Jews Under Muslim Rule: The Case of Persia," *Wiener Library Bulletin* 32, new series, nos. 49-50 (1979), 4 and 12.

[10] Cited in David Menashri, "The Jews of Iran," in *Antisemitism in Times of Crisis*, eds. Sander L. Gilman and Steven T. Katz (New York: New York University Press, 1991), 354.

is not Muslim is *najis* (impure). All contact with an unbeliever is regarded as a type of poisoning. The resulting fear of "infection" provoked periodic excesses and led to the development of a specific Shi'ite code of conduct. This code of conduct had a profound impact on the local Jewish minority, which unlike the Armenian Christians and the small Zoroastrian community was present throughout the country. Its members accordingly had to live in ghettoes and were not permitted to go out when it rained or snowed, in order to prevent their "impurity" from spreading to Muslims. For the same reason, they were prohibited from visiting public baths or coming into contact with food and drink consumed by Muslims.[11]

These rules were officially abolished when the Shah-Pahlavis came to power, but the orthodox clergy continued to insist on them. Thus, in 1962, Ayatollah Ruhollah Khomeini, the future Supreme Leader of the Revolution, explicitly propagated the *najis* doctrine in a widely disseminated handbook entitled *Clarification of the Problems: A Guide to Muslims in their Daily Life*, in which he observed that "there are eleven things which make unclean: 1. urine; 2. feces; 3. sperm; 4. carrion; 5. blood; 6. dog; 7. pig; 8. unbeliever; 9. wine; 10. beer; 11. the sweat of a camel which eats unclean things." In a gloss on number 8, he adds: "The entire body of the unbeliever is unclean; even his hair and nails and body moistures are unclean." There is, however, some hope: "When a non-Muslim man or woman is converted to Islam, their body, saliva, nasal secretions, and sweat are ritually clean. If, however, their clothes were in contact with their sweaty body before their conversion, these remain unclean."[12]

2. *Nazi propaganda*

The second root of Iranian antisemitism is Nazi propaganda.

During World War II, European antisemitic ideology was brought to Tehran in the Farsi language via a Berlin-based short-wave propaganda radio station called Radio Zeesen. This is a well-established, though rarely mentioned, fact.[13] I have found documents in the archives of the German Foreign Office showing that the Nazis incited hatred of Jews within the Iranian population by fusing early Islamic Jew-hatred with the European global Jewish conspiracy myth. In this context, it is worth quoting the recommendations that Erwin Ettel, the German ambassador to Tehran, sent to the Foreign Office in Berlin by letter in February 1941:

> The way to directly connect with Shi'ite ideas is through the treatment of the Jewish question, which the Muhammadan perceives in religious terms and which, precisely for this reason, makes him susceptible to National Socialism on religious grounds. A way to foster this (anti-Jewish) development would be to highlight Muhammad's struggle against the Jews in ancient times and that of the Führer in modern times. ... Additionally, by identifying the British with the Jews, an exceptionally effective anti-English propaganda campaign can be conducted among the Shi'ite people.

11 Bernard Lewis, *The Jews of Islam* (New Jersey: Princeton University Press, 1984), 33ff.; Menashri, "Jews of Iran," 356.

12 Ayatollah Ruhollah Khomeini, *Risala-i Tawzih al-Masa'il* (Tehran, 1962), cited in Lewis, *Jews of Islam*, 34.

13 See Matthias Küntzel, "National Socialism and Antisemitism in the Arab World," *Jewish Political Studies Review* (Spring 2005): Jeffrey Herf, *Nazi Propaganda for the Arab World* (New Haven: Yale University Press, 2009).

Ettel even picked out appropriate Qur'anic passages, such as *surah* 5, verse 82: "Truly you will find that the most implacable of men in their enmity to the faithful are the Jews and the pagans," which goes well with the final sentence of Chapter 2 of *Mein Kampf*: "In resisting the Jew, I do the work of the Lord." He further noted that "by successfully bringing the country's clergy under the sway of German propaganda, we can win over broad layers of the popular masses."[14]

Various testimonies from the period indicate that these broadcasts were widely heard. Iranian author Amir Cheheltan has written that it was common in Tehran for passers-by to stand on the sidewalk at the entrance to a tea house listening to Radio Zeesen's broadcasts on the progress of the German army. He notes that "these broadcasts inspired the fantasy of the masses on the street. Each German victory represented a defeat of the colonial powers, the Soviet Union and Great Britain, which they applauded."[15] Radio Zeesen thus encouraged growing numbers of Persians to view Jews and Zionists through the antisemitic perspective of the Germans. Among the regular listeners to Nazi Germany's radio propaganda was Ayatollah Ruhollah Khomeini, the founder of Islamism in Iran, which brings us to the third root of Iranian antisemitism.

3. Khomeini's antisemitism

During the reign of Reza Shah (1925-1941) and his son Mohammed Reza Shah (1941-1979), Iranian Jews enjoyed political equality, cultural autonomy, and an increasing level of economic security. Judeophobia nonetheless continued to exist, albeit unofficially.

From 1963 onwards, Khomeini, the most important opponent of the Shah, recognized the mobilizing power of antisemitism and exploited it for his own purposes. "I know that you do not want Iran to be under the boot of the Jews," he cried out to his supporters in April 1963.[16] In the same year, he called the Shah a Jew in disguise and accused him of taking orders from Israel. The response was enormous; Khomeini had found his theme. Khomeini's biographer Amir Taheri writes: "The Ayatollah was by now convinced that the central political theme of contemporary life was an elaborate and highly complex conspiracy by the Jews—'who controlled everything'—to 'emasculate Islam' and dominate the world thanks to the natural wealth of the Muslim nations."[17] From this point on, hatred of Jews—both in its atavistic Shi'ite form and in the form of modern antisemitism—would remain a central component of the Islamist ideology of Iran.

After the Six-Day War of 1967, antisemitic agitation, which did not differentiate between Jews and Israelis, intensified. "It was [the Jews] who first established anti-

---

14 Political Archive of the German Foreign Office, "Deutsche Gesandtschaft Teheran an das AA Berlin, Teheran den 2. Februar 1941: Propagandistische Möglichkeiten unter der iranischen Bevölkerung im Hinblick auf die religiösen Erwartungen der Schiiten," R 60690, Orient, Juden um Roosevelt (1941), 2.

15 Amir Hassan Cheheltan, "Warten auf den Verborgenen Imam," *Frankfurter Allgemeine Zeitung*, March 12, 2008.

16 Cheryl Benard and Zalmay Khalilzad, *Gott in Teheran: Irans Islamische Republik* (Frankfurt a. M.: Suhrkamp, 1988), 260 n. 26.

17 Amir Taheri, *The Spirit of Allah: Khomeini and the Islamic Revolution* (New York: Adler and Adler, 1986), 158.

Islamic propaganda and engaged in various stratagems, and as you can see this activity continues down to the present," Khomeini wrote in 1970 in his main work on Islamic government.[18] "The Jews ... wish to establish Jewish domination throughout the world," he continued, "Since they are a cunning and resourceful group of people, I fear that ... they may one day achieve their goal."[19] In September 1977, he finally declared: "The Jews have grasped the world with both hands and are devouring it with an insatiable appetite, they are devouring America and have now turned their attention to Iran and still they are not satisfied."[20]

Two years later, Khomeini was the unchallenged leader of the Iranian Revolution. His antisemitic tirades found favor with the opponents of the Shah—both Leftists and Islamists. Khomeini's antisemitism ran along the same lines as the *Protocols of the Elders of Zion*, which were republished in Persian in the summer of 1978 and widely disseminated in order to serve as a weapon against the Shah, Israel, and the Jews.

Nevertheless, after the victory of the revolution in 1979, such rhetoric was toned down. Khomeini could not ignore the signs of submission emerging from the Jewish community or the precept of tolerance laid down in the Qur'an. In May 1979, he declared: "We distinguish between Jews and Zionists. Zionism has nothing to do with religion."[21] From then on, Jews were treated as *dhimmis*, like the Armenian Christians and Zoroastrians, but the foundations of Iranian antisemitism, remained unchanged. Thus, in 2005, I was able to purchase an English edition of the *Protocols of the Elders of Zion*, published by the Islamic Propagation Organization of the Islamic Republic of Iran, at the Iranian stand at the Frankfurt Book Fair. Other antisemitic literature, such as Henry Ford's *The International Jew*, was also available.[22]

In conclusion, it is true that Ahmadinejad was the first president of a powerful state to make Holocaust denial a hallmark of its foreign policy. However, antisemitism has always been an inherent component of Khomeini's ideology, which is deeply rooted in Islamic anti-Judaism and European antisemitism.

III. What has changed since Iran's new president Hassan Rouhani took power in August 2013?

In September 2013, in an apparent contrast to Ahmadinejad's overt antisemitism and Holocaust denial, the new foreign minister of Iran, Mohammad Javad Zarif, wished Christine Pelosi, the daughter of US congresswoman and former speaker of the House of Representatives Nancy Pelosi a "Happy Rosh Hashanah" on his English-language Twitter account. Christine responded: "Thanks. The New Year would be even sweeter

18 Ayatollah Ruhollah Mousavi Khomeini, *Islamic Government: Governance of the Jurist* (Tehran: Institute for the Compilation and Publication of the Works of Imam Khomeini, International Affairs Division, n.d.), 7. Page references are to the PDF version made available by the Iran Chamber Society at http://www.iranchamber.com/history/rkhomeini/ayatollah_khomeini.php.

19 Ibid., 79.

20 *Kauthar: An Anthology of the Speeches of Imam Khomeini, 1962-1978*, vol. 1 (Tehran: Institute for the Compilation and Publication of the Works of Imam Khomeini, International Affairs Division, 1995), 370.

21 Menashri, "Jews of Iran," 363.

22 Matthias Küntzel, "The Booksellers of Tehran," *Wall Street Journal*, October 28, 2005.

if you would end Iran's Holocaust denial, sir." To which Mr. Zarif responded: "Iran never denied it. The man who did is now gone. Happy new year."[23]

Let us take a closer look at Mr. Zarif's words. He claims that Iran never denied the Holocaust. However, as we have already seen, this denial of the denial is utterly misleading. Iran is the first and only country in the world that has made Holocaust denial a central matter of foreign policy. Mr. Zarif's second claim: "The man who did is now gone" is partly true, since Mahmoud Ahmadinejad is fortunately no longer president. But what about Ali Khamenei, the supreme leader of the Islamic revolution, who has also ridiculed "the myth of the massacre of Jews known as the Holocaust"?[24]

It is true, on the one hand, that the tone of Holocaust denial has changed since Rouhani and Zarif entered office. Previously, denial of the Holocaust was the leitmotif of Iran's foreign policy. Today, it is still an undisputed part of Iran's state ideology, but it is no longer the centerpiece of its public diplomacy. On the other hand, even the internationally presentable Rouhani is still far from acknowledging the real scope and nature of the Holocaust. Asked, for example, whether the Holocaust was real, Iran's new president responded: "I am not a historian. I'm a politician."[25] To pretend that the facts of the Holocaust are a matter of serious historical dispute that should only be addressed by historians is a classic rhetorical evasion. Later, Rouhani admitted that "a group of Jewish people" had been killed by the Nazis during World War II.[26] This is also typical of Holocaust deniers, who commonly acknowledge that Jews were killed while insisting that the number of Jewish victims was relatively small and that a systematic effort to wipe them out did not take place.

The mainstream thinking among Iran's rulers is even worse. They leave no doubt that the complete denial of the Holocaust remains an essential part of Iran's state ideology. For example, foreign minister Zarif's tweet stating that Iran had never denied the Holocaust was met with a wave of angry protests.[27] According to the chief editor of the *Kayhan* newspaper, which is considered to be the mouthpiece of Iran's Supreme leader, "the Holocaust is nothing but a myth created by the Zionists. … There is not a shred of doubt that the story of the Holocaust is false." He added that on this issue Ahmadinejad "crushed the false legitimacy of the Zionist regime, and for this he is worthy of esteem and praise."[28]

---

[23] Rick Gladstone and Robert Mackey, "Iran Signals an Eagerness to Overcome Old Impasses," *New York Times*, September 5, 2013.

[24] Office of the Supreme Leader Sayyid Ali Khamenei, "Leader Receives Air Force Serviceman," July 2, 2006.

[25] "Rohani: Atomstreit schnell beilegen," *Frankfurter Allgemeine Zeitung*, September 27, 2013.

[26] Rick Gladstone, "Iranian President Softens Condemnation of Holocaust," *New York Times*, September 26, 2013.

[27] "70 Iranian Lawmakers Want Zarif to Explain Why He Said the Holocaust 'Should Not Happen Again,'" *the algemeiner*, February 16, 2014; "President's Advisor: Holocaust Never Used by Rouhani," *Fars News Agency*, September 29, 2013: "While the Iranian president did not recognize the Holocaust, the [sic] CNN aired a translation that contained several words and sentences not uttered by the Iranian president."

[28] "Criticism in Iran of Foreign Minister Zarif Tweet Claiming Iran Never Denied the Holocaust," MEMRI Special Dispatch Series, no. 5450, September 18, 2013.

In addition to statements in support of Holocaust denial, there have also been numerous symbolic acts, including but not limited to the following. In November 2013, an Internet journal with close to the Iranian leadership published an exhibition of so-called fake pictures of the Holocaust.[29] Also in November 2013, *Fars News Agency*, Iran's official state news agency, condemned the UNESCO-sponsored Aladdin Project, which provides information about the Holocaust in Arabic and Persian, claiming that it was "fulfilling the goals of the Zionists" and that its purpose was "to persuade Muslim countries to recognize the Zionists' fabricated narrative about the Holocaust."[30] Finally, in December 2013, Khamenei, the Supreme Leader, honored Roger Garaudy, the famous French Holocaust denier.[31]

Thus, although the tone of Holocaust denial may have changed its substance clearly remains the same. The same applies to the regime's rants against "international Zionism," which have not disappeared. At his first press conference in August 2013, Hassan Rouhani referred to unspecified "war-mongering pressure groups" that were confusing the White House at the behest of an unidentified country in order to sabotage the negotiations about Iran's nuclear program:

> Unfortunately, a pressure group in the US, which is a warmongering group and is against constructive talks, is [pursuing] the interests of a foreign country and mostly receives its orders from that foreign country. ... The interests of one foreign country and one group have been imposed on the members of the US Congress. And we can see that even the interests of the United States are not considered in such actions.[32]

Guess which country he meant. Despite the fact that several UN Security Council resolutions on the Iranian nuclear program were adopted unanimously or almost unanimously and with the consent of all the veto-holding powers, and despite the fact that the whole world wanted Iran to stop its weapon-related nuclear enterprise, Rouhani accused just one country—Israel—of pulling the strings against the interests of the American people. He accuses Israel of giving orders to the US Israel lobby not for the sake of peace but for the sake of war; not in order to foster constructive talks but in order to prevent successful negotiations; and not in support of the American people but in opposition to American interests. "The Jews are our misfortune," was the battle cry of the German antisemitic newspaper *Der Stürmer*, which helped pave the road to Auschwitz. "Israel—the war-mongering Jew—is our misfortune," appears to be the gist of Rouhani's remarks at his first press conference. Once again, it is clear that he differs from Ahmadinejad in tone but not in substance.

Rouhani has abandoned the regime's extreme antisemitic tirades and replaced them with somewhat more sober antisemitic ranting. Does this constitute an im-

---

29 "Holocaust Denial in Iran: Iranian Website Claims Holocaust Photos Are Forgeries," MEMRI Special Dispatch Series, no. 5571, December 20, 2013.

30 Aladdin Project, "Aladdin Project President Tells President Rouhani to Stop Iran's Policy of Holocaust Denial, Anti-Semitic Statements in State-Run Media," press release, November 14, 2013.

31 "Ayatollah Khamenei Tweets Support for French Anti-Semite," *the algemeiner*, December 17, 2013.

32 "Rouhani: US officials still do not fully grasp Iran's realities," *Iran Daily Brief*, August 9, 2013.

provement? Yes and no. There is a disturbing tendency in the West to be relieved about or even satisfied with anything that is less radical than Ahmadinejad. Thus, while the totalitarian character of this regime has remained the same, the world media's attitude toward the Islamic Republic of Iran has changed dramatically. Most politicians and journalists in the West have a good feeling about the new Iranian president. They do not want to spoil this feeling by looking too closely at what Rouhani or his boss Khamenei actually say or do. They would rather allow themselves to be taken in by the new Iranian government's public relations spin than acknowledge the unchanging policy that underlies it. Ahmadinejad was terrible but he did create a certain team spirit among the Western powers and Israel. Rouhani is not much better but seems to be succeeding in isolating Israel by luring the Western powers over to his side.

In November 2013, for example, Ali Khamenei ranted and raved at the Jewish state, calling it a "sinister, unclean rabid dog" and added that "Israelis should not be called humans." Khamenei used this language just hours before the negotiations on Iran's nuclear program were set to resume in Geneva. Previously, such ranting would have prompted Western diplomats to walk out of the UN General Assembly. Now, the Western powers did not even address Khamenei's inflammatory language during the Geneva talks. The fact that the leader of an American negotiating partner had used language that strongly recalled Nazi incitement went unheeded.[33]

IV. Conclusion

In conclusion, Iranian antisemitism exists. It is deeply rooted in history and has formed a key part of the regime's ideology since 1979. Under Rouhani, it has changed its appearance but not its character. The Holocaust is still denied, "international Zionism" is still held responsible for all the evils of the world, and Israel's annihilation continues to be propagated—though in a less radical form. The West cherishes the delusory hope that Iran has already undergone a fundamental change in this respect—or that such change is genuinely possible—under Rouhani. As demonstrated in this paper, however, this is clearly not the case. History shows the folly of failing to take antisemitism seriously. It reminds us that false hope eventually leads to all-out conflict. That is what we must bear in mind. That is what we must prevent.

[33] According to Marie Harf, Deputy Speaker of the State Department, "The negotiations had not addressed the topic ... of inflammatory language used by Iranian officials against Israel." See Rebecca Shimoni Stoil, "P5+1 talks on Iran's nukes to resume on Monday," *Times of Israel*, December 7, 2013.

Antisemitism in the Public and Private Discourse of Hezbollah

Matthew Levitt with Kelsey Segawa*

> If we search the entire globe for a more cowardly, lowly, weak, and frail individual in his spirit, mind, ideology, and religion, we will never find anyone like the Jew—and I am not saying the Israeli: we have to know the enemy we are fighting.
>
> Hassan Nasrallah, 1997

> Most assuredly our attitude toward Israel is not an attitude toward Jews or Judaism.
>
> Hassan Nasrallah, 1998

Introduction

Founded in the early 1980s by a group of young Shi'a militants, Hezbollah—the Party of God—was the product of an Iranian effort to aggregate under one roof a variety of militant Shi'a groups in Lebanon, themselves the products of the domestic and regional instability of the time. On the one hand, Hezbollah was the outgrowth of a complex and bloody civil war, during which the country's historically marginalized Shi'a Muslims attempted to assert economic and political power for the first time. But Hezbollah was also the product of outside elements, specifically Iran. Shortly after the Israeli invasion of southern Lebanon in 1982, approximately 1,500 Islamic Revolutionary Guard Corps (IRGC) advisors set up a base in the Beqaa Valley as part of Iran's goal to export the Islamic Revolution to the Arab world.[1] All Hezbollah members were required to attend IRGC-run camps in the valley, according to Hezbollah Deputy Secretary-General Naim Qassem, which taught them how to confront the enemy.[2]

Iran's logistical and financial support was crucial, but it supplied much more than that. The founding manifesto of Hezbollah contained a commitment to establish an Islamic state in Lebanon and recognized the rule of *velayet e-faqih* (guardianship of the jurist)—in other words, it promised to obey Iran's ruling Shi'ite clerics. Hezbol-

---

* Dr. Matthew Levitt is the Fromer-Wexler fellow and director of the Stein Program on Counterterrorism and Intelligence at the Washington Institute for Near East Policy. Kelsey Segawa is a research intern in the Washington Institute's Stein program.

[1] Daniel Byman, *Deadly Connections: States that Sponsor Terrorism* (Cambridge: Cambridge University Press, 2007), 82.

[2] Naim Qassem, *Hizbullah: The Story from Within* (London: Al Saqi Books, 2005), 66.

lah's ideology has closely mirrored Iran's ever since—including its ingrained antisemitism. As a running theme, antisemitism can be found at all levels of the Hezbollah enterprise: leaders, members, formal organizations, individual followers, and so forth. It is both an official, sanctioned phenomenon and an unsanctioned layperson phenomenon. And as new media platforms became available, Hezbollah adapted its antisemitic statements in order to take advantage of them. From public lectures reported in the press, to radio, television, satellite television, and now social media outlets, Hezbollah's messaging—including its antisemitic material, both audio and visual—has developed over time. Indeed, it has also shifted with the times. With the advent of global media, antisemitic statements not only reach the ears of Hezbollah's core constituents and followers but those of Western audiences as well. For a while, Hezbollah leaders proactively held their tongues and refrained from making blatantly antisemitic statements. This self-restraint would prove to be short lived, however, and Hezbollah's antisemitic messaging continues today.

I. HEZBOLLAH'S ANTISEMITIC LEXICON

Antisemitism has been present in Hezbollah since its inception in the 1980s. A religious edict in the mid-1980s legitimized drug trafficking for the purpose of killing Jews (see below). Antisemitic sentiment from official sources was curtailed a couple of times, including in the late 1990s and again after the September 11 attacks, when Hezbollah did not want to be placed in the same basket as al-Qaeda, which it denounced.[3] In March 1998, Hezbollah's Secretary-General, Hassan Nasrallah, explicitly denied any animosity toward the Jews as a people. "Most assuredly our attitude toward Israel is not an attitude toward Jews or Judaism," he said. "[O]ur war is not against Judaism or Jews but against Zionism."[4] Much of Hezbollah's more noxious antisemitic material predates the year 2000. Indeed, Hezbollah's official website posts almost none of Hassan Nasrallah's speeches before that year.

In 2002, the news director for Hezbollah's al-Manar satellite television station told an American journalist that antisemitic remarks had been banned from its broadcasts. Yet, in the very same breath, the director mentioned that he was considering a program on "scholars who dissent on the issue of the Holocaust."[5] Hezbollah went even further in 2005, when four anti-Zionist rabbis spoke at a pro-Palestinian conference in Beirut, also attended by Hamas. At the time, Abdullah Qusseir, a Hezbollah MP, said: "Hezbollah has never been against religions. Hezbollah supports all religions, it supports interfaith dialogue, and it has no problem with any religion. Hezbollah considers Zionism to be the enemy, not the Jews as a people or a religion."[6] Then, in 2009, Hezbollah issued a new manifesto.

---

3 Bilal Y. Saab and Bruce O. Riedel, "No Love Lost: Hezbollah and Al Qaeda," *New York Times*, April 9, 2007, http://www.nytimes.com/2007/04/09/opinion/09iht-edsaab.1.5198514.html.

4 Sayyed Hassan Nasrallah, "On Conditional Withdrawal," trans. Nicholas Noe, in *Voice of Hezbollah: The Statements of Hassan Nasrallah*, ed. Ellen Khouri (London: Verso, 2007), 185-86.

5 Jeffrey Goldberg, "A Reporter at Large: In the Party of God," *New Yorker*, October 14, 2002.

6 "Anti-Zionist Rabbis Join Hizbullah and Hamas at Beirut Pro-Palestinian Convention," MEMRI TV Clip no. 570, February 23, 2005, http://www.memritv.org/clip/en/570.htm.

The party maintained that it was a national Lebanese organization protecting the country against the Israeli threat, thereby de-emphasizing its Islamist goals. In a country with a large Christian population, parts of which had formed a political alliance with Hezbollah, an official platform calling for the establishment of an Islamic state could undermine support within the Christian community. Opposing Israel, on the other hand, is still a widely popular stance in the Arab Middle East.

While there is no way of knowing for certain why Hezbollah has adopted this stance, the fact remains that the majority of Nasrallah's speeches on the group's main Arabic-language news website (www.moqawama.org)[7] do not even mention Jews. Meanwhile, in 1992, Nasrallah was making statements that pledged eternal animosity toward Jews:

> You Jews, leave our land, you have no home among us, go back from where you came, for there will never be peace or reconciliation between us, only war, resistance, and the language of war and bullets.[8]

And while Hezbollah obviously opposes Israel's existence in word and deed, not all of its antisemitic statements are tied to Israel. In 1997, Hezbollah expressed concern about the movie *Independence Day*, in which a Jewish actor played a Jewish scientist (alongside a US Air Force pilot played by Will Smith) defending the planet against an alien invasion. It was "propaganda for the so-called genius of the Jews and their alleged concern for humanity," Hezbollah asserted in a statement, and called on Muslims to boycott the movie. Interestingly, it appears few people heeded the boycott call. The film was a worldwide hit and did just fine in Lebanon, raking in only a little less than it did in Egypt, a country with a population fifteen times larger than Lebanon's. The *New York Times* called its $600,000 earnings "an impressive showing for any film."[9]

Hezbollah institutions employ expressly antisemitic motifs as well, such as the fundraising brochure produced by the Islamic Resistance Support Organization (IRSO), designated by the US Treasury Department as "a key Hezbollah fundraising organization." IRSO stood out in part for not bothering to obfuscate its support for violence, as many charities tied to terrorism financing tend to do. "IRSO's fundraising materials present donors with the option of sending funds to equip Hezbollah fighters or to purchase rockets that Hezbollah uses to target civilian populations," a Treasury official noted, adding that "IRSO works to inflict suffering rather than alleviate it."[10] The IRSO's solicitation materials made it clear to prospective donors that funds would be used to purchase weapons and conduct operations. But the message was clear enough from the organization's fundraising brochure, which

---

[7] "Terrorism in Cyberspace: Hezbollah's Internet Network" (Meir Amit Intelligence and Terrorism Information Center 2013), http://www.terrorism-info.org.il/Data/articles/Art_20488/E_276_12_739632364.pdf.

[8] Sayyed Hassan Nasrallah, "Elegy for Sayyed Abbas Mussawi," trans. Nicholas Noe, in Khouri, *Voice of Hezbollah*, 52-55.

[9] Judith Miller, "Making Money Abroad, and Also a Few Enemies," *New York Times*, January 26, 1997.

[10] US Department of the Treasury, "Treasury Designates Key Hizbullah Funding Organization," press release, August 29, 2006, http://www.treasury.gov/press-center/press-releases/Pages/hp73.aspx.

depicted coins falling into a collection box in the shape of Jerusalem's al-Aqsa mosque (with a picture of Hezbollah chief Nasrallah superimposed on the mosque). Falling out the bottom of the collection box—clearly the product of those donations—were bullets targeting a broken Star of David. To top it all off, the same image appeared in a children's activity kit, next to a pre-printed envelope the children could cut out and use to send in their own donations. The brochures and kits were part of a fundraising campaign nicknamed "savings account" and were discovered by Israeli forces during the 2006 Lebanon War.[11]

Hezbollah's antisemitic tendencies have other practical uses beyond raising funds for explicitly militant behavior, such as justifying the group's criminal and violent activities. For example, one *fatwa* or religious edict (presumably issued by Iranian clerics) provided Lebanese Shi'ite drug dealers with a theological basis for their business with Western consumers: "We are making drugs for Satan—America and the Jews. If we cannot kill them with guns, so we will kill them with drugs."[12] An FBI report noted that "Hezbollah's spiritual leader has stated that narcotics trafficking is morally acceptable if the drugs are sold to Western infidels as part of the war against the enemies of Islam."[13]

II. Breaking down Hezbollah's Jew-hating

Despite its periodic self-restraint, Hezbollah's antisemitic worldview has continued to appear in a variety of ways and from a range of sources. The most clear-cut examples are verbal attacks, which can usually be grouped into denigrations of the Jewish character, abuse of Judaism as a religion, and accusations of Jewish conspiracies. All three angles are reminiscent of medieval European antisemitic motifs.

Character insults seize upon and propagate the old Shylockian stereotypes of greedy, power-hungry, and cowardly Jews. "If we search the entire globe for a more cowardly, lowly, weak, and frail individual in his spirit, mind, ideology, and religion," proclaimed Hassan Nasrallah in 1997, "we will never find anyone like the Jew—and I am not saying the Israeli: we have to know the enemy we are fighting."[14] Even after Nasrallah's March 1998 declaration, in which he asserted that Hezbollah had nothing against the Jews, subsequent statements gave the lie to those words. One year later, he was boasting about the decline of the Israeli army.

---

11 Islamic Resistance Support Organization fundraising brochure, image (Meir Amit Intelligence and Terrorism Information Center, August 2006), http://www.terrorism-info.org.il/data/articles/Art_18699/hezbollah_funds_1.jpg.

12 LaVerle Berry et al., *A Global Overview of Narcotics-Funded Terrorist and Other Extremist Groups*, report prepared by the Federal Research Division, Library of Congress (Washington, DC: Library of Congress, 2002), https://www.loc.gov/rr/frd/pdf-files/NarcsFundedTerrs_Extrems.pdf; Ron Ben Yishai, "Hizbullah's Drug Link: The Ayatollahs Allowed Drug Traffic as a Weapon against Israel," *Yediot Ahronot* (Tel Aviv), June 6, 1997.

13 US Department of Justice, Federal Bureau of Investigation, "International Radical Fundamentalism: An Analytical Overview of Groups and Trends," November 1994, declassified on November 20, 2008.

14 Sayyed Hassan Nasrallah, "The Martyrdom of Hadi Nasrallah," trans. Nicholas Noe, in Khouri, *Voice of Hezbollah*, 171.

> Where are the impressive and easy victories? Where is the iron power for the invincible army? … These questions are not an exercise in romantic delusions about a complete defeat for the Israeli army, but an unquestionable gateway to understanding the pace of degeneration, which has struck the psychological mindset that is absolutely dependent on power. Power is one of the most import aspects of the Jewish psyche. … Power is an existential issue, even for the very identity of Israel. Jewish history embraces symbols like the story of Samson, who from defeat and death drew his last strength.[15]

In any case, it took Nasrallah less than a year to return to Jew-bashing. Barely two months after his denial of antisemitism, Nasrallah gave a speech dedicated to the villainy and odiousness of Jews. Describing them as "the descendants of apes and pigs," he decried Israel as "a few million vagabonds from all over the world, brought together by their Talmud and Jewish fanaticism."[16] The list goes on.

Judaism itself also comes in for a fair amount of abuse. Hezbollah officials and representatives have sought to discredit Judaism by misrepresenting the Old Testament and reviving the myth of Jewish blood libel. Hezbollah's al-Manar satellite television station broadcast several programs purporting to educate its viewers about the "true" nature of Judaism. In one, al-Manar displays pictures of Israeli leaders with the label "terrorist," ending with these words misrepresented from the book of Isaiah: "When you enter a village, stab those you encounter, kill with a sword those you capture, pulverize children on sight, take homes by force, and rape the women."[17] The original passage, verses 15 and 16 from chapter 13, are in fact a prophecy of the retribution that would fall upon Babylon. The text is actually in the passive voice, not an active command, though al-Manar's interpretation implies that it is commanding the Jewish people to do these terrible things.

In another program, al-Manar brings in a guest who is said to be an expert on Israeli weapons of mass destruction. He informs viewers that "there are Torah-based reasons for many Americans to use WMD. … Therefore, it is essential that there be a world and Arab movement against this Torah-based project. This is a Torah-based plan to finish all Islam."[18] Judaism is frequently portrayed as an inhumane religion whose adherents seek to dominate and oppress the rest of the world. On a program called *Files*, Sheikh Taha al-Sabounji, a leading cleric in northern Lebanon, warned in April 2002 that Judaism was "a project against all humanity." He also denied the premise on which Hezbollah officials had recently begun to rely, namely that Zionism was a separate issue from Judaism: "There is no such thing as Zionism … there is only Judaism … Zionism is a legend, a myth."[19]

Despite these programs, al-Manar continued to broadcast freely in Europe. Finally, in February 2004, al-Manar aired a series that galvanized Western governments to

---

15 Hassan Nasrallah, speech, March 6, 1999, http://www.moqawama.org/essaydetails.php?eid=7279&cid=142#.UtfyU_RduCk.

16 Sayyed Hassan Nasrallah, "On Jews," trans. Nicholas Noe, in Khouri, *Voice of Hezbollah*, 188.

17 Avi Jorisch, *Beacon of Hatred: Inside Hizballah's al-Manar Television* (Washington, DC: The Washington Institute for Near East Policy, 2004), 66.

18 Ibid., 59.

19 Ibid., 64.

take action. Eventually, France (2004), the Netherlands (2005), Spain (2005), and Germany (2008) banned the station,[20] and the United States listed it as a Specially Designated Global Terrorist entity in 2006 for inciting terrorist activity.[21] The series in question, *al-Shatat* (The Diaspora), revived the concept of blood libel, one of the most notorious antisemitic libels, which claimed that Jews abducted Christian children and used their blood to make their Passover matza (unleavened bread). In the relevant scene, a Jewish rabbi plots to find a sacrificial Christian child. The chosen boy begs for mercy, addressing one of the Jews by name, only to have his throat slit and his blood collected for the matza.[22]

Hezbollah's antisemitism also parlays *modern-day conspiracy theories*. Less than a week after 9/11, an al-Manar broadcast posited that Israelis and Jews were complicit in the attacks. By this account, some 4,000 Jews survived the attacks because Israeli intelligence warned them of the impending disaster ahead of time and they did not go into work on September 11.[23] Similarly, Hezbollah leaders alternately deny the Holocaust or claim that the Jews themselves intentionally incited it. In 1998, Muhammad Ra'id, the head of Hezbollah's Political Council, said: "From what we know of the Jews, their tricks and their deceptions, we do not think it unlikely that they partook in the planning of the Holocaust. … [At a minimum,] they prepared the foreground which incited the Nazis to the Holocaust killings, so that they could serve their settlement project in Palestine."[24] The Jews are also attempting to Judaize Jerusalem, forcing out Muslims and Christians and destroying their holy places. "Jerusalem, for the Israelis, is a critical issue," Nasrallah says, "and their plan for it is for it to become a Jewish city."[25]

At times, Hezbollah tries to *portray Judaism as being in conflict with Islam*, with the former trying to oppress or supplant the latter. An influential Shi'ite cleric credited as being one of Hezbollah's early ideological guides, Mohammed Hussein Fadlallah,[26] described Israel's supporters as "a group which wants to establish Jewish culture at the expense of Islamic culture," and the country was meant to gather "all the Jews in the world to this region, to make it the nucleus for spreading

---

20 Ben Saul and Daniel Joyce, "International Approaches to the Regulation of Al-Manar Television and Terrorism-Related Content" (Australian Communications and Media Authority, 2011), http://www.acma.gov.au/webwr/_assets/main/lib310780/intntl_approaches-regulation-al-manar_tv_and_terrorism-related_content.pdf.

21 United States Treasury Department, "U.S. Designates Al-Manar as a Specially Designated Global Terrorist Entity Television Station is Arm of Hizballah Terrorist Network," press release, August 23, 2006, http://www.treasury.gov/press-center/press-releases/Pages/js4134.aspx.

22 Palestinian Media Watch, "Blood Libel on Hizbollah TV: Jews Take Blood of a Christian Child for Passover Matzah, Nov. 18, 2003," YouTube video, September 24, 2009, http://www.youtube.com/watch?v=mnYJGX4mCw8.

23 Avi Jorisch, "Al Manar: Hizbullah TV, 24/7," *Middle East Quarterly* 11, no. 1 (2004): 17-31.

24 Amal Saad-Ghorayeb, *Hizbu'llah: Politics and Religion* (London: Pluto Press, 2001), 182.

25 Hassan Nasrallah, interview, al-Manar TV, March 31, 2010, http://www.moqawama.org/essaydetails.php?eid=21598&cid=140#.UtapWfRDuCk.

26 For a discussion of Fadlallah's relationship with Hezbollah, see Matthew Levitt, *Hezbollah: The Global Footprint of Lebanon's Party of God* (Washington, DC: Georgetown University Press, 2013), 24-28.

their economic and cultural domination."[27] Nasrallah has alternately propagated the conspiracy theory of a Jewish-Christian alliance against Muslims and of an exclusively Jewish plot against Christians and Muslims alike. Speaking about the 2003 Iraq War, Nasrallah told followers: "The Jews have long hoped for a war that pits a Jewish-Christian alliance against the Muslim nation."[28] But three years earlier, Nasrallah peddled a different message: "In the eyes of these Zionists, we Christians and Muslims are mere servants and slaves to God's chosen people."[29] The truth apparently varies according to the nature of Hezbollah's alliance and the sectarian balance in Lebanon at any given time.

Antisemitism on al-Manar continues today, as noted in the State Department's recently released Annual Country Report on Human Rights.[30] In 2014, al-Manar aired a program claiming that Jews had invented a number of Hollywood movies, and even Hollywood itself, in order to subversively insert Jewish superiority into American and global culture. Because Jews "felt rejected by real American society," the narrator says, "they tried to change society's opinion of them by inventing cinematic characters that would serve as role models." She cites the example of Superman, who only fit into society by taking on the pathetic persona of Clark Kent. The Jews, according to the narrator, slyly implied that their weak public face hid their true superhuman identity. "Hollywood is a Jewish invention that changed the way Americans view America," she continues. "Undoubtedly, the goal was to take over the greatest superpower in the world."[31] Though a Western audience would likely find the program laughable, it is presented with all seriousness. And the fact that such a claim could be made with a straight face suggests a deep underlying assumption of Jewish insidiousness and scheming ambition.

III. Hezbollah's Antisemitism as Portrayed by Its Followers

The trickle-down effect of Hezbollah's antisemitic corporate culture, as it were, is evident in the actions and attitudes of its grassroots supporters. Even when the party's official stance denied any antisemitic leanings, insisting its beef was limited to Israel and Zionism, the shift has not been reflected among its followers. In part, this may be an indication of how deeply ingrained antisemitism is in the culture of Hezbollah and how early on in a young follower's development the group begins to instill such sentiments.

The Imam al-Mahdi Scouts is Hezbollah's radical version of America's Boy Scouts youth movement. According to Lebanon's *Daily Star*, it "teaches young boys

---

[27] Martin Kramer, "The Oracle of Hizbullah," in *Spokesmen for the Despised*, ed. R. Scott Appleby (Chicago: University of Chicago Press, 1996), 116.

[28] Sayyed Hassan Nasrallah, "The Impending Iraq War and 'Muslim-Christian Alignment,'" trans. Nicholas Noe, in Khouri, *Voice of Hezbollah*, 286.

[29] Sayyed Hassan Nasrallah, "Victory," trans. Nicholas Noe, in Khouri, *Voice of Hezbollah*, 238.

[30] Bureau of Democracy, Human Rights and Labor, *Lebanon 2014 Human Rights Report* (Washington, DC: US State Department, 2014), 32-33, http://www.state.gov/documents/organization/236822.pdf.

[31] "Hizbullah TV: Jews Invented Superman in the Service of Global Jewish Goals," MEMRI TV Clip no. 4157, February 10, 2014, http://www.memritv.org/clip/en/4157.htm.

the basics of religion, jihad and the ways of the revolution as a prelude to carrying weapons in the anti-Israeli resistance in the South."[32] But it is far more than that. "Religious and moral instruction—rather than physical activity—occupy the vast bulk of the Mahdi Scouts' curriculum," the *New York Times* reports, including distinctly antisemitic themes. Text books for the Mahdi Scouts' 12- to 14-year-old age group include a chapter entitled "Facts about Jews" in which Jews are described as "cruel, corrupt, cowardly and deceitful, and they are called the killers of prophets." It goes on to state "their Talmud says those outside the Jewish religion are animals."[33]

It should not come as a surprise, therefore, that antisemitism is prevalent not only among Hezbollah's official members and operatives but among its followers and sympathizers as well. Consider, for example, the comments of a young Hezbollah guerilla fighter who escorted a reporter writing for the *New Yorker* magazine around southern Lebanon in 2002. Looking out over the red-roofed houses of an Israeli community just across the border, the guerilla informed that "the Jews are sons of pigs and apes."[34]

Intercepted phone calls from an FBI investigation into a Hezbollah fundraising cell in North Carolina recorded speakers condemning an undesirable news outlet back home in Lebanon: "God damn everything that they show, they are Jews! They are Jews!" Discussing a fellow Lebanese individual who they were told had been executed as a traitor, the Hezbollah sympathizers in Charlotte cursed the turncoat by referring to him as a Jew. Evidence from the same North Carolina case included propaganda videotapes. In one, Hassan Nasrallah lambasts then-Palestinian Authority president Yasser Arafat for giving "the land of the Palestinians to the Zionist Jews, the Murderers, the Savages, the Racists who committed every crime against the people of Palestine."[35] A reporter for *Vice* related a story about going paintballing with several Hezbollah fighters in 2012, one of whom showed off his marksmanship by firing bullets at a rope and saying "Yahud," or "Jew," with each shot.[36]

Hezbollah's antisemitic rhetoric, however, echoes far beyond the immediate circle of its official militants and operatives to include like-minded followers and sympathizers as well. At a Montreal rally in 2009, protesters waved the Palestinian and Hezbollah flags and burned Israeli flags. A teenage boy took up the catchy Arabic chant of "Filastin biladna, w'al-Yahud kilabna," meaning "Palestine is ours, and the Jews are our dogs."[37] That same day, at another rally featuring the flags of

---

32 Mohammed Zaatari, "Hizbullah Scout Movement Trains Young Soldiers," *Daily Star* (Beirut), August 24, 2004.

33 Robert Worth, "Hezbollah Seeks to Marshal the Piety of the Young," *New York Times*, November 20, 2008, http://www.nytimes.com/2008/11/21/world/middleeast/21lebanon.html?hp=&pagewanted=all.

34 Goldberg, "Reporter at Large."

35 *United States of America v. Mohamad Youssef Hammoud and Chawki Youssef Hammoud*, Case: 265B-CE-82188, item: S01052002, 1B: 268, translated by LS Hesham A. Elgamiel, March 16, 2001.

36 Mitchell Prothero, "Paintballing with Hezbollah is the Path Straight to Their Hearts," *Vice*, March 26, 2012.

37 "Montreal Rally of Hate; Islamists, Trade Unionists, and PQ Monique Richard: Jan 10th 2009," YouTube video, January 12, 2009, http://www.youtube.com/watch?v=6UWPeK-uydk.

Hezbollah and Palestine, in Toronto, a woman shouted: "Jewish child, you're going to f***ing die!"[38]

Conclusion

Hezbollah today faces a variety of challenges stemming from both its actions and its words. The group's greatest challenge stems from its active participation in the war in Syria. By siding with the Assad regime, the regime's Alawite supporters, and Iran and taking up arms against Sunni rebels, Hezbollah has placed itself at the epicenter of a sectarian conflict that has nothing to do with the group's purported raison d'être: "resistance" to Israeli occupation. The ugly, sectarian language Hezbollah and other Shi'ite militias have employed demeaning Sunni Muslims is no less disgusting than its antisemitic rhetoric denigrating Jews.[39] Shi'a invectives brand Sunnis as *nasabi* (pl. *nawasib*), or those who hate the Prophet Muhammad and his family, while the Shi'a in turn are labeled as worse than Jews. Yusuf al-Qaradawi, an influential Sunni cleric, accused the Shi'a of being "bigger infidels than even the Jews or the Christians."[40] The vicious back-and-forth between Shi'a and Sunnis does not bode well for future sectarian harmony in the region.

Meanwhile, Hezbollah operatives have also been indicted for the murder of former Lebanese prime minister Rafiq Hariri at the UN Special Tribunal for Lebanon (STL) in The Hague, arrested on charges of plotting attacks in Nigeria, and convicted on similar charges in Thailand and Cyprus. The European Union has blacklisted the military wing of Hezbollah, and the Gulf Cooperation Council similarly banned any support for the group from GCC countries and started deporting suspected supporters.

The demonization of Jews that is reflected in Hezbollah's antisemitic language and that of its supporters is in large part an effort to provide moral justification for the organization's terrorism and political violence. Hezbollah has demonstrated both the motivation and the capability to attack not only Israeli but also distinctly Jewish targets. This should not come as a surprise. Fadlallah said in October 1992 that "it must be made clear to Israel that when one of our civilians is killed by its rockets, a Jewish civilian will also be killed by one of our rockets."[41] In 2002, Nasrallah remarked: "If they [the Jews] all gather in Israel, it will save us the trouble of going after them worldwide."[42]

As that has yet to happen, Hezbollah seems content to target Israeli and Jewish interests around the world. In the 1990s, for example, Hezbollah operatives blew up the AMIA Jewish community center in Buenos Aires. In more recent years, Hezbollah terrorist plots have proliferated on a scale and scope not seen since the late 1980s

---

38 "Canadian Jewish Congress exposes incitement to hatred and violence at pro-Hamas rallies," YouTube video, January 14, 2009, http://www.youtube.com/watch?v=eXgMbZwUBeI.

39 Aaron Y. Zelin and Phillip Smyth, "The Vocabulary of Sectarianism," *Foreign Policy*, January 29, 2014, available at http://www.washingtoninstitute.org/policy-analysis/view/the-vocabulary-of-sectarianism.

40 Ibid.

41 Martin Kramer, "Oracle of Hizbullah," 155.

42 Jorisch, *Beacon of Hatred*, 65.

and early 1990s. Some plots, such as assassination attempts targeting Israelis in Azerbaijan, Thailand, and Nigeria have failed. But one in Bulgaria succeeded in killing several Israeli tourists and a Bulgarian bus driver, spurring the European Union to finally consider blacklisting Hezbollah's military and terrorist wings. When the EU finally did ban Hezbollah's militant wings in July 2013, it did so for a variety of reasons ranging from Hezbollah's involvement in the Syrian war to its terrorist plots and logistical and financial support activities in Europe.

But in one European plot in Cyprus, Hezbollah's antisemitic fixation on targeting Jews—not Israelis, but Jews—may also have factored into the calculus of some Europeans as they decided to ban the group's military and terrorist wings. In this plot a European Hezbollah operative—a Swedish-Lebanese dual citizen—carried out surveillance of Israelis and Jews in Cyprus. At one point, Hezbollah tasked its agent "to spot Israeli restaurants in Limassol, where Jews eat kosher" in an apparent attempt to locate Jewish targets. Later, the Hezbollah operative would deny any wrongdoing when questioned by Cypriot police. In an effort to explain his behavior, he explained that he was not doing anything wrong, "it was just collecting information about the Jews, and this is what my organization is doing everywhere in the world."[43] In other words, Hezbollah's antisemitism is not only alive and well, not merely conceptual, but operational as well.

43 Matthew Levitt, "Hizb Allah Resurrected: The Party of God's Return to Tradecraft," *CTC Sentinel* 6, no. 4 (April 2013), available at http://www.ctc.usma.edu/posts/hizb-allah-resurrected-the-party-of-gods-return-to-tradecraft.

Arab and Muslim Antisemitism: Reconsideration, Reflection, and Some Propositions

Salim Mansur*

In Islamic society hostility to the Jew is non-theological.

Bernard Lewis, *The Jews of Islam*

The contemporary resurgence of post-Shoah antisemitism in Europe is an indisputable and menacing reality.[1] It is also an indisputable and menacing reality that the resurgent antisemitism in Europe rides, or is fuelled by, the even more menacing spread of Arab and Muslim antisemitism globally. Muslim antisemitism is driven by anti-Jew and anti-Israeli hatred packaged as religiously sanctioned by Muslim clerics such as Sheikh Yusuf al-Qaradawi, the Qatari-based leader of the Muslim Brotherhood in Egypt, and the clerical-based political leadership of the Islamic Republic of Iran. Hence, the moot question in discussing Muslim antisemitism is in finding to what extent it is traceable to or rooted in the Qur'an and in the life of Muhammad, and to what extent it is a modern phenomenon that is in part imported from the West and in part a symptom of the deep-seated civilizational crisis within the Muslim world.

It is important, I believe, to examine forthrightly whether or not the Qur'an and the Sira (the biographical literature on the Prophet) sanction Islamic bigotry toward the Jews for the following reasons. First, if Muslim antisemitism is religiously based, then it can be said that there is no reprieve from the cycle of Islamic Judeophobia and that a future catastrophe for the Jews and Muslims can only be postponed but not averted. Secondly, it then follows that any relationship with Israel and Israelis based on mutual respect and interest, as sought by the late President Anwar Sadat of Egypt, is mistaken from a Muslim perspective and contrary to the traditionally scripted relationship instituted in the early years of Islamic history in which the Jews were accorded the status of *dhimmi* or protected people subordinate to the status of Muslims. And thirdly, opposition to Muslim antisemitism by the Jews, Christians, other non-Muslims, and even by Muslims, invariably leads to a conflict with more or less the entirety of Islam.

---

* Associate Professor of Political Science, University of Western Ontario, Canada.

1 See European Union Agency for Fundamental Rights, *Discrimination and Hate Crime against Jews in EU Member States: Experiences and Perceptions of Antisemitism* (Luxembourg: Publications Office of the European Union, 2013).

I approach this subject from the perspective that Arab and Muslim antisemitism is a modern phenomenon and that attempts by Muslims to give legitimacy to this politics and culture of hate by citing the Qur'an or the traditions of the Prophet as references are not merely misguided but constitute an abuse of Islam and its sacred texts. When non-Muslims, particularly the Jews for very understandable reasons, give credence to the thesis of Muslim hate-mongers that their derogatory views about the Jews are derived from the Qur'an and the biography of the Prophet, they are paradoxically legitimating Muslim antisemitism with potentially lethal consequences for Israel. It is also ominous that, in the early decades of the twenty-first century, Israel finds itself in the middle of the raging conflicts of the Middle East that are in origin tribal and sectarian and whose causes are internal to the fractious and schismatic nature of Arab-Muslim history; and even though Israel has neither a role in nor any responsibility for these conflicts it cannot insulate itself from their effects.

I believe that in confronting Muslim hate-mongers and antisemites, the paramount urgency is to deny and delegitimize their abusive reading of Islam's sacred texts. Indeed, the quelling of Muslim hate-mongers is inseparable from advancing modernist reform of Islam, and this is why non-Muslims are mistaken when they make allowances for the thesis of Arab and Muslim antisemites or agree with them that Islam obliges Muslims to vilify and fight the Jews as enemies of Allah.

Robert Wistrich has rightly described Muslim antisemitism as "a clear and present danger."[2] He painstakingly describes the vile characterizations of the Jews by Muslims. Those most guilty of spewing bigotry against the Jews are Palestinian Arabs and their religious, political, and intellectual leaders.[3] The role of Haj Amin al-Husseini, the Mufti of Jerusalem, as Hitler's collaborator in importing European antisemitism into the Middle East is well documented.[4] The Mufti's ideology and politics have not been disavowed openly and in public by Palestinians or by the religious and political leaders of Arabs or Muslims in general. On the contrary, the Mufti's ideology of hate-mongering against the Jews and the Zionist project has been emulated by an array of other leading Arab and Muslim intellectuals, activists, and religious leaders, including Hasan al-Banna, the founder of the Muslim Brotherhood; Sayyid Qutb, the intellectual heavyweight of the Muslim Brothers; Sheikh Ahmed Yassin, the founder of Hamas; the rulers, religious leaders, and imams of Saudi Arabia; the clerics of Cairo's al-Azhar, the most renowned and prestigious Sunni Muslim religious institution; Abul A'la Mawdudi, the Indo-Pakistani founder of the Jamaat-i-Islami; Ayatollah Khomeini, the Iranian architect of the Islamic Republic, its current Supreme Leader Ayatollah Ali Khamenei, and, notably, former presidents Akbar Rafsanjani and Mahmoud Ahmedinejad; the leaders of Hezbollah in Lebanon; Sheikh Yusuf al-Qaradawi, the popular Egyptian cleric on the Al Jazeera television network based in Qatar; the leadership and ranks of al-Qaeda and other "jihadi"

---

2 Robert S. Wistrich, *Muslim Anti-Semitism: A Clear and Present Danger* (American Jewish Committee, 2002).

3 See David Pollock, "Beyond Words: Causes, Consequences, and Cures for Palestinian Authority Hate Speech," Policy Focus 124 (Washington Institute for Near East Policy, 2013), http://www.washingtoninstitute.org/uploads/Documents/pubs/PolicyFocus124_Incitement.pdf.

4 See, for instance, David D. Dalin and John F. Rothmann, *Icon of Evil: Hitler's Mufti and the Rise of Radical Islam* (New York: Random House, 2008).

(holy war) organizations, such as the Taliban in Afghanistan and Pakistan; and non-clerical or secular Muslim leaders like Mahathir Mohamad, the former prime minister of Malaysia. Clearly, the front of Muslim antisemitism is wide and deep.

It might be supposed that so many prominent Muslims cannot all be wrong in insisting that their hatred for the Jews, Zionists, and Israel is sanctioned by Islam. History, however, is replete with examples of people proven wrong in their beliefs and politics, who were eventually faced with the evil consequences of their errors. In this regard, Islamic history itself bears testimony to the wrongs done by Muslims, for which they have suffered grievously.

I.

The Jewish-Muslim relationship, as the historical record from the earliest years of Islam shows, has been difficult and marked by quarrels that turned ugly. Muhammad's engagement with the Jews of Arabia who settled in Yathrib (later known as Medinat-un-nabi, the Prophet's city, or simply Medina once the Prophet permanently settled there) turned uneasy and culminated in their expulsion and massacre. There are references to these events in the Qur'an and in the earliest biography of the Prophet. We are nevertheless compelled to ask if these references can be construed as evidence of Islam's "Ur-antisemitism" that Muslim hate-mongers deploy in sanctifying their vilification of the Jews. According to Neil Kressel, "[t]he problem goes way beyond the Nazi-like rants of extremist clerics. And far from being a by-product of the Arab-Israeli conflict, Jew hatred has roots in the long history and complex theology of Islam."[5]

In expanding on his thesis, Kressel points to Sheikh Mohamed Sayyid Tantawi, the former Grand Imam and Rector of al-Azhar who died in 2010, as an example of a contemporary Muslim antisemite who validated his bigotry by appealing to traditional Muslim Judeophobia based on negative references to the Jews in the Qur'an and in the traditions of the Prophet. Tantawi was viewed by many as a liberal Muslim reformer, and from his position of influence and authority he condemned suicide-bombings after 9/11, defended the Egyptian-Israeli peace treaty signed by President Anwar Sadat and Prime Minister Menachem Begin, denounced female circumcision common in Egypt, supported the ban on *niqab* (the full face cover worn by some Muslim women), and promoted inter-faith meetings with Christian and Jewish religious leaders. But when it came to the Jews and Israel, Tantawi displayed antisemitism masked as traditional Muslim Judeophobia prevalent across the Muslim world. Kressel writes,

> His [Tantawi's] doctoral dissertation, written in 1969, disparaged Jews with an abundance of quotations from the Quran and other religious sources. In this lengthy theological work, he detailed the Jews' supposedly evil ways and how they purportedly endeavored to entrap the Muslims during Muhammad's era. Tantawi's reading of the Quran ascribes to the Jews a slew of unflattering characteristics, including wanton envy, lasciviousness, religious fanaticism, murderous-

---

[5] Neil J. Kressel, *"The Sons of Pigs and Apes": Muslim Antisemitism and the Conspiracy of Silence* (Washington, DC: Potomac Books, 2012), 1.

ness, and a tendency toward "semantic bickering." Jews, collectively, are accused of corrupting Allah's word, consuming the people's wealth, and most ominously, murdering Allah's prophets.[6]

Kressel then observes that "[e]ven if one assumes that the Qur'anic text offers some basis for Tantawi's inferences, a true religious moderate might have argued that the verses in question apply only to particular Jews living in Muhammad's day."[7] Tantawi did not; instead, in a sermon delivered in April 2002, he called out the Jews as "the enemies of Allah, descendants of apes and pigs."[8] This phrase refers to a verse in the Qur'an (2:65), and it is commonly deployed by Muslim hate-mongers against the Jews and Israelis.

The depiction of the Jews as loathsome by Tantawi or Khomeini[9] or Sayyid Qutb is done, as Wistrich writes, "not simply to morally delegitimize Israel as a Jewish state and a national identity in the Middle East, but to dehumanize Judaism and the Jewish people as such."[10] Such depiction with reference to the Qur'an and early Muslim history is, according to Bassam Tibi, the Islamization of European antisemitism.[11] And this could occur, in Tibi's view, because Judeophobia is present in Islamic history just as it is found in European history. But genocidal antisemitism, writes Tibi, is "a specifically European, primarily German, disease that never existed in Islam before the twentieth century."[12] Similarly, Wistrich observes,

> The persistence, integrity, and depth of this hatred should not blind us, however, to the fact that, historically speaking, anti-Semitism is a relatively new phenomenon in Arab culture and among Muslims in general. It did not exist as a significant force in the traditional Islamic world, although, as we shall see, some of the seeds of contemporary anti-Jewish attitudes can be found in the Koran and other early Islamic sources.[13]

There is a distinction to be made, as both Tibi and Wistrich observe, between pre-modern Judeophobia in general and modern antisemitism that arose in Europe, specifically in Germany. Antagonism toward the Jews among Christians and Muslims in the pre-modern world was common, and both Christians and Muslims took recourse to their faith-traditions as a warrant for their Judeophobia. But despite this commonality Bernard Lewis has argued a distinction needs to be made between Christians and Muslims in their respective attitudes toward the Jews. According to Lewis,

> The story of a golden age of complete equality is, of course, nonsense. No such thing was possible or even conceivable. Indeed, among Christians and Muslims alike, giving equal rights or, more precisely, equal opportunities to unbelievers

6 Ibid., 3-4.

7 Ibid., 4.

8 Ibid.

9 See references to the Jews by Khomeini in *Islam and Revolution: Writings and Declarations of Imam Khomeini*, trans. and ann. Hamid Algar (Berkeley: Mizan Press, 1981).

10 Wistrich, *Muslim Anti-Semitism*, 4.

11 See Bassam Tibi, *Islamism and Islam* (New Haven/London: Yale University Press, 2012), 56.

12 Ibid., 55-56.

13 Wistrich, *Muslim Anti-Semitism*, 5.

would have been seen not as a merit but as a dereliction of duty. But until fairly modern times there was a much higher degree of tolerance in most of the Islamic lands than prevailed in the Christian world. For centuries, in most of Europe Christians were very busy persecuting each other; in their spare time, they were persecuting Jews and expelling Muslims—all at a time when, in the Ottoman Empire and some other Islamic states, Jews and several varieties of Christians were living side by side fairly freely and comfortably.[14]

The fusion of traditional Muslim Judeophobia and European antisemitism occurred in the shadow of Nazi Germany, with the import of the entire corpus of Russian and German antisemitism, from the fabricated *Protocols of the Elders of Zion* to support for Hitler's policy of extermination of the Jews, into the Middle East. This was the period during the inter-war years when the victors of World War I were precariously positioned in the Middle East, as the League of Nations' so-called Mandatory Powers, while the former subject peoples of the Ottoman Empire restlessly aspired to their own independence and statehood.

The collapse of the Ottoman Empire brought political instability to that part of the Arab-Muslim world ruled directly by (or under the nominal authority of) the Ottoman Caliph-Sultan residing in Istanbul. And when the Caliphate was abolished in 1924 by Mustapha Kemal and his supporters in post-Ottoman Turkey, which was reconstituted as a modern republican state, an entirely new problem arose for Muslims. The issue of legitimate order was at the heart of the dispute that broke out among the companions of the Prophet following his death, and what emerged through the ensuing discord was the institution of the Caliphate. The abolition of Caliphate by the Turkish leader meant Muslims were faced with the question not only how to eventually acquire independence from European colonial rule, but also how to reach a consensus in respect of the nature of legitimate authority in the new and unsettled age of post-Caliphate Islam. The argument over restoration of the Caliphate in some form or other, or the creation of a Sharia-based Islamic state as its approximation, became the distinguishing feature of political Islam, or Islamism, the ideology of socio-political movements such as the Muslim Brotherhood.

The Muslim distress that spread over the long period of decline of Islamic rule and loss of lands to European powers turned more bitter, especially among Arabs, in the twentieth century, following the partition of Palestine, the establishment of Israel, and the repeated defeats suffered by Arabs in their wars against the Jews. Arabs and Muslims view this history as insufferable, as deeply humiliating—bitter feelings that find expression in the vilest denunciation of the Jews as enemies of Islam and Muslims. As Lewis writes,

> Why then this special anger in the Muslim response to the end of Palestine and the birth of Israel? Part of this is certainly due to its position, in the very center of the Arab core of the Islamic world, and to its inclusion of the city of Jerusalem, which—after long and sometimes bitter disputes—was finally recognized as the third Holy City of Islam after Mecca and Medina. But most of all, the sense of outrage, as is clearly shown in countless speeches and writings, was aroused by the identity of those who inflicted these dramatic defeats on Muslim and Arab

14 Bernard Lewis, "The New Anti-Semitism," *The American Scholar* 75, no. 1 (Winter 2006).

> armies and imposed their rule on Muslim Arab populations. The victors were not the followers of a world religion or the armies of a mighty imperial power, by which one could be conquered without undue shame—not the Catholic kings of Spain, not the far-flung British Empire, not the immense and ruthless might of Russia—but the Jews, few, scattered, and powerless, whose previous humility made their triumphs especially humiliating.[15]

This recent history explains in part the nature of Arab and Muslim antisemitism, and why it continues to be ratcheted up in inverse relation to the repeated failures of Arabs to defeat Israel. It is also aggravated by the continuing discord over the nature of Islamic society, by the general economic, political, and cultural malaise across the Muslim world, by the discrediting of secular-nationalist regimes, and by sectarian conflicts that have spilled over into civil war across the Middle East and beyond into the wider Muslim world. The unwillingness to examine the causes internal to Muslim culture and history for this civilizational crisis has fostered among Muslims a culture of denial and a pathological proclivity to blame others, especially the Jews.

While Arab and Muslim antisemitism might be explained as symptomatic of Islamic civilization in disarray, what is not—and, I submit, cannot—be explained is Muslim bigotry against the Jews on the basis of Islam. If the argument that the Qur'an and the Prophet sanction Muslim Judeophobia is as true as Muslim hate-mongers insist, then what logically follows is unavoidable. Just as a few drops of lemon juice can curdle a bowl of milk, Judeophobia sanctioned by the Qur'an and the Prophet would mean that Islam as a religion of mercy is a falsehood. As a Muslim I recoil at this thought as should any Muslim reflecting upon the fallacy of the argument that those few references in the Qur'an about some Jews, or a segment of the Jewish population with whom Muhammad had a bitter encounter, can be read, as Muslim hate-mongers have done and continue to do, as divine wrath directed toward all the Jews till the end of time and that it is incumbent upon Muslims to fight them as enemies of God. Such a reading of the Qur'an is plainly wrong and indefensible. The question therefore arises how the Qur'anic references to the Jews should be interpreted in accordance with the Qur'an's overall message that Muslims believe is a sign of God's mercy for mankind.

The Qur'an is also the testimony and record of Muhammad's life. The few biographical references to Muhammad in the Qur'an represent what we indisputably know about him. These references constitute the core narrative or the bare outline of a life that was later much embroidered and embellished through the imaginative writings of his biographers, who assembled volumes of oral reports about the Prophet, most of them unreliable or of dubious merit, as supporting evidence of their scholarship. If Shakespeare's life remains contested despite the proximity of his age to ours, it is of no surprise that what we know of the Prophet with any degree of certainty is very little given the distance in time and, especially, since the people among whom he was born, the Arabs of the desert, lived at the margin of existing civilizations barely mentioned in recorded history.[16] But it might also be said that, since the Qur'an is the

---

15 Bernard Lewis, "The New Anti-Semitism," *New York Review of Books*, April 10, 1986.

16 See Clinton Bennett, *In Search of Muhammad* (London/New York: Cassell, 1998); see also Tarif Khalidi, *Images of Muhammad: Narratives of the Prophet in Islam across the Centuries* (New York: Doubleday, 2009).

most authentic source of the little we know about the Prophet, it vouchsafes the truthfulness of his life. It is a matter of Muslim belief that the Prophet conducted his affairs and lived his life consistent with the directives given to him as revealed in the Qur'an.

II.

Islam is not a new religion that sprouted in the relative barren soil of Arabia among a people at the margin of civilization. It is instead an expression of man's primordial faith in God—as narrated in the Hebrew Bible—renewed and restated at an inflection of history that proves providentially to be immensely fertile, which in seizing the imagination and devotion of a people propels them forward into the world as a new force bearing the old message of monotheism. The manner in which events surrounding this history unfolded was so remarkable that the shockwaves from that moment in time in the early decades of the seventh century of the Christian era still resonate more than fourteen centuries later.

In *Moses and Monotheism*, Sigmund Freud speculated about Moses' life and origin. This book, published in 1939, was his last before his death, and in it he described Judaism as a Father religion and Christianity as a Son religion. This description of Judaism and Christianity is striking, and following Freud we might describe Islam as a return to the Father religion that, as Judaism, had evolved into a strict and uncompromising monotheism relative to the Christian belief in which the idea of One God was somewhat diluted due to the Greek-Roman influence. Though an atheist till the end, Freud's last work as a testimony of a thinker deeply influenced by the religion and culture of his Jewish ancestors was packed with striking insights and was written while he witnessed Europe sink into a new age of barbarism. Freud made one reference to Islam, which reads as follows,

> [T]he founding of the Mohammedan religion seems to me to be an abbreviated repetition of the Jewish one, in imitation of which it made its appearance. There is reason to believe that the Prophet originally intended to accept the Jewish religion in full for himself and his people. The regaining of the one great primeval Father produced in the Arabs an extraordinary advance in self-confidence which led them to great worldly successes, but which, it is true, exhausted itself in these.[17]

Freud was not a scholar of Islam and, though there is no indication given by his biographers that he ventured into any study of Islam, it would not be outside the realm of possibility that he had heard of, or come across, the writings of those Jewish scholars—for instance, Rabbi Abraham Geiger (1810-74) or Freud's contemporary, Ignaz Goldziher (1850-1921)—who made significant contributions in the study of Islam and its sacred texts, the Qur'an, and the traditions of the Prophet. Freud's observations, which I have quoted above, uncannily echo a theme advanced by Geiger in his prize-winning monograph of 1833, the title of which, rendered into English, asks "What Did Muhammad Take from Judaism?"[18]

---

[17] Sigmund Freud, *Moses and Monotheism* (New York: Vintage Books, 1967), 118.

[18] Geiger's monograph was translated into English by F.M. Young in 1896 in Bangalore, India, and published two years later. The same edition was reissued as *Judaism and Islam* in 1970.

The thesis, according to Geiger, that "Muhammad in his Quran has borrowed much from Judaism as it presented itself to him in his time,"[19] is not strange given the numerous references to Hebrew prophets, their stories, and the highly elevated place Moses occupies in the Qur'an. Indeed, it might be said that the Qur'an is very much a Jewish text insomuch as the Jews were not merely the "People of the Book" (*ahl al-Kitab*) but the *first* people in the Semitic tradition called upon to worship the one and only God. The religion of the Jews and their stories were familiar to the pagan Arabs, who had lived in Arabia for nearly a millennium before Muhammad's time.[20] And since Muhammad preached the message of worshipping one God, the God of Abraham, it was only natural and reasonable that he held up the Jews, the Arabs' most proximate neighbors, as an example of a people subscribing to a monotheistic faith.

But the pagan Arabs, despite the length of time the Jews had lived among them, did not embrace the Jewish faith, nor did they accept Christianity, with which they were also familiar. It took a revelation from God to a man born among them, belonging to them by blood and customs, to wrench them away from polytheism and embrace the idea of one God, the single, unique Lord of Mankind—Allah in Arabic—whom Abraham discovered, Moses encountered and spoke with, Jesus manifested by his miraculous birth, and whose messenger among the Arabs was Muhammad.

Muslims believe that Muhammad did not borrow from Judaism or Christianity but that he revealed that which came to him from the same source that the Jews and the Christians hold as truth. There is one truth revealed time and again under different circumstances to different people at different places, and what was revealed to Muhammad was that one truth in the circumstances of the time and place in which his divinely ordained mission occurred.

God's revelation to Muhammad is the Qur'an, and for Muslims the Qur'an is God's Word. As Frithjof Schuon (1907-1998), a German philosopher, poet, and teacher or sage of the "perennial philosophy," has written, "[t]he great theophany of Islam is the Quran; it presents itself as being a 'discernment' (*furqan*) between truth and error."[21]

Before a text of the revelation was compiled, there was only the Word of God as heard by Muhammad, and it was through him that others received the Word. Whether or not Muhammad fabricated the Qur'an is an old controversy, one that surfaced during his lifetime. On this issue, the Qur'an itself states,

> [They fail to understand that] thou art only a warner, whereas God has everything in His care; and so they assert, "[Muhammad himself] has invented this [Qur'an]!"
>
> Say [unto them]: "Produce, then, ten surahs of similar merit, invented [by yourselves], and [to this end] call to your aid whomever you can, other than God, if what you say is true!" (11:12-13).

---

19 Abraham Geiger, *Judaism and Islam* (New York: Ktav Publishing House, 1970), 1.

20 See Gordon D. Newby, "The Jews of Arabia at the Birth of Islam," in *A History of Jewish-Muslim Relations: From the Origins to the Present Day*, ed. Abdelwahab Meddeb and Benjamin Stora (Princeton/Oxford: Princeton University Press, 2013), 39-51.

21 Frithjof Schuon, *Understanding Islam* (Bloomington, IN: World Wisdom Books, Inc., 1994), 39.

Fazlur Rahman (1919-1988), a Muslim scholar and philosopher of Pakistani origin, proposed the pristine Qur'an was Muhammad's divinely inspired speech collected into the Uthmanic codex—the authorized text of the Qur'an compiled during the rule of Uthman, the third caliph and companion of the Prophet. Rahman wrote,

> But orthodoxy (indeed, all medieval thought) lacked the necessary intellectual tools to combine in its formulation of the dogma the otherness and verbal character of the Revelation on the one hand, and its intimate connection with the work and the religious personality of the Prophet on the other, i.e. it lacked the intellectual capacity to say both that the Qur'an is entirely the Word of God and, in an ordinary sense, also entirely the word of Muhammad. The Qur'an obviously holds both, for it insists that it has come to the "heart" of the Prophet, how can it be external to him?[22]

This opinion got Rahman into deep trouble with the orthodoxy, and he was forced into exile. But Rahman's thesis of the Qur'an as simultaneously divine and human speech holds the key to explaining those Qur'anic verses admonishing the Jews in polemical tones.

The Qur'an describes itself as revelation that "makes things clear" (15:1). Nevertheless, it is difficult to grasp the full meaning of divine texts like the Qur'an. And the same goes for the Bible. Referring to the various texts of the Bible, Schuon observes:

> The seeming incoherence of these texts—for instance the Song of Songs or certain passages of the Pauline Epistles—always has the same cause, namely the incommensurable disproportion between the Spirit on the one hand and the limited resources of human language on the other: it is as though the poor and coagulated language of mortal man would break under the formidable pressure of the Heavenly Word into a thousand fragments, or as if God, in order to express a thousand truths, had but a dozen words at his disposal and so was compelled to make use of allusions heavy with meaning, of ellipses, abridgements and symbolic syntheses. A sacred Scripture—and let us not forget that for Christianity Scripture includes not only the Gospels but the whole Bible with all its enigmas and seeming scandals—is a totality, a diversified image of Being, diversified and transfigured for the sake of the human receptacle; it is a light that wills to make itself visible to clay, or wills to take the form of that clay; or still in other words, it is a truth which, since it must address itself to beings compounded of clay, has no means of expression other than the very substance of the nescience of which our soul is made.[23]

Hence, how to read the Qur'an—how to distinguish between what is the universal and timeless truth embedded in the particular, how to go beyond the explicit (*zahir*) statements and grasp or discover the implicit or hidden (*batin*) meaning of the text, how not to misuse and abuse the allegorical language of the Qur'an for partisan purposes—has been contentious ever since the Prophet's demise. From the earliest

[22] Fazlur Rahman, *Islam*, 2nd ed. (Chicago/London: University of Chicago Press, 1979) 31.
[23] Schuon, *Understanding Islam*, 40-41.

discord that ruptured the community of believers Muhammad left behind to the sectarian conflicts that eventually led to the massacre of his family, the proliferation of sects among Muslims, the tribal wars fought in the name of Islam, and the raging conflicts across the Arab-Muslim world in our time, the history of the House of Islam reflects abiding disagreements among Muslims over how the Qur'an is read—differences in the sacred text of Islam that all too frequently erupted in violence. Islam's success in history ironically exacerbated the differences among its followers; politics inevitably corrupted faith when pagan Arabs as recently converted Muslims carved out a vast empire and their tribal chiefs emerged as imperial rulers in the manner of the Byzantine and Persian oriental despots.

But differences among Muslims, especially among the religious scholars, the *ulema,* also stimulated the variety and richness of Muslim learning during the expansive phase of Islamic civilization during the first half millennium of Muslim history. The innumerable commentaries on the Qur'an produced in this period were indicative of the need to make non-Arab Muslims familiar with the language of the sacred text they were required to learn and enable them to comprehend what they were reading. Yet regardless of how the text was read, the one incontrovertible fact is that the Qur'an, revealed in a world filled with strife, teaches that man can find the path to repose, equilibrium, peace, and blessings despite all conflicts, provided he bears witness to one God and His message. The Qur'an warns, reminds, explains, and provides lessons from history, but it is not vindictive, because God, as the Qur'an repeatedly affirms, is ever merciful. Hence, the seeds of contemporary anti-Jewish attitudes found in the Qur'an should be read, as they were understood when revealed to the Prophet, as lessons to be learned from what follows when a people, in this case the Jews, squanders the trust placed in them by the higher power—the God of Abraham who spoke with Moses.

The few negative references to the Jews in the Qur'an tell of how a segment among them in Arabia mounted opposition against Muhammad and how he responded. This Jewish opposition located in Medina turned into collusion with the Meccan enemies of the Prophet, as in the case of the indictment and punishment of the Jews of Banu Qurayza. If this collusion had succeeded, it would have meant defeat, death, and the end of Muhammad's divinely ordained mission. These references are to particular events; they are elliptical, and they bear universal lessons. Moreover, the Jews specifically addressed in the Qur'an—the Jews in the time of Muhammad who opposed him—understood the allusions made in these verses to their own sacred text.

The Qur'anic admonishment "Be ye apes, despised and rejected," which is hurled at the Jews by Muslim hate-mongers is found in a verse that reads as follows in Muhammad Asad's translation:

> [F]or you are well aware of those from among you who profaned the Sabbath, whereupon we said unto them, "Be as apes despicable!"—and set them up as a warning example for their time and for all times to come, as well as an admonition to all who are conscious of God (2:65-66).

The admonishment is figurative and it cannot be read literally as Muslim hate-mongers do. There is reference here to the Mosaic Law that condemns those Jews violating the Sabbath with death as punishment according to the Hebrew Scripture.[24] These words were a warning to the Jews opposing Muhammad and, with reference to their own Scripture, a reminder of what would befall those who turn away from righteousness after God has shown mercy to them—a lesson also emphasized in preceding verses of the Qur'an. Verse 2:62, the most significant in this section—the second and longest chapter in the Qur'an called "Al-Baqarah" (The Cow)—reads as follows in Asad's translation:

> Verily, those who have attained to faith [in this divine writ], as well as those who follow the Jewish faith, and the Christians, and the Sabians—all who believe in God and the Last Day and do righteous deeds—shall have their reward with their Sustainer; and no fear need they have, and neither shall they grieve (2:62).

In his commentary on this verse, Asad writes,

> The above passage—which recurs in the Qur'an several times—lays down a fundamental doctrine of Islam. With a breadth of vision unparalleled in any other religious faith, the idea of "salvation" is here made conditional upon three elements only: belief in God, belief in the Day of Judgment, and righteous action in life.[25]

I refer here to Asad's translation of the Qur'an and the accompanying commentary because of his excellence in both languages, Arabic and English, as well as his personal history. Asad (1900-1992), born Leopold Weiss, was a Polish Jew and grandson of a rabbi. As an adult, he became a Muslim, lived in Saudi Arabia and later in Spain, and devoted his life to the study of the Qur'an and Islam.[26] In his prologue to *The Message of the Qur'an*, Asad writes,

> It is axiomatic from the Islamic perspective that the Qur'an cannot be translated, because the *form* of God's revelation, that is the Arabic itself, is not merely incidental to its meaning, but essential to it. ... A rendering into another language, therefore, is not and never can be the Qur'an as such, but merely an interpretation of it.

Asad devoted his life to learning the Qur'an's Arabic, or the closest living approximation to it spoken by those dwindling numbers of Bedouin of the Arabian Desert who have still not assimilated into the rapidly changing world around them or succumbed to the reach of "modernized" Arabic disseminated in radio and television broadcasts from the urban centers of the Arab world.

According to Asad's commentary, verse 2:62 bears the universal message of the Qur'an. It belies any justification of Muslim anti-Jewish bigotry; it nullifies any suggestion that the Jews, as a result of opposition by some against Muhammad, are condemned as enemies of God and the Prophet. The idea that the sins of one generation, or one individual, might be visited upon another is explicitly rejected in

---

24 See Exodus 31:14, "Ye shall keep the sabbath therefore; for it is holy unto you: everyone that defileth it shall surely be put to death: for whosoever doeth any work therein, that soul shall be cut off from among his people." *The Bible: Authorized Version* (Swindon: Bible Society).

25 Muhammad Asad, *The Message of the Qur'an* (Bristol, UK: The Book Foundation, 2003), 21n50.

26 See Ismail Ibrahim Nawwab, "Berlin to Makkah: Muhammad Asad's Journey into Islam," *Saudi Aramco World* (January-February 2002): 6-32.

the Qur'an in the following words: "And no bearer of burdens shall be made to bear another's burden" (35:18). The ill will toward the Jews in the pre-modern world could not be derived from the Qur'an. Nonetheless, many Muslims—followers of a faith-tradition that turned triumphantly imperial and yet was open and inviting to non-Muslims—viewed the Jews negatively because, as devout Muslims, they could not understand why the Jews as a people did not embrace Islam.

The story about the Jews of Banu Qurayza—their collusion with the Meccans, the resistance they offered after the pagan confederates were beaten, their surrender, and their punishment—is briefly referred to in the Qur'an as follows: "and He brought down from their strongholds those of the followers of earlier revelation who had aided the aggressors, and cast terror into their hearts; some you slew; and some you made captive" (33:26). Ibn Ishaq, the first biographer of the Prophet, writing some 145 years after the events relating to the Banu Qurayza, embroidered and embellished this brief reference in the Qur'an by gathering together oral reports of what presumably occurred. According to Ibn Ishaq, following the judgment of the arbitrator, Sa'd ibn Mu'adh, that the men of Banu Qurayza be put to death and the women and children given to slavery, Muhammad oversaw the execution of the verdict. The estimates for the men killed on that day vary between 400 and 900. The validity of this story, the veracity of Ibn Ishaq, and the meaning of this event in relation to the Prophet and his teaching have all been disputed.[27]

From a present-day perspective, the judgment looks harsh, but was it harsh under the circumstances and customs of the time? Although the story of the Banu Qurayza stands as a rebuke of the Prophet among his critics regardless of any explanation, explaining the history surrounding the story is not to indulge in an apology for or a rationalization of Muslim Judeophobia. As noted earlier, if the treachery of the Banu Qurayza in colluding with the pagan confederates led by the Meccan enemies of the Prophet had turned out as planned, it would have likely spelled the end for the Prophet and Islam. The stakes were immensely high, and the leaders of the Banu Qurayza were fully aware that this would be the outcome if their plan succeeded. It was also exceedingly ironic that the Jews of Banu Qurayza, a people of the Book and monotheists, colluded with polytheists against Muhammad, who was bringing a monotheistic message to the pagan Arabs. From the Qur'an's point of view, it was providential that Muhammad prevailed, thereby teaching a timely lesson to those still maintaining their hostility to his message and mission. Moreover, the punishment meted out to the men of Banu Qurayza was also in keeping with the tenets of Hebrew Scripture. Here reference might be made to the judgment of Moses delivered when he came down from Mount Sinai and saw his people, as if engaged in treason against God who had delivered them from their captivity in Egypt, worshipping a golden calf sculpted out of their jewelry. Moses called out upon his men, the Levites, and ordered them to draw their swords and slay the men who had done wrong, and some three thousand were put to death.[28]

---

27 See, for instance, Walid N. Arafat, "New Light on the Story of Banu Qurayza and the Jews of Medina," *Journal of the Royal Asiatic Society of Great Britain and Ireland*, no. 2 (1976): 100-107; and M.J. Kister, "The Massacre of the Banu Qurayza: A Re-examination of a Tradition," *Jerusalem Studies in Arabic and Islam* 8 (1986): 61-96.

28 See Exodus 32:26-28.

Moses was a Jewish prophet, and having referred to Freud's striking description of Judaism and Christianity I shall quote him here again: "And since we know that behind the God who chose the Jews and delivered them from Egypt stood the man Moses, who achieved that deed, ostensibly at God's command, I venture to say this: it was one man, the man Moses, who created the Jews."[29] Moses is a towering presence in the Hebrew Scripture, just as he is in the Qur'an. Muslims revere him and refer to him as *"kalimullah"*—the one who spoke with God. The reference to Moses and the punishment he meted out to those responsible for making and worshipping an image is neither inapt nor improper in discussing the penalty carried out against the Jewish men of Banu Qurayza, especially as Moses' draconian punishment of the idol worshippers would have been readily understood at the time by all involved in the story of the Banu Qurayza. Just as much of the *hadith* literature about the Prophet is of dubious merit, the accounts of what occurred with the Jews of Banu Qurayza remain doubtful.

Nevertheless, if the story of the Banu Qurayza was so egregious and out of proportion to the norms of the time, it would have reverberated beyond the confines of Arabia and been reported, or at least mentioned, in the contemporary chronicles of the Jewish and Christian centers of the Byzantine and Persian empires. Yet there is no independent record of the story of the Banu Qurayza outside of Muslim sources, beginning with Ibn Ishaq's first biography of the Prophet. The earliest mention of Islam in Christian records is found in the *History of Heraclius*, which was compiled by the Armenian bishop Sebeos and completed around 661, that is, less than thirty years after the death of Muhammad. In this account, Sebeos recorded that the Jews sought assistance from Arabs to defend Edessa against the Byzantines. He also referred to the Arabs as the children of Ishmael and mentioned that Muhammad preached to the Arabs about the God of Abraham and the connection of Islam's origins with the Jewish faith. Sebeos made no mention of the Banu Qurayza or of any other event or matter related to Islam that displayed Arab hostility to the Jews. Instead, as John Moorhead notes, "Sebeos' evaluation of Islam was positive."[30] When the Arab armies conquered Palestine and captured Jerusalem—events that took place a few years after the Jews of Banu Qurayza were punished—the Jews celebrated the defeat of the Byzantines and saw the new rulers as a positive change in terms of their own situation in Palestine. Such a receptive attitude by the Jews toward Arabs would have been at best odd, even scandalously hypocritical, if they had known about the Banu Qurayza and, as a result, nurtured enmity against Islam. Until Ibn Ishaq narrated this story and very likely embellished it, as W.N. Arafat has indicated,[31] there was nothing about it except for the Qur'anic reference that might have alarmed the people outside of Arabia. Yet there was no such alarm; and the Jews, despite their long tradition of recording events that affected them for good or ill, did not even record it.

We might ask if there is any lesson in these events as recorded in scriptures beyond the generic rule that men are answerable for their deeds? For believers in God,

---

29 Freud, *Moses and Monotheism*, 136.

30 See John Moorhead, "The Earliest Christian Theological Response to Islam," *Religion* 11, no. 3 (1981): 265-74.

31 See Arafat, "Banu Qurayza."

history can be providential. Yet even the prophets were liable to make mistakes and were accordingly accountable for their errors on the Day of Reckoning. Lesser men should not presume to act as divine agents. Consequently, since for Muslims the revelation came to an end with Muhammad as the last of God's prophets, any Muslim who claims to emulate the Prophet or acts as if he has God's sanction is simply regarded as suffering from gross presumptuousness and delusion.

It is this presumptuousness and delusion that fill the minds of the intemperate and self-described "jihadis" or "holy warriors" in the ranks of al-Qaeda, the Islamic State of Iraq and Syria (ISIS), Lashkar-e-Taiba, Hamas, the Taliban, and others who selectively seize hold of verses from the Qur'an to sanction their violence. This is not a new development, and it can be traced back to the earliest years of discord following the Prophet's demise, which divided the community of believers. Islamists in recent years have prioritized Chapter 9—"At-Tawbah" or "Repentance"—of the Qur'an as God's sanction to wage war on the infidels, including the Jews and the Christians. The verse invoked by Islamists, and variously known as the War Verse or the Sword Verse, reads as follows in Asad's translation:

> [And] fight against those who—despite having been vouchsafed revelation [aforetime]—do not [truly] believe either in God or the Last Day, and do not consider forbidden that which God and His Apostle have forbidden, and do not follow the religion of truth [which God has enjoined upon them], till they [agree to] pay the exemption tax with a willing hand, after having been humbled [in war] (9:29).

According to the Franco-Tunisian scholar Abdelwahab Meddeb, this verse was

> invoked, for example, by the Armed Islamic Group (GIA) terrorists who massacred the monks of Tibhirine in Algeria in 1996. The same verse is said to grant religious legitimacy to the suicide bombers of Hamas in Israel. The same reference may well have been involved in galvanizing the criminals responsible for the horrifying attacks on September 11, 2001, in New York and Washington, D.C.[32]

There is little that can be done to prevent those Muslims and their hate-mongering teachers, such as Hasan al-Banna, Sayyid Qutb, Khomeini, Sheikh Yusuf al-Qaradawi, or Mullah Omar, who cite the Sword Verse, or similar verses, as an excuse to precipitate and justify violence. Violence begets violence, and we have witnessed how Algeria, for example, descended into the nightmare of terrorist atrocities in the 1990s, when a brutal war between the state and the Islamists gave rise to mounting civilian casualties. There are too many similar examples from recent Muslim history that might be mentioned. The point to emphasize is that the traditional exegesis of Chapter 9, which contains the Sword Verse, was overwhelmingly one of caution. The revelation of Chapter 9 is from the Medina period of the Prophet's life, a period of warfare with the pagan confederacy in which segments of the Jewish population, notably the Jews of Banu Qurayza, colluded against Islam and Muhammad. In his commentary on Chapter 9, particularly in reference to the Sword Verse, Asad notes that "it must be read in the context of the clear-cut

32 Abdelwahab Meddeb, *Islam and the Challenge of Civilization* (New York: Fordham University Press, 2013), 14.

Qur'anic rule that war is permitted only in self-defence."[33] Accordingly, we might state here that the wars Israel has fought since 1948 were mostly in self-defense and, therefore, consistent with the Qur'anic directives. If any of these wars the Jews of Israel have had to fight against the Arab states and terrorists had ended in a loss, it would have meant an existential defeat for the Jewish state. Moreover, within the Muslim community, the authority responsible for initiating war in self-defense must be legitimate, or seen to be legitimate by a majority of Muslims. Since the end of the Prophetic era, the arc of Muslim history has had to cope with a crisis of legitimacy. During the age of Islamic expansion in the early centuries of Islam, the Sword Verse was invoked to justify instituting the exemption tax or *jizya* on Jews and Christians living among Muslims, but that period of Muslim history ended a long time ago. In the post-Caliphate age, the historic religio-political challenge for Muslims lies in constructing the basis of a legitimate order consistent with democracy, freedom, human rights, gender equality, and science. The universal message of the Qur'an that might assist Muslims in meeting this challenge is not found in the verses Muslim fanatics extol; it is found in those verses that they seek to deliberately downgrade in priority or even go so far as to declare abrogated.

The Sudanese reformer Mahmoud Mohamed Taha suggested that the universal message of Islam was yet to be fully understood by Muslims. Taha was optimistic and saw the modern age as being propitious for Muslims in terms of reforming Sharia, since their society's progress would demand of them to comprehend the universality of Islam. In *The Second Message of Islam*, Taha explained his thinking and methodology for the reform of Muslim societies. His message was built around the proposition that there is a natural progression in Muslim understanding of the Qur'an and that it is therefore incumbent on the Prophet's followers to be open and receptive to the universal message revealed to him, which was not fully comprehensible to his immediate followers and those who came after them. This landed Taha in serious trouble with the authorities. He was hanged by the regime headed by President Numeiri, the Sudanese dictator, in 1985.

The tragic fate of Taha illustrates the immense problems and perils faced by Muslim reformers. Reform of Islam means, in effect, either reforming the Sharia code—the corpus of Islamic laws derived from the Qur'an, the *hadith* or traditions of the Prophet, and the *ijma* or consensus of the *ulema* (Muslim scholars)—or setting it aside entirely and beginning afresh in terms of modern legal-political philosophy, hermeneutics, comparative religion, theology, and cosmology. In Sunni Islam, to which the overwhelming majority of Muslims belong, the Sharia is a fixed and inviolate code of law based on the accumulated wisdom, knowledge, and consensus of the *ulema* from the classical period of Muslim history during the first three centuries of Islam. The need for independent reasoning or *ijtihad*, which scholars had used to formulate the Sharia, was declared closed by a consensus of Sunni *ulema* either in the twelfth century following the death of Al-Ghazali, the revered scholar-jurist turned mystic, in 1111,[34] or, at the latest, in the thirteenth century following the

---

33 Asad, *Message of the Qur'an*, 295n40.

34 See, for instance, Sadakat Kadri, *Heaven on Earth: A Journey Through Shari'a Law from the Deserts of Ancient Arabia to the Streets of the Modern Muslim World* (New York: Farrar, Straus and Giroux, 2012), 99-105.

sack of Baghdad by the Mongol armies in 1258. The Sunni leader, the Caliph of Islam, held, as enjoined by the Sunni *ulema,* that there was no more need for *ijtihad* because there was nothing more to be added as new insights to the existing corpus of laws. Consequently, Muslim scholars were obligated to replace independent reasoning with *taqlid* or imitation in the application of the Sharia. As Robert Reilly has demonstrated convincingly, this closing of the Muslim mind effectively doomed the Islamic civilization once Europe emerged from its own relative state of backwardness into the making of the modern world.[35]

As Taha had maintained, the prerequisite for reforming Islam is a fresh reading of the Qur'an in keeping with the spirit of the age in which people live. The Qur'an, which is literally God's Word to Muslims, cannot be a closed or frozen text with a fixed meaning determined by the dead weight of men from another time long past. However, this need to read the Qur'an with fresh eyes and insight threatens the orthodoxy, the Islamists, the defenders of the status quo, and all other Muslims who dread or disapprove of change and openness in closed societies. A reading of the Qur'an that relies only, as Islamists insist, on an explicit and literal meaning of the text will fail to comprehend the essential unity of the Qur'anic message due to the prevalence of apparent contradictions scattered across the text. It is only by openness to reading the Qur'an as a text with a hierarchy of implicit meanings that Muslims can be prepared to comprehend the universal message of the Qur'an and set it apart from the subsidiary meanings in the text.

In the *surah* (chapter) "Al-Maa'idah" or "The Repast" (Chapter 5 of the Qur'an), we read, "O You who have attained to faith! Do not take the Jews and the Christians for your allies" (5:51). Like the Sword Verse in Chapter 9, this is another favorite passage of Islamist and fundamentalist Muslims. It happens that "Al-Maa'idah" is one of the last chapters of the Qur'an revealed in Medina sometime after the Prophet's farewell pilgrimage a decade after the *hijra* (flight) from Mecca to Medina, or in the tenth year of Islam. This chapter also contains a verse declaring: "Today have I perfected your religious law for you, and have bestowed upon you the full measure of My blessings, and willed that self-surrender unto Me [al-Islam] shall be your religion" (5:3). And as we read further in "Al-Maa'idah," we come across the following verse: "[V]erily, those who have attained to faith [in this divine writ], as well as those who follow the Jewish faith, and the Sabians, and the Christians—all who believe in God and the Last Day and do righteous deeds—no fear need they have, and neither shall they grieve" (5:69). Thus what we have here in "Al-Maa'idah" or Chapter 5, revealed after the Sword Verse found in "At-Tawbah" or Chapter 9, is a negative reference to the Jews and the Christians that is diluted, or set aside, by a universal message that is inclusive and unambiguously stated. According to Meddeb, "it is here that the ethical vocation becomes the criterion for salvation, beyond any consideration of belief in any so-called true religion."[36] It is here also, and even more importantly, that the Qur'an's universal message nullifies the presumptuousness, or hubris, of fanatical monotheists (be they Muslims, Christians, or Jews) who insist their religion is the only true belief. And to emphasize this

35 See Robert R. Reilly, *The Closing of the Muslim Mind: How Intellectual Suicide Created the Modern Islamist Crisis* (Wilmington, DE: ISI Books, 2010).

36 Meddeb, *Islam and the Challenge of Civilization,* 30.

universal message so that there is no mistaking that ethical conduct is the measure of the quality of faith, the Qur'an states in "Al-Maa'idah" that differences between faiths are by heavenly design:

> Unto every one of you have We appointed a [different] law and way of life. And if God had so willed, He could surely have made you all one single community: but [He willed it otherwise] in order to test you by means of what He has vouchsafed unto you. Vie, then, with one another in doing good works! Unto God you all must return; and then He will make you truly understand all that on which you were wont to differ (5:48).

Moreover, according to the methodology of traditional exegesis, the Sword Verse is abrogated by the relevant verses of "Al-Maa'idah." This principle of abrogation (*naskh*) was developed by early Muslim jurists as a remedy for apparent inconsistencies in the Qur'an by giving precedence to a verse revealed later over one revealed earlier. As Carl Ernst explains, the "harmonizing approach acknowledges a chronological dimension to the unfolding of the Qur'an, as is evident from the traditional labelling of suras as belonging to the earlier Meccan period or the later Medinan period."[37] While "At-Tawbah," which contains the Sword Verse, and "Al-Maa'idah" were both revealed in Medina, "Al-Maa'idah" was revealed in the final year of the Prophet's life and, consequently, takes precedence over "At-Tawbah." And while the idea of abrogation is faulty, as Muhammad Asad argued,[38] and goes against the spirit of the Qur'an, as Taha the Sudanese reformer taught,[39] it remains the methodology of traditionalism in Islamic jurisprudence, which, by its own reasoning, must conclude that the Sword Verse was abrogated by the universal message reiterated in "Al-Maa'idah."

Regardless, Islamist hate-mongers, such as Sheikh Yusuf al-Qaradawi, habitually insist upon the principle of abrogation when it serves their purpose and void it when it does not. Clearly, though, on the basis of traditional exegesis, there is no justification even in pre-modern times for anti-Jewish bigotry among Muslims in the Qur'anic references to the Jews. What we are left with, therefore, when trying to explain Muslim Judeophobia in pre-modern history is that such behavior reflects inherent flaws in the nature of man as well as certain traits of Islamic history that perpetuated the pathology of tribalism and tribal conflicts. Muslim Judeophobia was a form of tribal paranoia, which has remained with Muslims until today. To justify Arab and Muslim bigotry against the Jews, Muslims have wrongly cited negative references to the Jews, which only pertain to specific historical disputes with the Prophet, in the Qur'an.

III.

Violence is not specific or limited to Islam and Muslims. It is embedded in "the crooked timber of humanity"—a phrase coined by Immanuel Kant, which Isaiah

---

37 Carl W. Ernst, *How to Read the Qur'an: A New Guide, with Select Translations* (Chapel Hill: University of North Carolina Press, 2011), 16-17.

38 See Asad, *The Message of the Qur'an*, 31n87.

39 Mahmoud Mohamed Taha, *The Second Message of Islam*, trans. and with an introduction by Abdullahi Ahmed An-Na'im (Syracuse, NY: Syracuse University Press, 1987).

Berlin, the Anglo-Jewish philosopher, adopted as a motif in his work—that religion, ethics, moral philosophy, and education seek to remedy. On the basis of his psychoanalytic theory, Freud explained that civilization is coercion writ large. The "replacement of the power of the individual by the power of a community," Freud wrote, "constitutes the decisive step of civilization."[40] Violence is contained, repressed, and redirected as civilized life evolves. And, according to Freud, the grand project of civilization can only be realized, if at all, at some future date, when men will cast aside their illusions and bring about a reordering of relations that makes coercion unnecessary and leads to its renunciation.[41]

Freud held that civilizations differ as a result of the specific history of each people and what recourse they have sought in striving for a legitimate and just socio-political order. Islamic history stands apart from that of the Jews and the Christians by the manner in which its founding drama and its success in emerging as a global power within the first century after Muhammad's death in 632 unfolded. Paradoxically, the speed with which the frontiers of Islam spread fostered repression of the memory of the violence that surrounded it.

The Qur'an is filled with general warnings about man's nature as prone to forgetfulness and ingratitude and his inclination to follow the instincts of his lower self. The warnings from the Hebrew Scripture about the reprobate characteristics of man reverberate in the Qur'an. But apart from the general nature of these warnings, there was also a specific warning to the Prophet to be wary of tribal Arabs when, after having been finally defeated in their campaigns against him and his followers, they came to swear allegiance in person to him. The relevant verse warns,

> The Bedouin say, "We have attained to faith." Say [unto them, O Muhammad]: You have not [yet] attained to faith; you should [rather] say, "We have [outwardly] surrendered"—for [true] faith has not yet entered your hearts. (49:14).

Beyond the immediacy of this warning to the Prophet, the verse also underscores the reality of hypocrites in society and the dangers they pose. The hypocrites eventually get exposed by their conduct, but the damage they cause in the meantime can be immensely costly.

The dispute over leadership of the Muslim community, or the embryonic Medinan state at the time of the Prophet's death, marked the beginning of the war within Islam. Those involved were companions of the Prophet, yet their intemperate behavior displayed an insufficiency of belief or rightful conduct that ignited schismatic wars and violently severed the unity of the believers in Islam. The repressed memory of this blood-soaked history has haunted Muslims from the earliest times to the present.[42]

---

40 Sigmund Freud, *Civilization and Its Discontents* (New York/London: W.W. Norton & Co., 1961), 47.

41 See Sigmund Freud, *The Future of an Illusion*(New York/London: W.W. Norton & Co., 1961), 7-8.

42 See Wilferd Madelung, *The Succession to Muhammad: A Study of the Early Caliphate* (Cambridge: Cambridge University Press, 1997). See also Lesley Hazleton's book based on early Muslim sources, *After the Prophet: The Epic Story of the Shia-Sunni Split* (New York: Random House, 2009).

Tribalism remained deeply embedded in the first generation of Muslims, the people among whom the Prophet was born and to whom he brought Islam. Political power passed into the family of the Prophet's most ardent foe when Abu Sufyan's son Mu'awiya seized the Caliphate following the murder of Ali, the cousin and son-in-law of Muhammad. Mu'awiya founded the Ummayad dynasty based in Damascus, Syria, and his son Yazid approved of the action his men took against Hussein—the grandson of the Prophet through his only surviving daughter Fatima, married to Ali—when he asserted his claim to succeed his father as the Caliph. Hussein was brutally killed in Kerbala, Iraq, in 680, his body disfigured by trampling horses and his severed head carried on the point of a lance to the Caliph's palace. In her account of the killing of Hussein and the great schism in Islam based on the earliest Muslim sources, Lesley Hazleton writes,

> As with the death of Christ, the death of Hussein soars beyond history into metahistory. It enters into the realm of faith and inspiration, of passion both emotional and religious.[43]

But Hussein's murder was also much more; it was a crime of such proportions that Muslims buried their grief and shame within themselves even as they became divided. A minority of Muslims became partisans of the family of the Prophet through Fatima and her sons, Hasan and Hussein, and came to be known as Shi'a. The majority, known as Sunni, preferred to accept the authority of the Ummayad dynasty rather than further deepen the violent tribal discord that had seized the rapidly growing Muslim community. In time, the Sunni majority came to look down upon the Shi'a minority with near contempt for their role in perpetuating discord and undermining the unity of the believers, while the actual crime of the massacre of members of the Prophet's family receded into the "collective unconscious" as a repressed Muslim memory.

However, as Freud has pointed out, the collective guilt over such a monstrous crime cannot be washed away, and the repression of such a collective memory resulted in a collective neurosis. The pathology of violence among Muslims and Muslim violence directed at non-Muslims may be traced back to this record of violence, such as the war against apostasy launched by Abu Bakr, the first Caliph, even as the Qur'an categorically states that "[t]here shall be no coercion in matters of faith" (2:256), and the tribal conflicts culminating in Hussein's murder, which stain the early years of Islamic history. In *Moses and Monotheism*, Freud writes

> We must not forget that all the peoples who now excel in the practice of anti-Semitism became Christians only in relatively recent times, sometimes forced to it by bloody compulsion. One might say they all are "badly christened"; under the thin veneer of Christianity they have remained what their ancestors were, barbarically polytheistic. They have not yet overcome their grudge against the new religion which was forced on them, and they have projected it on to the source from which Christianity came to them. The facts that the Gospels tell a story which is enacted among Jews, and in truth treats only of Jews, has facilitated such a projection. The hatred for Judaism is at bottom hatred for Christianity, and it is

43 Hazleton, *After the Prophet*, 191-92.

> not surprising that in the German National Socialist revolution this close connection of the two monotheistic religions finds such clear expression in the hostile treatment of both.[44]

Freud touched a raw nerve that is readily inflamed in speculating on the origins of genocidal European antisemitism. This hatred was imported into the Middle East, and Muslim anti-Jewish bigotry that had been present since pre-modern times "Islamized" it. But even though there was no basis or record in Islam or among Muslims of the sort of anti-Judaism that existed beneath the "thin veneer of Christianity" in Europe, yet the phenomenon of "badly christened" Christians has its parallel in the Islamic history of Bedouin Arabs outwardly accepting Islam without faith entering their hearts, just as the Prophet was warned. The lesson from the Qur'an's reference to Bedouin Arabs also relates to Muslims in general, since their hypocrisy is writ large across the Muslim world despite repeated warnings about it in their sacred texts. The customs of Bedouin Arabs remained unreformed despite their forceful conversion and their repression in the war against apostasy launched by Abu Bakr following the Prophet's death. The Bedouin mentality left its pagan mark on the body politic of the Islamic civilization, since beneath the "thin veneer of Islam" the Bedouin culture remained resilient. Muslim Judeophobia in pre-modern times reflected tribal narrow-mindedness against the outsider, and the disdain shown toward the Jews buttressed the Arab and Muslim sense of tribal envy and superiority contrary to the teachings of Islam. Moreover, given their collective neuroses and the repressed memory of violence, anti-Jewish bigotry provided Muslims with an excuse for blaming others for their own failings and instilled in them a proclivity to look for non-Muslim conspiracies against the idealized notion of Muslim unity, while denying the bleak reality of their own, self-generated tribal conflicts.

The world of Islam stretches far beyond the Arab region and the Middle East, with its diverse ethnicity of Afghans, Arabs, Berbers, Kurds, Iranians, Turks, and others. The largest concentration of Muslims is found in South Asia, and the largest Muslim country—Indonesia—is far from the Middle East. Most Muslims outside the Middle East have little or no personal contact with Jews, and only know of them through the lens of the religious-based history they were taught within the confines of their local religious schools and mosques. In modern times, Arab and Muslim antisemitism has been exported from the Middle East to the wider world of Islam in the form of religious propaganda sweetened by the largesse of petrodollars. Just as non-Arab and non-Middle Eastern Muslims defer to Arabs on Islam, so they have readily and unquestioningly absorbed the entire tradition of antisemitism propagated by Arab hate-mongers. The result is the undeniable reality of the deplorable extent to which Islamist Judeophobia fused with genocidal European antisemitism has become part of contemporary Islam.

Islamism is a pathology propelling a significant segment of the global Muslim population into conflict with Islam's perceived enemies, with a particular emphasis on the Jews. Not surprisingly, this inner compulsion of Islamists to wage war against others has also resulted in Muslim-on-Muslim violence, a raging sectarian conflict

44 Freud, *Moses and Monotheism*, 116-17.

between Sunnis and Shi'ites and a range of ethnic conflicts between tribes and nations. Islamists have shredded their "thin veneer of Islam" and displayed their "jihad" as a neo-pagan belief in the cult of violence. The world at the end of the twentieth century was not prepared to encounter Islamism as an ideology of hate and terror. The terrorist acts of war unleashed by Islamists on September 11, 2001 came as a shock. Since that fateful day, the world has been informed about Islamists and now needs to recall from history that violence born of Jew-hatred or antisemitism does not end with the Jews and is not only about the Jews. Antisemitism was, and remains, a plague that endangers all. There is an urgent need to quell, rather than appease, Muslim antisemitism. The suicidal acts of terrorism that Islamists have engaged in since the September 11 attacks demonstrate their willingness, if they acquire the wherewithal, to bring about their own version of the *Götterdämmerung* in their fanatical desire to destroy the enemy. The world stands warned.

Radical Islamism and the Arab Upheaval

Meir Litvak*

I. Introduction

Radical Islamic movements have emerged as major players following the upheaval, optimistically referred to as the Arab Spring, that engulfed several Arab countries in 2011 and 2012. The mainstream Muslim Brotherhood movements, which scored electoral successes in Tunisia and Egypt, suffered major setbacks once they took over governments and had to govern states. In contrast, Salafi-jihadist movements, which resorted to arms, have so far scored greater success.[1] These movements have perpetrated large-scale atrocities against civilians and prisoners of war, partly motivated by their extremist ideology and partly as a calculated means of intimidation. Their activities have also jeopardized the territorial integrity and even existence of at least four states: Syria, Iraq, Yemen, and Libya. If the fall of Saddam Hussein in Iraq in 2003 marked the emergence of the so-called Shi'i Crescent or the Iran-led resistance axis, the Arab upheaval can be seen as the Sunni backlash. Consequently, the rise of the Salafi-jihadist organizations exacerbated the sectarian Sunni-Shi'i rift in the region into a transnational violent conflict that has cost the lives of over 200,000 people, the displacement of millions of others, and the suffering of even more.[2]

The root cause of the region-wide crisis is the failure of state authorities to control their borders and their territories, provide services to their populations, and, ultimately, forge a common political identity that could form the basis of a political community. The crisis erupted in the form of spontaneous uprisings of mostly young people from all walks of life against the abuse of dictatorial regimes, socio-economic despair, and excessive corruption. Islamists did not initiate these uprising, though in Egypt they played a significant role behind the scenes in the mass protests that led to the removal of President Hosni Mubarak on February 11, 2011.

---

* Associate Professor at the Department of Middle Eastern History, Director of the Alliance Center for Iranian Studies, and Senior Research Fellow at the Dayan Center for Middle Eastern Studies at Tel Aviv University.

1 The literature on the ideas of and differences between these two denominations is vast. For two somewhat different typologies, see Quintan Wiktorowicz, "Anatomy of the Salafi Movement," *Studies in Conflict and Terrorism* 29, no. 3 (2006): 207-239; Guilain Denoeux, "Navigating Political Islam," *Middle East Policy* 19, no. 2 (June 2002): 56-81.

2 For an historical analysis of this rift, see Ofra Bengio and Meir Litvak, eds., *The Sunna and Shi'a in History Division and Ecumenism in Islam* (New York: Palgrave-McMillan, 2011).

Whatever the motivations behind these protests, Islamist parties emerged as the major victors in the democratic processes that followed, thanks to a combination of several factors, including the decades-long discrediting of secular ideologies, such as liberalism and socialism, on the grounds of their failure to address the region's problems and their association with the West. In contrast, Islamism, which relied on the symbolic repertoire of religion—the dominant cultural force in the region —seemed to offer simple and comprehensive solutions to the crisis of modernity. In other words, the Islamists represented for many Arabs the only authentic cultural and communal identity. Just as importantly, the Islamist movements had established networks of religious and social-welfare institutions that provided religious proselytism (*da'wah*) and social services, which the inefficient and indifferent governments failed to provide. These networks prospered in countries like Egypt and survived even in countries like Syria, providing the Islamists with a mobilization apparatus far superior to that of the moribund legal opposition parties in Egypt or the new parties that sprung up after the removal of Ben Ali and Mubarak.

The Tunisian Ennahda Movement, the most moderate of the Muslim Brotherhood-affiliated movements, won more than 41 percent of the vote in the first free elections held in that country since independence in 1956, securing 90 seats in the 217-member parliament, and headed the first coalition government in its history.[3] In Egypt, where the Brotherhood was founded 1928, it won 37.5 percent of the vote (235 seats out of 508), while the more radical Salafi al-Nour Party won 27.8 percent of the vote (123 seats). The more moderate al-Wasat Party received only 3.7 of the vote (10 seats). Altogether, Islamist parties garnered 69.7 percent of the vote.[4]

In June 2012, Mohamed Morsi, the Brotherhood's candidate, won 51.7 percent of the vote in the presidential elections and become the first democratically elected president of Egypt. But Morsi's majority was significantly slimmer than the movement's parliamentary gain, as voter turnout was only 51 percent. In other words, most Egyptians either did not want him or were too indifferent about the outcome. This was an ominous sign, which the Brotherhood failed to take seriously.

In Jordan, the Brotherhood played a leading role in recurring demonstrations protesting the country's dire socio-economic situation, but they were either too cautious or the tribal nature of local society precluded an escalation into a full-fledged uprising. Similarly, in Morocco, Islamist parties won the elections, which King Mohammed VI held following a series of reforms, and consented to play within the monarchical system.

The Brotherhood did well in countries that are relatively homogenous as far as religion and ethnicity are concerned. While two regimes were toppled, and two others faced considerable challenges, the states did not collapse. In these countries, they fared better than the less organized and less experienced Salafi parties or groups that had historically shunned integration in the political and international arenas. Conversely, the Brotherhood proved unsuccessful in countries where the state was deeply divided along sectarian, ethnic, or tribal lines, where the armed radical Salafi-jihadist groups emerged as major forces.

---

3 "Final Tunisian Election Results Announced," *Al Jazeera*, November 14, 2011, http://www.aljazeera.com/news/africa/2011/11/20111114171420907168.html.

4 "Egypt's Islamist Parties Win Elections to Parliament," *BBC News*, January 21, 2012, http://www.bbc.com/news/world-middle-east-16665748.

II. The Failure of the Muslim Brotherhood

After assuming power, the Muslim Brotherhood faced a daunting task in tackling Egypt's structural economic predicament, which grew worse during the months of political turmoil. Before entering office, the Brotherhood promised that they had an elaborate plan, referred to as the *nahda* (revival) plan, for governing Egypt, which they claimed was the "result of a tremendous effort and hard work that lasted well over fifteen years" and, if implemented, would uplift Egypt in four years. In the short term, Morsi published an ambitious plan that included some sixty-four distinct "promises," which sought to address Egypt's most pressing problems within 100 days, including the traffic problem, accumulated garbage, fuel and bread shortages, and the security vacuum. In reality, the *nahda* plan proved to be "more rhetoric than substance."[5] Similarly, and as was to be expected considering Egypt's structural problems, the 100-day plan achieved little.[6]

Facing the challenges of governance, the Egyptian Brotherhood exhibited flexibility and pragmatism on several key issues during their first months in power. They recognized and preserved the peace treaty with Israel after forty years of fierce opposition to it, though Morsi himself avoided any contact with or mention of Israel. They sought to cultivate working relationships with Western countries despite a history of anti-Western diatribes.[7]

Most importantly, the Brotherhood moved cautiously in the Islamization process. The new constitution approved in November 2012 contained two provisions that risked turning Egypt into a religious state, but were less than what the Salafis had aspired to beforehand. Article 4 buttressed the role of al-Azhar University, the bastion of mainstream conservative Islam, which had been unfriendly to Salafism. And Article 219 defined the "principles of the Islamic sharia" with a far greater deference to centuries of Islamic jurisprudence than Salafis had ever shown, given their preference to go straight to foundational texts and downplay traditional jurisprudence.[8] Moreover, a new Article 10 empowered the state to "preserve the genuine character of the Egyptian family, its cohesion and stability, and to protect its moral values," thereby providing a constitutional basis for future legislation that could have undermined women's rights.

Equally problematic was the government's policy toward the Christian minority. The number of individuals accused of "contempt of religion" rose significantly. The government also showed incompetence or indifference in acting against Islamist

---

5 Samuel Tadros, "Victory or Death: The Brotherhood in the Trenches," in *Current Trends in Islamist Ideology*, vol. 15, ed. Hillel Fradkin et al. (Washington, DC: Hudson Institute, 2013), 8.

6 Salma Shukrallah, "Morsi's First 100 Days: The Balance Sheet," *Ahram Online*, October 8, 2012, http://english.ahram.org.eg/News/54962.aspx; "'Morsi Meter' Indicates Only One of Egyptian President's 64 Promises Kept So Far," *Al Arabiya*, August 1, 2012, http://english.alarabiya.net/articles/2012/08/01/229743.html.

7 Ashraf El-Sherif, "What Path Will Egypt's Muslim Brotherhood Choose?," *Carnegie Endowment for International Peace*, September 23, 2013, http://carnegieendowment.org/2013/09/23/what-path-will-egypt-s-muslim-brotherhood-choose/gnx6#.

8 Nathan J. Brown, *Islam and Politics in the New Egypt*, The Carnegie Papers (Washington, DC: Carnegie Endowment for International Peace, 2013), http://carnegieendowment.org/files/islam_politics.pdf.

gangs that attacked Christians in southern Egypt. Sexual harassment, abuse, and rape of women increased to alarming rates, with the authorities usually blaming the victims for their "immoral" conduct.[9]

Salafi politicians and clerics, although taking part in the democratic process, persisted in calling for strict intolerant legislation and treatment of perceived offenders against Islam. Sheikh Yasser Borhamy, spokesman of the Da'wah group in the Egyptian parliament, complained in October 2012 that the freedoms established in the draft of the new Egyptian constitution "suggest the freedom of paganism, Satanism, and apostasy." Going further, the preacher Mazen Sirsawi stated in a TV sermon that "anyone who wants to affront the sharia [Islamic law] and become a heretic" should be executed, adding that "beheading them should be easier than cutting the buttons off their shirts."[10]

Overall, the Brotherhood's pragmatism proved to be far from genuine moderation, and their declared commitment to democratic rule proved to be merely tactical. On November 22, 2012, following the decision of Egypt's Constitutional Court to disband the elected parliament, Morsi transferred full executive and legislative authority to his office. In addition, he launched a process popularly called the "Brotherization of the state" (*akhwanat al-dawla*), in which large numbers of Brotherhood members took over official institutions at all levels.[11] In the words of Ashraf El-Sherif, the movement's solidarity networks—predominantly based on religious mobilization, identity politics, and the Brotherhood's closed, hierarchical organization—transformed into power-hungry networks. These networks capitalized on religious and social linkages to solicit blind grassroots support for the leadership in its clashes with those it deemed enemies of the Brotherhood, the Islamic movement, and the Islamic identity of Egypt.[12]

Within one year after taking office, the Brotherhood's abuse of power and failure to address Egypt's dire socio-economic situation produced mass alienation. A broad ad hoc coalition of angry opponents, including non-Islamists, Salafis, and Copts, held massive demonstrations in late June and early July 2013.[13] The army, which

---

9 Raymond Ibrahim, "Victimization of Egypt's Christians Worse After Revolution," *Jihad Watch*, September 4, 2012, http://www.jihadwatch.org/2012/09/victimization-of-egypts-christians-worse-after-revolution; Raymond Ibrahim, "The 'Epidemic' of Sexual Harassment—and Rape—in Morsi's Egypt," *FrontPageMag*, February 15, 2013, http://www.frontpagemag.com/fpm/177672/epidemic-sexual-harassment%E2%80%94and-rape%E2%80%94-morsis-egypt-raymond-ibrahim.

10 "Salafi Leader: Constitution Should Restrict Rights and Freedoms," *Egypt Independent*, October 16, 2012, http://www.egyptindependent.com/news/salafi-leader-constitution-should-restrict-rights-and-freedoms; "Egyptian Cleric Mazen Sirsawi in Favor of Killing Apostates: 'Beheading Them Should Be Easier Than Cutting the Buttons off Their Shirts," transcript of clip no. 3307, Middle East Media Research Center (MEMRI), September 4, 2011, http://www.memritv.org/clip_transcript/en/3307.htm.

11 Nathan J. Brown, "Egypt's Ambiguous Transition," *Carnegie Endowment for International Peace*, September 6, 2012, http://carnegieendowment.org/2012/09/06/egypt-s-ambiguous-transition/drsi.

12 El-Sherif, "Egypt's Muslim Brotherhood Choose."

13 For an analysis of the Muslim Brotherhood's failures, see, inter alia, Ashraf El-Sherif, *The Egyptian Muslim Brotherhood's Failures* (Washington, DC: Carnegie Endowment for International Peace, 2014); Tadros, "Victory or Death," 5-24.

resented the Brotherhood's threat to its own influence and privileges, took advantage of this anger and carried out widely supported military coup that ousted Morsi and the Brotherhood from power.

The Brotherhood refused to concede defeat and staged a series of protests aimed at reinstating the former government, trying to motivate grassroots supporters with messages of defiance while simultaneously sending out more conciliatory messages to the international community. Their efforts failed as the new authorities stormed their sit-in compound, killing over 700 Brotherhood members and arresting almost the entire leadership of the movement. Within two years of assuming power, the Brotherhood had reached one of the lowest point in its history: the movement was outlawed as a terrorist organization; thousands of its members were arrested; hundreds were condemned to death for charges of terrorism (although the verdicts were not implemented but rather served as a deterrent); and the movement's social network was subject to systematic repression. Even worse, as Nathan Brown observes, the "hatred for the Brotherhood expressed by so many in Egyptian public life [was] overwhelming and likely unprecedented."[14]

The Tunisian Ennahda Movement adopted a more cautious approach than their Egyptian colleagues. Following a prolonged political battle with other parties, it presided over the adoption of a new, fairly liberal constitution in January 2014. Although the constitution promoted the country's Islamic nature, it gave Islam a limited role in the legislative process. The constitution recognized the acquired rights of women, thus closing the door to a future rollback of personal status laws, and made parity the basis for women's participation in the political and economic arenas—a first for any Arab country. Ennahda also kept its promise not to criminalize "attacks on the sacred." The party's leader, Rached Ghannouchi, justified the concessions as a tactical move in light of both the current balance of power between the different political groups in the country and the opposition's control of key sectors, such as the media and the economy.[15] At the same time, Ennahda failed to tackle Tunisia's structural socio-economic problems and was largely unsuccessful in improving national security. It was accused of being soft toward extreme Muslim movements whose militias tried to impose an Islamist way of life on Tunisia. In February 2014, the movement decided to relinquish power in the face of growing public disapproval and accepted an interim technocratic government in the hope of obtaining a stable majority in the forthcoming elections.[16]

Overall, it appears that the Brotherhood was built primarily for politics but not for governing. The belief that Islam, as a moral system or ideology, would be the

---

[14] Nathan J. Brown, "The Future Of Egyptian Democracy: Political Islam Becomes Less Political," *The Immanent Frame*, http://blogs.ssrc.org/tif/2014/03/11/political-islam-becomes-less-political.

[15] "Tunisia's Islamists Compromise to Secure Legacy," *Gulf News*, January 8, 2014, http://gulfnews.com/news/region/tunisia/tunisia-s-islamists-compromise-to-secure-legacy-1.1275048; Maha Yahya, "Beyond Tunisia's Constitution: The Devil in the Details," *Carnegie Middle East Center*, April 28, 2014, http://carnegie-mec.org/2014/04/28/beyond-tunisia-s-constitution-devil-in-details/h9da#.

[16] "Tunisia's New Constitution a 'Victory over Dictatorship,'" *Al-Akhbar*, January 27, 2014, http://english.al-akhbar.com/node/18402; Synda Tajine, "Tunisia Suffers Bloodiest Day in 50 Years As Terror Strikes Border," *Al-Monitor*, July 21, 2014, http://al-monitor.us3.list-manage2.com/track/click?u=f1566964eaf39ab18387973ed&id=8b138dcef1&e=37a609d1fe.

panacea to Egypt's structural social and economic problems proved to be an illusion. Just as importantly, despite the hopes and probably illusions of various Western observers, the Brotherhood did not shed its authoritarian worldview. It appears that for most Brotherhood leaders democracy was never a value in itself but more a means to assume power that could be discarded when it was no longer useful. Another reason for the Brotherhood's poor record in government was its failure to promote younger and more pragmatic leaders, instead allowing old-guard-type dogmatic figures to prevail.[17]

III. The Salafi-jihadist war in Syria

In Syria, the popular revolt began in March 2011 with peaceful demonstrations in the Sunni periphery against the Allawi-dominated Ba'ath regime. This protest was primarily motivated by economic grievances: the destruction of the Syrian countryside by a devastating eight-year drought, coupled with economic stagnation and growing gaps, in the words of Sadiq Jalal al-Azm, between the "insolent, Brahman-like upper caste that sees itself beyond all accountability" and the masses.[18] For various reasons, however, the conflict quickly assumed a sectarian character. While Hafez al-Assad cultivated Sunnis from the periphery, they apparently felt forgotten by his son Bashar, who could no longer provide sufficient jobs to the younger Sunni generation nor allocate sufficient resources to the increasingly impoverished Sunni periphery. In addition, Assad played the sectarian card, and even helped inflame sectarian tensions, in order to rally the Christian and Druze minorities behind the regime out of fear of Sunni reprisals.

Contrary to Egypt, the radical Salafi-jihadist organizations in Syria became the major players in the Islamist arena as a result of three inter-related developments First, systematic repression in earlier years prevented the Brotherhood from building a state-wide organization. This policy exacerbated the existing fissures within Syrian society along regional, sectarian, class, and familial lines. More importantly, the brutal suppression of the popular uprising by the Assad regime pushed the protesters to resort to arms as the only way to defend themselves and resist the system. Finally, as opposition parties consisted mainly of groups of old politicians living in exile without any real grass-roots support or infrastructure, leadership of the popular uprising was taken by local coordinating committees.[19] Consequently, the opposition suffered from deep political and organizational divisions. At one point, there were over 114 militias operating in Syria, most of them local organizations. The Free Syrian Army (FSA) received only meager support from the outside.

Initially, the FSA, which was comprised of defectors from the regular army, emerged as the major rebel force, but gradually it was overshadowed by Islamist groups. Unlike the FSA, these movements enjoyed more generous financial and military support from Arab countries. For example, Saudi Arabia supported the

---

17 Ammar Ali Hassan, "Why Did Morsi Fall?" *Al-Ahram Weekly*, August 1-7, 2013; Raphaël Lefèvre, "A Falling-Out Among Brothers?," *Sada*, July 30, 2013, http://carnegieendowment.org/sada/2013/07/30/falling-out-among-brothers/ggtj.

18 Sadik J. Al-Azm, "Syria in Revolt: Understanding the Unthinkable War," *Boston Review*, August 8, 2014.

19 Ibid.

umbrella group Jabhat Tahrir Suriya al-Islamiyyah (Syrian Islamic Liberation Front), while Qatar supported the Ahfad al-Rasul Brigade (Grandsons of the Prophet), which was closer to the Muslim Brotherhood.[20]

The violent escalation and weakness of the relatively secular FSA and local militias helped the Salafi-jihadists, most prominently Jabhat al-Nusra, which was affiliated with al-Qaeda and its mother organization the Islamic State in Iraq and the Levant (also known as Daesh, ISIS, or ISIL), to emerge as the most important force in the region, as it could bring in activists from Iraq and other Muslim countries to fight in Syria. Since the fall of Afghanistan in 2001, the Salafi-jihadists have been looking for territories in which there was no effective government and where they could establish the base for a true Islamic emirate. In this regard, Syria was seen as the ideal place, being situated in the heart of the Middle East.

Moreover, between late-2011 and mid-2014, Syria became a a major front for the Salafi-jihadist organizations and the main arena for the escalating Sunni-Shi'i conflict. Ever since 2003, the Salafi-jihadists had waged a bloody struggle against the Shi'is in Iraq, whom they regard as apostates deserving of death. However, after suffering a setback as a result of the 2006 US military surge and their own brutal conduct, which alienated many Sunni tribes, they viewed the revolt in Syria as a golden opportunity to roll back Shi'i gains. Whereas the fall of Iraq in 2003 created the so-called Shi'i Crescent, the Salafi-jihadists believed that, in toppling the Assad regime, they would break this power bloc and consolidate the Sunni camp. The struggle in Syria has also reawakened the Salafi-jihadists' latent anti-Persian animosity, which is based on the accusation that the Persians have distorted true Arab Islam.

Although the Salafi-jihadists advocate an extreme anti-Jewish and anti-Israeli ideology, they have refrained from attacking Israel. Historically, religious radicals often view lapsed or deviating members of their own religion as more dangerous—at least in the short term—than members of other religions, on account of their supposed deviousness, which threatens the community from within and prevents it from attaining its spiritual and political goals. If the West and the Jews serve as the ultimate external "other" for the Salafis, the Shi'is and Sufis fulfill this role within Islam. Salafi polemicists have often branded the Shi'is as "worse than Jews," the reason being that the Jews did not hide their evil character, whereas Shi'is pretend to be good Muslims.[21] Thus, an ISIL spokesman explained in mid-2014 that Jerusalem would not be liberated from Jewish rule prior to the extermination of the *rafida* (a pejorative alluding to the Shi'i rejection of the first three Caliphs).[22]

Moreover, internal rivalries between the various Islamist organizations sometimes superseded their animosity toward Israel. Thus, during the July-August 2014

---

20 "Syrian Crisis: Guide to Armed Groups in Syria," *BBC Arabic*, January 21, 2014 (in Arabic), http://www.bbc.co.uk/arabic/middleeast/2014/01/131213_syria_rebels_background.shtml.

21 For an analysis of the Salafis' ideological attitude toward the Shi'is, see Meir Litvak, "'More harmful than the Jews': Anti-Shi'i Polemics in Modern Radical Sunni Discourse," in *Le Shi'isme imamite quarante ans après: hommage à Etan Kohlberg*, ed. Muhammad Ali Amir-Moezzi et al. (Paris: Presses Universitaires de France, 2008), 285-306.

22 "Daesh: Jerusalem Will Not Be Liberated by the Disagreeing Judiciary," *Al-Mayadeen*, July 11, 2014 (in Arabic), http://www.almayadeen.net/ar/Newscast/aJBlw0H1SkaTZaNlAHxKyw/17/2014-07-11.

Gaza War between Israel and Hamas, jihadists and pro-jihadist Salafis issued video clips and tweets explaining their lack of assistance to the Palestinians. One tweet accused the Hamas government of being an "apostate, and what it is doing does not constitute jihad, but rather a defense of democracy [which Salafis oppose]." On a few occasions, ISIL's fighters even burnt the Palestinian flag, which they consider a symbol of the decline of the Islamic world, which has succumbed to national divisions through the creation of independent political states. In addition, while Hamas focuses on Israel as its enemy, al-Qaeda and its affiliates see the United States as the main enemy of Islam.[23]

As Syria emerged as the major arena for the Salafi jihad and the focal point of the Sunni-Shi'i sectarian conflict, it attracted thousands of volunteers from other Arab and Muslim countries, most notably Chechnya, Uzbekistan, and Pakistan, as well as from Xinjiang, China. Particularly significant were volunteers from Europe and North America, both descendants of Muslim immigrants and recent converts to Islam. Considering past experience, as Aaron Zelin has observed, the new networks of fighters forged by a shared experience in Syria are likely to continue their activities in their home countries in future years.[24]

Contrary to the Salafis, the Shi'is refrained from declaring all Sunnis to be infidels or apostates. As a minority group, they had always sought to convert Sunnis to their cause through polemics and religious preaching. They believed that declarations of apostasy would have alienated mainstream Sunnis. Rather, the Shi'is have focused their criticism on the Wahhabis, a euphemism for Saudis and Salafis, whom they have called deviant Muslims, thereby trying to drive a wedge between them and mainstream Sunnis. In practical terms, prior to the Arab upheaval, Shi'is refrained from violent attacks against Sunnis, except in Iraq, where the Sadrist movement launched concerted attacks to drive Sunnis from mixed neighborhoods in Baghdad, in retaliation for Salafi terrorist attacks against Shi'is.[25]

As the situation in Syria escalated, Iran was instrumental in mobilizing Shi'i volunteers from Iraq, and possibly Yemen, and sending them to fight in support of the Syrian regime.[26] Most importantly, Iran apparently forced Hezbollah to dispatch

---

23 Ali Mamouri, "Why Islamic State Has No Sympathy for Hamas," *Al-Monitor*, July 29, 2014, http://www.al-monitor.com/pulse/originals/2014/07/islamic-state-fighting-hamas-priority-before-israel.html; Dalit Halevi and Ari Soffer, "ISIS Spokesman Explains Why 'Islamic State' Not Supporting Hamas," *Arutz Sheva*, October 7, 2014, http://www.israelnationalnews.com/News/News.aspx/182751#.VCgd-ptxnok.

24 Aaron Y. Zelin, "Syria: The Epicenter of Future Jihad," Policy Watch no. 2278, Washington Institute, June 30, 2014, http://www.washingtoninstitute.org/policy-analysis/view/syria-the-epicenter-of-future-jihad; Emil A. Souleimanov, "Globalizing Jihad? North Caucasians in the Syrian Civil War," *Middle East Policy* 21, no, 3 (Fall 2014): 154-62; Mairbek Vatchagaev, "Recruits From Chechnya and Central Asia Bolster Ranks of Islamic State," *Eurasia Daily Monitor* 11, no. 154, September 4, 2014, http://www.jamestown.org/programs/edm/single/?tx_ttnews%5Btt_news%5D=42785&tx_ttnews%5BbackPid%5D=756&no_cache=1#.Vsl9RH195dg.

25 Ofra Bengio and Meir Litvak, "Epilogue," in *The Sunna and Shi'a in History*, ed. Ofra Bengio and Meir Litvak (New York: Palgrave-MacMillan, 2011), 246-48.

26 "IRGC Commander: Iran not to forestall military action against Israel," *Iranian Students' News Agency (ISNA)*, September 16, 2012, http://isna.ir/en/news/91062615337/IRGC-Commander-Iran-not-to-forestall-military.

thousands of its troops to fight alongside Assad's forces, an intervention which, at the time of writing, has helped produce a strategic stalemate in the Syrian war.[27]

Seeking to justify the fight against other Muslims rather than against Israel, Hezbollah Secretary General Hassan Nasrallah employed both sectarian and revolutionary arguments. He stressed the need to protect Shi'i holy sites—such as the tomb of Sayyida Zaynab, the granddaughter of the Prophet Muhammad, located near Damascus—from Salafi desecration. At the same time, he presented the struggle in Syria as a war declared by extremist Sunnis, the United States, and Israel against the "axis of resistance." He warned that "if the *takfiri* [i.e. Salafi] stream takes over [Syria], then the future of that country, of Lebanon, and of the region will be grim and dark."[28]

Hezbollah's military intervention in the Syrian war gave rise to vitriolic counterattacks by Sunni clerics, in a sharp turn from their previous support of or sympathy for its fight against Israel. Sheikh Yusuf al-Qaradawi, the most prominent Sunni authority in the Arab world and the spiritual authority of the Muslim Brotherhood, called on Sunni Muslims to head to Syria for a jihad against the Assad regime, Hezbollah, and other "heretics." He also accused Iran of seeking "continued massacres to kill Sunnis."[29] Qaradawi charged that "Alawites and Shi'is are even worse than Christians and Jews," and further slammed Iran and Hezbollah as "parties of Satan" (a play on words since Hezbollah literally means "party of God"). He expressed regret for defending Hezbollah in 2006, when Saudi clerics vilified its war with Israel as the posturing of Shi'i infidels, admitting that he had been deceived by Hezbollah, and praised the Saudis for being "more mature" when it came to the reality of this party.[30]

Seeking to deter Hezbollah or force it to devote its attention to Lebanon, Salafi-jihadist groups exploded car bombs in the Shi'i neighborhoods of Beirut in 2013. In mid-2014, Jabhat al-Nusra launched an attack on the northern Shi'i town of Arsal, in practice threatening to expand the Sunni-Shi'i war into Lebanese territory and perhaps even reignite a civil war in Lebanon.[31]

---

[27] Itamar Rabinovich, "The Changing of the Tide in the Syrian Civil War," INSS Insight no. 499, Institute for National Security Studies (INSS), December 17, 2013, http://www.inss.org.il/index.aspx?id=4538&articleid=6213.

[28] Nasrallah's speech on May 25, 2013, cited in "Lebanon Openly Enters Fighting in Syria," MEMRI Inquiry and Analysis Series Report no. 980, June 13, 2013. See also "Nasrallah: Hezbollah in Syria for Long Haul," *Al Jazeera*, November 15, 2013, http://www.aljazeera.com/news/middleeast/2013/11/nasrallah-hezbollah-syria-long-haul-2013111414617430132.html.

[29] "Top Muslim Cleric al-Qaradawi Urges Sunnis to Join Syria War," *Ahram Online*, June 1, 2013, http://english.ahram.org.eg/NewsContent/1/64/72857/Egypt/Politics-/Top-Muslim-cleric-AlQaradawi-urges-Sunnis-to-join-.aspx.

[30] "Sheikh Qaradawi makes U-turn, says Hezbollah is 'Party of Satan,'" *Al Arabiya*, June 9, 2013, http://english.alarabiya.net/en/News/middleeast/2013/06/09/Sheikh-Qaradawi-renews-call-for-holy-war-against-Hezbollah.html.

[31] Esperance Ghanem, "Could Arqoub Be the Next Arsal?," *Al-Monitor*, September 8, 2014, http://www.al-monitor.com/pulse/originals/2014/09/lebanon-arqoub-south-syrian-displaced-clashes.html?utm_source=; "Hezbollah Calls for Resistance against IS," *Al-Monitor*, August 27, 2014, http://www.al-monitor.com/pulse/originals/2014/08/hezbollah-resistance-arsal-counter-islamic-state-attacks.html?utm_source=.

While the Iranian state sought to downplay the sectarian element, the worsening strife in Syria has hardened the positions of regime-affiliated Shi'i clerics in Qom. In an unprecedented ruling (*fatwa*), Ayatollah Kazem al-Haeri stated that "the struggle in Syria is not about protecting the tomb of the Sayyida Zaynab," but a "war waged by the infidels against Islam." Hence, Islam needs to be defended, and those who are killed in this defense are martyrs (*shuhada*).[32] In other words, radicalism eventually produced total negation on both sides.

A major consequence of the deepening sectarian strife was increasing brutality from both sides. The Salafi-jihadists who regard those who do not adhere to their strict interpretation of religion as apostates deserving of death resorted to genocidal rhetoric advocating the annihilation of the Alawites. Following the intervention of Hezbollah fighters in the battle of al-Qusayr in Syria, local Sunni activists stated that while "the Shi'ites shout at us that we are the killers of Hussein ... [w]e will call them the killers of women and children." Others charged that Hezbollah placed "a burden on the shoulders of generations" of Shi'is, like the one borne by Germans after their leaders "committed massacres against the Jews." Following the capture of the town of Raqqah, heads of executed prisoners were displayed on spikes on street fences.[33]

The sectarian animosity was also directed at Christians and lead to brutal executions of prisoners, including crucifixion and beheading, in addition to the rape and enslavement of women and forced conversions. On at least one occasion, a woman was stoned to death for adultery. Jihadi fighters also desecrated churches and demolished icons and statues of Christian saints as symbols of paganism.[34] Christians living in ISIL-controlled territory in Syria were forced to pay the *jizya* (poll) tax, which had been levied in the early Islamic period on "protected minorities" (*ahl al-dhimma*), or face expulsion. These measures drew the Christians and Druze closer to the regime.[35]

IV. The Rise of "Islamic State"

As typical of religious radicals elsewhere, the Salafi-jihadists suffered from internal splits over ideology as well as personal and organizational rivalries. These divisions prevented the rebels from forging a united front against the Syrian regime and focusing their efforts in crucial areas, thereby precluding a decision on the battlefield.[36]

---

32 *Al-Sharq al-Awsat*, December 16, 2013, http://khabarnew.ir/NSite/FullStory/News/?Serv=0&Id=43159&Sgr=0 (URL no longer valid).

33 *New York Times*, June 5, 2013.

34 Sharona Schwartz, "Syrian Christians Accuse Islamist Rebels of Destroying Church Crosses, Pillaging Homes During Town Seizure,' *TheBlaze*, March 27, 2014, http://www.theblaze.com/stories/2014/03/27/syrian-christians-accuse-islamist-rebels-of-destroying-church-crosses-pillaging-homes-during-town-seizure; "Syrian Rebels Damage, Desecrate Churches," *CBN News*, October 23, 2013, http://www.cbn.com/cbnnews/world/2013/October/Syrian-Rebels-Damage-Desecrate-Churches.

35 M. Khayat, "The Islamic State's Treatment Of Christians," MEMRI Inquiry and Analysis Series Report no. 1112, August 20, 1994, http://www.memri.org/report/en/print8119.htm.

36 Jeffrey White, Andrew J. Tabler and Aaron Y. Zelin, *Syria's Military Opposition: How Effective, United or Extremist?*, Policy Focus no. 128, Washington Institute for Near East Policy, September 2013; Yezid Sayigh, "Unifying Syria's Rebels: Saudi Arabia Joins the Fray," *Carnegie Middle East Center*, October 28, 2013, http://carnegie-mec.org/publications/?fa=53436.

The most fateful split took place between ISIL and Jabhat al-Nusra in early 2014. ISIL had evolved from the al-Qaeda in Iraq (AQI) organization led by Abu Musab al-Zarqawi, which had played a key role in the fight against the American forces there. At this time, it had already acquired notoriety for killing Sunni and Shi'i civilians in suicide attacks, bombing Shi'i mosques, uploading videos of beheadings on jihadist forums, and forcing local Sunnis to abide by its strict interpretation of Islamic law. It maintained tense relations with al-Qaeda's leadership in Afghanistan, which viewed these activities as alienating Sunnis and harming the broader global jihadist strategy of driving the United States out of the Muslim world. Abu Bakr al-Baghdadi, who had become the organization's leader in 2010, changed its name to the Islamic State of Iraq (ISI), probably in order to highlight its local and independent stance. In 2011, Baghdadi dispatched fighters to Syria to set up a new jihadist organization under his overall command. Among them was Abu Mohammad al-Jawlani, the leader of what would become Jabhat al-Nusra, which officially announced itself in January 2012. By November 2012, Jawlani had built it into one of the opposition's best fighting forces. In April 2013, in view of this success, Baghdadi changed the name of his group to the Islamic State in Iraq and the Levant (ISIL), in order to signal that his organization and Jabhat al-Nusra had been the same group. However, Jawlani rebuffed the change and reaffirmed his allegiance to al-Qaeda leader Ayman al-Zawahiri as a separate organization. As the friction between the two organizations grew, Baghdadi moved from Iraq and established his base in Syria. ISIL also began to attract a growing number of fighters from Jabhat al-Nusra and foreign countries.[37]

Zawahiri, who sought to assert his own authority over the loose network of al-Qaeda–affiliated organizations, demanded that ISIL stay in Iraq and allow Jabhat al-Nusra to be the preferred actor in Syria. In response, ISIL leaders accused Zawahiri of splitting the jihadist front and, even worse, of affirming "the Sykes-Picot division of the Arab Middle East into artificial nation-states like 'Iraq' and 'Syria,' a division without basis in Islam." In July 2013, ISIL's official spokesman, Abu Mohammad al-Adnani, declared that the organization's goal was "the formation of an Islamic state on the prophetic model that acknowledges no boundaries" and does not "distinguish between Arab and non-Arab."[38]

Zawahiri's attempts to manage the jihadists in Syria in the summer and fall of 2013 failed. On 2 February 2014, al-Qaeda's general command officially dissociated itself from ISIL, stating it was not "a branch of the Qa'idat al-Jihad [al-Qaeda's official name]." This was the first time that the movement had publicly dissociated itself from a group previously associated with it.[39] The move aggravated pre-existing

---

[37] Aaron Y. Zelin, "Al-Qaeda in Syria: A Closer Look at ISIS (Part I)," Policy Watch no. 2137, Washington Institute, September 10, 2013, http://www.washingtoninstitute.org/policy-analysis/view/al-qaeda-in-syria-a-closer-look-at-isis-part-i.

[38] Cole Bunzel, "The Islamic State of Disobedience: al-Baghdadi Triumphant," *Jihadica*, October 5, 2013, available at http://www.aymennjawad.org/13909/the-islamic-state-of-disobedience-al-baghdadi.

[39] Clint Watts, "ISIS's Rise After al Qaeda's House of Cards," *Geopoliticus: The FPRI Blog*, March 22, 2014, http://www.fpri.org/geopoliticus/2014/03/isis-rise-after-al-qaedas-house-cards-part-4-smarter-counterterrorism; Aaron Y. Zelin, "Al-Qaeda Disaffiliates with the Islamic State of Iraq and al-Sham," Policy Alert, Washington Institute, February 4, 2014, http://www.washingtoninstitute.org/policy-analysis/view/al-qaeda-disaffiliates-with-the-islamic-state-of-iraq-and-al-sham.

divisions within the global jihad movement that have long been apparent. As a result, the two jihadist groups Jama'at Ansar Bayt al-Maqdis and the Majlis Shura al-Mujahideen, which were active in both the Sinai Peninsula and the Gaza Strip, moved away from al-Qaeda and affirmed their support for ISIL.[40] Conversely, at least three of the most radical Salafi scholars, Abu Basir al-Tartusi, Abu Hamid al-Maqdisi, and Ibn Qatada, who served as mentors for the Salafi-jihadist movement as a whole, came out against ISIL on the grounds of its extremism and excesses.[41]

Unlike other Islamist organizations in Syria, ISIL exerted more effort in consolidating the territory under its control as a rudimentary Islamic state and fighting rival Islamist organizations than in combating the Syrian regime. By mid-2014, it had carved out a de facto state in the borderlands of Syria and Iraq, stretching in an extended ellipse roughly from Raqqah in Syria to Fallujah in Iraq, where it provided limited social services and dispensed its interpretation of Islamic justice. In the Raqqah region, for example, it banned smoking, music, and singing and mandated all men to take part in public prayers and all women to adorn the veil covering their faces (*niqab*). ISIL's major source of revenue consisted of the oil and gas fields in eastern Syria. Significantly, it traded this oil with the Syrian government, which it had considered an apostate regime. As in the case of the radicals' attitude toward Shi'is and Jews, the enemy within, i.e. other Salafi organizations, was perceived as more dangerous than the enemy without.[42]

In Iraq, ISIL took advantage of the increasing resentment of the Sunni minority against the exclusionary policies of Shi'i Prime Minister Nouri al-Maliki to forge alliances with Sunni tribal fighters and former officers and soldiers of Saddam Hussein's army and expand its territorial hold in the western Anbar region.[43] In June 2014, ISIL scored its greatest military victory when it captured Mosul, the second largest city in Iraq.

As in Syria, the conquests in Iraq led to new atrocities. In Mosul, ISIL executed hundreds of Shi'i soldiers, forcing them to lie down in ditches before being shot. After taking the town of Sinjar in northern Iraq, it executed hundreds of civilians from the Yazidi minority, reportedly burying some alive, and took scores of Yazidi women as spoils of war.[44] In addition to religious fanaticism, the rationale behind

---

40 Aymenn Jawad al-Tamimi, "ISIS, al-Qaeda Compete for Supremacy in Global Jihad," *Al-Monitor*, February 11, 2014, http://www.al-monitor.com/pulse/ar/originals/2014/02/isis-qaeda-zawahri-baghdadi-jihadist-syria-iraq.html#.

41 Cole Bunzel, "Caliphate Now: Jihadis Debate the Islamic State," *Jihadica*, November 25, 2013, http://www.jihadica.com/caliphate-now-jihadis-debate-the-islamic-state (URL no longer valid); Joas Wagemakers, "A Purity Contest: Abu Basir and al-Maqdisi Slug It Out," *Jihadica*, September 12, 2014, http://www.jihadica.com/a-purity-contest-abu-basir-and-al-maqdisi-slug-it-out (URL no longer valid). For an elaboration of the doctrinal disagreements between some of the sheikhs and lay activists, see Eli Alshech "The Doctrinal Crisis within the Salafi-Jihadi Ranks and the Emergence of Neo-Takfirism," *Islamic Law and Society* 21, no. 4 (2014): 419-52.

42 Douglas A. Ollivant and Brian Fishman, "State of Jihad: The Reality of the Islamic State in Iraq and Syria, *War on the Rocks*, May 21, 2014, http://warontherocks.com/2014/05/state-of-jihad-the-reality-of-the-islamic-state-in-iraq-and-syria.

43 Raed El-Hamed, "ISIS and the Anbar Crisis," *Sada*, June 12, 2014, http://carnegie endowment.org/sada/2014/06/12/isis-and-anbar-crisis/hdli.

44 Mohammed A. Salih, "After Taking Sinjar, IS Draws Iraqi Kurds into Full-Scale War," *Al-Monitor*, August 7, 2014, http://www.al-monitor.com/pulse/originals/2014/08/iraq-kurdistan-yazidis-peshmerga-isis-islamic-state.html#.

these acts was to instill dread among future rivals and make them flee from advancing ISIL forces. In June, ISIL destroyed seven Shi'i places of worship in the Turkmen city of Tal Afar, 50 kilometers west of Mosul. It also destroyed the tomb of the Prophet Yunis (Jonah) in Mosul, where Sunnis went to worship, since it regards the visitation of graves as idolatry.[45]

The conquest of Mosul and its environs, which provided ISIL with considerable resources, allowed it to emerge as the most formidable Islamist force in the history of the modern Middle East. It reportedly seized over $400 million from the city's banks as "war booty" and captured large stocks of heavy weapons left by the disintegrating Iraqi army. It extracts an estimated 35,000 barrels of oil per day in Iraq, selling it to middle men in Iraq, Turkey, Jordan, and Iran. It also controls the oil pipeline between Kirkuk and the Turkish port of Ceyhan. In addition, it is collecting about $8 million a month from taxes in Mosul alone. The aura of success and material resources surrounding ISIL has further increased its prestige among Islamists and brought thousands of new volunteers to its ranks. By September 2014, it had a fighting force of close to 50,000 men.[46]

The capture of Mosul and its environs marked the formation of a new political entity whose territory cut across the borders of two major states, thereby posing an unprecedented challenge to the continued territorial integrity and survival of those states, as well as to the entire political-territorial map established after the collapse of the Ottoman Empire at the end of World War I.

On June 30, flush with success and reflecting its broader ambitions and self-perception, ISIL proclaimed a caliphate headed by Abu Bakr al-Baghdadi, who was henceforth known as Caliph Ibrahim. In his first sermon as caliph, Baghdadi promised all Muslims that the new caliphate would "restore your dignity, might, rights, and leadership" and that it was "a state where the Arab and non-Arab, the white man and black man, the easterner and westerner are all brothers." He insisted that the Islamic state had satisfied the conditions for the establishment of a caliphate, which included, among other things, the practical implementation of sharia law in territories under its rule, with Islamic courts set up to mete out sentences in accordance with Islam. He rejected accusations that the Islamic state was engaged in terrorism by arguing that "terrorism is to worship Allah as He ordered you. Terrorism is to refuse humiliation, subjugation, and subordination." Baghdadi vowed to "take revenge" against the enemies of Islam and called upon the Muslims to stand up and rise up in the face of "tyranny, against the treacherous rulers—the agents of the crusaders and the atheists, and the guards of the Jews!"[47]

---

[45] "Iraq: ISIS Kidnaps Shia Turkmen, Destroys Shrines," *Human Rights Watch*, June 27, 2014, http://www.hrw.org/news/2014/06/27/iraq-isis-kidnaps-shia-turkmen-destroys-shrines; "Video Shows Blowing Up of Shrine of Nabi Yunis by Daesh," *CNN Arabic*, July 25, 2014 (in Arabic), http://arabic.cnn.com/middleeast/2014/07/25/me-250714-iraq-isis-jonah-tomb-blown.

[46] "Report: ISIS Steals $429m from Central Bank after Capturing Mosul," *Al Arabiya*, June 13, 2014, http://english.alarabiya.net/en/News/middle-east/2014/06/13/Report-ISIS-steals-429mn-in-Mosul-capture.html; "ISIS Using Oil to Create Its Own State, Say Experts," *Daily Sabah*, July 10, 2014, http://www.dailysabah.com/energy/2014/07/11/isis-using-oil-to-create-its-own-state-say-experts; Mona Alami "The Islamic State and the Cost of Governing," *Sada*, September 4, 2014, http://carnegieendowment.org/sada/index.cfm?fa=show&article=56534&solr_hilite=.

[47] "What did Abu Bakr al-Baghdadi say?," *Middle East Eye*, July 5, 2014, http://www.middleeasteye.net/news/what-did-baghdadi-say-320749010.

The declaration of the caliphate has been an unprecedented event in modern times. It signified a claim to the political and religious leadership of the entire Muslim nation, as was the case following the death of the Prophet Muhammad in 632 CE. Since the 1924 abolition of the Ottoman Caliphate by the Turkish Republic, no Muslim group in control of any territory had made such a bid. Attempts by a few Arab rulers in the 1920s, most notably King Hussein of the Hijaz, or Kings Fuad and Farouk in Egypt, met widespread opposition. Even al-Qaeda and the Taliban in Afghanistan made a more modest claim in establishing an emirate (an undefined political-territorial entity, which they hoped would eventually coalesce into a caliphate once conditions were ripe).[48]

Following the declaration, ISIL changed its name to the "Islamic State" shedding the territorial designation of Iraq and the Levant. The change indicated that it rejected the division of the Muslims into different states on a national basis and signified its ambition to expand to other countries as well. Indeed, in a speech, Baghdadi addressed the plight of Muslims from Burma to Europe and concluded with aspirations for the Islamic State's conquest of "Rome" and the whole world.[49]

The declaration of the caliphate and the claim to pre-eminence and leadership of the entire Muslim world elicited broad opposition across the Islamist spectrum. Sheikh Abbas Shuman of al-Azhar university stated that "all those who are today speaking of an Islamic state are terrorists," adding that the "Islamic caliphate cannot be restored by force, occupying a country and killing half of its population." Other al-Azhar scholars accused ISIL of fomenting discord among the Muslims and of committing various crimes, branding their actions as "corruption on earth," a sin punishable by death according to Islamic law. They also maintained that only "those in authority" are eligible to declare and establish a caliphate, but remained vague as to whether this referred to the rulers or established clerics like themselves. Al-Azhar's rector, Sheikh Ahmadel-Tayeb, charged ISIL with tarnishing Islam by its crimes and claimed that ISIL and all other terrorist organizations were "the product of imperialism and working in the service of Zionism."[50]

The World Union of Muslim Clerics, headed by Yusuf al-Qaradawi, dismissed the declaration as legally invalid. It maintained that the caliph was a representative and agent of the Islamic nation based on an oath of allegiance (*bay'ah*), and that this deputization lacked any legal or rational basis unless it came from the entire nation or through its representatives, that is to say the clerics—the eligible senior decision-makers of Islamic societies. The union warned of anarchy should any group decide to declare its own caliphate, with the inevitable degradation of the noble ideal.[51]

---

48 Bernard Haykel and Cole Bunzel, "A New Caliphate?," *Project Syndicate*, July 10, 2014, http://www.project-syndicate.org/commentary/bernard-haykel-and-cole-bunzel-consider-the-implications-of-the-islamic-state-s-declaration-of-a-caliphate?barrier=true.

49 Aymenn Jawad Al-Tamimi, "Abu Bakr al-Baghdadi's Message as Caliph," *Gatestone Institute*, July 2, 2014, http://www.gatestoneinstitute.org/4387/baghdadi-isis-caliphate.

50 "French: The Islamic State Is Accused of Distorting the Concept of Succession," *Al Shorouk*, July 2, 2014 (in Arabic), http://www.shorouknews.com/news/view.aspx?cdate=02072014&id=bbf8b100-83d6-4e34-964c-978de63f04e3; Islam Abdul Zahir, "Al-Azhar Scholars and Salafi Theorists: Daesh Succession Void," *Al Ahed*, July 16, 2014 (in Arabic), http://www.alahednews.com.lb/essaydetails.php?eid=98530&cid=76#.VB75Tq1xnok.

51 "Union of Muslim Scholars: Daesh Announcement of Caliphate Legally Void," July 5, 2014 (in Arabic), http://www.islammemo.cc/akhbar/arab/2014/07/05/202318.html. For similar

Radical Salafi clerics lashed out at ISIL's caliphate as increasing discord within the jihadist camp and questioned Baghdadi's scholarly credentials for making such a momentous step.[52]

Needless to say, Shi'i Iran and Hezbollah vehemently attacked the caliphate's declaration and charged that the crimes committed by the *takfiri* groups were "supported by Tel Aviv and Washington." Interestingly, the Iranian media chose to cite Sunni condemnations of the declaration, including those of Salafi scholars, seeking to show that it shared the broad Islamic consensus, and downgraded its sectarian approach to the regional conflict. Various Iranian sources even claimed that Baghdadi was a Jew named Simon Elliot who was an "agent for the Zionist intelligence agency the Mossad." His supposed mission was to invade countries that pose a threat to Israel in order to establish the biblical "Greater Israel."[53]

The build-up of a US-led international coalition against ISIL in September 2014 could put an end to the organization's advancement but will not necessarily lead to its demise. It could also lead to an important tactical regional realignment whose first signs are already visible at the time of writing. One can speak of tacit US-Iran cooperation against ISIL and an attempt at Saudi-Iranian rapprochement, though it is too early to tell whether either move will advance beyond tactics. Significantly, mainstream Islamists led by Qaradawi, who had denounced ISIL, opposed any US-led military action against ISIL, claiming that they did not trust US motives.[54] Apparently, suspicion and animosity toward the leading Western power still runs deeper than internal Muslim struggles.

V. Conclusion

The Arab upheaval raised the Islamist movements to new heights but also placed them in a serious predicament. The swift electoral win of the Muslim Brotherhood in Egypt proved to be a pyrrhic victory, as once in power they failed in almost every aspect. Their short tenure in government demonstrated that their ideology was not the solution to the serious socio-economic and political problems plaguing the Arab world. Moreover, they proved to be as authoritarian as their opponents had feared and appeared to be more focused on advancing their narrow party interests than on forging a national consensus. The setback that they suffered following their forced removal from power cannot be underestimated given the hundreds of casualties they suffered and the authorities' ongoing efforts to crush their organizational infrastructure. Just as importantly, the widespread support in Egypt for the coup shows how quickly they lost popularity among wide segments of society. However, this defeat does not mean the end of the movement, since a substantial minority still

---

arguments by the Muslim Brotherhood in Syria, see http://www.muslm.org/vb/showthread.php?534957 (in Arabic).

[52] Zahir, "Al-Azhar Scholars"; "Conclave Launches an Attack on Militants, Warns Daesh: Silent No More," July 2, 2014 (in Arabic), http://www.islammemo.cc/akhbar/arab/2014/07/02/202142.html.

[53] Yuram Abdullah Weiler, "'Caliph' al-Baghdadi is Jewish Mossad Agent 'Simon Elliot,'" *Tehran Times*, September 10, 2014, available at http://worldmeets.us/tehrantimes000043POST.shtml#ixzz3E8HtIdzG.

[54] *Al-Hayat*, September 15, 2014.

supports it and the appeal or power of religion has not disappeared. It remains to be seen whether the Brotherhood will embark on a process of organizational and ideological renewal and moderation, as some younger activists advocate, or whether they will cling to their old practices and ideas as if nothing has changed and/or turn to organized and persistent violence.

Even more troubling has been the role of the radical Salafi-jihadist movements. While they scored major military gains, their actions—and those of the Syrian army—have brought widespread misery to Syria and Iraq. The brutality that they have practiced against prisoners and civilians is reminiscent of the darkest ages eras of human history. Their actions have exacerbated sectarian and ethnic animosities in the region and precipitated the disintegration of several Arab countries that may require many years to repair. Typical of radicals elsewhere, they have experienced internal divisions and splits stemming from ideological and personal differences. Their declaration of a caliphate and claim to leadership of the Muslim world have encountered broad opposition, reflecting not only ideological, organizational, and personal rivalries but also the fact that the territorial and ideological fragmentation of the Muslim world has become deeply entrenched, superseding aspirations for worldwide Muslim unity. The animosity within the Salafi-jihadist camp has seemed on occasion to be even deeper than its opposition to the Syrian regime and even Israel, the ultimate outsider in the region. Like the Muslim Brotherhood, the Salafi-jihadists do not offer any real practical remedy to the problems that the Arab world had been suffering from in recent decades. On the contrary, in many ways, they have pushed the Arab world back and brought even more suffering to the region. Only time will enable us to assess the extent of the human and material cost of their actions and the years it will take to repair.

Antisemitism among Muslims in Europe

Günther Jikeli*

Antisemitism in Europe has increased dramatically since the beginning of the twenty-first century. Antisemitic acts have increased in number and in terms of their severity and violence, even if European governments regularly condemn antisemitism and little or no institutionalized discrimination takes place. However, antisemitic parties are currently represented in the European Parliament and some national parliaments. Antisemitic stereotypes get high approval rates in surveys. In certain countries, some antisemitic assumptions are even endorsed by the majority of the population. Many Jews in Europe feel under threat and consider leaving Europe. While Muslims are far from being the only perpetrators of antisemitic acts, the most violent acts in recent years were committed by individuals of Muslim background. However, little is known about their attitudes and why many of them have such negative views of Jews.

I. Muslims in Europe

The vast majority of Muslims in Europe are immigrants, or descendants of immigrants, who settled in Europe after World War II. Together with other immigrants, they came to work in the growing Western European economies during the 1950s, 1960s, and early 1970s. They were subsequently joined by their families, and later others arrived as refugees. Out of the European Union's present population of 500 million, 15 to 20 million are Muslim. Approximately 70 percent live in France, Germany, and the United Kingdom.[1] France has the highest share of Muslims, but

---

* Visiting Associate Professor, Justin M. Druck Family Scholar, Institute for the Study of Contemporary Antisemitism at Indiana University. Jikeli is also a Research Fellow at ISGAP, the Moses Mendelssohn Center for European-Jewish Studies at Potsdam University, and the Groupe Sociétés, Religions, Laïcités at the Centre National de la Recherche Scientifique (GSRL/CNRS), Paris.

[1] Pew Forum on Religion and Public Life, *Mapping the Global Muslim Population: A Report on the Size and Distribution of the World's Muslim Population* (Washington, DC: Pew Research Center, 2009), http://www.pewforum.org/files/2009/10/Muslimpopulation.pdf; Open Society Institute, *Muslims in Europe: A Report on 11 EU Cities* (New York/London/Budapest, 2010), 22, https://www.opensocietyfoundations.org/sites/default/files/a-muslims-europe-20110214_0.pdf; European Monitoring Centre on Racism and Xenophobia, *Muslims in the European Union: Discrimination and Islamophobia* (2006), 29, http://fra.europa.eu/fraWebsite/attachments/Manifestations_EN.pdf.

they still comprise only 6-7.5 percent of the population.[2] However, the proportion is significantly higher in some urban agglomerations and among young people.

The history of migration to Europe has resulted in a diverse landscape of Muslim communities in each European country. The majority of the estimated 5.5 million Muslims in Germany are immigrants or the descendants of immigrants from Turkey; about a quarter are ethnic Kurds. The second largest group comes from the former Yugoslavia[3] and, after the arrival of more than one million refugees in Germany in 2015, from Syria, Afghanistan, and Iraq.[4] Most Muslims in Germany are Sunni, but about 10 percent adhere to Alevism, a particular liberal current of Islam. Shi'ites form less than 7 percent of Muslims in Germany, while others, such as Ahmadiyas and Sufis, comprise less than 6 percent of the Muslim population.[5] Some 80 percent of the 4-5 million Muslims in France have a Maghreb background, mostly Arab but also Berber, coming from Algeria, Morocco, and Tunisia. Other ethnicities include groups from Turkey, Sub-Saharan Africa, and Middle Eastern countries.[6] Most of the roughly 3 million Muslims in the United Kingdom are immigrants or descendants of immigrants from former colonies in South Asia, today's Pakistan, Bangladesh, and India.[7] Muslims make up the country's second largest religious community, comprising 4.8 percent of the population, with a higher percentage in urban areas.[8] Approximately one million Muslims live in London.

---

2 The estimation based on a 2008-2009 representative survey of 18-60 year-old individuals in France is 4-4.3 percent. Simon, Patrick and Vincent Tiberj, "Sécularisation ou regain religieux: la religiosité des immigrés et de leurs descendants," Working Document 196 (Paris: Institut national d'études démographique, 2013), 6; see also Open Society Institute, *Muslims in the EU: Cities Report—France: Preliminary Research Report and Literature Survey* (2007), 11-14, http://www.opensocietyfoundations.org/sites/default/files/museucitiesfra_20080101_0.pdf; Jonathan Laurence and Justin Vaïsse, *Integrating Islam: Political and Religious Challenges in Contemporary France* (Washington, DC: Brookings Institution Press, 2006), 15-48; Gilles Couvreur, *Musulmans de France: diversité, mutations et perspectives de l'islam français* (Paris: Éditions de l'Atelier/Éditions Ouvrières, 1998), 10-13; Thomas Vampouille, "France: Comment est évalué le nombre de musulmans," *Le Figaro*, April 5, 2011.

3 Open Society Institute, *Muslims in the EU: Cities Report—Germany: Preliminary Research Report and Literature Survey* (2007), 14, https://www.opensocietyfoundations.org/sites/default/files/museucitiesger_20080101_0.pdf; Bundesamt für Migration und Flüchtlinge, *Muslimisches Leben in Deutschland* (Nuremberg, 2009), 13, 57-93, http://www.bamf.de/SharedDocs/Anlagen/DE/Publikationen/Forschungsberichte/fb06-muslimisches-leben.pdf?__blob=publicationFile; Martin Sökefeld, *Aleviten in Deutschland. Identitätsprozesse einer Religionsgemeinschaft in der Diaspora* (Bielefeld: Transcript, 2008).

4 Bundesministerium des Innern, "2015: Mehr Asylanträge in Deutschland als jemals zuvor," press release, January 6, 2016, http://www.bmi.bund.de/SharedDocs/Pressemitteilungen/DE/2016/01/asylantraege-dezember-2015.html.

5 Katrin Brettfeld and Peter Wetzels, *Muslime in Deutschland* (Berlin: Bundesministerium des Innern, 2007), 13.

6 Jonathan Laurence and Justin Vaïsse, *Integrating Islam: Political and Religious Challenges in Contemporary France* (Washington, DC: Brookings Institution Press, 2006); Open Society Institute, *Muslims in the EU: Cities Report—France: Preliminary Research Report and Literature Survey* (2007), 11, http://www.opensocietyfoundations.org/sites/default/files/museucitiesfra_20080101_0.pdf.

7 Office for National Statistics, *Focus on Religion* (October 2004), http://www.ons.gov.uk/ons/rel/ethnicity/focus-on-religion/2004-edition/focus-on-religion-summary-report.pdf.

8 Figures are for England and Wales.

Today, the majority of European Muslims are an integral part of the fabric of their cities, regions, and countries. Although there have been vociferous discussions about terrorist plots by young European Muslims, the introduction of Shari'a, the violent response to cartoons mocking the Prophet Muhammad, and issues concerning Muslim women, such as the wearing of the veil and the outlawing of the burkha, forced marriages, and "honor killings," these matters mostly concern a minority of Muslims and have not led to a general alienation of Muslims from mainstream society. Even if some surveys reveal high approval rates for antidemocratic attitudes and approval of Shari'a law,[9] the large majority of European Muslims do not put such attitudes into practice and are law-abiding citizens. It is important to bear in mind that Islam, far from being a homogeneous religion, varies according to doctrine, ideological streams, and individual preferences. However, religious identity is of growing importance to European Muslims. Most Muslims strongly identify with Islam but also with their country of residence.[10]

The diversity of the Muslim population is reflected in the diversity of Muslim organizations. However, the majority of Muslim organizations in Europe are affiliated with or linked to global Islamist movements, such as the Muslim Brotherhood. In Germany, the second-largest Muslim organization, Millî Görüş, is thought to be a non-violent Islamist organization[11] with strong links to Turkey that is ideologically close to the Brotherhood. In France, the majority of Muslim organizations of the Conseil français du culte musulman, created as a representative body for Muslims in France, have strong ties to Islamist organizations.[12] The Muslim Council of Britain (MCB) is linked to the international Islamist organizations Muslim Brotherhood and Jamaat-e-Islami.[13] On a European level, the most prominent Muslim organization is the European Council of Fatwa, headed by Yusuf al-Qaradawi, a prominent Egyptian Islamic theologian and one of the main ideologues of the Muslim Brotherhood. These and other Islamist organizations have published antisemitic statements and some have close contacts to openly antisemitic organizations. Millî Görüş in Germany, for instance, has not severed its links to the antisemitic

[9] Ruud Koopmans, "Religious Fundamentalism and Hostility against Out-Groups: A Comparison of Muslims and Christians in Western Europe," *Journal of Ethnic and Migration Studies* 41, no. 1 (2015): 33-57; Pew Research Center's Forum on Religion and Public Life, *The World's Muslims: Religion, Politics and Society* (Washington, DC: Pew Research Center, 2013).

[10] Gallup, *The Gallup Coexist Index 2009: A Global Study of Interfaith Relations—With an in-depth analysis of Muslim integration in France, Germany, and the United Kingdom* (Washington, DC: Gallup, 2009), available at https://ec.europa.eu/migrant-integration/librarydoc/the-gallup-coexist-index-2009-a-global-study-of-interfaith-relations.

[11] Bundesministerium des Innern, *Verfassungsschutzbericht 2011*, 290-304; Günther Jikeli, Robin Stoller, and Hanne Thoma, *Proceedings: Strategies and Effective Practices for Fighting Antisemitism among People with a Muslim or Arab Background in Europe* (Berlin/London: IIBSA, 2007), 57-65.

[12] Samir Amghar, "Les mutations de l'islamisme en France. Portrait de l'UOIF, porte-parole de l'«islamisme de minorité»," *La Vie des idées* (October 2007), http://www.laviedesidees.fr/Les-mutations-de-l-islamisme-en.html.

[13] Martin Bright, *When Progressives Treat with Reactionaries: The British State's Flirtation with Radical Islam* (London: Policy Exchange, 2006); John Ware, "MCB in the Dock," *Prospect Magazine*, no. 129 (December 2006).

pro-Hamas organization IHH,[14] even after the latter was outlawed in Germany. Book fairs in mosques associated with Millî Görüş have displayed blunt antisemitic literature.[15] Similarly, the orthodox Sunni Union des Organisations Islamiques de France (UOIF) supports the pro-Hamas Committee for Charity and Assistance to Palestinians (CBSP).[16] The leading Deobandi figure in the United Kingdom, Abu Yusuf Riyadh ul Haq, is known for the blunt antisemitic statements he has uttered in public.[17] The list goes on. The Muslim Association of Britain gained prominence after organizing a pro-Palestinian rally that equated Israel with Nazi Germany.[18] An investigation of the literature available in mosques, Islamic schools, and Islamic cultural centers in the United Kingdom found that some of Britain's mainstream Islamic institutions provide cause for concern. The literature available in a number of British mosques contains hatred against Jews and the West, as well as antisemitic conspiracy theories, including positive references to *The Protocols of the Elders of Zion*.[19] However Islamist organizations are hardly representative of the Muslim population in Europe, despite their prominence and influence in many European mosques. In fact, Muslim organizations in general are not very representative of Muslims. Fifty percent of Muslims in Germany and 51 percent of Muslims in the United Kingdom do not feel represented by any existing Islamic organization.[20] In France, the representativeness of the Muslim umbrella organization Conseil français du culte musulman (CFCM) is disputed because only 25 percent of French Muslims regularly visit a mosque.

Muslim communities face a number of social and economic challenges, including particularly high unemployment rates, relatively poor housing conditions, and lower levels of formal work qualifications. Discrimination is also a factor. In addition to racism and xenophobia, Muslims are increasingly confronted with negative stereotypes of Islam and Muslims. In 2008, one in three Muslims in the European Union had suffered discrimination in the previous twelve months.[21] However, discrimination varied according to country and ethnic background and was even higher in the case of other minority groups: 47 percent of Roma and 41 percent of people of Sub-Saharan African background suffered discrimination in the previous

---

14 Sabine Am Orde et al., "Islamismus in Deutschland: Die netten Herren von Millî Görüs," *Die Tageszeitung*, July 18, 2010.

15 Aycan Demirel, "Kreuzberger Initiative gegen Antisemitismus," *DAVID—Jüdische Kulturzeitschrift* (June 2006), http://www.david.juden.at/kulturzeitschrift/66-70/69-demirel.htm.

16 Stephen Roth Institute, *Country Report: France 2007* (2008), http://www.tau.ac.il/Anti-Semitism/asw2007/france.html.

17 Riyadh ul Haq, "Riyadh Ul Haq Sermon on 'Jewish Fundamentalism' in Full," *Times* (London), September 6, 2007.

18 Michael Whine, "The Advance of the Muslim Brotherhood in the UK," *Current Trends in Islamist Ideology*, no. 2 (2005).

19 Denis MacEoin, *The Hijacking of British Islam: How Extremist Literature Is Subverting Mosques in the UK* (London: Policy Exchange, 2007).

20 Katrin Brettfeld and Peter Wetzels, *Muslime in Deutschland* (Berlin: Bundesministerium des Innern, 2007); Munira Mirza, Zain Ja'far, and Abi Senthilkumaran, *Living Apart Together: British Muslims and the Paradox of Multiculturalism* (London: Policy Exchange, 2007).

21 European Union Agency for Fundamental Rights (FRA), *Data in Focus Report: Muslims* (Luxembourg: Publications Office of the EU, 2009), 5, http://fra.europa.eu/fraWebsite/attachments/EU-MIDIS_MUSLIMS_EN.pdf.

twelve months,[22] indicating that racism is still the dominant factor in discrimination against ethnic and religious minorities. Ten percent of Muslim respondents believed that the discrimination they experienced was based on religion or belief, 32 percent believed that it was a result of ethnic or immigrant origin, and 43 percent believed that it was a combination of all of the above.[23] However, there is a growing sense of victimhood based on Islamic belief. Public debate on Islamic fundamentalism and increased anti-terror measures are often viewed as anti-Muslim bias.[24]

II. Muslim Antisemitism in Europe

Antisemitism is present in a number of groups in Europe today. Antisemitism among Muslims has added weight to antisemitism from the far right, the left, and mainstream society and poses an additional security risk.[25] Antisemitism among European Muslims and Muslim organizations is frequently visible in anti-Israel demonstrations and has sometimes led to veritable antisemitic riots, such as in Oslo at the beginning of 2009[26] and in Paris in the summer of 2014.[27]

Several violent antisemitic incidents were perpetrated in recent years by youths of Muslim background. The most infamous of these were the jihadist terror attacks in Paris, Copenhagen, Brussels and Toulouse. Mohamed Merah slaughtered three children and a teacher at a Jewish school in Toulouse, France.[28] The cold-blooded

---

22 FRA, *European Union Minorities and Discrimination Survey* (2009), 36, http://fra.europa.eu/fraWebsite/attachments/eumidis_mainreport_conference-edition_en_.pdf.

23 FRA, *Data in Focus Report: Muslims* (Luxembourg: Publications Office of the EU, 2009), 5.

24 The term "Islamophobia" is often used to blur the distinction between anti-Muslim bias and criticism of Islamic doctrine and practice.

25 Robert Wistrich provides an excellent overview with numerous examples. Robert S Wistrich, *A Lethal Obsession: Anti-Semitism from Antiquity to the Global Jihad* (New York: Random House, 2010); Wistrich, *Muslimischer Antisemitismus. Eine aktuelle Gefahr* (Berlin: Edition Critic, 2012). See also Pierre-André Taguieff, *Rising from the Muck: The New Anti-Semitism in Europe* (Chicago: Ivan R. Dee, 2004). Surveys regularly show that antisemitic attitudes are widespread in mainstream society. A comparative study of eight European countries reveals that 24.5 percent agreed with the statement that Jews have too much influence in their country and 41.2 percent supposed that "Jews try to take advantage of having been victims during the Nazi era." However, there are significant differences among the countries. See Andreas Zick, Beate Küpper, and Hinna Wolf, *European Conditions: Findings of a Study on Group-focused Enmity in Europe* (Institute for Interdisciplinary Research on Conflict and Violence, University of Bielefeld, 2009), http://www.amadeu-antonio-stiftung.de/w/files/pdfs/gfepressrelease_english.pdf.

26 Eirik Eiglad, *The Anti-Jewish Riots in Oslo* (Porsgrunn, Norway: Communalism Press, 2010).

27 "Dark Days," *Economist*, July 22, 2014, http://www.economist.com/blogs/charlemagne/2014/07/anti-semitism-france; Jessica Elgot, "France's Jews Flee As Rioters Burn Shops To Chants Of 'Gas The Jews,'" *Huffington Post UK*, July 22, 2014, http://www.huffingtonpost.co.uk/2014/07/22/france-jewish-shops-riot_n_5608612.html.

28 On March, 19, 2012, Mohamed Merah opened fire at the *Ozar Hatorah* school in Toulouse. The gunman chased people inside the building and shot at them. He grabbed a 7-year-old girl, shooting her at close range. He then retrieved his moped, and drove off. Gabriel (4), Arieh (5), their father and teacher at the school, Jonathan Sandler, and Myriam Monsonégo (7) were killed and a 17-year-old student was gravely injured. The perpetrator, who also killed three unarmed French soldiers some days earlier, filmed his crimes, intending to publish them on the internet and on *Al Jazeera*. "Mohammed Merah and Abdelkader Merah (Shootings in Toulouse, France)," *New York Times*, April 4, 2012.

shooting at the Jewish museum in Brussels, Belgium, on May 24, 2014, left four dead. The presumed murderer is French jihadist Mehdi Nemmouche, who grew up in France and was radicalized in prison. He then participated in the Syrian civil war, most likely on the side of the Islamic State of Iraq and the Levant (ISIS). Violence further escalated with a wave of jihadist terror attacks in Paris in January 2015. On January 7, two of the three perpetrators murdered twelve people at the *Charlie Hebdo* offices, most of them journalists and cartoonists. A third gunman shot a police officer on January 8 and took hostages at a kosher supermarket the next day, killing four Jewish customers. Only a month later, jihadists attacked a meeting on "Art, Blasphemy and Freedom of Expression" and a synagogue in Copenhagen, killing two people. Subsequent Islamist terror attacks, such as in Paris in November 2015, in Brussels in March 2016, and in Nice in July 2016, have shown that Jews are far from being the only target group, although they are still a prime target. But extreme violence against Jews already started with an act of insanity in 2003 when Sébastien Selam was murdered in a Parisian suburb. The killer was quoted as shouting "I killed a Jew. I will go to paradise" after he brutally stabbed his victim. In 2006, Ilan Halimi was tortured and murdered in Paris by a group of mostly Muslim youths calling themselves the "gang des barbares."[29] In addition, other incidents in which young Muslims or Arabs were involved became public, such as the assault on a rabbi and his six-year-old daughter in Berlin in August 2012[30] and an attack on Jewish dancers at a local festival in Hanover, Germany, in 2010.[31] Muslim antisemitism is also a problem in the context of schools and education, as reports and teachers' testimonies in Germany,[32] France,[33] and Britain[34] have shown. Problematic views are often voiced in the context of education about the Holocaust.[35]

---

29 The self-named "gang des barbares" abducted Ilan Halimi because he was Jewish. Members of the gang tortured him for three weeks and eventually murdered him in a Parisian suburb. "Meurtre d'Ilan Halimi: le 'gang des barbares' jugé en appel, sans son leader," *Le Monde*, October 25, 2010.

30 Günther Jikeli, "Der neue alte Antisemitismus: Müssen Juden sich wieder verstecken?," *Stern*, September 14, 2012.

31 Johannes Wiedeman, "Angriff auf Tanzgruppe: Der alltägliche Antisemitismus in Hannover-Sahlkamp," *Welt*, June 26, 2010. For other examples, see Christine Schmitt, "Bei Gefahr 0800 880280," *Jüdische Allgemeine*, February 25, 2010; "Un rabbin agressé à la gare du Nord," *Le Monde*, April 21, 2007; Nick Cohen, "Following Mosley's East End Footsteps," *Observer* (Manchester), April 17, 2005; Leon Symons, "Teacher 'Sacked for Challenging Antisemitism,'" *Jewish Chronicle*, February 9, 2010; Léa Khayata, "Battles of Paris," *Tablet Magazine*, February 11, 2010.

32 Amadeu Antonio Stiftung, *"Die Juden sind schuld". Antisemitismus in der Einwanderungsgesellschaft am Beispiel muslimisch sozialisierter Milieus. Beispiele, Erfahrungen und Handlungsoptionen aus der pädagogischen und kommunalen Arbeit* (Berlin, 2009), http://www.amadeu-antonio-stiftung.de/w/files/pdfs/diejuden.pdf.

33 Emmanuel Brenner, *Les territoires perdus de la République: antisémitisme, racisme et sexisme en milieu scolaire* (Paris: Mille et une nuits, 2002). An English translation is available at http://www.ajc.org/atf/cf/%7B42d75369-d582-4380-8395-d25925b85eaf%7D/LOST%20TERRITORIES.PDF.

34 The Historical Association, *T.E.A.C.H. Teaching Emotive and Controversial History 3-19* (2007), 15, https://www.education.gov.uk/publications/eOrderingDownload/RW100.pdf.

35 Günther Jikeli and Joëlle Allouche-Benayoun, eds., *Perceptions of the Holocaust in Europe and Muslim Communities: Sources, Comparisons and Educational Challenges.* (Dordrecht/New York: Springer, 2013).

Discussing Muslim antisemitism is politically challenging. This became apparent when a study commissioned by an EU agency in 2002, which revealed that "physical attacks on Jews and the desecration and destruction of synagogues were acts mainly committed by young Muslim perpetrators mostly of an Arab descent in the monitoring period,"[36] was not published by the agency. It was feared that naming the problem would contribute to further stigmatization of Muslim minorities.[37] We believe that scholarly discussions about antisemitism among Muslims in Europe are necessary for a detailed understanding of the phenomenon and its sources, which might inform the development of effective tools for fighting antisemitism in Europe. It is only if Muslims are essentialized, that is, if it is assumed wrongly that people of Muslim background *necessarily* or "naturally" adhere to certain attitudes, that they become further stigmatized. Neglecting specific forms of antisemitism and groups of antisemitic perpetrators, on the other hand, is detrimental to the struggle against antisemitism.

The total number of antisemitic incidents in France and the United Kingdom (and worldwide) has increased considerably since the 1990s.[38] Many of the peaks in antisemitic incidents are related to eruptions of violence in the Israeli-Palestinian conflict but also to other events such as the Iraq war. Even the murders at a Jewish school in Toulouse triggered further antisemitic acts.

1. *What percentage of attacks come from Muslim perpetrators?*

Systematic data on the ethnic background of perpetrators of antisemitic acts is available mainly for Britain and France. However, perpetrators often remain unidentified.[39] The available numbers suggest that, in recent years, more than 30 percent of perpetrators of violent antisemitic incidents in those two countries were Muslim, with a higher percentage in France. Data from Germany indicate that the percentage of right-wing perpetrators of antisemitic attacks is particularly high there (about 80 percent of the violent antisemitic acts).[40] The statistics do not allow for an accurate estimation of the percentage of Muslim perpetrators,[41] but it seems to be lower in

---

36 Werner Bergmann and Juliane Wetzel, *Manifestations of Anti-Semitism in the European Union: First Semester 2002*, Synthesis Report on Behalf of the EUMC (2003), 25.

37 Some populists essentialize Muslims in their criticism of Muslim antisemitism. See Peter Widmann, "Der Feind kommt aus dem Morgenland. Rechtspopulistische 'Islamkritiker' um den Publizisten Hans-Peter Raddatz suchen die Opfergemeinschaft mit Juden," *Jahrbuch für Antisemitismusforschung* 17 (Berlin: Metropol, 2008), 45-68.

38 According to figures published annually by the Community Security Trust (UK), the Commission nationale consultative des droits de l'homme (France), and the Kantor Center for the Study of Contemporary European Jewry (Tel-Aviv University).

39 The percentage of incidents in which perpetrators have been identified at all varies from year to year. In France, the number of identified perpetrators of violent antisemitic acts was above 26 percent from 1997 to 2011, although their total number is relatively small. In Britain, the percentage of ethnically identified perpetrators of all incidents varied between 26 percent (2012) and 44 percent (2007).

40 Bundesministerium des Innern, *Antisemitismus in Deutschland. Erscheinungsformen, Bedingungen, Präventionsansätze. Bericht des unabhängigen Expertenkreises Antisemitismus* (Berlin, 2011), 36.

41 Günther Jikeli, "Der neue alte Antisemitismus Müssen Juden sich wieder verstecken?," *Stern*, September 14, 2012.

Germany than in France and the United Kingdom.[42] While the share of Muslim perpetrators in all three countries is disproportionately high for violent antisemitic attacks, there are indications that it is disproportionately low for other forms of antisemitism, such as desecration of cemeteries, written threats, and abusive letters.[43]

The annual reports of the French Commission nationale consultative des droits de l'homme (CNCDH) provide figures for the percentage of identified Arab-Muslim perpetrators of all antisemitic acts in France for the years 1994-2007, as illustrated in Table 1. The percentage was roughly 30 percent in that period, with a drop to less than 10 percent in 1997 and 1998 and a notable peak of 83 percent in 2000. It should be noted that these numbers refer to the identified Arab-Muslim perpetrators. The actual percentage of Arab-Muslim perpetrators is higher because it can be assumed that many of the non-identified perpetrators also have a Arab-Muslim background. However, the overall figures indicate that the rise of antisemitism since 2000 cannot be blamed solely on Muslim or Arab perpetrators. The percentage of identified Arab-Muslim perpetrators was just under 30 percent from 1994 to 1997, similar to the period from 2002 to 2006. Unfortunately, the CNCDH has not published these figures since 2007.

Table 1: Percentage of identified Arab-Muslim Perpetrators of all antisemitic acts (threats and violence) in France, 1994-2007 (Source: CNCDH)

Year	Percentage	Year	Percentage
1994	28	2001	35
1995	28	2002	27
1996	29	2003	27
1997	6	2004	27
1998	7	2005	28
1999	19	2006	27
2000	83	2007	18

42 However, a report on Berlin shows that 12 of 33 acts of antisemitic and anti-Israeli violence between 2003 and 2005 were committed by "foreigners" and 15 by right-wing extremists. Senatsverwaltung für Inneres und Sport, *Antisemitismus im extremistischen Spektrum Berlins* (Berlin, 2006), 53, http://www.berlin.de/imperia/md/content/seninn/verfassungsschutz/fokus_antisemitismus_2._aufl..pdf?start&ts=1234285743&file=fokus_antisemitismus_2._aufl..pdf.

43 The perpetrators of threats, including graffiti, often remain unknown, but according to figures from the French CNCDH for the year 2009 13 percent of antisemitic threats in France were related to neo-Nazi ideology and 5 percent were committed by people of Arab or Muslim background. Commission nationale consultative des droits de l'homme (CNCDH), *La lutte contre le racisme, antisémitisme et la xénophobie. Année 2009* (Paris: La Documentation Française, 2010), 45, http://www.ladocumentationfrancaise.fr/var/storage/rapports-publics/104000267.pdf. Bergmann and Wetzel observed already in 2003 that different forms of antisemitic actions can be assigned to different groups of perpetrators. Werner Bergmann and Juliane Wetzel, *Manifestations of Anti-Semitism in the European Union: First Semester 2002*, Synthesis Report on Behalf of the EUMC (2003), 25-26. The share of "Islamists" sending antisemitic letters and emails to the Israeli Embassy in Germany and to the Central Council of Jews in Germany is only 3 percent. The vast majority comes from the center of society. Monika Schwarz-Friesel and Jehuda Reinharz, *Die Sprache der Judenfeindschaft im 21. Jahrhundert* (Berlin/Boston: De Gruyter, 2013), 21.

Table 2 presents the number of identified perpetrators of violent antisemitic acts in France from 1997 to 2015. Since 2000, the number of identified Arab-Muslim perpetrators has exceeded the number of identified perpetrators of the extreme right (see Table 2). Since 2000, the majority of identified perpetrators of violent antisemitic acts in France have been Arab-Muslims. The figures also show the sharp rise in antisemitic violence since 2000 in France.

Table 2: Perpetrators of violent antisemitic acts in France, 1997-2015
(Source: CNCDH)

Year	Violent acts by Arab-Muslim perpetrators	Violent acts by unidentified/other perpetrators	Violent acts by extreme right perpetrators	Total
1997	0	2	1	3
1998	0	0	1	1
1999	3	1	8	12
2000	109	5	5	119
2001	10	21	1	32
2002	51	143	3	197
2003	44	77	6	127
2004	67	119	14	200
2005	41	48	10	99
2006	38	81	15	134
2007	36	58	12	106
2008	33	56	11	100
2009	20	138	14	172
2010	31	80	20	131
2011	19	95	15	129
2012	–	167	10	177
2013	–	–	–	105
2014	–	–	–	241
2015	–	–	–	207

Since 2012, the reports have not divulged any information on perpetrators of Arab-Muslim background in France, although Arab-Muslims have been identified as perpetrators in a number of incidents. Among the most violent antisemitic incidents in France in 2012 were the murder of three small children and a teacher at the Jewish school *Ozar Hatorah* in Toulouse by French Jihadist Mohamed Merah and the hand grenade attack on a kosher supermarket in Sarcelles, also involving a Muslim perpetrator.[44] An analysis of antisemitic incidents in France from 2000 to 2012 by Marc Knobel confirms the significant role played by Muslims in antisemitic acts.[45] Since 2013, the CNCDH's reports do not provide any information on the background of perpetrators.

In the United Kingdom, the Community Security Trust (CST) collects figures on the ethnicity of identified perpetrators. The CST reports show that, since 2005, 27 to 43 percent of perpetrators of antisemitic incidents whose ethnicity was identified were classified as being of (South) Asian or Arab appearance, while the majority of the perpetrators were white. The percentage of black perpetrators ranged between 5 and 14 percent.[46] Based on these figures and religious allocations of "whites," "blacks," "Arabs," and "Asians" in the UK census,[47] the percentage of Muslim perpetrators can be estimated at between 20 and 30 percent, while the percentage of Muslims in the general population stands at 5 percent. This disproportion is only partly explained by the geographic proximity of the two communities in cities such as London and Manchester, where most incidents were reported.

Another source of data points even more clearly to the relatively large share of Muslim perpetrators. Jews who fell victim to antisemitic incidents were asked to provide details of their victimizers. The European Union Agency for Fundamental Rights (FRA) published a survey in 2013 on experiences of antisemitism in eight countries: Belgium, France, Germany, Hungary, Italy, Latvia, Sweden, and the United Kingdom.[48] The survey included 5,847 self-identified Jews. One-third of those surveyed had experienced antisemitic harassment in the past five years and seven percent reported antisemitic violence or threats against them. The most important group of perpetrators of harassment, violence, and threats were of Muslim background.

---

44 At the time of writing, the two individuals who actually threw the hand grenade were still at large, but the Muslim convert and jihadist Jérémie Louis-Sidney had handled the explosives.

45 Marc Knobel, *Haine et violences antisémites. Une rétrospective: 2000-2013* (Paris: Berg International, 2013). See also the interview with Richard Prasquier, chairman of CRIF, the umbrella organization of French Jewry, at the time in Manfred Gerstenfeld, *Demonizing Israel and the Jews*, Kindle edition (RVP Publishers, 2013), loc. 2507.

46 The Community Security Trust (CST) regularly publishes reports on antisemitic incidents. The reports are available on the CST website: http://www.thecst.org.uk.

47 In the 2001 census, 56 percent of Asians, 90 percent of Arabs, 11 percent of blacks, and 0.5 percent of whites identified as Muslim. Office for National Statistics (UK), *Focus on Ethnicity and Religion*, ed. Joy Dobbs, Hazel Green, and Linda Zealey (Basingstoke: Palgrave Macmillan, 2006).

48 European Union Agency for Fundamental Rights (FRA), *Discrimination and Hate Crime against Jews in EU Member States: Experiences and Perceptions of Antisemitism* (Luxembourg: Publications Office of the European Union, 2013), http://fra.europa.eu/sites/default/files/fra-2013-discrimination-hate-crime-against-jews-eu-member-states_en.pdf. Other citable victim testimonies are rare, but some of those that exist also point to the fact that perpetrators of Muslim background are often responsible for harassment and even violence against Jews in public places. Manfred Gerstenfeld, "Nederlands: Harassment of Recognizable Jews," *Arutz Sheva 7*, April 8, 2013, http://www.israelnationalnews.com/Articles/Article.aspx/13113#.UWrI4df7s5Y.

Table 3: Background of perpetrators of the most serious antisemitic violence or threats: Responses by Jewish victims in Belgium, France, Germany, Hungary, Italy, Latvia, Sweden, and the United Kingdom (Source FRA Survey 2013)

Background	Percentage*	Background	Percentage*
Muslim	40	Right-wing	10
Teenagers	25	Neighbor	9
Unidentified	20	Colleague or supervisor	9
Left-wing	14		

* Multiple answers were possible.

Forty percent of the victims of antisemitic violence or threats across these eight countries said that the perpetrators of the worst incidents in the past five years had a Muslim background.[49] Given the fact that there are only a few thousand Muslims in Hungary and Latvia, it can be assumed that the percentage is higher for Belgium, France, Germany, Italy, Sweden, and the United Kingdom. (The FRA report does not provide detailed figures on perpetrators for each country.) However, respondents could give multiple answers, and about one-third used this category in combination with "teenagers," the second largest group of perpetrators of violent incidents and threats (25 percent). Perpetrators from the political left (14 percent) or right (10 percent) are relatively few.

Table 4: Background of perpetrators of the most serious antisemitic harassment: Responses by Jewish victims in Belgium, France, Germany, Hungary, Italy, Latvia, Sweden, and the United Kingdom (Source FRA Survey 2013)

Background	Percentage*	Background	Percentage*
Muslim	27	Teenager	15
Left-wing	22	Colleague or supervisor	14
Unidentified	20	Neighbor	10
Right-wing	19	Christian	7

* Multiple answers were possible.

The differences between these groups of perpetrators are somewhat smaller when it comes to harassment. While Muslims remain the largest group of perpetrators (27 percent), they are closely followed by perpetrators of the political left (22 percent) and the political right (19 percent). Interestingly, there are more perpetrators identified with the left than with the right, both for harassment and violence and threats.

49 Respondents could choose from a number of categories, including "someone with Muslim extremist views," "someone with extremist Christian views," "teenagers," "someone with left-wing political views," "someone with right-wing political views," "a colleague or a supervisor at work," and "a neighbor." There was no distinction between perpetrators "with Muslim extremist views" and people of Muslim background.

2. *Antisemitic attitudes among Muslims in Europe*

Surveys demonstrate that antisemitic attitudes are stronger and more widespread among Muslims in Europe than among non-Muslims. The Pew Global Attitudes Project published the only internationally comparative survey that distinguishes between Muslims and non-Muslims in 2006. Muslims and non-Muslims in a number of countries were asked whether they had a "favorable or unfavorable opinion of Jews." In the United Kingdom, 7 percent of the general population and 47 percent of Muslims stated that they had an unfavorable opinion of Jews. In France, the figures were 13 percent of the general population and 28 percent of Muslims and, in Germany, 22 percent of the general population and 44 percent of Muslims. The contrast is even greater when "very unfavorable" opinions are compared.[50] Another international survey, published in 2013 by the WZB Berlin Social Science Center, reveals similar tendencies. In Germany, 28 percent of Muslims and 10.5 percent of Christians agreed with the statement that "Jews cannot be trusted." In France, 43.4 percent of Muslims and 7.1 percent of Christians agreed with this statement. The survey shows similar results for the Netherlands, Belgium, Austria, and Sweden. The authors explicitly exclude socio-economic marginalization, exclusion, alienation, and a lack of religious rights for Muslims as explanatory factors for religious fundamentalism and out-group hostility.[51] Country-specific surveys that include a distinction between Muslims and non-Muslims confirm and specify these results.

In Germany, two studies commissioned by the German Ministry of the Interior came to similar results. Katrin Brettfeld and Peter Wetzels (2007) conducted a non-representative study of 2,683 students, including 500 Muslims, from Cologne, Hamburg, and Augsburg. According to this study, 15.7 percent of Muslims of migrant background, 7.4 percent of non-Muslims of migrant background, and 5.4 percent of non-Muslims with no migration background strongly believed that "people of Jewish faith are arrogant and greedy."[52] The second study commissioned by the Germany Ministry focused on radicalization of young Muslims (14-32 year olds). Two hundred German Muslims, 517 non-German Muslims, and a representative sample of 200 non-Muslim Germans were surveyed in 2009 and 2010. The questionnaire included two items on antisemitic attitudes, both related to Israel:

1. Israel should be blamed exclusively for the origin and continuation of the Middle East conflict.
2. It would be better if the Jews left the Middle East.

About 25 percent of both German and non-German Muslims and less than 5 percent of non-Muslim Germans agreed with both statements.[53]

---

50 Pew Global Attitudes Project, *The Great Divide: How Westerners and Muslims View Each Other* (2006). The survey was conducted before the Lebanon War in the summer of 2006.

51 Ruud Koopmans, "Religious Fundamentalism and Out-Group Hostility among Muslims and Christians in Western Europe" (presentation at the 20th International Conference of Europeanists, Amsterdam, June 25-27, 2013), http://www.wzb.eu/sites/default/files/u8/ruud_koopmans_religious_fundamentalism_and_out-group_hostility_among_muslims_and_christian.pdf.

52 Katrin Brettfeld and Peter Wetzels, *Muslime in Deutschland* (Hamburg: Bundesministerium des Innern, 2007), 274-75.

53 Wolfgang Frindte et al., *Lebenswelten junger Muslime in Deutschland* (Berlin: Bundesministerium des Innern, 2012), 245-47.

In 2010, Jürgen Mansel and Viktoria Spaiser carried out a survey of 2,404 students with different ethnic backgrounds in Bielefeld, Cologne, Berlin, and Frankfurt. About one-third of those surveyed were Muslims. Antisemitic attitudes relating to Israel, religious antisemitism, classic antisemitism, and comparisons between Israel and the Nazis were significantly higher among Muslim students than among other students.[54] The researchers also found differences regarding ethnic background: 24.9 percent of students of Turkish-Muslim background and 40.4 percent of those of Arab background agreed "completely" with the statement "Jews have too much influence in the world." Among those with no migrant background, the rate was only 3 percent. Some based their antisemitic views on their religion: 15.9 percent of Muslim students of Turkish background and 25.7 percent of those of Arab background agreed unreservedly with the statement "In my religion it is the Jews who drive the world to disaster." Looking at a different dimension, in response to the statement "I am tired of hearing about the crimes against the Jews over and over again," 20.2 percent of those without a migrant background, 14.7 percent of Turkish background, and 26 percent of Arab background were in complete agreement.[55] This was also confirmed in another German study from 2012, which only included a small number of Muslim participants. Muslims endorse classic antisemitic statements more often than their non-Muslim counterparts; approval of so-called "secondary" antisemitism, which is related to the Holocaust, was slightly weaker.[56] An earlier survey published in 1997 asked youths of Turkish background in Germany whether they thought that Zionism threatened Islam; 33.2 percent agreed.[57]

A 2009 Danish study based on interviews with ethnic Danes and immigrants from countries and regions with Muslim majorities (Turkey, Pakistan, Somalia, Palestinian Territories, and the former Yugoslavia) found that a number of anti-

---

[54] These attitudes were measured using the following indicators:
- "Because of Israeli policies, I increasingly dislike Jews."
- "Regarding Israel's policy, I understand someone who is against Jews."
- "In my religion, the Jews bring disaster to the world."
- "Jews have too much influence in the world."
- "What the State of Israel is doing to the Palestinians is basically no different from what the Nazis in the Third Reich did to the Jews."
- "Jews throughout the world feel more strongly attached to Israel than to the country where they live." (Translated from German by the author.)

[55] Jürgen Mansel and Victoria Spaiser, *Abschlussbericht Forschungsprojekt: "Soziale Beziehungen, Konfliktpotentiale und Vorurteile im Kontext von Erfahrungen verweigerter Teilhabe und Anerkennung bei Jugendlichen mit und ohne Migrationshintergrund"* (University of Bielefeld, 2010), http://www.vielfalt-tut-gut.de/content/e4458/e8260/Uni_Bielefeld_Abschlussbericht_Forschungs projekt.pdf and http://www.vielfalt-tut-gut.de/content/e4458/e8277/Uni_Bielefeld_Tabellen anhang.pdf.

[56] Oliver Decker, Johannes Kiess, and Elmar Brähler, *Die Mitte im Umbruch. Rechtsextreme Einstellungen in Deutschland 2012*, ed. Ralf Melzer (Bonn: Dietz, 2012), 79. The study found "primary" antisemitism among 11.5 percent of the overall population and 16.7 percent among Muslims, but 23.8 percent of "secondary" antisemitism among the overall population and 20.8 percent among Muslims. However, the poll included only 86 Muslims out of a sample of 2,510 people.

[57] Wilhelm Heitmeyer, Joachim Müller, and Helmut Schröder, *Verlockender Fundamentalismus. Türkische Jugendliche in Deutschland* (Frankfurt am Main: Suhrkamp, 1997), 181, 271.

semitic stereotypes were significantly more widespread among immigrants than among ethnic Danes. It revealed that 65.8 percent of respondents of migrant background and 18.2 percent of ethnic Danes agreed that "one cannot be careful enough in relation to Jews in Denmark." The study also showed that anti-Jewish attitudes were more common among Muslim immigrants than among Christian immigrants of the same ethnic origin (Palestinian and former Yugoslavian background).[58] In Britain, Muslims were interviewed by the polling institute Populus in December 2005. Although the survey does not provide comparative figures for non-Muslims, antisemitic attitudes seem particularly high. Of those surveyed, 53 percent agreed with the allegation that "Jews have too much influence over foreign policy"; 46 percent concurred that "Jews are in league with the Freemasons to control the media and politics"; and 37 percent even supported the statement that "Jews are legitimate targets as part of the ongoing struggle for justice in the Middle East."[59]

A comprehensive survey on prejudices and stereotypes among students in Sweden identified Muslim students as the group with the highest percentage of strong antisemitism (8.3 percent compared to 3.7 percent among Christians). However, the group of nonreligious students followed closely with 7.6 percent.[60]

In France, 33 percent of citizens of African and Turkish background and 18 percent of the general population exhibited antisemitic attitudes according to a poll from 2005. However, antisemitic attitudes were lower in the second generation born in France (17 percent). Interestingly, antisemitism among French citizens of African and Turkish background was only weakly related to conservative attitudes, ethnocentrism, and authoritarianism, but correlated strongly with the level of Islamic practice.[61] One of the authors of the study, Vincent Tiberj, argued that the social envy hypothesis, education, and even negative attitudes toward Israel are not explanatory factors, as respective correlations are relatively weak. The level of hostility toward Israel (in contrast to antisemitic attitudes) was similar among people of African and Turkish origin and the general population in France.[62]

A 2011 Belgian study by Mark Elchardus in thirty-two Dutch-speaking high schools in Brussels revealed that about half of Muslim students agreed with the following statements:

---

58 Peter Nannestad, "Frø af ugræs? Antijødiske holdninger i fem ikke-vestlige indvandrergrupper i Danmark," in *Danmark og de fremmede: Om mødet med den arabisk-muslimske verden*, ed. Tonny Brems Knudsen, Jørgen Dige Pedersen, and Georg Sørensen (Århus: Academica, 2009), 43-62.

59 Populus, "Muslim Poll" (December 2005), http://www.populus.co.uk/wp-content/uploads/Muslim_Poll-Times.pdf.

60 Living History Forum, *Intolerance: Anti-Semitic, Homophobic, Islamophobic and Xenophobic Tendencies among the Young* (Stockholm: Brottsförebyggande rådet (Brå), 2005), 59 and 152-53, http://www.levandehistoria.se/files/INTOLERANCEENG_0.pdf.

61 Among French people of African or Turkish origin antisemitism reaches 46 percent among practicing Muslims, 40 percent among "infrequently" observant Muslims, 30 percent among non-practicing Muslims, and 23 percent among those who have no religion. Sylvain Brouard and Vincent Tiberj, *Français comme les autres? Enquête sur les citoyens d'origine maghrébine, africaine et turque* (Paris: Presses de la fondation nationale des sciences politiques, 2005), 104.

62 Vincent Tiberj, "Anti-Semitism in an Ethnically Diverse France: Questioning and Explaining the Specificities of African-, Turkish-, and Maghrebian-French," Working Paper no. 33 (American University of Paris, 2006), http://www.aup.fr/pdf/WPSeries/AUP_wp33-Tiberj.pdf.

1. Jews want to dominate everything (total: 31.4 percent; Muslims: 56.8 percent; non-Muslims: 10.5 percent).
2. Most Jews think they're better than others (total: 29.9 percent; Muslims: 47.1 percent; non-Muslims: 12.9 percent).
3. If you do business with Jews, you should be extra careful (total: 28.6 percent; Muslims: 47.5 percent; non-Muslims: 12.9 percent).
4. Jews incite to war and blame others (total: 28.4 percent; Muslims; 53.7 percent; non-Muslims: 7.7 percent).

The antisemitic attitudes were unrelated to educational level or social status.[63] Elchardus confirmed the findings in 2013 with a study of 863 students from Gent and Antwerp, including 346 Muslim students. While 45-50 percent of Muslim students reveal antisemitic attitudes, "only" about 10 percent of non-Muslims do so.[64]

To conclude, all available data, including statistics on antisemitic incidents and attitude surveys, suggest that antisemitism is stronger and more widespread among Muslims in Europe than among non-Muslims. Why is this so?

III. What Rationales Are Used by Young European Muslims? Results from an Empirical Study

Some of the above-mentioned surveys show that socio-economic marginalization or exclusion are not explanatory factors. To find out more about the reasons why many European Muslims have negative attitudes toward Jews, we conducted an international study, interviewing more than 100 young male[65] Muslims in Berlin, Paris, and London. The sample was "saturated" across the three cities, meaning that the arguments started repeating themselves in new interviews; additional interviews did not bring new insights.[66] This method does not guarantee that there were no other rationales, but because of the repetition in three different cities with very different contexts, and in two different neighborhoods in each city, it is unlikely that we missed significant arguments by young male Muslims.

---

63 Mark Elchardus, "Antisemitisme in de Brusselse Scholen," in *Jong in Brussel. Bevindingen uit de JOP-monitor Brussel*, ed. Nicole Vettenburg, Mark Elchardus, and Johan Put (Leuven/The Hague: Acco, 2011), 265-96.

64 Antisemitic attitudes were somewhat stronger among "conservative Muslims" than among "progressive Muslims." Nicole Vettenburg, Mark Elchardus, and Stefaan Pleysier, eds., *Jong in Antwerpen en Gent* (Leuven/The Hague: Acco, 2013), 187-222.

65 We also interviewed a small number of female interviewees but the analysis is restricted to male interviewees for methodological reasons. The role of gender in attitudes toward Jews is unclear. Different surveys show contradictory results. The study by Frindte et al. on young Muslims in Germany found no gender differences, whereas the study by the Living History Forum found significant gender differences among young Muslims in Sweden. Cf. Frindte et al., *Lebenswelten junger Muslime in Deutschland* (Berlin: Bundesministerium des Innern, 2012), 226 and Living History Forum, *Intolerance: Anti-Semitic, Homophobic, Islamophobic and Xenophobic Tendencies among the Young* (Stockholm: Brottsförebyggande rådet (Brå), 2005), 59 and 152-53.

66 This approach is used in Grounded Theory ("saturation" of arguments). However, the analytical strategy might be considered too focused for an orthodox method of Grounded Theory. See Jane C. Hood, "Orthodoxy vs. Power: The Defining Traits of Grounded Theory," in *The SAGE Handbook of Grounded Theory*, ed. Antony Bryant and Kathy Charmaz (Thousand Oaks, CA: Sage Publications, 2010), 151-64.

The interviewees had various ethnic and educational backgrounds (from early school leavers to university graduates). The majority of interviewees in Germany were of Turkish origin, most interviewees in France had a Maghreb background, and in the United Kingdom most originated in South Asia. Thus, the ethnic backgrounds largely represented those of the Muslim population in each country. It can be assumed that the attitudes of the participants in this study can also be found among other young (male) European Muslims.[67]

Whereas the focus here is on negative views of Jews, it should be kept in mind that many European Muslims do not exhibit any antisemitic attitudes. In fact, some interviewees in the sample spoke out explicitly against antisemitic views among their friends and family.[68] However, the analysis of the arguments shows four distinct patterns of antisemitic argumentation used by young Muslims in all three cities:

1. "Classic" antisemitism (conspiracy theories, "Jews are rich," etc.)
2. Negative views of Jews with reference to Israel (allegations such as "Jews/Israelis kill children")
3. Negative views of Jews with reference to Muslim or ethnic identity or to Islam ("Muslims dislike Jews")
4. Negative views of Jews without rationalization (attitude that it is "natural" to loathe Jews, use of the word "Jew" as an insult)

1. Attitudes of "classic" antisemitism

This category comprises antisemitic conspiracy theories and well-known stereotypes of Jews. The trope of the rich Jew, including related stereotypes such as the belief that Jews are stingy or greedy, is very popular among interviewees from all countries and backgrounds. Jews have also been portrayed as clannish, treacherous, and clever. More rarely, certain physical characteristics have been attributed to them. Common themes of antisemitic conspiracy theories are "Jewish power" in the world, "Jewish influence" in the United States, the terrorist attacks of September 11, 2001, "big business," the Holocaust, the media, suicide attacks, the Middle East conflict, the alleged war against Muslims, and, occasionally, even topics such as AIDS and tsunamis.

There are many reasons why people want to believe in conspiracy theories. A central rationale among interviewees seems to be the wish to explain and personalize complicated processes. "For everything that must happen, there is a reason," declared Neoy from London, after stating that, "it's obvious now that there is someone, and not just someone but a group of people ... like a ruling class we hardly see." This is a textbook illustration of the tendency to seek out simplistic worldly explanations.[69] The same interviewee holds conspiracy theory beliefs about the terrorist attacks of September 11, 2001, the Holocaust, and Israeli power. Neoy also assumes that "all these other big channels they are owned by Jews and they do control the majority of the media."

---

67 For more information on the sample and methods, see Günther Jikeli, *European Muslim Antisemitism: Why Young Urban Males Say They Don't Like Jews*, Studies in Antisemitism (Indianapolis: Indiana University Press, 2015).

68 For a detailed analysis of these anti-antisemites' rationales, see ibid.

69 Wolfgang Benz, *Was ist Antisemitismus?* (Bonn: Bundeszentrale für politische Bildung, 2004), 192.

Such "classic" antisemitism is also widespread in mainstream society. In a survey conducted by the Anti-Defamation League (ADL) in December 2008 and January 2009, 21 percent of respondents in Germany, 33 percent in France, and 15 percent in the United Kingdom believed that it is "probably true" that Jews have too much power in the business world.[70] Classic antisemitic stereotypes and conspiracy theories connect to well-known negative tropes of Jews within mainstream society. They are also expressions of psychological mechanisms in modern societies[71] and serve as simplistic explanations of the world's problems.

2. *Negative views of Jews with reference to Israel*

Antisemitic attitudes with reference to Israel involve: (a) conflation of Jews with Israelis; and (b) Manichean views of the Israeli-Palestinian conflict. Negative views of Israel thus serve as justification for general hatred against Jews, including German, French, and British Jews. Almost all interviewees who show hostile attitudes toward Israel or Israelis conflate Jews and Israelis at one point or another and also exhibit negative attitudes toward Jews. This confirms surveys in Germany and other European countries.[72]

One of the most common antisemitic tropes with reference to Israel is "Jews/Israelis kill children," including the allegation that "the Israelis" or "the Jews" (usually the latter) kill children on purpose, out of cruelty and evilness. It is part of a Manichean view of the Middle East conflict and vilifies Israel. It also relates to the old antisemitic trope of the blood libel.[73] According to Kassim from Berlin: "The Israelis, they are warriors, they kill children, and the Palestinians are such poor people ... and they [the Israelis] come and just attack them." Such dualistic perspectives on the Middle East conflict, however, can also be found in European media and are generally widespread in Europe.[74]

Fundamental delegitimization of Israel is another issue. Various rationales are used to deny Israel's legitimacy, which can be identified as an antisemitic trope in itself, for example according to the working definition of antisemitism of the International Holocaust Remembrance Alliance (IHRA), an intergovernmental body with

---

70 Anti-Defamation League, *Attitudes toward Jews in Seven European Countries* (February 2009), http://www.adl.org/Public%20ADL%20Anti-Semitism%20Presentation%20February%20 2009%20_3_.pdf.

71 Theodor W. Adorno and Max Horkheimer, *Dialectic of Enlightenment* (London: Verso, 1972).

72 Andreas Zick and Beate Küpper noted that 90 percent of Germans who criticized Israel in 2004 also endorsed antisemitic statements. Andreas Zick and Beate Küpper, "Traditioneller und moderner Antisemitismus," *Bundeszentrale für politische Bildung*, November 28, 2006, http://www.bpb.de/politik/extremismus/antisemitismus/37967/traditioneller-und-moderner-antisemitismus?p=all. The fact that antisemitism often appears in the guise of criticism of Israel is also reflected in comparative surveys in a number of European countries. Andreas Zick, Andreas Hövermann, and Beate Küpper, *Intolerance, Prejudice and Discrimination: A European Report* (Berlin: Friedrich-Ebert-Stiftung, Forum Berlin, 2011), 162, http://library.fes.de/pdf-files/do/07908-20110311.pdf.

73 Léon Poliakov, *The History of Anti-Semitism: From the Time of Christ to the Court Jews* (Philadelphia: University of Pennsylvania Press, 2003).

74 Andreas Zick, Andreas Hövermann, and Beate Küpper, *Intolerance, Prejudice and Discrimination: A European Report* (Berlin: Friedrich-Ebert-Stiftung, Forum Berlin, 2011), 162, http://library.fes.de/pdf-files/do/07908-20110311.pdf.

thirty-one member countries.[75] The main argument used is that since Jews built Israel on what is regarded as "Muslim (or Palestinian or Arab) land," the establishment of a Jewish state in Palestine wronged them from the outset. Others accept the Jewish State of Israel as a reality.

However, hostility against Israel is rarely a question of borders or specific policies by the Israeli government or "settlements." The topos "Jews have taken over Muslim/Palestinian/Arab land" is often used to deny the legitimacy of the State of Israel entirely.

The intensity of hostility against Jews justified by the Middle East conflict is related to identification with "the Palestinians," either via an Arab or Muslim identity, or both. Not all interviewees identify with Palestinians, but most respondents of Arab background do. Arab identity is an important additional factor that can enhance hostility against European Jews, on the basis of claims related to the Israeli-Palestinian conflict, which is often understood as a conflict between Arabs and Israel/"the Jews."

3. Negative views of Jews with reference to religious or ethnic identity

The interviews demonstrate that some Muslims relate their negative views of Jews to their ethnic or religious identity or to their perception of Islam. The assumption of a general enmity between Muslims and Jews is widespread. Somewhat less frequently, interviewees believe that there was an eternal enmity between their own ethnic community and Jews. Such views are voiced approvingly in statements such as "Muslims and Jews are enemies" or "the Arabs dislike Jews."[76] As such, the Israeli-Palestinian conflict merely serves as an example. The enmity is understood in much wider terms. "As a Muslim you have problems, not with Israelis, [but] with Jews." said Ümit explicitly, an interviewee of Turkish origin from Berlin. However, justifications are often vague.

Such generalizing and essentializing assumptions of enmity deny different views among individuals within the community and different interpretations of Islam and also wrongly portray Muslims as a unitary category regarding their attitudes toward Jews.[77] Moreover, such assumptions that are bound to the collective religious identity make it difficult for individuals to distance themselves from them.

The same goes for rationales related to ethnic identity. It has been argued that anti-Zionism and antisemitism are part and parcel of Arab nationalism.[78] Many

---

75 The IHRA definition of antisemitism cites "Denying the Jewish people their right to self-determination" as an example of the ways in which antisemitism manifests itself with regard to the State of Israel. See https://www.holocaustremembrance.com/sites/default/files/press_release_document_antisemitism.pdf. The term "delegitimization" is explained in Natan Sharansky, "3D Test of Anti-Semitism: Demonization, Double Standards, Delegitimization," *Jewish Political Studies Review* 16, nos. 3-4 (October 2004).

76 Religious and ethnic identities often get blurred in this context. The enmity is seen as one between "us" and "the Jews."

77 Tarek Fatah is probably the most prominent contemporary scholar who writes from a Muslim perspective against the assumption that Muslims and Jews are enemies. See Tarek Fatah, *The Jew Is Not My Enemy: Unveiling the Myths That Fuel Muslim Anti-Semitism* (Toronto: McClelland & Stewart, 2010).

78 Jochen Müller, "Von Antizionismus und Antisemitismus. Stereotypenbildung in der arabischen Öffentlichkeit," in *Antisemitismus in Europa und in der arabischen Welt. Ursachen und*

participants of Arab background believe that their Arab identity encompasses negative views of Jews. This underlying assumption is often uttered in passing: "In any case, we, the Arabs, we never get along with them [the Jews]," said Hafid, from Paris, who is of Algerian origin. Two main rationales are used for this justification. It is either argued that such hostility is a reaction to the alleged hatred of Jews against Arabs, or the Middle East conflict is used to explain why (all) Arabs allegedly dislike Jews.

Religious rationales, on the other hand, are intertwined with arguments based on both religious sources and Muslim identity. In young Muslims' discussions about an "interdiction" of befriending or marrying Jews, for example, alleged religious reasons and pressure from other Muslims are mixed. Interviewees' references to a long history of animosity between Muslims and Jews can be related to the historical perspectives of confrontations between the two groups or to an interpretation of Islamic scriptures, which highlights the conflicts between Muhammad and Jewish tribes. Direct references to the Qur'an or to the belief that suicide bombers go to paradise for killing Jews, on the other hand, are rooted in certain views of Islam. References to the Qur'an have a particularly strong authority as it is regarded as the word of Allah, dictated to the Prophet Muhammad. It is thus seen as reflecting divine truth, often in a literal understanding of fragmented scriptures.

The level of animosity against Jews with reference to Islam or Muslim identity can vary. This also holds true for those who see similarities between Judaism and Islam or who regard Muslims and Jews as "cousins." "Muslims are supposed to be the Jewish's worst enemies," said Sabir from London, who saw Muslims and Jews (and Christians) as being involved in a global war. Some root their notions of Jewish enmity in apocalyptic visions and conspiracy theories. Others assume the existence of a mutual antipathy but reject notions of war. Patterns of argumentation with reference to Islam include direct references to God's perception of the Jews, who allegedly condemns them for their materialistic and life-affirming lifestyle.

However, it is important to note that it is particular perceptions of Islam and Muslim (and ethnic) identity that are relevant for such forms of antisemitism. As in all purported rationales for Jew-hatred, these notions are chimerical;[79] they are not the actual reason for antisemitic attitudes.

4. No rationalization

All antisemitic attitudes are, by definition, irrational. There is no "reason" to hate "the Jews." As shown in the description of the three previous categories of argumentation, participants often try to justify their hostile attitudes toward Jews by making negative claims about them which they assert to be true or by extrapolating particular traits or behaviors of some Jews to "the Jews." But some participants do not even attempt to offer justifications for their hostility. In their minds, negative views of Jews are self-evident.

Wechselbeziehungen eines komplexen Phänomens, ed. Wolfgang Ansorge (Paderborn: Bonifatius, 2006), 163-82.

[79] I borrowed this term from Gavin I. Langmuir, "Towards a Definition of Antisemitism," in *The Persisting Question: Sociological Perspectives and Social Contexts of Modern Antisemitism*, ed. Helen Fein (Berlin: Walter de Gruyter, 1987), 86-127.

"Jewish people are Jewish, that's why we don't like them," said Ganesh from London. And Bashir from Berlin confirmed his outspoken hatred of all Jews "[b]ecause they are Jews nevertheless. Jews are, a Jew is a Jew anyway."

The "argument" of hating Jews because they are Jews points to the essence of antisemitism: its irrationality. Endorsing such irrationality is radical but consistent. The antisemite longs for the extermination of the Jews. Bashir wishes "that the damned Jews should be burnt."

Antisemitic resentments stem not only from learned stereotypes but also from unconscious projections onto Jews, the actual behaviors or lives of whom may shape only the nature of antisemitic expressions. The argument of hating Jews because they are Jews is rarely bluntly voiced, but this irrational "cause" often shines through when hatred against "all Jews" is justified by accusations for which only some Jews can possibly be responsible. Others consider their negative feelings toward Jews to be "common sense" and normal. This finds expression in a peculiar use of language. The very term "Jew" is understood among many interviewees but also in general among many young people in Germany and France as bearing negative connotations.[80] The words for "Jew" (*Jude* in German and *Juif* and *Feuj* in French) are used as insults or in an otherwise pejorative way by interviewees in France and Germany. (Such usage appears to be less frequent in Britain today.[81])

IV. The Relationship between Antisemitism and Perceptions of Discrimination and Exclusion

Some scholars have linked prejudice against Muslims and Muslim antisemitism, alleging that a key cause of antisemitism among European Muslims lies in their marginalization, discrimination, and exclusion.[82] The theoretical assumptions of such allegations remain unclear. One could also deduce the contrary: that suffering discrimination and exclusion would lead to criticism of prejudices against other minorities, including Jews. However, it also does not explain the fact that other

80 Günther Jikeli, "Anti-Semitism in Youth Language: The Pejorative Use of the Terms for 'Jew' in German and French Today," *Conflict & Communication Online* 9, no. 1 (2010): 1-13; Günther Jikeli, "'Jew' as a Slur in German and French Today," *Journal for the Study of Antisemitism* 1, no. 2 (2009): 209-32.

81 The interviews in London indicate that this usage of the word "Jew" in Britain is not as common as in France and Germany among youths. Stenström, Andersen, and Hasund did research on common insults among youths in London and did not report usage of the term "Jew" as an insult. Anna-Brita Stenström, Gisle Andersen, and Ingrid Kristine Hasund, *Trends in Teenage Talk* (Amsterdam/Philadelphia: John Benjamins, 2002). However, there were reports of such usage in the United Kingdom in the late 1990s. David Margolis, "Anti-Semitism in the Playground," *Independent* (London), February 1, 1999.

82 See Matti Bunzl, *Anti-Semitism and Islamophobia: Hatreds Old and New in Europe* (Chicago: Prickly Paradigm Press, 2007), 26-27. Paul A. Silverstein wrote a "Comment on Bunzl" in the same volume. See also Esther Benbassa, "Jewish-Moslem Relations in Contemporary France," *Contemporary French and Francophone Studies* 11, no. 2 (2007): 189-94. Klaus Holz adopted a similar argument and mentioned the social, racist, and religious exclusion of Muslims as indirect reasons for the manifestation of antisemitism. Klaus Holz, *Die Gegenwart des Antisemitismus. Islamistische, demokratische und antizionistische Judenfeindschaft* (Hamburg: Hamburger Edition, 2005), 9.

minorities that experience similar or even stronger discrimination show antisemitic attitudes to a lesser degree. In our sample, we could not find a correlation between discrimination and antisemitism.[83] The same is true for a relation between antisemitism and the sense of belonging to the national society. Self-identification with the nation is very different in Germany, France, and Britain,[84] but the level of antisemitism is similar, and, according to surveys, even stronger in Britain, where most interviewees identify themselves as British.

Focusing only on statistical correlations, however, may be misleading, for two reasons: (a) possible relations between discrimination and antisemitism are complex and not a straightforward result of cause-and-effect; and (b) some perceptions of global discrimination against Muslims include antisemitic conspiracy theories. This was shown above in an example by the interviewee who believes there is a global war against Muslims in which Jews (and Christians) are seen as the enemies. Similarly, the rhetoric of victimhood competition can contain antisemitic arguments.[85] Correlations between such attitudes would only confirm that antisemitic perceptions of discrimination and victimhood are linked to antisemitic world views. However, the formation of complex attitudes such as antisemitism are unlikely to be rooted in a single factor anyway.

V. Sources and Factors of Influence

The formation of any attitude is a multidimensional process.[86] This is also true in the case of antisemitism. The genesis of antisemitic attitudes among European Muslims cannot be reduced to religious beliefs or affiliation. Nor are they a result of deprived living conditions. Exposure to antisemitic remarks or propaganda, or to antisemitism in the media, enhances antisemitic beliefs but does not necessarily lead to antisemitic attitudes, as proved by some interviewees who, despite these factors, ultimately reject antisemitic views. The eventual adoption of antisemitic stereotypes and ways of thinking is a choice made by individuals.[87]

---

[83] I explore a number of possible links (such as comparing negative attitudes toward Jews and toward their own community, comparing the minorities, exclusion as a factor for an emphasis on religious identity, etc.) in more detail in Günther Jikeli, *European Muslim Antisemitism: Why Young Urban Males Say They Don't Like Jews*, Studies in Antisemitism (Indianapolis: Indiana University Press, 2015).

[84] Günther Jikeli, "Discrimination of European Muslims: Self-Perceptions, Experiences and Discourses of Victimhood," in *Minority Groups: Coercion, Discrimination, Exclusion, Deviance and the Quest for Equality*, ed. Dan Soen, Mally Shechory, and Sarah Ben-David (New York: Nova Science, 2012), 77-96.

[85] Bernard Henri Lévy, *Ce grand cadavre à la renverse* (Paris: Grasset, 2007). See also Jochen Müller, "Auf den Spuren von Nasser. Nationalismus und Antisemitismus im radikalen Islamismus," in *Antisemitismus und radikaler Islamismus*, ed. Wolfgang Benz and Juliane Wetzel (Essen: Klartext, 2007), 85-101.

[86] William D. Crano and Radmila Prislin, *Attitudes and Attitude Change* (New York/London: Psychology Press, 2008).

[87] Cf. Jean-Paul Sartre, *Réflexions sur la question juive* (Paris: Gallimard, 1954). However, the notion of free choice is disputed. For a critical debate on free choice and antisemitism, see Thomas Maul, "Dialektik und Determinismus. Zum Verhältnis von Adorno, Sartre und Améry," *Bahamas* 64 (2012): 46-52.

Along with a number of other factors, antisemitic attitudes are related to worldviews and individual psychological processes and mechanisms.[88] The interviews provide some insights into projections onto Jews. In some cases, participants directly linked their fantasies, which they know are immoral and thus have to be suppressed, to antisemitic assumptions. Hussein from London, for instance, explained the events of September 11, 2001 based on his own wish to have more money and to do whatever it takes to obtain some. He suspects similar wishes and motives on the part of the alleged Jewish conspirators of 9/11. Other examples in which Jews were blamed for terrorist attacks can also be interpreted as expressions of pathological projection. Many interviewees had difficulty in accepting that Muslims were the perpetrators of terrorist attacks and that they used their religious convictions to justify their deeds. The terrorist attacks are still seen as evil, but some projected the responsibility of Muslim perpetrators onto the Jews and thus blamed the Jews. However, Ümit from Berlin, who is convinced that people who believe in Islam cannot undertake suicide attacks, took this a step further. He feels that Muslims are unjustly accused of terrorism, and stated that Jews or Americans disguised as Muslims might have blown themselves up in Israel. Another area of projection is the wish for solidarity or social stability. Some envy Jews for their alleged solidarity and accuse them of being clannish. This can take on a positive tone: "The Jews are really smart.... They can get work really easily, not like us, they can do a lot of things that we can't do," said Omar from Paris.

Interviewees explicitly mentioned a number of sources for their antisemitic beliefs, including anti-Jewish views of friends and family, as well as perceptions linked to religious and ethnic identities, conversations in mosques, the influence of media such as television, the internet, music, books, and newspapers, and, in some cases, schools.[89] The level of education influences the form of expression of antisemitic attitudes. Those with a higher level of formal education tended to voice negative views of Jews in more socially acceptable ways, such as insinuations and allegations about Jewish influence in the finance sector and media, conspiracy theories, or demonization of Israel, instead of open approval of hatred or violence against Jews.

---

88 Scholars have discussed a number of reasons for the development of antisemitic attitudes, such as transmission of stereotypes and beliefs and psychological mechanisms of group dynamics or unreflected projections. For a discussion of different theories, see Samuel Salzborn, *Antisemitismus als negative Leitidee der Moderne. Sozialwissenschaftliche Theorien im Vergleich* (Frankfurt: Campus Verlag, 2010). Projection is a psychological defense mechanism whereby one "projects" one's own undesirable thoughts, motivations, desires, and feelings onto someone else. Psychoanalytical theories on antisemitism have identified projection as the main mechanism of antisemitism. Hermann Beland, "Psychoanalytische Antisemitismustheorien im Vergleich," in *Antisemitismusforschung in den Wissenschaften*, ed. Werner Bergmann and Monika Körte (Berlin: Metropol, 2004), 187-218.

89 For similar findings based on a survey of social workers in Berlin, see Gabriele Fréville, Susanna Harms, and Serhat Karakayalı, "'Antisemitismus—ein Problem unter vielen'. Ergebnisse einer Befragung in Jugendclubs und Migrant/innen-Organisationen," in *Konstellationen des Antisemitismus. Antisemitismusforschung und sozialpädagogische Praxis*, ed. Wolfram Stender, Guido Follert, and Mihri Özdogan (Wiesbaden: VS Verlag für Sozialwissenschaften, 2010), 185-98.

VI. Conclusions

Many young Muslims in Europe exhibit antisemitic attitudes; some resort to violence and pose a serious threat to Jewish communities in Europe. While polls reveal that fewer European Muslims endorse antisemitic views than Muslims in Islamic countries,[90] they also show that the level of antisemitism is significantly higher among Muslims than among non-Muslims. This study of young male Muslims from Berlin, Paris, and London provides some insights into the sources of and reasoning behind negative views of Jews among young Muslims.

The genesis of antisemitic views cannot be reduced to a single factor. Ethnic or religious identity and interpretations of Islam are a factor for many. In this sense, use of the term *Muslim antisemitism* is apt and meaningful. Others relate their hostility toward Jews to their hatred of the State of Israel. Many use classic antisemitic attitudes that are also widespread in mainstream European society. However, negative views of Jews have become the norm in some young Muslim social circles so that they do not feel the need to justify them. This facilitates radical forms of antisemitism and antisemitic violence.

Sources of antisemitic attitudes include the stereotypes and beliefs held by friends, family members, religious circles in and around mosques, foreign and domestic television, and the internet. Projections onto Jews of fears and wishes also play an important role. While discrimination and exclusion of Muslims in Europe is still a reality, this does not seem to be a relevant factor influencing antisemitic attitudes.

---

[90] Anti-Defamation League, "ADL GLOBAL 100: An Index of Anti-Semitism" (2014), http://global100.adl.org.

Muslim Antisemitism: A Litmus Test for the West

Neil J. Kressel*

I. A BLIND SPOT

In January 2013, many reasonable people in the West were shocked and disturbed to learn that Mohamed Morsi, then president of Egypt, had a bit earlier described the Jews as "the descendants of apes and pigs." Quite a few political leaders and analysts in Western nations, especially liberals and moderates, had been doing their best to discern constructive elements in Morsi's government and in the associated Muslim Brotherhood. When it became known that the elected Egyptian president had recently urged his countrymen to "nurse our children and our grandchildren on hatred" for Jews and Zionists, some response seemed necessary. Thus, *New York Times* editorialists sharply condemned the blatant prejudice in Morsi's 2010 speech. Then, however, they proceeded to wonder whether he really believed what he had said. The *Times* also asked whether becoming president had possibly made the man "think differently about the need to respect" all people.[1] President Obama's spokesman Jay Carney similarly objected to Morsi's bigoted "rhetoric."[2] At the same time, though, the Obama administration reaffirmed official American enthusiasm for the Egyptian president and his alleged pro-peace role. Despite the ambiguity of these responses, those of us concerned about antisemitism in the Islamic world had at least some small basis for hope that the problem might now acquire a place on the public agenda; previously, prominent instances of Muslim anti-Jewish bigotry had drawn far more muted reactions from most Westerners in high places.

Now, as a consequence of his political demise, questions about Morsi's personal character have become moot, but antisemitism in the Islamic world remains intense and dangerous. Indeed, during the past few years, it has skyrocketed in intensity and virulence.[3] The *New York Times*, in one uncharacteristically frank article on the

---

* Professor of Psychology and Director, Honors Program in the Social Sciences, William Paterson University of New Jersey.

1 "President Morsi's Repulsive Comments," editorial, *New York Times*, January 16, 2015, A22.

2 David D. Kirkpatrick, "U.S. Criticizes Egypt's Leader for Anti-Semitic Remarks," *New York Times*, January 16, 2013, A6. See also Neil J. Kressel, "Laughing Off Jew-Hatred: Our Leaders Ignore the Obvious," *New York Post*, January 17, 2013, 29.

3 See, for example, Anti-Defamation League, *Violence and Vitriol: Anti-Semitism around the World during Israel's Operation Protective Edge—July-August 2014* (New York: Anti-Defamation League, 2014), http://www.adl.org/assets/pdf/anti-semitism/international/adl-report-on-anti-semitism-during-ope-july-aug-2014.pdf (accessed October 31, 2014).

topic, reported in the autumn of 2014 that "scattered attacks have raised alarm about how Europe is changing and whether it remains a safe place for Jews…." The article further noted that some Jews "describe 'no go' zones in Muslim districts of many European cities where Jews dare not travel."[4] Yet, for the mainstream media, antisemitism in Muslim-majority countries and among Muslims in the West still appears as a minor, backburner issue—when it is mentioned at all. And we can identify in the now-distant spate of reactions to President Morsi's "apes and pigs" remarks a common but dysfunctional mindset regarding hostility toward Jews when it comes from Muslim sources.

For starters, many mainstream analysts—especially those likely to define themselves as progressives—seem to react to antisemitism in the Muslim world *only* when averting one's gaze has become an untenable strategy. Moreover, those manifestations of Jew-hatred that demand attention are generally conceptualized as discrete incidents, unconnected to any broad or dangerous movement. Denunciations, when they occur, frequently are accompanied by suggestions that—for one reason or another—the utterers of bigoted language do not really mean what they say. There is also a near-universal avoidance of references to past and present religious roots of hostility, preferring to insulate Islam the religion from analysis and to focus instead on the political, social, or economic grievances of those who express prejudice or engage in discriminatory behavior. Along these lines, one often hears that anti-Jewish eruptions have their origins in the Arab-Israeli conflict or—depending on the analyst's Middle East politics—in Israel's inappropriate conduct. What we rarely see is the flipside of this causal theory, that is, any suggestion that antisemitic beliefs might be the cause of orientations to the Arab-Israeli conflict or that antisemitism, historically, may be responsible for the pernicious hatred of Arabs for the Jewish state and their unwillingness to move toward a peaceful resolution of what would otherwise be a negotiable dispute over land.[5]

There is, in short, a dangerous Western blind spot concerning Muslim antisemitism. Despite recent efforts by a few writers and activists to raise consciousness, most mainstream political leaders, journalists, scholars, and human rights activists continue to ignore, misunderstand, or downplay the significance of anti-Jewish hostility in the Islamic world.[6] This failure is complicated; it arises from many sources, some benign and some malignant. Thus, the mentality has its roots in a mixture of apathy, ignorance, confusion, bigotry, ideology, supposed pragmatism, and misguided multiculturalism. On some occasions, the need to avoid engaging the challenge of antisemitism in the Islamic world becomes an all-out effort to sweep the

---

4 Jim Yardley, "Europe's Anti-Semitism Comes Out of Shadows," *New York Times*, September 24, 2014, 1.

5 Neil J. Kressel, *"The Sons of Pigs and Apes": Muslim Antisemitism and the Conspiracy of Silence* (Washington, DC: Potomac Books, 2012), 164-70.

6 Some recent efforts to raise consciousness of Muslim antisemitism include: Rusi Jaspal, *Antisemitism and Anti-Zionism: Representation, Cognition and Everyday Talk* (Burlington, VT: Ashgate, 2014); Mitchell Bard, *Death to the Infidels: Radical Islam's War against the Jews* (New York: Palgrave Macmillan, 2014); Robert S. Wistrich, *A Lethal Obsession: Anti-Semitism from Antiquity to the Global Jihad* (New York: Random House, 2010); Martin Gilbert, *In Ishmael's House: A History of Jews in Muslim Lands* (New Haven: Yale, 2010); Tarek Fatah, *The Jew Is Not My Enemy* (Toronto: McClelland and Stewart, 2010).

hatred under the rug. Thus, speakers, professors, and writers who call attention to the prejudice may find themselves occasionally under various forms of attack.[7] Shockingly, all of the misconceptions and dysfunctional tendencies with regard to understanding Muslim antisemitism can be observed prominently in the works of Western Middle Eastern studies scholars—so the experts who, in theory, might guide us through the morass have—with a few exceptions—become a part of the problem.[8]

My primary goal in this essay is to refute some common arguments that have been made against those who call attention to the problem of Muslim antisemitism.[9] I contend that while Islam *can be* compatible with a tolerant outlook and a friendly relationship with Jews, the Jewish people, and the Jewish state, the Muslim religious tradition also contains many sources that can be used by those seeking justification for their hatred.

II. Abundant Evidence

This is not the place for a comprehensive review of data establishing the scope and intensity of antisemitism in the Muslim world; still, some evidence must be summoned to refute the oft-heard contention that pro-Israel partisans have fabricated the problem or exaggerated it beyond all semblance of reality. One place to start is by examining the content and tone of some recent public remarks by Muslim political, religious, and academic leaders at varying levels of status and importance. In Denmark, for example, in September 2014, Sheik Muhammad Khaled Samha asked how, when Allah in the Koran deemed Palestine a blessed and sacred land, "can we—or any free Muslim with faith in his heart—accept the division of Palestine between [the Palestinians] and a gang of Jews, the offspring of apes and pigs."[10] Speaking in Damascus that same month, Sheik Muhammad Ma'moun Rahma voiced an accusation that is heard again and again throughout large parts of the Muslim world: "Those [Twin Towers] ... were destroyed by the Jews, and the most significant evidence of that is that 5,000 Jews were absent from work when the towers collapsed."[11]

---

[7] Kressel, *"Sons of Pigs and Apes,"* 58-64, 188-96.

[8] Ibid., 88; See also *The Morass of Middle Eastern Studies: Title VI of the Higher Education Act and Federally Funded Area Studies* (Washington, DC: The Louis D. Brandeis Center for Human Rights under the Law, 2014), http://brandeiscenter.com/publications/research_articles/morass_of_middle_east (accessed October 31, 2014).

[9] A detailed refutation of the logic of antisemitism minimization can be found in my book, *"The Sons of Pigs and Apes,"* 99-151. Some arguments presented below have been revised, adapted, and updated from that work.

[10] *Denmark Sermon: There Can Be No Division of Palestine with the Offspring of Apes and Pigs—The Internet—September 19, 2014*, Middle East Media Research Institute (MEMRI) TV Monitor Project Clip #4545 (Washington, DC: MEMRI, 2014), http://www.memritv.org/clip/en/0/0/0/0/0/0/4548.htm (accessed October 31, 2014). Although several groups monitor media in the Muslim world, MEMRI has produced the most useful and consistently reliable documentation of Muslim antisemitism.

[11] *Damascus Friday Sermon: The Americans Established ISIS to Destroy Syria Sama—TV (Syria)—September 19, 2014*, MEMRI TV Monitor Project Clip #4511 (Washington, DC: MEMRI, 2014), http://www.memritv.org/clip/en/4511.htm (accessed October 31, 2014).

Still that same month, former Jordanian Member of Parliament Abd Al-Mun'im Abu Zant spoke about the Talmudic origins of Jewish cannibalism, reviving medieval blood libel charges and saying: "if they cannot find a Muslim to slaughter, and use drops of his blood to knead the matzos they eat, they slaughter a Christian in order to take drops of his blood…."[12] A similar allegation was made on television by Osama Hamdan, a top Hamas official, who argued that the killing of women and children was "engraved in the historical Zionist and Jewish mentality…. We all remember how Jews used to slaughter Christians…. It is a fact, acknowledged by their own books and by historical evidence…."[13]

Hamdan, Samha, Rahma, Abu Zant, and others made their antisemitic statements during or slightly after the 2014 fighting in Gaza. On the other hand, Mustapha Tlass was a high-level politician in Syria for more than thirty years until he left office in 2004—well before Israel's fight in Gaza. He too was a fan of the blood libel, having published a vile book in the 1980s called *The Matza of Zion*. Tlass's literary effort had no discernible negative impact on his prominent political career; he spoke proudly of his anti-Jewish writing during his tenure as defense minister and in other high posts.[14]

In the summer of 2014, Turkish President Recep Tayyip Erdoğan—ostensibly a NATO ally and staunch opponent of antisemitism in Turkey—spoke at a political rally, saying: "Just like Hitler tried to create a pure Aryan race in Germany, the State of Israel is pursuing the same goals right now." The crowds responded by chanting: "Damn Israel! Down with Israel!"[15] One may argue whether this constitutes antisemitism or merely a political response to the fight in Gaza. Until recently, however, Turkey had much friendlier relations with Israel and would have been listed as one of the most pro-Jewish of Muslim majority countries. Erdoğan's adoption of the frequently-observed habit of equating Israeli behaviors with those of the Nazis is at least questionable. But whatever one makes of the Turkish president's position, it is hard to argue that norms among Muslim leaders reject antisemitism.

A particularly poignant illustration of mainstream Muslim receptivity to Jew-hatred in the early twenty-first century can be found in the pattern of reaction to Malaysian Prime Minister Mahathir Mohamad's 2003 speech to an audience of high-level Islamic political leaders. Mahathir said:

---

12 *Former Jordanian MP Abd Al-Mun'im Abu Zant: Jews Permit Cannibalism, Use Human Blood In Passover—Al-Aqsa TV (Hamas/Gaza)—September 7, 2014*, MEMRI TV Monitor Project Clip #4498 (Washington, DC: MEMRI, 2014), http://www.memritv.org/clip/en/4498.htm (accessed October 31, 2014).

13 *Top Hamas Official Osama Hamdan: Jews Use Blood for Passover Matzos—Al-Quds TV (Lebanon)—July 28, 2014*, MEMRI TV Monitor Project Clip #4384 (Washington, DC: MEMRI, 2014), http://www.memritv.org/clip/en/4384.htm (accessed October 31, 2014).

14 *The Damascus Blood Libel (1840) as Told by Syrian Defense Minister Mustafa Tlass*, Inquiry and Analysis Series Report No. 99 (Washington, DC: MEMRI, 2002), http://www.memri.org/report/en/0/0/0/0/0/51/688.htm (accessed October 31, 2014).

15 *Erdoğan Compares Israel to Hitler, Says: They Will Drown in the Blood They Shed*, MEMRI TV Monitor Project Clip #4484 (Washington, DC: MEMRI, 2014), http://www.memritv.org/clip/en/4484.htm (accessed October 31, 2014).

> We [Muslims] are actually very strong, 1.3 billion people cannot be simply wiped out. The Nazis killed 6 million Jews out of 12 million [*sic*].... But today the Jews rule the world by proxy. They get others to fight and die for them. They invented socialism, communism, human rights and democracy so that persecuting them would appear to be wrong so they may enjoy equal rights with others. With these they have now gained control of the most powerful countries.[16]

Mahathir's words were essentially a paraphrase of notions embodied in the world's most famous antisemitic forgery, *The Protocols of the Elders of Zion*, which has been a source for the worst antisemites throughout the years since it was created by the Tsarist secret police in the late nineteenth century. Although Mahathir was considered by many to be progressive, pragmatic, and religiously moderate, his 2003 comments could have been uttered by any of the very worst European antisemites ever. Still, his remarks "received a standing ovation from Muslim leaders of many nations ... at the 57-nation Organization of the Islamic Conference, the world's largest Muslim group."[17] Possibly, some of the many leaders who applauded did so not out of genuine conviction but, rather, because of peer pressure and an unwillingness to assume the unpopular role of defender of the Jews. Or maybe some were caught up in the moment. But few, if any, later reversed their initial positions on the speech.

Moreover, Muslim religious leaders who have used the "pigs and apes" epithet publicly are far too numerous to list. The insult comes from a tale in the Koran—which while hardly flattering to Jews—need not be read as applying to contemporary Jews.[18] As with difficult verses in the source materials of many faiths, this one could conceivably be interpreted in a benign manner. But this has not been the intent of those who hurl "pigs and apes" language so freely in Islamic countries today. Among those who have used the widely-understood label, one finds Sheik Mohammed Sayed Tantawi, the Sunni head of the prestigious Al-Azhar University who was described at his death in 2010 by the Western media as the quintessential Muslim moderate.[19] Similarly, the dangerous and defamatory *Protocols of the Elders of Zion* are so widely accepted as true that parts of the document are included essentially verbatim in the Hamas Charter and cited repeatedly as academic sources by so-called scholars in many parts of the Muslim world. Far from being an obscure document known only to experts, however, it has been the basis for several multi-part television series in various parts of the Muslim world, including Iran and Egypt.[20] This suggests that, at least for some people powerful enough to get television programs produced, antisemitism is seen as good business.

Nonetheless, the appearance of television series and declarations of leaders do not conclusively establish the extent to which sentiments or behavioral inclinations

---

16 Mahathir Mohamad, "Speech by Prime Minister Mahathir Mohamad of Malaysia to the Tenth Islamic Summit Conference, Putrajaya, Malaysia," Anti-Defamation League, October 16, 2003, http://www.adl.org/Anti_semitism/malaysian.asp (accessed July 10, 2010).

17 David Sanger, "Malaysia Talk Attacking Jews Draws Bush Ire," *New York Times*, October 21, 2003, http://www.nytimes.com/2003/10/21/world/malaysia-talk-attacking-jews-draws-bush-ire.html (accessed October 31, 2014).

18 Kressel, "*Sons of Pigs and Apes*," 26-33.

19 Ibid., 3-5.

20 Ibid., 156-57.

have penetrated a population. It is possible—at least in theory—that relatively tolerant populations are led by those who are far less open-minded. Moreover, public statements do not even prove beyond dispute the internal sentiments of the people who issue them. And one cannot rule out the possibility that they are short-term emotional reactions to dramatic events like the recent military conflicts in Gaza and elsewhere as opposed to lasting orientations. At a minimum, however, one can conclude that strong, loud, sustained, public denunciations of antisemitism to local audiences are rare in the Muslim world. In addition, few seem to regard forays into anti-Jewish invective as particularly dangerous to their future prospects.

Ayaan Hirsi Ali, the noted Somali-born author, reported of her childhood time in Saudi Arabia that:

> Everything bad was the fault of the Jews. When the air conditioner broke or suddenly the tap stopped running, the Saudi women next door used to say the Jews did it. The children next door were taught to pray for the health of their parents and the destruction of the Jews. Later when we went to school, our teachers lamented at length all the evil things Jews had done and planned to do against Muslims. When they were gossiping, the women next door used to say, "She's ugly, she's disobedient, she's a whore—she's sleeping with a Jew." Jews were like djinns [evil spirits], I decided. I had never met a Jew. (Neither had these Saudis.)[21]

The Syrian-educated psychiatrist Wafa Sultan reports that "members of the educated class, thinkers and writers—none of them are immune to this [anti-Jewish and anti-Zionist] conspiracy theory: Whenever a writer comes up with an idea that does not conform to prevailing opinion, the rumor mill accuses him of being a Zionist agent."[22] And speaking about his days as a Muslim student activist in Britain in the 1990s, Ed Husain recalled that: "Without question we despised the Jews."[23] Of course, Hirsi Ali, Sultan, and Husain are controversial. But perhaps that is the point. One immediately becomes controversial in the Muslim world by acting in any capacity that might be interpreted as friendship to the Jews. Those few members of the political, cultural, and intellectual elites who have opposed overt anti-Jewish bigotry have often done so in the context of strongly expressed opposition to Israel. When that component is missing, expressions of tolerance for Jews and Jewry can lead to social ostracism or even physical danger. Still, we can cite the testimony regarding the pervasiveness of Islamic antisemitism of brave writers such as Bassam Tibi, Tarek Fatah, Khaleel Mohammed, Haras Rafiq, Morad El-Hattab El-Ibrahimi, Rachid Kaci, Irshad Manji, Amir Taheri, Nonie Darwish, Irfan Khawaja, Salim Mansur, and Mark Gabriel. Works by these individuals vary greatly in style, academic quality, religious orientation, and political affiliation, but all have value as testimony to the pervasiveness of anti-Jewish hostility in the Muslim and Arab world. If the authors were brought together, perhaps the only thing they would agree on is the destructiveness of Muslim and Arab antisemitism.

Additional evidence supporting the existence of widespread and destructive anti-Jewish bigotry can be seen in the widespread use of the labels "Jew" and Zionist" as a

---

21 Ayaan Hirsi Ali, *Infidel* (New York: Free Press, 2007), 47.

22 Wafa Sultan, *A God Who Hates* (New York: St. Martin's, 2009), 194.

23 Ed Husain, *The Islamist* (New York: Penguin, 2007), 54.

means of discrediting those with whom one disagrees. For example, associates of Shi'ite Iranian Supreme Leader Ali Khamenei recently denounced the Sunni Al-Saud family that rules Saudi Arabia for its "Jewish" origins.[24] A play presented on post-Morsi Egyptian television claims that Israeli Mossad agents were behind the Arab Spring.[25] A Shi'ite imam from Kuwait claims that the Islamic State in Iraq and Syria has been selling women and children to the Jews in Israel. "What kind of religion," he asks, "allows the capturing of a Muslim woman, and on top of that, allows her to be sold to a Jew?"[26] When Ashraf Ghani, the newly elected president of Afghanistan, wanted to give his wife a public role in advocating for women and children, a regional governor who opposed the move denounced her as an "Israeli agent."[27]

Also consider the sales success of translated antisemitic classics like *Mein Kampf* and *The Protocols of the Elders of Zion*, prevalent Holocaust denial and minimization, and—increasingly—violent attacks on the Jews and Jewish institutions by Muslim terrorists in the West. Volumes could be filled with documentation of these points.

But still there are social scientists who might describe all of this evidence as "anecdotal." Where, they might inquire, is the hard scientific research? If world antisemitism were studied the way the US electorate is studied during a presidential election year, we might possess detailed statistics on how many people in each of dozens of countries with substantial Muslim populations accept various antisemitic beliefs; we might also be able to calculate reasonable estimates of how these beliefs might likely impact behavior and other attitudes, such as support for terrorism, hostility toward the United States, support for freedom of religion, support for freedom of the press, and support for democratic elections. We might further possess quantitative breakdowns of Jew-hatred by education, socioeconomic status, region, age, and other relevant dimensions. But, of course, strong social pressures would likely prevent people from providing honest answers, and in any case current knowledge does not even begin to approach this level of sophistication.

As I have discussed elsewhere, there are many reasons why even rudimentary studies of antisemitism in most Muslim-majority nations have not been carried out.[28] Some of these reasons are political, some ideological, some methodological, some practical. As the US State Department's 2008 report to Congress on global antisemitism acknowledged,

---

24 *Associates of Iranian Supreme Leader Khamenei: Saudi Arabia Is the Source of Scheming against the Islamic World; The Al-Saud Family Is of Jewish Origin—and Its Turn to Fall Has Come*, MEMRI Special Dispatch #5858 (Washington, DC: MEMRI, 2014), http://www.memri.org/report/en/0/0/0/0/0/0/8178.htm (accessed October 31, 2014).

25 *Antisemitic Egyptian Play on TV: Mossad Agents behind Arab Spring—Al-Hayat (Egypt)—January 31, 2014*, MEMRI TV Monitor Project Clip #4153 (Washington, D.C: MEMRI, 2014), http://www.memritv.org/clip/en/4153.htm (accessed October 31, 2014).

26 *Shiite Kuwaiti Imam: ISIS Sold Thousands of Women, Girls, and Children to the Jews in Israel*, MEMRI TV Monitor Project Clip #4549 (Washington, DC: MEMRI, 2014), http://www.memritv.org/clip/en/4549.htm (accessed October 31, 2014).

27 Declan Walsh and Rod Nordland, "Jolting Some, Afghan Leader Brings Wife into the Picture," *New York Times*, October 15, 2014, A4.

28 Neil J. Kressel, "The Urgent Need to Study Islamic Anti-Semitism," *Chronicle of Higher Education*, March 12, 2004, B14-B15; Neil J. Kressel, "Antisemitism, Social Science, and the Muslim and Arab World," *Judaism* 52, nos. 3-4 (Summer/Fall 2003).

> It is important to note the challenge of collecting [relevant] information, particularly in closed societies, as we must rely on reported anti-Semitic incidents. Thus, available statistics tend to reflect anti-Semitic incidents that occur in open, democratic countries that allow transparent monitoring of societal conditions such as anti-Semitism. In contrast, information about anti-Semitic incidents in closed societies is largely unavailable, particularly because nongovernmental groups and scholars reporting from closed societies risk persecution.[29]

The problems noted here should not be construed as a mere footnote to an otherwise sound endeavor. The inability to gather data in precisely those places where Jew-hatred is most pronounced is a threat to the overall enterprise and has created misleading impressions about the global distribution of anti-Jewish beliefs. (Far more has been written about antisemitism in America—one of the world's most philosemitic countries—than about Jew-hatred in Saudi Arabia.) Moreover, as the State Department report noted, "[s]ince statistics focus on actual attacks against Jews and facilities used by Jews, they do not capture more generalized antisemitic attitudes or restrictions, such as those reflected in anti-Semitic political cartoons, or anti-Semitic behavior in countries where there is not a significant Jewish population."[30] The lure of life in Israel combined with persecutory conditions in some Arab and Muslim states has, during the past six decades, led to a drastic reduction in the Jewish population of Arab and Muslim-majority countries. Thus, most Jew-hatred occurs in countries that are not home to many Jews.

Despite all this, there has still emerged a body of convincing—if not definitive—empirical research. For example, a 2011 poll of Palestinians in the West Bank and Gaza found that 73 percent endorsed an antisemitic hadith (i.e., a saying attributed to Muhammad) that is quoted in the Hamas Charter. In translation, this section reads, "The Day of Judgment will not come about until Moslems fight the Jews.... [W]hen the Jew will hide behind stones and trees[:] The stones and trees will say O Moslems, O Abdulla, there is a Jew behind me, come and kill him. Only the Gharkad tree ... would not do that because it is one of the trees of the Jews." In addition, 53 percent favored teaching songs about hating Jews in Palestinian schools.[31]

A 2005 report by the Pew Global Attitudes Project, a group with no readily apparent agenda with regard to the topic, explored feelings toward the Jews in numerous countries around the world.[32] The study found that the percentage of Jordanians and Lebanese holding favorable views of Jews was about zero, whereas 99-100 percent held unfavorable views. In Morocco, a moderate, pro-Western Arab country, 88 percent of people hold negative views of Jews. In Pakistan, 74 percent

---

29 US Department of State, *Contemporary Global Anti-Semitism: A Report provided to the United States Congress* (Washington, DC, 2008), 3.

30 Ibid.

31 Gil Hoffman, "6 in 10 Palestinians Reject 2-State Solution, Survey Finds," *Jerusalem Post*, July 15, 2011, http://www.jpost.com/Diplomacy-and-Politics/6-in-10-Palestinians-reject-2-state-solution-survey-finds (accessed October 31, 2014).

32 Pew Global Attitudes Project, "Little Enthusiasm for Many Muslim Leaders: Mixed Views of Hamas and Hezbollah in Largely Muslim Nations," (Washington, DC: Pew Research Center, 2010), http://www.pewglobal.org/2010/02/04/mixed-views-of-hamas-and-hezbollah-in-largely-muslim-nations (accessed October 31, 2014).

hold negative views, and in Indonesia, 76 percent. Even in Turkey, 60 percent of the population holds negative views of Jews. For comparison, the Pew poll found that 77 percent of Americans hold favorable views of Jews and only 7 percent hold unfavorable ones. Such data is telling, and a similar 2010 study essentially corroborated the findings. It is also important to keep in mind that some bigoted respondents are unwilling to confess negative feelings to survey researchers; usually, pollsters believe that the real level of prejudice is greater than the reported level.

Moreover, Hamas—an organization which openly expresses antisemitism, and considers the destruction of Israel to be its raison d'être—receives favorable ratings from 60 percent of Muslims in Jordan, 39 percent in Indonesia, 49 percent in Nigeria, 49 percent in Lebanon, and 49 percent in Egypt. If the people who provide these ratings are not antisemitic, they certain do not regard Jew-hatred as a disqualifier in the political arena.[33]

In 2014, the Anti-Defamation League (ADL)—a century-old activist organization that fights antisemitism as well as many other forms of bigotry—released the results of a well-funded and extensive survey of global antisemitism.[34] Respondents included 53,100 people, aged 18 and over, from 101 countries as well as from the Palestinian Territories in the West Bank and Gaza. In-person and telephone interviews were conducted in 96 languages and—while a genuinely random sample was impossible for such a broad study—researchers devoted much effort to obtaining full national coverage in the countries that were studied and close-to-random samples whenever possible. The study assessed agreement with eleven traditional antisemitic stereotypes including items such as "Jews have too much power in international financial markets," "People hate Jews because of the way Jews behave," and "Jews have too much control over the global media." The ADL summarized their findings by classifying a person as an antisemite if he or she said that at least six of the eleven negative stereotypical items were "probably true." Using this approach, the ADL classified 1.09 billion people worldwide as antisemites. According to the data, Middle Eastern and Muslim-majority countries scored highest in self-reported antisemitic opinions; for example, 92 percent of Iraqis and 69 percent of Turks scored above the antisemitism threshold. However, antisemitic belief systems were also common in many non-Muslim, non-Middle Eastern countries with, for example, 69 percent of Greeks scoring antisemitic, 53 percent of South Koreans, 52 percent of Panamanians, 45 percent of Poles, 44 percent of Bulgarians, 38 percent of Peruvians, 37 percent of French people, 30 percent of Russians, 27 percent of Germans, and 20 percent of Chinese. Relatively good news came from the United States (9 percent), the United Kingdom (8 percent), the Netherlands (5 percent), and the Philippines (3 percent).[35]

---

33 Ibid.

34 *ADL Global 100: An Index of Anti-Semitism*, Report of the Anti-Defamation League (New York: ADL, 2014), http://global100.adl.org/public/ADL-Global-100-Executive-Summary.pdf (accessed October 31, 2014).

35 It is worth noting that the US Department of State and some other organizations have incorporated various aspects of extreme hostility to the State of Israel into their definition of antisemitism, but the ADL measures generally avoided items tapping into such attitudes and relied on measures of traditional anti-Jewish stereotypes. Still, some critics have objected to

Empirical research findings also suggest that Muslims in Europe tend to be substantially more hostile to Jews than members of other European religious groups. One study of the British population, for example, found that Muslims were nearly eight times as likely as members of the general public to hold negative opinions of Jews. Another study found that more than one-third of British Muslim respondents viewed Jews as legitimate targets in the struggle for justice in the Middle East. Yet another study in the United Kingdom found that Muslims perpetrated 30 percent of antisemitic incidents, even though Muslims make up only 3 percent of the general population. Disproportionate anti-Jewish sentiment is even found among Muslims who have come to the West from non-Arab Muslim countries. Christians who hail from Arab countries also tend to be more anti-Jewish than Christians from other countries.[36]

So—with all this evidence—why has the problem of Muslim antisemitism not received the attention it deserves? This question can be answered at many levels. But the simplest one is that those who deny or minimize the significance of Muslim and Arab Jew-hatred nearly always maintain that the problem lies with the anti-antisemites—those whom they charge with misreading, misinterpreting, and misrepresenting the relevant facts. Antisemitism minimizers offer arguments that follow many different tacks, but they all end up concluding that, despite occasional appearances to the contrary, most Muslim and Arab negativity toward Jews is not really bigotry or, even if it is, does not merit much attention or concern.

Critics of the anti-antisemites often start by proclaiming their opposition to prejudice in all its forms, including antisemitism. Thus, a denier or minimizer of contemporary Muslim antisemitism may denounce instances of Jew-hatred drawn from Christian history, Nazism, or contemporary groups to which he or she is politically opposed (e.g., skinheads). Such declarations may be little more than ritualistic, credential-enhancing ploys, or they may be sincere. One often cannot know.

The most superficial of the minimization arguments is that Arabs cannot be antisemitic because they themselves are Semites. This argument fails historically and semantically—partly because the category of Semite is, in the main, meaningless, a

---

elements of the ADL methodology. Some do not like the dichotomous classification of antisemites versus non-antisemites, arguing that a continuous spectrum of hostility would be more reflective of reality. Others suggest that the study might have included other groups for assessment in order to provide a comparative perspective. Still others objected to inclusion of particular items in the antisemitism scale. The belief that "Jews have too much power in international financial markets" may, for example, be a measure first and foremost of attitudes toward the power of international financial markets. The belief that "Jews still talk too much about what happened to them in the Holocaust" need not, in itself, indicate hostility toward Jews and may, in fact, be expressed by many Jews themselves. Finally, the notion that Jews are more loyal to Israel than to the countries they live in may also tap beliefs other than antisemitism. Of course, the ADL has not advanced any of these items individually as the definitive indicator of anti-Jewish bigotry; it is when they are assessed in conjunction with other beliefs that a pattern emerges.

36 Günther Jikeli, "Anti-Semitism among Young Muslims in London" (paper presented at the International Study Group on Education and Research on Anti-Semitism, London, December 5, 2009), http://iibsa.org/cms/fileadmin/downloads/london_symposia/Gunther_Jikeli.pdf (accessed July 10, 2010).

half-baked fabrication of racists and pseudoscientists in the late nineteenth century. Mostly, however, the argument falls apart because there has never been a bigotry specifically targeting "Semites," whether thought of as speakers of Semitic languages or in any other way. Antisemitism has always been directed at Jews.

When someone uses the "Arabs cannot be antisemites" argument, they are usually not attempting to convince the unconvinced or to make a sustainable argument. Rather, they are signaling their politics to their audience, demonstrating their ignorance, or trying to push opponents on to the defensive. They imply that whatever happens now in the Muslim and Arab world by definition bears no resemblance to the long and dishonorable history of Jew-hatred in the Christian world. The extent to which such resemblance exists must, of course, be assessed on the evidence, regardless of whether the word "antisemitism" is used. But by denying the appropriateness of the word "antisemitism," critics attempt to circumvent discussion through what is, in effect, a public relations ploy.

III. What You Say Is Antisemitism Is Not Really Antisemitism

One frequently hears that the hostility observed in the Muslim and Arab world is not really antisemitism. Usually this argument assumes one of the following forms: (1) "Muslims and Arabs do not hate Jews; they just hate Israelis," (2) "Muslims and Arabs do not hate Jews; they just hate Zionists," (3) "not all criticism of Israel is antisemitic," or (4) "the 'new' antisemitism is a myth." The first two contentions are empirically incorrect, the third irrelevant, and the fourth at bottom a matter of semantics.

As Canadian human rights lawyer David Matas has pointed out, "[t]aking a racial slur or stereotype directed against someone who is Jewish and replacing the word Jew with the word Zionist does not change the slur into acceptable discourse."[37] One must search far and wide to locate Islamists who maintain a clear and credible distinction between Jews, Zionists, and Israelis. Aside from overtly anti-Jewish declarations—of which there are tons—one finds in various Middle Eastern and Muslim media many instances in which "Zionists" commit offenses well before the start of the Zionist movement. Moreover, Zionists and Israelis are frequently seen by Islamists to act from motivation that is religiously Jewish rather than political. It is hard to determine how many non-Islamist Muslims and other Arabs draw clear distinctions between Jews, Zionists, and Israelis. Certainly, specifically anti-Jewish rhetoric is less common in these groups than it is among the Islamists. However, the previously cited data from the Pew studies does not counsel optimism; it shows widespread unfavorable attitudes toward "Jews."

Perhaps, also, it is necessary to point out that hatred directed against all or most of the people in a country, even Israel, is still bigotry. And while Israelis are the primary targets of the prejudice, Jews outside Israel usually come under fire because they are believed to support Israel unless they publicly distance themselves. Thus, from the perspective of the ardent anti-Israeli, a criterion for Jewish rights and the acceptability of being Jewish becomes public rejection of the Jewish state. No other people faces this sort of conditional acceptance.

---

37 David Matas, *Aftershock: Anti-Zionism and Antisemitism* (Toronto: Dundurn, 2005), 113-14.

British scholar David Hirsh has voiced the best response to the complaint that "all criticism of Israeli policies is not antisemitic." He answers: "No, of course not, but who says that it is? There are very few Jewish communal spokespeople or Israeli politicians who are prepared to make such an evidently false claim. The contention that criticism of Israel is necessarily anti-Semitic nearly always functions as a straw-man argument."[38]

It makes sense to reframe the issue. Should criticism of Israel ever lose legitimacy because it contains antisemitism? What, for example, is one to make of "criticisms" of Israel that justify or explain away suicide bombings directed against civilians in Israel? And consider that political cartoonists frequently criticized Israel by portraying its leaders as Nazis or with inaccurate and stereotypically Jewish physical features—or by invoking thinly-veiled or overt blood libel charges. Moreover, criticism of the Israel lobby in the United States may rest on readily discernible aspects or imagery from the *Protocols*. Another form of "policy criticism" involves denying academic privileges to all Israeli academics because of the way Israel has allegedly behaved, even though citizens of other countries are not held to any similar standard. Sometimes it seems the Israeli policy to which critics object is Israel's policy of existing.

For my argument, there is no need for new definitions of antisemitism—those based on the so-called "new" antisemitism—or for expansion of old definitions. What I have been talking about is straightforward bigotry. The portrait of the Jew that too often appears in the contemporary Middle East includes heinous character traits, unappealing physical features, malignant motives, insinuations of inappropriate power, calls for discrimination, and even exterminationist sentiment—all of which have turned up notoriously in other cultures and times.

All in all, it seems fair to conclude: (1) that there is a tremendous amount of traditional antisemitism in the Muslim and Arab world; (2) that there is tremendous amount of fairly obvious antisemitism that simply uses the word "Zionist" as a synonym for Jew; (3) that there is much legitimate criticism of Israel; and (4) that much criticism of Israel is extreme, unfair, and illegitimate. This final category of criticism assumes the characteristics of a prejudice. However, whether or not it makes sense to expand the traditional meaning of antisemitism to include it is a complex matter about which reasonable people may disagree—although everyone should understand that this is more a matter of nomenclature than substance.

IV. Political Spillover Arguments

Some minimizers attribute Muslim and Arab anti-Jewish hostility to the politics of international conflict and thereby seek to diminish its significance as prejudice. Two frequently encountered arguments include: (1) "The real issue is not hostility toward Jews, but sometimes there is a little unavoidable spillover from the Arab-Israeli conflict"; and (2) "How else would we expect people to react to all those Israeli transgressions against human rights and morality."

---

[38] David Hirsh, *Anti-Zionism and Antisemitism: Cosmopolitan Reflections*, YIISA Working Paper No. 1 (New Haven, CT: Yale University, 2007), 139, http://eprints.gold.ac.uk/2061/1/Hirsh_Yale_paper.pdf (accessed April 4, 2012).

We must acknowledge the impact that the rise of Zionism, the birth of Israel, and the Arab-Israeli conflict have obviously had on the development of Muslim Jew-hatred. Every time the conflict flares up—regardless of the reason—fuel is tossed on to the bonfire of the antisemites. It is impossible to speculate about how Muslim-Jewish relations might have progressed had there never been a State of Israel or had the majority of Arabs followed the few in the early years of Zionism who welcomed the Jews back into the neighborhood. But those who see the politics of conflict as a contributing factor in the growth of anti-Jewish bigotry are certainly right.

The problem lies in the next step, concluding from this that such bigotry is *just* politics. To do so would require us to implicitly validate a great deal of past and present prejudice and discrimination around the world. Some would have us believe, especially with regard to Muslim antisemitism, that when history, politics, and economics have something to do with anger and hate, then it's not "classic" bigotry.

But what exactly is classic bigotry? Politics, economics, real and perceived competition for scarce resources (like land), real and perceived past grievances, manipulation by unsavory leaders—all of these have played a key role in many types of prejudice. For example, the Turks perpetrated the Armenian genocide in part because they perceived a threat to the state from Armenians, longstanding Hutu resentment of Tutsis had roots in the system of Tutsi overlordship that prevailed in Rwanda prior to the arrival of the European colonialists and that persisted under colonial rule, and high crime rates in the American black community feed stereotypes about blacks. There probably is no such thing as pure, classic prejudice. Nearly all instances of prejudice have something to do with the political, economic, and psychological needs and desires of the perpetrators. And there has never been a requirement that victims of prejudice establish their absolute innocence.

Along with Israel, the United States, Britain, and perhaps a few other nations are carefully watched and held to high standards of conduct. But most nations in the world do not appear to be judged at all in international forums. Freedom House, an organization that carefully collects data on a variety of human rights abuses has rated China, Kazakhstan, Syria, Angola, Congo, Burma, Vietnam, Cambodia, Belarus, Saudi Arabia, Zimbabwe, Cuba, Pakistan, and many other countries "not free." Tanzania, Malaysia, Bangladesh, Thailand, Bolivia, Colombia, and many more have been rated "partially free." Israel is rated "free," as is the United States, Western Europe, Canada, Australia, and Japan.[39] Yet nearly all the relatively unscrutinized and unfree nations join enthusiastically in the chorus of condemnation of Israel.

To the extent that any nation is judged, it should in principle be by the totality of its record and against standards that are universally applied. For people not blinded by ideology, it ultimately becomes clear that the worst charges against Israel are nearly always baseless. Those accusations with substance generally show Israel to be behaving imperfectly but in line with how we would expect a functioning liberal democracy to act in the midst of a long-term struggle to survive. And, needless to say, there is no case for the sometimes-heard charges of genocide, apartheid, or

---

[39] Freedom House, *A Catalyst for Freedom and Democracy: 2007 Annual Report* (Washington, DC, 2007), http://www.freedomhouse.org/report/freedom-world/freedom-world-2007 (accessed October 31, 2014).

indiscriminate military targeting of civilians. The purpose of such accusations is to instill hatred and emotionality, not to further objective analysis.

Despite their lack of merit, the most extreme charges hurled against Israel are making headway in the West as well as in the Middle East largely by repetition and the power of the big lie. The constant drumbeat of accusations against Israel is being received unthinkingly in well-regarded places, even after charges are exposed as groundless. The international community has many Muslim states and one Jewish one, so on the basis of numbers alone, Israel loses all international votes. Human rights organizations seem naturally to prefer losers over winners and to reject military force, regardless of its justification. And these are only a few of the reasons why the focus on Israeli transgressions in the world media has been out of proportion to the dimensions of these transgressions.

At a minimum, the far left's propensity for extreme opposition to Zionism and Israel creates fertile ground for antisemitism. David Hirsh, speaking the language of the academic left, notes that "antiracist anti-Zionism is creating commonsense discourses which construct antisemitism as thinkable and possible. There are some people who are prepared to experiment openly with antisemitic ways of expressing themselves and are nonetheless accepted as legitimate by some antiracist organizations and individuals."[40] The actual deeds of Israel (and the United States) may themselves fertilize Jew-hatred, but more often it is not the deeds themselves but rather the view people take of them that feeds the bigotry.

For many, Israel has become a central element in a collective obsessional delusion. With no shortage of injustices close to home in countries such as Pakistan, Indonesia, Sudan, Libya, and Saudi Arabia, one wonders how so many people in these places find so much energy to devote to a far-away conflict. Even if Israel were conducting itself as unjustly as its detractors maintain, it remains to be explained why these particular infractions should loom so large in Muslim and Arab public consciousness.

Moreover, anger is not necessarily directed at the true sources of one's problems. The many misfortunes, injustices, and "narcissistic wounds" experienced by large numbers of people in the many parts of the Arab world have a plethora of causes. Most (but not all) of the time, blaming Israel has been little more than a form of irrational scapegoating rather than an accurate direction of anger toward the source of the troubles.

It is hard to imagine how a more accurate diagnosis of the reasons for Palestinian suffering might have emerged in the Middle East. Try to envision the fortunes of a Muslim journalist or professor who stands up to advance the argument that Israel had, for the most part, acted reasonably. In Israel, not only have speakers advancing clearly self-critical perspectives on the Arab-Israeli conflict been tolerated, but more than few have also ended up in the Knesset, led departments at major universities, or headed human rights organizations in Israel dedicated to helping Israeli Arabs and Palestinians in the territories. Yet, in much of the Arab world, the person who publicly announces that "Israel hasn't been so bad" is likely to lose his or her domestic platform quickly.

---

40 Hirsh, *Anti-Zionism and Antisemitism: Cosmopolitan Reflections.*

Finally, even if Israel were guilty of major transgressions, that would not seem to justify antisemitism.

V. CHARGES OF BAD HISTORY

Critics not infrequently respond to those who express concern about contemporary Muslim antisemitism by alluding to a benign history of Muslim-Jewish relations. Such thinking in turn supports antisemitism minimization via two arguments: (1) "Muslims have always treated Jews well so how can we say that what we are now witnessing is a serious instance of dangerous bigotry?"; and (2) "It is historically inaccurate to say that Islam contains the seeds of contemporary antisemitism."

The first answer to both of these arguments is, even if the roots of Muslim and Arab antisemitism were all recent, it would not negate, or even much reduce, the danger of the current manifestation of hatred. The second, more important answer is that the "rosy past" scenario greatly overstates Islam's historic open-mindedness toward Jews.

Informed experts disagree about the historical precedents for contemporary Muslim antisemitism. The most common perspective, the received wisdom, sees Jew-hatred as mainly alien to Islamic history and culture. Experts may acknowledge a variety of negative references to Jews in the Islamic religious literature and occasional antisemitic incidents through the years, but they portray Islamic political and social traditions as fundamentally tolerant, at least when judged by the standards of their day.[41] They call attention to religious verses that they interpret as respectful of Jews and supportive of peaceful coexistence. They see antisemitism mainly as a European import, brought to the Muslim world by manipulative European antisemites and fueled by the Arab-Israeli conflict. As historian Mark R. Cohen suggests, for example, "it is precisely because classical Islamic sources have so little that can be construed as anti-Semitic that the *Protocols of the Elders of Zion* are so popular in the Muslim world today."[42]

Historian Jeffrey Herf focuses on the importance of documents he has unearthed that detail conscious Nazi efforts to spread antisemitism through the Middle East as a means of mobilizing Muslims in the war effort.[43] Bernard Lewis also focuses on

---

41 See, for example, Mark R. Cohen, *Under Crescent and Cross: The Jews in the Middle Ages*, rev. ed. (Princeton, NJ: Princeton University Press, 2008); Mark R. Cohen, "Modern Myths of Muslim Anti-Semitism," in *Muslim Attitudes to Jews and Israel*, ed. Moshe Ma'oz (Eastbourne: Sussex Academic Press, 2010), 31-47; John L. Esposito, *What Everyone Needs to Know about Islam: Answers to Frequently Asked Questions, from One of America's Leading Experts* (New York: Oxford University Press, 2002), 81; Reuven Firestone, *An Introduction to Islam for Jews* (Philadelphia: Jewish Publication Society, 2008). Numerous Jewish historians from the past shared a belief in the relative benevolence of Muslim rule through the ages. See, for example, Léon Poliakov, *The History of Anti-Semitism*, vol. 2, *From Mohammed to the Marranos*, trans. Natalie Gerardi (Philadelphia: University of Pennsylvania Press, 2003).

42 Cohen, "Modern Myths," 41.

43 Jeffrey Herf, *Nazi Propaganda for the Arab World* (New Haven, CT: Yale, 2009). Herf does not take a strong position on the situation of the Jews in Islamic history. But he argues that contemporary Islamists remain heavily influenced by Nazi efforts to spread their antisemitic doctrine.

modern European colonialist contributions to Muslim antisemitism.[44] Some say the magnanimity of the essentially tolerant Islamic faith began to crack in the twentieth century, when Zionism, European colonialism, globalization, and other modern movements disrupted the natural course of Islamic history. Present-day hostility toward Jews, these experts maintain, is consequently without deep indigenous roots.

The challengers of the received wisdom generally acknowledge that Jews at times fared tolerably well under Muslim rule in some places; however, they emphasize that Islamic environments were, as a rule, difficult places for Jews. The challengers of the received wisdom include Norman Stillman, Martin Gilbert, Bat Yeor, and Andrew Bostom, each of whom has his or her own specific take on the matter.[45] These scholars assign more weight to hostile statements and incidents concerning Jews in the Qur'an, hadiths, and other religious documents of Islam. Moreover, they reject as historically untrue the notion that Islam has been a fundamentally tolerant culture, calling attention to burdensome, discriminatory, and degrading rules Jews and Christians had to abide by in order to survive. The *dhimmi*, the protected Jew or Christian under Muslim rule, was often subject to special taxes, clothing requirements, rules about riding horses and bearing arms, and limitations on religious observance.

Writers in this tradition sometimes argue that the vision of a tolerant Islam is, despite a few prominent exceptions, mainly (or to some extent) an idyllic fairy tale created partly by poorly informed European Jewish historians who were dismayed by conditions in the West and seeking—for various political, ideological, and psychological reasons—greener grass on the other side. Scholars such as Stillman, Bostom, and Gilbert argue that a considerable body of anti-Jewish material, significant anti-Jewish discrimination, and substantial violence preceded the modern Israeli state and Zionism for centuries and sprouted from seeds planted at the very inception of Islam.

Islamic history covers a great many people, many years, and many places. The story is complex and does not fit either perspective perfectly. Polemics aside, there is considerable basis for agreement among reasonable people on both sides of the debate.

In my view, the best summary is that Jews, under Islam, were treated considerably better much of the time than Jews in Christian Europe—but also that such a conclusion is unfortunately not saying all that much.[46] Until recent times, Christianity set a very low standard for treatment of Jews, varying from bad to worse to intolerable to genocidal. Islam, by contrast, created a political and religious world that, despite some violent episodes, did sometimes provide a degree of tolerance for

---

44 Bernard Lewis, *Semites and Anti-Semites* (New York: Norton, 1986). Lewis argues that some degree of "normal" prejudice existed in traditional Islam but that full-blown, lethal, obsessive antisemitism was largely a European import.

45 See, for example, Andrew Bostom, ed., *Legacy of Islamic Anti-Semitism* (Amherst, NY: Prometheus, 2008); Martin Gilbert, *In Ishmael's House*; Norman A. Stillman, *The Jews of Arab Lands in Modern Times* (Philadelphia: Jewish Publication Society, 2003); Norman A. Stillman, *Jews of Arab Lands: A History and Source Book* (Philadelphia: Jewish Publication Society, 1979); Bat Yeor, *Islam and Dhimmitude: Where Civilizations Collide*, trans. Miriam Kochan and David Littman (Madison, NJ: Fairleigh Dickinson University Press, 2002).

46 Lewis, *Semites and Anti-Semites*, 121.

Christians and Jews. This tolerance was based on second-class citizenship and often—but not always—came at a high price.

As is the case in many religions that believe they possess the one true faith for everyone, one can find in Islamic theology—or, more accurately, parts of Islamic theology—significant disdain for nonbelievers. Muhammad initially had high hopes for converting the Jews and considerable respect for their traditions. Like Martin Luther, however, his initial favorability turned into anger when Jews did not flock to convert. Some stories about the founder of Islam show him endorsing very unfavorable treatment of the Jews; for example, he presides over the mass killing of the Jewish Banu Qurayza tribe, thereby providing twenty-first century extremists with the ability to draw upon a religiously-sanctioned precedent for very destructive behavior.

Not inconsistent with Muhammad's message, Muslim leaders after Muhammad continued to believe that Islam had been ordained to dominate the world, and in most Muslim lands complete acceptance of this domination was generally the cost of survival for Jews. However, even taking all this into account, the distant religious and historic tradition is only one source of contemporary Jew-hatred in Muslim and Arab countries. Those who focus primarily on ancient religious traditions are omitting an important part of the story. One need not probe very deeply before the substantial overlap between antisemitism in the Christian and Muslim worlds becomes apparent, and part of this was attributable to the importation of the European antisemitic culture. Almost every major theme from Christian and secular European antisemitism makes an appearance in the contemporary Islamic world, none more prominently than the dangerous idea that rich, powerful, ubiquitous, immoral Jews are conspiring to control the world.[47]

The argument concerning the extent and depth of anti-Jewish discrimination under Islam is partly an argument over which sources to trust and partly a "glass half full or half empty" problem. About the status of Jews under Islam in the distant past, there is, however, room for reasonable people to debate. About the prevalence of Jew-hatred in the contemporary Muslim world, there is no such room.

Some argue that extremist Christians are the deeper enemies of the Jews. Based on an overall quantitative assessment over two thousand years of history, I would agree. Moreover, based on the centrality of pernicious anti-Jewish imagery in the traditional theology, I would also agree. However, Christianity has taken many constructive steps during the past half century to limit and control its antisemitic potential.

A related objection is that Jews, Christians, and Muslims should get together and fight the right-wingers and neo-Nazis who are the real enemies of both the Jews and the Muslims. It is true that no one knows where the next wave of antisemitism might originate. And there has long been a disturbing amount of hatred coming from the extreme right and neo-Nazis. In the United States, some evidence from opinion polls suggests that a subset of the American population, fairly small in size, holds both

[47] Some Muslims do blame Jews for their purported attempts to harm Jesus, but this is obviously much less central to Islamic Jew-hatred than it is to Christian Jew-hatred. (Muslims view Jesus as a prophet, although they deny his divinity, the crucifixion, and, hence, the Jews' role as Christ-killers.)

Jews and Muslims in low regard.[48] So one need not be dismissive about right-wing Christian extremism, and certainly the dangers of one type of extremism should not be used as grounds to deflect interest in the other. But, in my view, though circumstances can change rapidly, Islamic Jew-hatred is the more pressing current concern.

VI. Disagreements about Commonality and Intensity

Some people may think charges of antisemitism in the Muslim world imply that all or nearly all Muslims are antisemitic or that Muslims are necessarily antisemitic. Such conclusions would be unjust, unwarranted, and insulting to millions of Muslims who do not harbor any such hatred. Moreover, it would reflect ignorance insofar as some Muslim theologians have found in Muhammad's message the basis for positive relations with Jews.

It is, therefore, logically, morally, and strategically important to establish in some detail an accurate topography of antisemitism in the Muslim world. Where is antisemitism more prevalent and why? Where has it not taken hold? Those who object to talk about the Islamic world as monolithic are certainly right.

Many have suggested that only a handful of Muslims endorse antisemitism. In a sense, of course, virtually every sociological generalization about a group is painting with too broad a brush. Generalizations rarely apply to everyone. For example, when people speak about the racist South in the United States during the late nineteenth and early twentieth centuries, they do an injustice to progressive-minded Southerners from that era. But the inability or unwillingness to speak of dysfunctional tendencies in social, political, ethnic, or national groups means the end of useful sociology. Although one cannot yet precisely quantify the diffusion of antisemitic hatred into various Muslim populations, enough evidence to say that the "handful" theorists are dead wrong is already available.

Indeed, if the "handful" designation applies to any subgroup of the Muslim population, it applies to those who speak out loudly and clearly in denunciation of antisemitism. Recognizing the reality of widespread hatred in a culture does not make one a hater.

VII. Arguments from Civility

Nice people, we are told, do not criticize other people's religious beliefs. The problem is that terrible things have been done throughout history under the banner of religion, and it is intellectually dishonest to say that religion has been causally irrelevant. Although many people like to assert that the source of evil behavior is never religion but rather the corrupters of religion, this semantic trick does not hold water. And to maintain that criticism of religion is out of bounds is to offer a screen behind which evil-doers may operate with impunity.[49]

---

48 Gallup Center for Muslim Studies, *Religious Perceptions in America: With an In-Depth Analysis of U.S. Attitudes toward Muslims and Islam* (Abu Dhabi: Gallup, 2009), 5, 15, http://www.abudhabigallupcenter.com/144335/Religious-Perceptions-America.aspx (accessed March 31, 2011).

49 See Austin Dacey, *The Secular Conscience: Why Belief Belongs in Public Life* (Amherst, NY: Prometheus, 2008).

Reinforcing the taboo against criticizing aspects of a religion is yet another taboo against denouncing anything associated with "diversity," especially diversity provided by non-Western groups who were once victims of Western colonialism. Perhaps especially since the publication in 1978 of Edward Said's *Orientalism*, Western scholars have felt that it was not their place to pass judgment of the ways of the East.[50]

Although those who argue from civility might be trying hard to bring about the right kind of world, they cannot succeed by simply assuming it is already here. Nor, as a general principle, will focusing on the positives do much to eliminate the negatives in the world. Recognizing a problem is widely and correctly acknowledged as the first step to solving it.

VIII. Charges of Islamophobia

Sometimes when one brings up the topic of Muslim antisemitism, the response is that, instead, we should be talking about Islamophobia. But why should attending to one prejudice lessen the importance of attending to another? We should, indeed, be talking about Islamophobia. The two bigotries do not cancel each other out; both merit concern. Beyond moral considerations, prejudice against Muslims and Arabs constitutes a problem for those who believe—as I do—that the long-term struggle against religious extremist violence turns largely on retaining the loyalty and cooperation of moderate Muslims in Western nations.

Sometimes people ask: "Aren't Jews just as bigoted against Muslims?" This question is really several questions. Do Jews hold unfavorable views of Muslims? Do Jews hold more negative views of Muslims than do others in the West? Does the Jewish religion provide a foundation for anti-Muslim bigotry, and, if so, does this tradition constitute part of contemporary Jewish attitudes toward Muslims? Do Jews hold bigoted or otherwise unfair prejudicial views concerning Muslims, and do they act on these views? In other words, are many Jews anti-Muslim bigots in the same sense that many Muslims are anti-Jewish?

To answer this last question first, of course some Jews are—but hardly any of these racists have political, social, or religious clout. And there is little reason to believe that Jews are any more prejudiced than members of any other Western group against Muslims and possibly some reason to suspect that Jews (or Jewish Americans) might be less prejudiced.[51]

Another question concerns whether elements in the Jewish religious and historical tradition might have a negative impact on contemporary Jewish attitudes toward Muslims and Islam. Looking back into the distant past, one will find many debates about the validity of Islam and Christianity, as well as many rules for how Jews should interact with the larger surrounding religions that generally possessed tremendous power over them. This is not the place to review this history. But most of the debates about the nature of Islam concerned whether the religion was merely untrue or was idolatry. The great Jewish scholar Maimonides concluded that Islam was not idolatry, and this view has generally prevailed. There were also debates

[50] Martin Kramer, *Ivory Towers on Sand: The Failure of Middle Eastern Studies in America* (Washington, DC: Washington Institute for Near East Policy, 2001), 27-43.

[51] Kressel, *"Sons of Pigs and Apes,"* 139-41.

about whether it was better to become a martyr or convert to Islam.[52] Beyond this, many scholars attempted to craft rules for dealing with Muslims; these rules reflected survival demands, theology, and tribal affinities. In the various deliberations, the Jewish scholars at times showed their lack of knowledge about the specifics of beliefs and practices associated with Islam. As a result of the power imbalance, however, Jews never had any power to harm Muslims with their religious decisions. And, in any case, the Jewish religious tradition—with its enlightened and unenlightened components—does not constitute a meaningful source of the contemporary attitudes of Jews toward Muslims, for better or worse.

Evidence may yet emerge showing Jews to be more prejudiced against Muslims than other Westerners, or it may turn out that Jews, with their prevailing tradition of tolerance, turn out be less anti-Muslim than Western populations as a whole. In any case, it is incumbent upon Jewish leaders to continue to fight the anti-Muslim bigotry that exists in their group, just as it is incumbent upon non-Jewish leaders to do the same. But opposing bigotry against Muslims does not require closing one's eyes to the murderous Jew-hatred that is being perpetrated by many Muslim religious leaders and large portions of their flocks in the name of the faith.

IX. Arguments Based on Benign Neglect

Sometimes minimizers acknowledge the existence of antisemitism in the Muslim world and then explain why we should deliberately ignore it. Some say that ignoring or downplaying Jew-hatred in the Muslim and Arab world is, for one reason or another, the best way to combat it in the long run. More often, minimizers say that fighting antisemitism must take a backseat to higher goals, such as resolving the Arab-Israeli conflict, pursuing better relations with the billion-strong Muslim world, or pursuing the West's interests in the war on terrorism. The arguments for "benign" neglect can be complex.

No one is arguing that foreign policy must be one-dimensional or monomaniacal with regard to antisemitism. There are, indeed, times when prudence dictates that the issue not be raised. However, the quiet strategy can be too quiet, and neglect of such venomous and potentially dangerous intergroup hostility can be anything but benign. Simple truth sometimes beats out wily sophistication in the pursuit of reasonable policy. And truth, maligned as it is by policy sophisticates, can prevent a less valid moral calculus from taking root.

Some argue that focusing on antisemitism does not promote the Arab-Israeli peace process, the only true path to reducing antisemitism. The basic argument here is that if only we could solve the Arab-Israeli conflict, Arab antisemitism would begin to dissipate and antisemitism in the non-Arab Muslim world would rapidly disappear. However, this approach underestimates the continuing impact of decades of massive antisemitic socialization in many parts of the Middle East and elsewhere in the Muslim world. Plus, the argument calls to mind the old story about landing on a desert island with only an economist for companionship and several crates of canned food for sustenance. How, you ask the economist, can we open the cans? He replies, "First, assume a can opener."

---

52 Marc B. Shapiro, "Islam and the Halakhah," *Judaism* 42, no. 3 (Summer 1993): 332-43.

How can the Arab-Israeli conflict be resolved when an irrational hostility to Jews who possess power and partial control over their destiny forms a key barrier to the resolution of that conflict? Shall we first assume a solution? Absent anti-Jewish irrationality and bigotry, the Arab-Israeli conflict would certainly have ended with the Israeli offer for a two-state solution in 2000, and probably much earlier.

Some also contend that America has many interests throughout the vast and diverse Muslim world, and these interests may not be advanced by keeping Israel and the Jews on the agenda. Precisely because delusional thinking about the Jews prevails, some argue that it would be best to make progress on other issues. Then, perhaps, there would be a cooperative foundation on which the matter of antisemitism might be addressed. If, for example, the Americans made progress with the Iranians, the Iraqis, the Libyans, the Egyptians, the Pakistanis, the Syrians, the Turks, or others, then America would be in a better position to discourage Jew-hatred. Similarly, if Europe could arrive at understandings with ever-so-slightly antisemitic—but otherwise moderate—Muslims at home and abroad, then such Muslims might be more willing and able to abandon their antisemitic ways.

In principle, this approach seems pragmatic, and in moderate doses, it might sometimes work. But there remains the possibility that delusional thinking also exists in the West. Putting aside the oxymoronic nature of the "antisemitic moderate," Europe and America may be misleading themselves about the extent to which such "moderates" will become partners on antisemitism or other matters. A realistic foreign policy is important, but too much realism can lead to deals with the devil, and for well-functioning democracies like America and others in the West such deals are never "pragmatic" for very long.

X. Why minimizers minimize

One cannot readily refute the contention that closet bigots exist among the deniers and minimizers. But in the absence of credible information about their relative numbers, this approach does not seem useful or convincing. In any event, there are better explanations. Lack of familiarity with the evidence can explain a lot. Many people in the West have arrived at their judgments about antisemitism in the Muslim world through various types of extrapolation. In the United States, for example, people reasonably infer from their observations and experiences that the local Jewish predicament is not all that bad, especially when compared with the situation of Jews in the past and other minorities nowadays. People further base their assessments on interactions with Muslims in the United States, most of whom are moderates. Extrapolations from observations of Muslims participating in interfaith initiatives—again, a disproportionately liberal, moderate, and well-intentioned bunch—can be even more misleading.

Some observers may minimize in their minds the threat of Muslim antisemitism primarily because they perceive—in some instances, accurately—a Jewish tendency to cry wolf. Thus, they overcorrect, presuming that complaints about Muslim and Arab antisemitism are yet another manifestation of the "overly defensive" Jewish psychology. These extrapolations are critically flawed, not least because circumstances in the Middle East, in Muslim-majority countries, and even in Europe are substantially different from those in the United States.

Most Westerners in America, Europe, and Israel—left, right, and center—strongly desire improved relations with the Muslim and Arab world. Poll data confirm this again and again. Politicians frequently elevate the desire for better relations to a first-order goal of international policy, as when—shortly after taking office in 2009—President Obama declared his intention to seek closer ties with Muslim nations. Clergy who try to improve interfaith relations are seen by many as heroes of our time. It is not only those on the left who hope to achieve a "just, peaceful, humane and sustainable world" by encouraging leading Islamic religious figures to broadcast statements of moderation. The objective in all of this is to keep the West from ending up in a conflict with Islam, Muslims, and Islamic states. It is a worthy goal, but it has a problem.

Gaining the cooperation of many Muslim religious and political leaders has proved far more difficult than expected, and hostility toward the United States appears more broad-based than initially believed in the days following 9/11. In this context, some see focusing attention on widespread bigotry emanating from large segments of the Muslim and Arab world as fanning the flames of conflict by identifying negative characteristics of the community with which the West wants to get along. There is a strong impulse to leave this one stone unturned in the battle against bigotry.[53]

Foreign policy realists, those who understand foreign affairs in terms of the cold-hearted pursuit of national interests, routinely downplay the ideological underpinnings of Hamas and Hezbollah and call on America to treat these non-state actors as normal participants in international politics.[54] Left-leaning Middle East Studies professors end up in a similar place, although for different ideological reasons; they have repeatedly pushed for negotiation with and, consequently, legitimation of Hamas.[55] How then should one expect them to address the presence of murderously antisemitic hadiths and straight-faced citations of the *Protocols of the Elders of Zion* in the Hamas Charter? And how should one expect them to deal with evidence suggesting that hostility toward Jews may be common even among some so-called moderates in the world of Islam.

Many on the moderate and mainstream left still see antisemitism as yesterday's news—a malady of the European past, a disease of nationalism and fascism, that has, for the most part, withered away in the new Europe. Such liberals are not necessarily naive; they may acknowledge the long tradition of antisemitism that stained the works of many socialist and leftist thinkers as well. They may retain some concern about the possibility of a resurgence of Jew-hatred, and they are also sensitive to other forms of bigotry. But, against these prospects, they counsel careful monitoring of right-wing groups in the West. To the extent that moderate liberals

---

53 See, for example, Michael Morris, "EU Whitewashes Muslim Anti-Semitism," *American Thinker*, April 1, 2004, http://www.americanthinker.com/2004/04/eu_whitewashes_muslim_antisemi.html (accessed October 31, 2014). Even when antisemitism is unearthed, some—especially in Europe—try hard to deflect blame from the Muslim community, although this may mean assigning it where it does not belong.

54 See Dennis Ross and David Makovsky, *Myths, Illusions, and Peace* (New York: Viking, 2009), 238.

55 See, for example, Janet Doerflinger, "Professors Push Israel to Negotiate with Hamas," *American Thinker*, February 6, 2011, http://www.americanthinker.com/2011/02/professors_push_israel_to_nego.html (accessed February 8, 2011.

misread Muslim hostility to Jews, it is largely because they have not been exposed to the evidence or because they are blinded by a desire to avoid conflict with Muslims and Arabs at all costs.

For elements of the radical left, the situation is different. Most are skeptical about Europe's antiracist declarations. The conservative writer Richard Baehr distinguished between liberals and leftists on basis of a test: "If you tend to regard America as a primarily flawed, evil, unjust racist country (or at least when Republicans are running it), and most importantly, believe that the US is the primary threat to world peace internationally, then you are a leftist, and not a liberal."[56] In any case, the radical left sees racism running rampant in Europe and the United States, especially racism against Muslims. But, for many, a new ideology has taken hold, with elements that undermine any attempt to perceive Muslim and Arab antisemitism clearly.

Sociologist Robert Fine explains:

> In recent years the European radical intelligentsia has become increasingly inclined to treat Israel as its primary enemy. Israel is represented as a racist state, a pariah people, an imperial power, the tail that wags the American dog, the extension of colonial Europe into the Middle East and so forth.[57]

According to David Hirsh and Jane Ashworth, Israel became "a symbol for all that is wrong with a world dominated by U.S. imperialism." There are no shades of gray in the radical left's worldview. Instead,

> [i]t is Manichaeism: the world is a great struggle between heroes and villains, only to be resolved by a great revelation and a final undoing. Conversely, the Palestinians have come to symbolise all victims, and their struggle has become the defining struggle against imperialism. Symbolic Zionists and victims replace real Jews and Palestinians in the left anti-Zionists' imagination.[58]

Such hostility, for most radical leftists, is not antisemitism, but it is obsessive—going far beyond a demand that Palestinians be treated fairly. Hirsh and Ashworth suggest that

> [a]nti-Zionism is not motivated by anti-semitism. It is motivated by concern for the oppressed. But it nevertheless creates a movement and a worldview that singles out Jews as being the central force for evil and imperialism in the world. Naturally, such movements are beginning to spawn people who are indeed motivated by anti-semitism.[59]

---

[56] Richard Baehr, "Why Does the Left Hate Israel?," *American Thinker*, January 22, 2004, http://www.americanthinker.com/2004/01/why_does_the_left_hate_israel.html (accessed April 12, 2011).

[57] Robert Fine, "New Antisemitism Theory and Its Critics" (unpublished paper prepared for Racism and Antisemitism Mid-Term Conference, European Sociological Association, Belfast, September 2010). See also Robert Fine, "Fighting with Phantoms: A Contribution to the Debate on Antisemitism in Europe," *Patterns of Prejudice* 43, no. 5 (2009): 459-79.

[58] David Hirsh and Jane Ashworth, "The State They're In," *Progress Magazine* (November-December 2005), http://www.progressonline.org.uk/2005/10/27/the-state-theyre-in (accessed April 12, 2011).

[59] Ibid.

Hirsh and Ashworth may be naive in accepting that most anti-Zionism stems from concern for the oppressed; there is much more to the psychology of hostility toward the Jewish state. But they are certainly correct that there has been much seepage of Jew-hatred into the anti-Zionist community.

It is hardly surprising that ideologically obsessed Israel-haters would fail to detect and denounce Jew-hatred in their ranks or in the Muslim and Arab world. It would require a tightrope walker to maintain the levels of anti-Israel hostility that are a central defining feature for much of the radical left and at the same time keep up sensitive antennae to those who cross over into overt antisemitism.

But several other factors reinforce antisemitism denial and minimization among radical leftists and sometimes others—liberals and conservatives—as well:

- a reluctance to incriminate those who are themselves the victims of racism and discrimination;
- the lack of a politically acceptable language with which one can speak accurately about a race, religion, or people;
- an unwillingness to judge the deeds of non-Western people by Western values because of the doctrine of moral relativism;
- a decline in sympathy for Jews as they lost the victim and underdog status that won support in the past; and
- a reluctance, especially in Europe, to alienate large blocks on Muslim voters important to political coalitions.

All of these problems contribute to the Western lack of clarity regarding Muslim antisemitism. And the blind spot is not a trivial one. Although the body count, thus far, has been low by the twentieth century standards of mass killing, we can probably expect an increase in terrorist attacks targeting Jews throughout the world. Aside from moral considerations and collateral damage, it is worth remembering that antisemites in the Muslim world and elsewhere frequently include under the category of Jews and their pawns many people who do not classify themselves as Jewish. Thus, for example, David Letterman and Lara Logan have been counted as Jews by those who tried to harass or attack them. For some Muslim antisemites, all of America is thought to be in the hand of the Jews. The violent risks associated with Muslim antisemitism will increase exponentially when Iran, a nation largely run by antisemites, becomes nuclear-armed.

At another level, the failure of the self-designated anti-racist and human rights communities to perceive clearly the nature of the contemporary antisemitic threat raises questions about the fundamental seriousness of these groups. Along with the Jews, genuinely moderate Muslims are the greatest victims of the inability to work realistically toward reform in the Muslim world. But the goals of those who fight antisemitism are, after all, likely to benefit everyone; these include a peaceful and respectful coexistence, a meaningful United Nations, an open and inquiring academic environment, an ability to perceive history accurately, and a capacity to call things by their rightful names.

Those who value human rights ignore Islamic antisemitism only at their own risk. As history has taught many times before, there never has been an antisemitic regime or movement that is otherwise reasonable or progressive. Muslim Jew-hatred, in effect, provides a litmus test to determine whether Western liberals are serious about their own values.

The Thinking Class and the Middle East: Pride and Prejudice vs. Intelligence

Michael Widlanski*

I. Introduction

From Franklin Roosevelt to Barack Obama, US leaders, policy makers, and analysts have shaped events in the Middle East, taking pride in American accomplishments. Is that pride justified, or, is there a pattern of a little too much pride combined with far too much prejudice, producing irrational policies, often with disastrous results?

While America influenced events in the Middle East, it produced academics and journalists who shaped how generations of Westerners and Western officials perceive the region. In the academic community, professors such as Edward Said of Columbia University and Noam Chomsky of MIT were particularly influential, while US journalism produced Fareed Zakaria, Christiane Amanpour, and Thomas Friedman.

With so many resources and so much putative talent, why was the picture on CNN, and the reports on the pages of the *New York Times*, so late, so skewed, and so out of focus? How is it that US officials reacted late repeatedly to major events? In short: how could America—its leaders, intelligence analysts, top academics, and journalists—have been so wrong so often—for over 60 years—regarding the Middle East?

How was the United States so astounded by 9/11, the worst-ever terror attack on American soil, which grew out of a decade of rising assaults on Americans in the Middle East? How could the Clinton and Bush II administrations miss the trend line? Even the US Department of State's annual "Patterns of Global Terrorism" report showed a clear rise in the number and ferocity of attacks, even though it was carefully vetted, for political reasons, to reduce embarrassment to the governments of Saudi Arabia and other Gulf states.[1]

Why did the US Department of Justice and the US Department of Transportation in the Clinton administration impose "anti-profiling" rules that made it easier to

---

* Schusterman Visiting Professor, University of California, Irvine; Lecturer, Bar-Ilan University.

[1] See United States Department of State, "Overview of State-Sponsored Terrorism," *Patterns of Global Terrorism: 2000* (Washington, DC: Office of the Coordinator for Counterterrorism, 2001), http://www.state.gov/j/ct/rls/crt/2000/2441.htm; see also US Department of State, "Middle East Overview—Saudi Arabia," *Patterns of Global Terrorism: 1999* (Washington, DC: Office of the Coordinator for Counterterrorism, 2000), http://www.state.gov/www/global/terrorism/1999report/mideast.html#Arabia.

hijack aircraft, and why did the Department of Justice impose rules that made it more difficult for the FBI and CIA to share intelligence data on potential terrorists?

The National Commission on Terrorist Attacks upon the United States, commonly known as the 9/11 Commission, discussed these matters, but its final report did not discuss them fully for political reasons. A penetrating and open discussion would have embarrassed former top officials, including one or two members of the Commission itself—a point later acknowledged by its chairman, Thomas Kean, and by its senior academic advisor, Professor Ernest May.[2]

One Commission member wanted a more public discussion. This was former Secretary of the Navy John Lehman, who later explained just how damning some of the material was:

> We had testimony … from the past president of United, and current president of American Airlines that kind of shocked us all. They said under oath that indeed the Department of Transportation continued to fine any airline that was caught having more than two people of the same ethnic persuasion in a secondary line for questioning, including and especially, two Arabs.[3]

Lehman felt that the "anti-profiling" rule had a critical impact, compromising security. "We're spending nine-tenths of the money we have on people who have 99/100ths of one percent of the likelihood of being terrorists, because we want to be politically correct. It's crazy." Such a rigid policy was an example of entrenched "political correctness," he averred.[4]

There have been more recent examples of not looking too closely at the Arab sphere or looking at it through rose-tinted lenses. President Obama, his top intelligence advisors, and many American intellectuals blithely believed in the Arab Spring, Arab moderation, Islamic democracy, and other mirages. Why?

Why and how could President Obama, Director of National Intelligence James Clapper, CIA director John Brennan, and other top officials believe in the moderation of Syria, Iran, and the Muslim Brotherhood? How could they ignore abundant evidence that these were *not* moderate forces? How could Obama and his aides possibly believe that new "elections" in Iran in 2009 would produce more "moderation," and how did they convince themselves not to speak out when the Iranian ayatollahs brutally repressed demonstrations and turned the elections into an authoritarian farce? How could Brennan, first as Obama's counter-terrorism advisor and then as CIA director, speak about jihad as spiritual yearning and not as holy war—its primary meaning in Arabic?

What can explain the way President Obama, who made outreach to Muslims a central policy plank of his administration, totally misread the leaders of several Islamic

---

2 The 9/11 Commission Report: Final Report of the National Commission on Terrorist Attacks upon the United States, Official Government Edition (Washington, DC: US Government Printing Office, 2004), available at https://www.gpo.gov/fdsys/pkg/GPO-911REPORT/pdf/GPO-911REPORT.pdf. See also Ernest R. May, "When Government Writes History: A Memoir of the 9/11 Commission," New Republic, May 23, 2005, 33.

3 Michael Smerconish, "Listen to Lehman," *National Review*, April 15, 2004, http://www.nationalreview.com/article/210278/listen-lehman-michael-smerconish.

4 Rod Dreher, "The Irrepressible John Lehman," *National Review*, August 6, 2004, http://www.nationalreview.com/corner/83581/irrepressible-john-lehman-rod-dreher.

countries? How did a leader who prided himself on knowing the Islamic world come to extol the virtues of Turkish Islamist leader Recep Erdoğan, who publicly spoke of leading a new Islamic caliphate, limited American access via Turkey to the military theater of Iran and Iraq, and helped Palestinian and Turkish terror groups assail America's ally Israel? How could Obama the democrat embrace Erdoğan as America's best friend in the region at a time when he was imprisoning more journalists than any other world leader?

Why did President Obama feel the time was ripe for a warm relationship with the Syrian regime just before Syrian despot Bashar al-Assad launched merciless attacks on his own citizens, leading to more than 250,000 deaths and more than five million refugees? President Obama's Middle East policies are his alone, but these huge American errors of judgment and analysis did not begin in recent years. They began much earlier.

President Jimmy Carter was caught flat-footed by the Egyptian-Israeli peace initiative in 1977 and, a year later, by the rise of militant Islamists in Iran. Carter's aides thought the ayatollahs were "moderates." Why were they so surprised by major developments? The short answer is that Carter and his State Department advisors did not have a clue about Egyptian-Israeli yearnings for peace, nor the strategic motivations and personal motives of Egyptian leader Anwar Sadat and Israeli Prime Minister Menachem Begin. Instead, they trusted the peaceful intentions of Soviet leader Leonid Brezhnev and hoped to impose a US-Soviet deal on Israel and Egypt at a Geneva summit. As for Iran, Carter's top advisors, including those at the State Department, believed Ayatollah Ruhollah Khomeini was a "moderate," and Carter's UN Ambassador, Andrew Young, actually called Khomeini "some kind of a saint."

Why did President Richard Nixon and top US officials hide how PLO leader Yasser Arafat ordered the murder of two US diplomats in Sudan in early January 1974? One answer is that many US officials felt Arafat was a potential intelligence asset and a "force for moderation"—much as British officials deluded themselves fifty years earlier about Haj Amin al-Husseini. The CIA and the State Department made similarly mistaken contentions about other Palestinian terrorists, such as "The Red Prince"—Ali Hassan Salameh, the man behind the 1972 Munich Olympics massacre, and Abu-Abbas, the leader of the *Achille Lauro* ship hijacking in which an elderly American, Leon Klinghoffer, was murdered.[5] How could they believe that Arafat would be a reliable intelligence source? To a certain extent, Nixon was influenced by the analysis of the CIA and the State Department, which cautioned against moving against "moderate" terror groups like Arafat's Fatah organization, which were erroneously believed to be moderate.

Why did President Ronald Reagan suspend shipments of fighter jets to Israel in 1981 after Israel destroyed Saddam Hussein's nuclear reactor and his hopes of obtaining nuclear weapons? Why did Secretary of Defense Caspar Weinberger consistently impede joint anti-terror operations with Israel, including the seizing of *Achille Lauro* hijackers?

---

[5] For an overview of these events and the evolution of US counter-terrorism policy, see Timothy Naftali, *Blind Spot: The Secret History of American Counterterrorism* (New York: Basic Books, 2005), 33, 70-72; and David C. Wills, *The First War on Terrorism* (Lanham, MD: Rowman and Littlefield, 2003), 147-52, 213.

In the middle of World War II, why did President Franklin D. Roosevelt link America's strategic interests and Middle East policies to a corrupt and weak Saudi ruling family?

The answers to many of these questions are linked to a few prejudicial ideas commonly referred to as Arabism, Islamophilia, and antisemitism or Jew-hatred. Let us define these terms and explain the problematic nature of what they represent.

II. Arabism

"Arabism" in this context does *not* refer to knowledge of Arabic or Arab culture. Such knowledge is more than welcome. The author of this article has proudly called himself an "Arabist" as well as "Orientalist." Arabism in this sense is not just beneficial but crucial for informed policy-making regarding the Middle East. For the purposes of this paper, however, Arabism is not a realm of area studies or specialization, because familiarizing oneself with or becoming an expert on a particular area is something to be welcomed. In this discussion, "Arabism" is a strong tendency to justify actions by Arab states or organizations not because they are intrinsically just but because they are Arab. It is used here, specifically, as "a pejorative for *he who intellectually sleeps with Arabs,*" as former US Assistant Secretary of State Richard Murphy once described it to author Robert Kaplan, who studied career Arabists in America's State Department.[6]

For the purposes of this discussion, "Arabism" refers to a simplistic or romantic indulgence of Arab nationalism, particularly of the pan-Arab kind known in Arabic as *qawmiyya.* This pan-Arab nationalism glosses over large non-Arab minorities such as Kurds, Berbers, and Armenians and sees the predominantly Arab states as subunits of an Arabic-speaking bloc—the "Arab people" or what is known euphemistically as the "Arab world."

Many American and British officials regarded the Arabs as natural allies because of the "free spirit" of Bedouin Arabs, who were sometimes referred to as "desert democrats." Another Arabist rationale was that God-fearing Arabs would oppose atheistic doctrines like communism and Nazism. British and American Arabists hoped the Arab bloc would safeguard Western interests, such as access to petroleum and the Suez Canal. Furthermore, they felt that an Arab bloc would be a bulwark, a physical and strategic barrier, against anti-Western extremism, particularly communism. The British championed the idea from World War I until World War II, hoping to groom a variety of local Arab leaders. When Britain's imperial presence faded, the concepts of Arabism passed to the Americans, who embraced them for another half century.

It was a simplistic, romantic notion cherished by generations of British and later American officials. One of the most famous was T.E. Lawrence, later lionized in the

---

6 The Arabist phenomenon includes romantics like Gertrude Bell, Freya Stark, and, of course, T.E. Lawrence ("Lawrence of Arabia"), as well as American diplomats who developed close ties with the Arab world. For a brilliant overview, see Robert D. Kaplan, *The Arabists: The Romance of an American Elite* (New York: The Free Press, 1993). Murphy's quote appears in this book (p. 7). Another fine and more recent work is Mitchell Bard, *The Arab Lobby: The Invisible Alliance that Undermines America's Interests in the Middle East* (New York: Harper, 2010).

epic British film *Lawrence of Arabia*. Britain hoped to install Prince Feisal of the Hashemite family at the head of an Arab bloc, leading a "Greater Syria," but this failed. For years thereafter, Hashemite rulers in Iraq and Jordan fought the stigma of being British stooges.

Later, the British hoped to use another pan-Arab leader, Haj Amin al-Husseini, as a kind of stalking horse for their interests in Palestine. This romantic notion also led to ruin. The British made Husseini a "Grand Mufti"—the chief Islamic jurist in Jerusalem—even though his knowledge of Islamic law was clearly inferior to the three other candidates for the post. British officials felt Husseini would be their pan-Arab puppet, and they were willing to overlook his incitement and attacks against Jews until he began to attack them as well. Amin al-Husseini fled Palestine and became the side-kick and chief propagandist of Adolf Hitler, aiding in the recruiting of Arab men and resources for Nazism from the Atlantic to the Gulf.

After World War II, British officials established the Arab League, planning it as a redoubt for pan-Arabism and Western interests, but the League was taken over by pan-Arab Egyptian president Gamal Abdel Nasser, who emerged as a strong ally of the Soviet Union. Nasser introduced a policy of "Arab socialism," a highly centralized and inefficient economic doctrine. In one fell swoop, Egypt, the most central and populous of all the Arab countries, became a client state of the USSR, a base for the Soviets on the Mediterranean. Just as Hitler turned the Arab nationalist to his cause, so the Soviets turned the pre-eminent Arab nationalists to their cause. President Dwight Eisenhower's secretary of state, John Foster Dulles, worked with Britain to construct "the Baghdad Pact" linking Iran, Iraq, Turkey, and Pakistan to the United States and Britain in some kind of military alliance. Secretary Dulles hoped to build a "northern tier" of pro-Western allies in South Asia to "contain" communism, but the charismatic Nasser had invited the Russians to leap-frog over the "northern tier" into the heart of the Arab world.[7]

The romantic preconceptions of Arabism—often promoted by officials with little or no real knowledge of Arabic or Arab culture—overlooked the cultural, religious, tribal, and even linguistic obstacles to real affinity with the United States and Western concepts of democracy. A hard look at the Arab sphere would have shown that, as individuals or as states, Arab society had a predilection for authoritarianism rather than democracy,[8] for endless border disputes rather than territorial stability, and for cultural and intellectual insularity rather openness. Arab economic historian Charles Issawi highlighted the Arab world's traditional lack of curiosity into the affairs of non-Arabs—a pattern that was substantiated by a series of major United Nations studies twenty years later.[9]

---

7 See J.C. Hurewitz, *Middle East Politics: The Military Dimension* (New York: Octagon Books, 1974), 87.

8 For the correlation between the harsh treatment of women and the tendency toward authoritarianism, see M. Steven Fish, "Islam and Authoritarianism," *World Politics* 55, no. 1 (October 2002): 24.

9 Charles Issawi, "The Change in the Western Perception of the Orient," *The Arab World's Legacy: Essays* (Princeton, NJ: Darwin Press, 1981), 363-72; UNDP, *The Arab Human Development Report 2002: Creating Opportunities for New Generations* (New York: United Nations Publications, 2002), http://www.arab-hdr.org/publications/other/ahdr/ahdr2002e.pdf.

A UN study entitled *Arab Human Development Report 2002: Creating Opportunities for New Generations* examined reading habits in Arabic-speaking countries and showed that the average Arab adult reads less than four pages per year and that the number of foreign works translated into Arabic by the entire community of Arabic speakers is equivalent to the number of translations in Greece. "Scientific expenditure in Arab countries was less than 0.5% of Arab GDP for 1996, compared to 1.26% for Cuba."[10]

These findings about the closed and backward nature of most Arab societies—some of which are even more backward than Africa in certain respects—is a horrible starting point for nurturing democracy, even a non-Western form of democracy. After all, many theorists of democracy note that building democracy is an evolutionary process that requires a notion of national sovereignty, a fairly large middle class, and a certain literacy level—elements that are often missing from Arab and Islamic societies. For example, Afghanistan is a collection of regions that each speak a different language and have never really had a national consciousness. Similarly, Iraq and Syria are plural societies that have been deeply divided along religious or clan lines for hundreds of years, including: Sunnis, Shi'ites, Druze, Allawites, Kurds, Christians, and Jews, among others. Like most Arab countries, Syria and Iraq only became national units after the end of World War I. Even the name "Syria," for example, is not as well-known or entrenched as the regional name al-Sham—the Levant: a name encompassing modern-day Syria, Lebanon, Israel, Gaza, Jordan, and the West Bank. Indeed, in the Levant and Iraq, people are often known by their towns or villages, such as al-Tikriti (from Tikrit) or al-Halabi (from Haleb or Aleppo), or by their ethnic background, such as al-Kurdi (the Kurd).

Even in Western societies like Britain and France, building the national idea and democratic institutions took hundreds of years. To expect a war-torn Arab state to become democratic in a matter of months is highly unrealistic. In addition, democracy is all about getting used to the idea of sharing power through models of election and separation of power, while most Arab-Islamic models show little of either trait.

Yet, too many American leaders and officials have been acting as if Arab democracy can be quickly implemented. The Bush administration succeeded in getting elections going in Iraq, but it was clear that maintaining Iraqi democracy required a tremendous US investment of money and manpower. When President Obama withdrew funds and forces, it was clear Iraq would revert to an older model of might makes right.

A tough examination of Arab-Islamic politics and culture would also have found a lingering tendency toward tribal behavior and concepts like "revenge," "group debt," and "family honor." US officials saw first-hand how tribal realities overwhelmed optimistic prognostications in Libya in 2012, when a US ambassador was assassinated, and in Iraq in 2002-2014, while trying to mend fences between rival communities. Over the last decade, US officials witnessed how these tribal concepts can erupt even when trying to manage border disputes, arms proliferation, or terror in Syria, Sudan, Sinai, and Yemen. Primitive tribal rule is a strong doctrine of group

10 See UNDP, *The Arab Human Development Report 2002: Creating Opportunities for New Generations—Executive Summary* (New York: United Nations Publications, 2002), 4-5, http://www.arab-hdr.org/publications/contents/2002/execsum-02e.pdf.

responsibility and group deterrence that does not respect the United Nations, the United States, or national borders.

Tribalism means "all group members may be called to fight in order to defend a member in a conflict, or to seek vengeance in the case of loss of property, injury, or death, or to pay compensation in the case of a group member causing injury to another, or would be a legitimate target for a member of the opposing group."[11] Being tribal means paying allegiance and debts at a tribal level, not necessarily to a municipality or a national tax authority. The traditional "Arabist" school of thought overlooks the enormous difficulties created by inveterate tribalism.

The pro-Arab sentiments among Western intellectual elites are not the special preserve of the left or the right, the religious or the secular. They have appeared across the political and cultural spectrum in the United States.

From the 1930s through the 1950s, Arabism, Islamophilia, and antisemitism were championed on the American right. These views were often linked to the oil industry, sometimes to missionaries in Lebanon and Syria, and sometimes to a sincere belief among US officials that America would lose influence among the Arabs and access to petroleum if it were to support Jewish statehood.

Often, these "Arabists" had little or no knowledge of Arabic or Arab-Islamic culture. They often adopted a romantic and overly optimistic attitude toward Arab intentions.

In recent years, some of these ideas seemed to be more strongly linked with the intellectual left, particularly with the ideas of two highly influential US academic voices—Edward Said and Noam Chomsky. Studying the Middle East is almost like trying to conquer it, Said has claimed, explaining that "political imperialism governs an entire field of study, imagination, and scholarly institutions."[12]

Various surveys have shown that, from the 1980s onwards, Said, the English literature professor, and Chomsky, the linguistics scholar, have been the academics most frequently cited on the syllabi of students studying the Middle East. Said's *Orientalism* (1978), which as practically become holy scripture for many Middle East studies faculties contends that Western scholars of the Middle East—orientalists—and Western inquiry into the Middle East are both part of a Western plot to overpower and subdue the Middle East, particularly the Arabs and Muslims.

For Edward Said, knowledge of the Middle East meant *control* of the Middle East. "To have such knowledge of such a thing," he avers, "is to dominate it."[13] By assailing orientalism, Said hoped to weaken the West and strengthen the East. Numerous events show how well he has succeeded.

One measure of Said's impact on Middle East studies in the West is that after the first fatal attack on the World Trade Center (WTC) in February 1993, Columbia University's Middle East Institute (MEI) convened a conference not to ponder terror but to pander to it. Professor Richard Bulliet, then head of MEI, did not examine the nature of the terror attack or the nature or identity of attackers but rather the purported persecution of the terrorists, who murdered six people and wounded more than 1,000. Rather than face terror on his doorstep, Bulliet discovered "a new

---

[11] Philip Carl Salzman, *Culture and Conflict in the Middle East* (Amherst, NY: Prometheus Books, 2007), 12.

[12] Edward W. Said, *Orientalism* (New York: Vintage, 1979), 14.

[13] Ibid., 32.

anti-Semitism against Muslims," driven by "the propensities of the non-elite news media to over-publicize, hype, and sell hostility to Islam."[14]

Months after the first WTC attack in 1993, Columbia's Bulliet expanded warnings against "alarmist" Islamophobes: "We at some point are going to reach a threshold where people no longer need evidence to believe a generic terrorist threat from religious Muslim fanatics." The Bulliet-Said vaccine against "Islamophobia" worked well. The 1993 WTC attack was committed by Arab-Islamic terrorists, but the Arab-Islamic aspect was downplayed and buried.

But the 1993 attack should have served as a warning for the attacks of September 11, 2001, because it could have been far more devastating. "Had they not made a minor error in the placement of the bomb, the FBI estimates, some 50,000 people would have died."[15] Ramzi Yousef, who planned the attack, later told interrogators he wanted to knock one tower into the other, killing all 250,000 people who worked in or visited the WTC each day.

This means the first WTC attack in 1993 could have been between ten to almost a hundred times more deadly than the 9/11 attacks. But this was not what troubled the head of Middle East studies at Columbia University.

Columbia student Barack Obama was influenced by the teachings of Columbia professor Edward Said and Professor Rashid Khalidi, both Palestinian activist-academics. Khalidi, who taught at the University of Chicago (as did Obama) later went to Columbia to become the first Edward Said Professor of Middle East Studies. Said and Khalidi are also alleged to have been members of Yasser Arafat's Palestine Liberation Organization.

Students of Said, Khalidi, Chomsky, and their disciples heard that the United States, Britain, France, and certainly Israel were terrorists, while the PLO, Hezbollah, revolutionary Iran, and Saddam Hussein were misunderstood Muslim leaders or Arab nationalists.

III. ISLAMOPHILIA

This paper uses "Islamophilia" like it does "Arabism"—not to describe love or knowledge of Arabic culture or Islam, not to describe a specialization in Islamic affairs, but rather to describe a conscious effort or unconscious tendency to overlook or minimize faults or problems in Islam, while substituting an almost-blind fealty to Islamic institutions, groups, or theology.

When President George W. Bush[16] or President Bill Clinton described Islam as "the religion of peace," they were being politically adroit, but they were also engag-

---

14 Richard Bulliet, cited in Fawaz A. Gerges, *America and Political Islam: Clash of Cultures or Clash of Interests?* (Cambridge: Cambridge University Press, 1999), 46; and Martin Kramer, *Ivory Towers on Sand: The Failure of Middle Eastern Studies in America* (Washington, DC: Washington Institute for Near East Policy, 2001), 51. Bulliet's claim that Muslims were victims of anti-semitism was an echo of Said's own rhetoric.

15 Jessica Stern, *The Ultimate Terrorists* (Cambridge, MA: Harvard University Press, 1999), 66. See also Dave Williams, "The Bombing of the World Trade Center in New York City," *International Criminal Police Review*, no. 469-471 (1998).

16 Bush's remarks are more understandable because he delivered them at the Islamic Center in Washington only six days after the 9/11 attacks, in a clear attempt to prevent reprisals

ing in Islamophilia, as they were stating something that was historically inaccurate. This is because Islam—from its founding in seventh-century Arabia to this day—is a religion that embraces the sword more than almost any other religion. Muhammad, Islam's messenger, was a general, not just a prophet. Muhammad won his place and his power by demonstrating success on the battlefield. His successors were also generals, and at least three of his four immediate successors, known as *al-khulafa al-rashidun*—the rightfully guided caliphs (deputies)—were assassinated in violent personal-theological feuds. As Muslims say, *sabil Allah fi-al-sayf* (the path of Allah is by way of the sword).

When Samuel Huntington wrote about "Islam's bloody borders" in his book *Clash of Civilizations*, he cited the frequency and intensity of conflict between Islamic countries and other countries, as well as the number of bloody conflicts between fellow Muslims.

"Wherever one looks along the perimeter of Islam, Muslims have problems living peaceably with their neighbors,"[17] writes Huntington, and he presents a wealth of statistics to prove his point:

> Muslims make up about one-fifth of the world's population but in the 1990s they have been far more involved in intergroup violence than the people of any other civilization. The evidence is overwhelming. ... There were, in short, three times as many intercivilizational conflicts involving Muslims as there were between non-Muslim civilizations.... Muslim states also have had a high propensity to resort to violence in international crises, employing it to resolve 76 crises out of a total of 142 in which they were involved between 1928 and 1979.... When they did use violence, Muslim states used high-intensity violence, resorting to full-scale war in 41 percent of the cases where violence was used and engaging in major clashes in another 39 percent of the cases. While Muslim states resorted to violence in 53.5 percent of their crises, violence was used the United Kingdom in only 1.5 percent, by the United States in 17.9 percent, and by the Soviet Union in 28.5 percent of the crises in which they were involved.... Muslim bellicosity and violence are late-twentieth-century facts which neither Muslims nor non-Muslims can deny.[18]

Huntington's work was prescient. It pointed to a historical pattern of aggressive probes by Islamic actors, particularly during the 1990s. Huntington's observations

---

or incitement against Muslims. In part, Bush said, "These acts of violence against innocents violate the fundamental tenets of the Islamic faith. And it's important for my fellow Americans to understand that." He added, "The face of terror is not the true faith of Islam. That's not what Islam is all about. Islam is peace. These terrorists don't represent peace. They represent evil and war." See Office of the Press Secretary, *"Islam is Peace," Says President: Remarks by the President at Islamic Center of Washington, DC*, September 17, 2001, http://georgewbush-whitehouse.archives.gov/news/releases/2001/09/20010917-11.html. Some former Bush administration officials, such as former Deputy National Security Advisor Elliot Abrams, feel that Bush's remarks were well intended but went too far. See Napp Nazworth, "Should Presidents Call Islam a 'Religion of Peace?' Two George W. Bush Officials Debate," *Christian Post*, November 21, 2014, http://www.christianpost.com/news/should-presidents-call-islam-a-religion-of-peace-two-george-w-bush-officials-debate-130014.

[17] Samuel P. Huntington, *The Clash of Civilizations and the Remaking of World Order* (New York: Simon and Schuster, 1996), 256-57.

[18] Ibid.

were carefully built on earlier findings by other researchers such as Bernard Lewis and Barry Buzan, but it was Huntington who sharpened them into a far-reaching synthesis that had tremendous strategic value. Yet, Huntington's work was ridiculed and insulted as "ignorant" by Edward Said, though he could not assail its underpinning, its research.

Two decades earlier, Said had responded similarly to another Islamist threat: the Islamic Revolution in Iran. The *New York Times* had given Said almost unprecedented exposure in a huge article in which he attacked scholars Bernard Lewis and Elie Kedourie, as well as the *New York Times* foreign policy columnist Flora Lewis (no relation to Bernard Lewis). At the time, Professor Lewis had found a copy of Khomeini's early work *Islamic Government*, which even the CIA did not possess. The *Times* refused to give Lewis space or even to report his findings. The *Washington Post* reported Khomeini's views, but the Carter administration treated the excerpts as a forgery or a hoax.[19]

It was amazing just how influential Edward Said had already become in 1979 (and how much damage he could do). The *New York Times* gave the English literature professor—a man virtually unlettered in Arabic—the kind of space it denied Professor Bernard Lewis, who was adept in Arabic, Farsi, and Turkish, and who had read Khomeini's writings. The *Times* even printed Said's attack on its foreign affairs columnist, Flora Lewis, less than a year after publication of *Orientalism*, a book without a single source in Arabic or Farsi.[20]

Professor Lewis tried to warn The *Times* and President Jimmy Carter that Khomeini was not a democratic reformer. "It became perfectly clear who he was and what his aims were. And that all of this talk at the time about [him] being a step forward and a move toward greater freedom was absolute nonsense," asserted Lewis. "The *New York Times* wouldn't touch it," recalled Lewis. "They said 'We don't think this would interest our readers.'"[21]

Revolutionary Iran became a vicious foe of the West and the foremost state sponsor of terror. The Carter administration was still looking for moderate Iranians even as fifty-two Americans were abducted at the US Embassy in Teheran. The Carter administration, the CIA, and the Iran desk at the State Department had made almost every possible error. First, they underestimated the weakness of the Shah of Iran, and then they misread the tenacity and far-reaching nature of Khomeini's anti-Western views. Some US officials felt the United States could win over Khomeini by apologizing to him for supporting the Shah in the 1953 Iranian coup that deposed Mohammed Mosaddeq. (This kind of thinking, we shall see, is a bit like thinking that Arab nationalists or the Muslim Brotherhood could be won over by apologizing for American recognition of Israel in 1948.)

---

19 For a detailed discussion focusing on Henry Pracht, head of the State Department's Iran Desk, see Dore Gold, *The Rise of Nuclear Iran: How Tehran Defies the West* (Washington, DC: Regnery 2009), 56-58.

20 Said referred to his critiques of Bernard Lewis, Flora Lewis, and Elie Kedourie on the question of Iran in his own book, Edward W. Said, *Covering Islam: How the Media and the Experts Determine How We See the Rest of the World* (London: Routledge and Kegan Paul, 1981), 84-86.

21 Cited in Bari Weiss, "The Tyrannies Are Doomed," *Wall Street Journal*, April 2, 2011, http://online.wsj.com/article/SB10001424052748703712504576234601480205330.html?mod=WSJ EUROPE_newsreel_opinion.

President Carter resisted the temptation to apologize, but Bill Clinton gave in to the itch in a public address by Secretary of State Madeleine Albright on March 17, 2000. It did not work. As Dore Gold observed, US officials had a disturbing habit of duping themselves about the ayatollahs and Iran and the depth of their enmity toward the West.[22] Some officials, like UN Ambassador Andrew Young, called Khomeini "some kind of saint." It was laughable that while Khomeini deemed the United States to be the "Great Satan," some top US officials saw him as a moderate or as a saint.

Twenty years later, on September 11, 2001, the *New York Times* and the US security community were again surprised by a massive Islamic attack on the United States. A month afterward, *The Nation* published a cover story by Edward Said, entitled "The Clash of Ignorance," that failed to cover-up Said's own ignorance. "Labels like 'Islam' and 'the West' serve only to confuse us about a disorderly reality," Said and *The Nation* told their readers.

Three thousand people had just been murdered in the worst attack on America since Pearl Harbor, and Said's self-serving conclusion was that "'The Clash of Civilizations' thesis is a gimmick like 'The War of the Worlds,' better for reinforcing defensive self-pride than for critical understanding of the bewildering interdependence of our time."[23] Exactly a year after this massive attack on the United States, on September 11, 2002, the Middle East Studies Association (MESA) formally bestowed a form of academic sainthood on Said by awarding its first annual Edward Said Prize.

Followers of Said at MESA tried to parody Huntington's work by using the word "clash" and "myth" in the titles of their articles and books. Shireen Hunter of Georgetown University penned *The Future of Islam and the West: Clash of Civilizations or Peaceful Coexistence?*, while John Esposito of Georgetown wrote *The Islamic Threat: Myth or Reality?* As the threat from Islamic terror was rising, both Hunter and Esposito suggested strongly that Samuel Huntington and Bernard Lewis were exaggerating the "threat." Similarly, Fred Halliday of the London School of Economics (LSE) spoke of "the myth of confrontation" between radical Islam and the West.[24]

"At times it seems that the West's attitude towards communism is being transferred to or replicated in the elevation of a new threat,"[25] writes Esposito, hinting that serious scholars like Huntington (who had been an advisor of Carter) were acting like Senator Joseph McCarthy in his communist-hunting days. "According to many Western commentators, Islam and the West are on a collision course. Islam is a triple threat: political, civilization and demographic," he continues, adding that both Lewis and Huntington stereotype Muslims, predisposing the Western reader "to view the relationship of Islam to the West in terms of rage, violence, hatred, and irrationality."[26] Of course, the real question is *not* how Esposito or Huntington or

---

22 See Gold, *Nuclear Iran*, 182-84.

23 Edward W. Said, "The Clash of Ignorance," *The Nation*, October 4, 2001.

24 See Fred Halliday, *Islam and the Myth of Confrontation: Religion and Politics in the Middle East* (London: I.B. Tauris 1996).

25 John L. Esposito, *The Islamic Threat: Myth or Reality?* 3rd ed. (New York: Oxford University Press, 1999), 218.

26 Ibid., 219.

Lewis or Said view Islam's relationship to the West. The real question is how Muslims—influential Muslims—like Ayatollah Ruhollah Khomeini, Sheikh Omar Abdul-Rahman (who was behind the WTC attack of 1993), Sayyid Qutb and Hassan al-Bannah (the chief ideologues of the Muslim Brotherhood), and Osama Bin-Laden (who learned from them) saw their relationship with the West. Esposito was not just another academic. He headed MESA and directed a program at Georgetown University's School of Foreign Service where many future US diplomats and CIA agents trained.

At least two CIA directors who figured prominently in the "war on terror" studied at Georgetown. George Tenet, who was CIA director at the time of 9/11, studied at Georgetown and Columbia. He was clearly not prepared for 9/11 or for executing the subsequent "war on terror." He had never been a field agent, and the only foreign language he knew was his native Greek. Tenet reached the CIA director's chair after being a consultant to the Democratic Party on arms control. When President George Bush first ordered the CIA to use drone attacks against al-Qaeda, Tenet responded angrily, "over my dead body." Tenet felt it was not CIA's place to use drones.

John O. Brennan, Obama's top counter-terror aide and later CIA director, speaks a little Arabic. He often sounds eerily like Obama himself—almost like his alter-ego—on Arab-Islamic matters. Like Obama, Brennan loves to dwell on the spiritual beauty of jihad or the sound of the Islamic call to prayer.

"As a boy, I spent several years in Indonesia and heard the call of the azaan at the break of dawn and at the fall of dusk," President Obama asserted in his major address at Cairo University, recalling what he called the beauty of the Islamic call to prayer.[27]

"While in college in the mid 1970s, I spent a summer traveling through Indonesia, where, like President Obama, I came to see the beauty and diversity of Islam,"[28] declared Brennan in a major policy speech at Georgetown University, setting the scene for one of the major themes of Obama's approach to the Middle East. One of the interesting portions of the speech involved Brennan explaining Obama's style and language—particularly his avoidance of the terms Islamic extremism or Arab-Islamic terror.

> Indeed, it was telling that the President was actually criticized in certain quarters in this country for not using words like "terror," "terrorism" or "terrorist" in that speech. This goes to the heart of his new approach. Why should a great and powerful nation like the United States allow its relationship with more than a billion Muslims around the world [to] be defined by the narrow hatred and nihilistic actions of an exceptionally small minority of Muslims? After all, this is precisely what Osama bin Laden intended with the Sept. 11 attacks: to use al Qaeda to

---

27 Office of the Press Secretary, *"On A New Beginning": Remarks by the President at Cairo University*, June 4, 2009, https://www.whitehouse.gov/the-press-office/remarks-president-cairo-university-6-04-09.

28 John O. Brennan, Assistant to the President for Homeland Security and Counterterrorism—Prepared Remarks for Delivery—"A New Approach to Safeguarding Americans," Center for Strategic and International Studies, Georgetown University, Washington, DC, August 6, 2009.

foment a clash of civilizations in which the United States and Islam are seen as distinct identities that are in conflict. In his approach to the world and in his approach to safeguarding the American people, President Obama is determined not to validate al Qaeda's twisted worldview.[29]

President Obama—like Edward Said, Noam Chomsky, and John Esposito—feels palpable distaste for the terms "Arab terror," "Islamic terror," "Islamist terror," or even "Arab extremism," but he has not really explained his feeling. Moreover, Obama and his top aides said there was no war on terror and that the United States had defeated al-Qaeda.

But events trumped ideology. A global terror surge made President Obama change his tone and his policy, *not* because he realized the error of his non-terror analysis but because the terror—including beheadings of Americans—made Obama look foolish and impotent. On September 10, 2014, the president announced a policy change after the successes of terrorists who called themselves Daesh, the Arabic acronym for the Islamic State in Iraq and the Levant (ISIL).

Yet Obama found it critically important to stress that he would stick to his terminology and his analysis:

Thanks to our military and counterterrorism professionals, America is safer. Still, we continue to face a terrorist threat. We can't erase every trace of evil from the world, and small groups of killers have the capacity to do great harm. That was the case before 9/11, and that remains true today. And that's why we must remain vigilant as threats emerge. At this moment, the greatest threats come from the Middle East and North Africa, where radical groups exploit grievances for their own gain. And one of those groups is ISIL—which calls itself the "Islamic State." Now let's make two things clear: ISIL is not "Islamic." No religion condones the killing of innocents. And the vast majority of ISIL's victims have been Muslim. And ISIL is certainly not a state.[30]

It is instructive to compare these remarks with the Obama-Brennan Islamophilic viewpoint that was stressed by Brennan only three years earlier:

Our strategy is also shaped by a deeper understanding of al-Qa'ida's goals, strategy, and tactics. I'm not talking about al-Qa'ida's grandiose vision of global domination through a violent Islamic caliphate. That vision is absurd, and we are not going to organize our counterterrorism policies against a feckless delusion that is never going to happen. We are not going to elevate these thugs and their murderous aspirations into something larger than they are.[31]

Three years later, part of al-Qaeda conquered three of Iraq's major cities, including Mosul and Faluja (where hundreds of US and British soldiers had died). ISIL—the al-Qaeda off-shoot—had declared itself a caliphate. So much for the "absurd"

---

29 Ibid.

30 Office of the Press Secretary, *Statement by the President on ISIL*, September 10, 2014, http://www.whitehouse.gov/the-press-office/2014/09/10/statement-president-isil-1.

31 "Ensuring al-Qa'ida's Demise," remarks of John O. Brennan, Assistant to the President for Homeland Security and Counterterrorism, Paul H. Nitze School of Advanced International Studies, Washington, DC, June 29, 2011.

becoming today's news. Obama himself had to admit that ISIL was a very successful off-shoot of al-Qaeda, which had apparently decided not to die or be "on the run," as Obama and Vice President Joe Biden had claimed in countless public appearances only three years earlier.

Another paragraph in Brennan's speech showed that it was personally vital for Brennan and Obama to show that they agreed with Edward Said and John Esposito and not, God forbid, with Samuel Huntington and Bernard Lewis. They viewed al-Qaeda and ISIL as non-Islamic, as tiny aberrations, even though ISIL controlled most of Syria and Iraq and was threatening Jordan. Brennan stressed that he and Obama did not believe in any "clash" with Islam, observing, "when we show that Muslim Americans are part of our American family, we expose al-Qa'ida's lie that cultures must clash. When we remember that Islam is part of America, we show that America could never possibly be at war with Islam."[32]

Like President Obama, Brennan spent a long time in Indonesia. Like Obama, Brennan seems to believe this gives him insights into the Islamic world. In fact, Indonesia is the world's most populous Muslim country, but it is certainly not a tone-setter like Egypt, Saudi Arabia, Iraq, Iran, or Syria. Indonesia is not a tone-setter because it is not an Arab country, and the Arab-Islamic world is traditionally led by caliphates or religious/political leaders who have emerged in places like Mecca, Baghdad, Cairo, Damascus, or Najaf-Karbala-Tehran. Like Obama, Brennan championed the idea of "engaging" Iran's leaders and finding the route to the soft part of their heart. Like Obama, Brennan was proved wrong.

> After nearly three decades of antagonistic rhetoric and diplomatic estrangement between the United States and Iran, the next president has the opportunity to set a new course for relations between the two countries. When the next president takes up residence at 1600 Pennsylvania Avenue, Iranian officials will be listening. The president must implement a policy of engagement that encourages moderates in Iran without implying tolerance for Tehran's historic support of terrorist activities.[33]

Brennan's comments in 2008 were like a strange mirror of Obama's own hopes vis-à-vis Iran and the entire Arab-Islamic world. It was and remains a "see-no-evil-in-Islam" view that was hammered home by John Esposito and Edward Said in the universities and also took root in the security community.

Sadly, wanting to engage the West-hating ayatollahs of Iran at all costs was not just a view held by President Obama and his terror advisor/CIA director John Brennan. Many other leading CIA and State Department officials who fit the same Arabist and/or Islamophile mold minimize the dangers of Arab-Islamic terror and prefer to see the kinder and gentler side of Arab-Islamic tyrants.

The US security community is always willing to supply an "intelligence expert" who claims that "they don't really mean what they say" or that "they will moderate, once they've been in power for a while." In 1992, the CIA's senior Middle East analyst,

---

32 Ibid.

33 John O. Brennan, "The Conundrum of Iran: Strengthening Moderates without Acquiescing to Belligerence," *Annals of American Academy of Political and Social Science* 618 (July 2008), http://ann.sagepub.com/content/618/1/168.refs.html.

Graham Fuller, said of the Islamist surge in Algeria: "It is time to demystify the phenomenon of Islamic fundamentalism and to see it for what it is: a movement that is both historically inevitable and politically 'tamable.'"[34] Twenty years after Fuller made his prediction, does it look like the Islamist movements are "moderate" or "tamable"? Many informed people would say no, but, in congressional hearings, James Clapper, Director of National Intelligence, used almost identical language to describe the Muslim Brotherhood as a "moderate" and "largely secular" organization with "franchises" around the Middle East. He might just as well have been describing McDonald's or Burger King, because he had just sold Congress a "whopper."[35]

Wishful thinking is the worst enemy of good intelligence analysis, and sadly the US security community is replete with such analysts. For example, Paul Pillar, one of CIA's top Middle East analysts, supported making a deal with Iran and also with Iran's ally, the blood-thirsty regime of Bashar al-Assad.

"Only a fraction of Islamic terrorism today can be blamed even indirectly on Iran,"[36] Pillar said in a book on terror in late 2000, in which he sounded more like a defense attorney than a counter-terror analyst. That was a misleading assessment even in 2000, when Iran had already carried out terror operations in Asia, Africa, South America, and, of course, the Middle East. Pillar's narrative included a superficial white-washing of Iran's role as the director and funder of Hezbollah, one of the world's worst terror groups, responsible for scores of American deaths in Lebanon and Saudi Arabia.

Pillar has been wrong on more matters than probably any other US intelligence official. He justified supporting Bashar al-Assad, said that Iran had no intentions of reaching a nuclear bomb, and argued that the terrorists who attacked the World Trade Center in 1993 were amateurs—what he called "ad hoc terrorists."[37]

Pillar, who knows no Arabic and never served in the field, was assistant to CIA director William Webster, deputy director of the CIA's Counterterrorist Center, and wrote the National Intelligence Estimate (NIE) for the Middle East in 2006-2007. The NIE said Iran was not pursuing nuclear bombs, when that was the only rational conclusion to reach for those who had followed Iran's nuclear development plans. Pillar later confessed that he wanted to prevent the Bush administration from attacking Iran.[38]

"Something akin to a normal relationship with the Islamic Republic of Iran can be envisioned, notwithstanding all there still would be to dislike and distrust about

---

[34] Graham E. Fuller, "Islamic Fundamentalism: No Long-Term Threat," *Washington Post*, January 13, 1992, A17.

[35] James Clapper, response to question at House Intelligence Committee hearings, February 10, 2011, available at http://abcnews.go.com/Politics/video/james-clapper-muslim-brother hood-largely-secular-12886575.

[36] Paul R. Pillar, *Terrorism and U.S. Foreign Policy* (Washington, DC: The Brookings Institution, 2001), 46.

[37] See Steve Coll, *Ghost Wars: The Secret History of the CIA, Afghanistan, and Bin Laden, from the Soviet Invasion to September 10, 2001* (New York: Penguin Books, 2004), 261.

[38] On Pillar's rationale for his NIE, see Tom Gjelten, "Iran NIE Reopens Intelligence Debate," *NPR Online*, January 17, 2008, http://www.npr.org/templates/story/story.php?storyId=18177103.

it," wrote Pillar in 2009.[39] Two years later, he was defending Iran's ally, Syria, as the Assad regime used tanks and snipers to kill its own citizens, working up to a full-scale civil war in which an estimated 250,000 were killed in three years and several million turned into refugees. "There is underestimation of how much worthwhile business could be conducted with the incumbent regime, however distasteful it may be," Pillar added.[40]

A few months before the September 2001 attacks on the United States, Pillar's new book on terrorism said a terror attack on the United States was less likely than being struck by lightning or falling and dying in the bathtub. Pillar writes prolifically, often sweeping disturbing facts under the carpet—such as Iran's direction of terror and atomic weapons building, the continued PLO assaults, or the implacability of Islamic terrorists. "Only a fraction of Islamic terrorism today can be blamed even indirectly on Iran," Pillar said in a book on terror in late 2000.

Today, Pillar is a lecturer at Georgetown University, alongside John Esposito, continuing Esposito's tradition of shining the best possible light on Arab-Islamic terror and tyranny. Esposito continues to be one of the most influential Middle East studies educators in the world, telling students, some of whom became or will become America's top officials, that the Islamic threat has been greatly exaggerated.

After 9/11, Professor Esposito, who had received millions of grant dollars from Saudi Arabia and other Arab countries, some of whose leaders aided terror, conceded Islamic terror was not a myth and modified the title of his book.[41] But Esposito could not admit that Islamic terror was a culturally-based or religiously-bred phenomenon with a special Arab or Islamic imprint. Just like Edward Said or CNN journalist Christiane Amanpour, he tried to show that there were just as likely to be Christian or Jewish terrorists lurking around the corner[42] and that Osama bin Laden was a victim of his upbringing.

"Master terrorist Osama bin Laden, like other religious extremists, is the product of his upbringing and experiences in life, of the religious world he inherited and which he reinvents for his own purposes,"[43] observed Esposito, adding "Muslims are our neighbors, colleagues and fellow citizens, and their religion, like Judaism and Christianity, rejects terrorism."[44] Of course, not all or even most Muslims are

---

39 Paul Pillar, "Iran and North Korea: Can They Be Deterred and Contained?," *National Journal* blog, June 22, 2009, http://security.nationaljournal.com/2009/06/iran-and-north-korea-can-they.php#1337516 (URL no longer valid).

40 Paul R. Pillar, "What Regime Change in Syria Would Mean," *The National Interest,* March 29, 2011, at http://nationalinterest.org/blog/paul-pillar/restrain-your-enthusiasm-about-syria-5089. At the time Pillar was writing, there was evidence that the Assad regime had gotten help from Iran's Revolutionary Guard and the Hezbollah militia to suppress Syrian demonstrations in cities across the country.

41 John L. Esposito, *Unholy War: Terror in the Name of Islam* (New York: Oxford University Press, 2002).

42 Christiane Amanpour's three-part documentary, "God's Warriors," tried to equate Jewish settlers and evangelical Christian preachers with Arab terrorists. It first aired over three successive days starting on August 22, 2007. Though generally not well received, it won a Peabody Award for documentary TV journalism. See http://edition.cnn.com/SPECIALS/2007/gods.warriors.

43 Esposito, *Unholy War*, ix.

44 Ibid., xi.

terrorists or condone terror, but a sizable number do. Surveys in Islamic countries done by the Pew organization prove it.

"Around the world, most Muslims also reject suicide bombing and other attacks against civilians. However, substantial minorities in several countries say such acts of violence are at least sometimes justified, including 26% of Muslims in Bangladesh, 29% in Egypt, 39% in Afghanistan and 40% in the Palestinian territories."[45] In a world of more than a billion Muslims, even 10 percent is a significant number, and here there are indications that the real support for terror may be higher still.

IV. Antisemitism or Jew-Hatred in the Security Community

Calling someone anti-Jewish or anti-Black or anti-woman is a serious charge, but sometimes one must make the charge and back it up. There is ample proof that antisemitic tendencies have been part of the US policy-making community and intelligentsia for years, sometimes influencing policy. From the days of Franklin Delano Roosevelt and his Department of State through today, a strain of bias against Jews and Israel is evident, bubbling to the surface at key moments.

For example, there is considerable evidence, which has recently become available, indicating that Roosevelt and several top State Department officials[46] stymied efforts to save thousands of Jews from the Holocaust, that existing US immigrant quotas were not filled, and that Roosevelt did not order any special efforts to slow the Nazi murder machine.[47] It is also clear (from documented conversations and letters) that Roosevelt held racist views (not just against Jews) and that he was molded in this matter by his mother, Sara Roosevelt.

"Roosevelt's statements indicate that he privately regarded Jews as potentially domineering, and often untrustworthy," notes Rafael Medoff. "Certain individual, assimilated Jews could be useful to him as political allies or advisers; but having a substantial number of Jews in the country, especially the less assimilated kind, was—in his mind—inviting trouble."[48] What Roosevelt and his wartime allies could have done to save Jews from the Holocaust is a matter of great controversy among historians. Some note that the US military was limited logistically, but those logistical problems did not stop the US government from mounting an operation to

---

45 Pew Forum on Religion and Public Life, *The World's Muslims: Religion, Politics and Society* (Washington, DC: Pew Research Center, 2013), 10, http://www.pewforum.org/files/2013/04/worlds-muslims-religion-politics-society-full-report.pdf.

46 The State Department officials usually blamed are Breckinridge Long and Sumner Welles, along with John J. McCloy, all of whom were close to Roosevelt. Their efforts to block movement of Jewish refugees stands in stark contrast to the activities of former President Herbert Hoover, who passed along evidence of mass murder early in World War II. This view is put forward in Arthur D. Morse, *While Six Million Died: A Chronicle of American Apathy* (New York: Random House 1968) and David Wyman, *The Abandonment of the Jews: America and the Holocaust, 1941-1945* (New York: Pantheon Books, 1984), among many others.

47 For the opposing viewpoint, see Richard Breitman and Allan J. Lichtman, *FDR and the Jews* (Cambridge, MA: Belknap, 2013).

48 Rafael Medoff, "Was FDR's Mother anti-Semitic—And Does It Matter?," *Jerusalem Post*, March 18, 2004. Medoff treats the whole theme at length in Rafael Medoff, *FDR and the Holocaust: A Breach of Faith* (Washington, DC: David S. Wyman Institute, 2013).

save some of Europe's great artworks.[49] Some say Roosevelt was hemmed in by antisemitism in Congress and that he felt the best way to shut down the gas chambers was to defeat Nazi Germany quickly. Yet, there is much evidence that Roosevelt could have done more—a lot more—despite lingering anti-Jewish feeling and nativist isolationism in the United States. He had a much freer hand, especially after winning his third election, and most specifically after Pearl Harbor. In addition, there is no doubt that some officials *and historians* concealed and falsified documents and discussions that show Roosevelt's racial prejudices and his anti-Jewish side in a very bad light.[50] The preponderance of historical material shows a very sad picture of antisemitism in America's highest councils—a prejudice that had fatal consequences.

Top allied military commander Dwight Eisenhower and President Harry Truman made sure pictures of the death camps became public, and both leaders said it was important because, otherwise, the awful truth of the mass murder would be denied. In the wake of the Holocaust, it is clear that even the genteel antisemitism of the upper Protestant society frequented by Sara Roosevelt and her son Roosevelt became unfashionable in public. But that does not mean that prejudice against Jews disappeared.

Antisemitism or Jew-hatred comes in many shapes and does not just consist of the killing of Jews. It also encompasses the view that Jews are inherently inferior members of society and/or tend to be dangerous to its other members. In the wake of the Holocaust, to borrow an ecological term, Jews were clearly one of Earth's endangered species. The birth of Israel was meant to help Jewish survival by creating a spiritual and physical refuge for Jews. However, even strong supporters of Israel must realize that criticizing Israel is not only permitted but desirable. All modern states need to be open to criticism. However, trying to destroy, hurt, or prevent Israel from surviving is, in the final analysis, also a form of Jew-hatred.

There have been many members of the US security community who disagree with Israel on policy questions, and there are many in the press and academia who critique Israel. This is perfectly legitimate and even necessary in democratic society. American officials such as Secretary of State George Marshall and leading State Department officials Dean Rusk and Loy Henderson opposed Harry Truman's recognition of Israel, believing it would harm US interests in the Arab world. Truman's

---

49 For a review of countervailing arguments, see Jack Schwartz, "Misreading History: FDR an anti-Semite?," *Haaretz*, July 5, 2013, http://www.haaretz.com/life/books/.premium-1.533801. Schwartz, an editor at the *New York Times* and *Newsday*, gives a good review to Breitman and Lichtman and largely dismisses Medoff. Jennifer Schuessler gives Breitman and Lichtman a favorable review but does not dismiss troubling questions. See Jennifer Schuessler, "Book Tries for Balanced View on Roosevelt and Jews," *New York Times*, March 9, 2013, http://www.nytimes.com/2013/03/09/books/book-tries-for-balanced-view-on-roosevelt-and-jews.html?pagewanted=all&_r=0.

50 Bedell Smith edited out a sentence at the Yalta Conference that was blatantly anti-Jewish, in which he told Stalin what Roosevelt had told King Ibn Saud regarding the Jews: "The President replied that there was only one concession he thought he might offer and that was to give him the six million Jews in the United States." One group of historians calls this merely an "ice-breaker," and not a true reflection of Roosevelt's thoughts or actions. See Brightman and Lichtman, *FDR and the Jews*, 301.

Secretary of Defense, James Forrestal, vehemently pursued the same line, contending that any support for Israel would alienate the entire Arab world from America. These officials, particularly Forrestal, were aware of America's need for petroleum. From the time of Roosevelt's meeting with King Saud in 1943, the United States had declared Arab petroleum reserves a vital American interest. Opposing Israel or Zionism on those grounds—what we might call "Oil-or-Israel"—may have been right or wrong analytically but is not necessarily a sign of prejudice.

Israel is a Western-style democracy, but its national interests are not identical to those of the United States or other countries. Policy-makers in those countries can make a good case why America should sell arms to Saudi Arabia or why Britain should provide financial aid to the PLO, among other matters. These decisions may be right or wrong, but they are *not* a priori evidence of animus against Israel or the Jews. As discussed earlier, decisions such as the Obama administration's backing of the Muslim Brotherhood in 2012 or its engagement with Iran in 2009 may be influenced by prejudices such as Arabism or Islamophilia but are not necessarily linked to antisemitism. They could, for argument's sake, be the result of foolishness or naiveté. Therefore, someone who backs such moves should not be called an antisemite.

However, when senior officials or academic analysts put forth factually preposterous theories—for example, that Israel or American Jews manipulate America and US foreign policy—then the antisemitic motif (the Jewish conspiracy) should be addressed. Professors John Mearsheimer and Steven Walt made precisely this claim in a major 2006 article first published in full in the *London Review of Books* (LRB), the same venue so favored by Edward Said.[51] The Mearsheimer-Walt motif, as two observers noted, was in the mold of classic Jew-hatred: "Accusations of powerful Jews behind the scenes are part of the most dangerous traditions of modern anti-Semitism."[52] Mearsheimer-Walt elaborated on their ideas in a book that had no more serious factual proof. "This is a conspiracy theory pure and simple, and scholars at great universities should be ashamed to promulgate it."[53] The Mearsheimer-Walt case was both unfactual and illogical, because if Israel and the Jews really did control US foreign policy, then how was it possible that the United States did so many things against Israel's wishes?

As former Secretary of State George Shultz concluded in a devastating response to Mearsheimer-Walt: "The United States supports Israel, not because of favoritism based on political pressure or influence, but because both political parties and virtually all our national leaders agree with the American people's view that supporting Israel is politically sound and morally just."[54] These words are especially telling because Shultz once worked for the Bechtel Corporation, which has large

---

51 John Mearsheimer and Steven Walt "The Israel Lobby," *London Review of Books* 28, no. 6 (March 23, 2006): 3-12, http://www.lrb.co.uk/v28/n06/john-mearsheimer/the-israel-lobby.

52 Jeffrey Herf and Andrei Markovits, letter in response to the Mearsheimer-Walt article, *London Review of Books* 28, no. 7 (April 6, 2006), http://www.lrb.co.uk/v28/n06/john-mearsheimer/the-israel-lobby.

53 George P. Shultz, foreword to *The Deadliest Lies: The Israel Lobby and the Myth of Jewish Control*, by Abraham H. Foxman (New York: Palgrave Macmillan, 2007), 16.

54 Ibid.

economic interests in Arab countries. Shultz added that "a number of examples can also be cited in which the U.S. rejected Israel's view of an issue, or the views of the American Jewish community."

The problem is that both Mearsheimer and Walt had strong academic reputations, and their book accordingly became a source for future generations, even though Mearsheimer marred his name further by endorsing the work of Gilad Atzmon, a known Holocaust minimizer and apologist for Hitler, whose book claimed that US Jews were responsible for spurring Hitler's assault on German Jews.[55]

However, when a senior US official—a president, a secretary of defense or state, or a chairman of the joint chiefs of staff—is shown to harbor anti-Jewish feeling, and is also shown to take anti-Jewish or anti-Israel actions, there is less need for a presumption of innocence. Defense Secretary Caspar Weinberger was a vehement opponent of Israel during the Reagan administration. Weinberger torpedoed joint US-Israel counter-terrorist operations, for example against the Palestinian hijackers of the *Achille Lauro* cruise ship in 1987.[56]

Secretary Weinberger went out of his way to interfere in the case of Jonathan Pollard, a US naval intelligence analyst who illegally transferred intelligence data to Israel. Weinberger sent a special letter to the trial judge, in violation of the plea-bargain agreement under which Pollard and Israel cooperated with US authorities, in which he provided an account of all the intelligence material that had been transferred. Weinberger's very unusual maneuver included accusing Pollard of "treason" and causing the deaths of many US agents. This led to a maximum sentence for Pollard, in violation of the agreement reached by US officials with Pollard under which Israel effectively ended the careers of two security officials tied to the Pollard affair.[57]

The truth is that US security officials, especially Weinberger, used Pollard as a fall-guy for the penetration of US intelligence by three different spy rings that had no ties to Israel, namely Aldrich Ames, the Walker family, and FBI counter-intelligence chief Robert Hanssen. US intelligence was slow to uncover those cases, which, unlike Pollard's case, involved a clear initial intent to help countries hostile to America (Russia) and hurt America.

---

55 See Jeffrey Goldberg, "John Mearsheimer Endorses a Hitler Apologist and Holocaust Revisionist," *The Atlantic*, September 23, 2011, http://www.theatlantic.com/national/archive/2011/09/john-mearsheimer-endorses-a-hitler-apologist-and-holocaust-revisionist/245518.

56 Assistant Secretary of State Richard Murphy, a former US ambassador to Syria, suggested letting the ship dock in Syria, where, he believed, Syrian leader Hafez al-Assad would surely capture the terrorists. Others in the State Department and the CIA consistently opposed the idea that the ship carrying the terrorists or the plane that later took them out of Egypt be forced into Israeli territory where the Israelis would gladly have captured them and extradited them to the United States. The CIA even lost track of the ship several times, but Secretary of Defense Caspar Weinberger specifically forbade asking the Israelis for intelligence help. Eventually, however, the Israelis tipped off Reagan's aides, and the ship was re-acquired by American intelligence and SEAL units. See Wills, *First War*, 147-52, 213. See also Naftali, *Blind Spot*.

57 Intelligence official Rafi Eitan and Israeli Air Force Colonel Aviem Sella.

Pollard himself not only got life imprisonment but was treated very harshly. He was denied permission to attend the funerals of his parents, and, more importantly, spent more than ten years in solitary confinement. Pollard's harsh treatment led former CIA director James Woolsey to publicly ask whether Pollard was not simply a victim of antisemitism. "I certainly don't think that it is universally true, but in the case of some American individuals, I think there is anti-Semitism at work here," Woolsey said.[58]

In addition, Pollard was repeatedly denied parole, despite the fact that his health was failing and that he was a model prisoner. Furthermore, CIA director George Tenet intervened to block President Bill Clinton's promise to commute Pollard's sentence in 1998.[59] All of this happened *after* the Ames, Walker, and Hanssen scandals revealed that Pollard had been blamed for the crimes of others.

Eight senior US officials took the highly unusual step of criticizing the most recent parole denial in 2014:

> The Commission's allegation that Mr. Pollard's espionage "was the greatest compromise of US security to that date" is false; and not supported by any evidence in the public record or the classified file. Yet it was this fiction that the Parole Commission cited to deny parole. We have learned that at the parole hearing, the government relied heavily on a stale, largely discredited, 28-year old classified memorandum written by former Secretary of Defense, Casper Weinberger, without any scrutiny or rebuttal since Pollard's security-cleared attorneys were denied access to the document and the Parole Commission is not cleared to review it. Mr. Weinberger himself discounted his original damage assessment of the Pollard case in a 2002 interview when he stated that the Pollard case had been exaggerated out of all proportion and that it was in fact "a very minor matter but made very important." The unreliability of the 1987 Weinberger document was known to and ignored by the Parole Commission. Worse, the Parole Commission ignored all other documentary evidence that mitigates in favor of Mr. Pollard's immediate release.[60]

Pollard was no hero. He deserved to be punished. However, he was punished out of all proportion to the crime of intelligence transfer to a friendly state. The United States and several of its allies—Britain, France, Germany, and even Egypt—have been involved in spying or data transfer affairs, but no other case has elicited

---

58 Interview with James Woolsey, Israel TV Channel 10, February 8, 2014, also cited in "Anti-Semitism Possible Factor in Pollard Case, Says ex-CIA Head," *Haaretz*, February 9, 2014, http://www.haaretz.com/news/diplomacy-defense/1.573178.

59 Tenet threatened to resign if Clinton commuted the sentence. Tenet subsequently denied this, but other officials, such as US mediator Dennis Ross, confirmed his threat.

60 Letter to President Barack H. Obama, dated November 14, 2014, from Robert C. MacFarlane, Former US National Security Advisor; Senator David F. Durenburger, Former Chair of Senate Intelligence Committee; Lawrence J. Korb, Former Assistant US Secretary of Defense; R. James Woolsey, Former Director of the CIA; Senator Dennis DeConcini, Former Chair of Senate Intelligence Committee; Angelo Codevilla, Prof. emeritus Boston University and Former Senate Intelligence Committee Staff; Bernard W. Nussbaum, Former White House Counsel; and Congressman Lee Hamilton, Homeland Security Advisor to President Obama and Former Chair of the Select Committee on Intelligence.

the same kind of extreme response, harsh sentence, and wholesale condemnation of the other state's security community.

German Chancellor Angela Merkel, for example, recently demanded and received a US apology for the bugging of her office, but neither side demanded the prosecution or extradition of any official. Similarly, when Egypt was caught trying to steal US missile technology, the matter was handled quietly: "The United States is expected to continue its close cooperative relationship with Egypt despite criminal charges against two Egyptian army colonels and three American accomplices accused of trying to steal U.S. ballistic missile technology, an Administration official said Saturday."[61] Weinberger's actions and the repeated actions of the US security community—including the Pentagon, the State Department, the CIA, and the FBI—raise tremendous questions about how and why US officials raise the question of the "dual loyalty" of US Jews as a regular policy tool. The Pollard case is the most extreme example, but the "dual loyalty" charge has been trotted out whenever some US officials feel the need to pressure Israel or US Jews on policy questions.

The "dual loyalty" charge figured prominently in the alleged "spying" by senior officials of AIPAC, the pro-Israel lobby group, in 2005. In fact, AIPAC officials had been involved in the usual Washington byplay of briefings and lunches with officials. After several highly publicized arrests and a huge build-up over four years, a US Defense Department official (Lawrence Franklin) who was sympathetic to Israel had his life ruined, but his sentence was dropped to time served of ten months' house arrest.[62] The trumped-up charges against the AIPAC officials were dropped: "A case that began four years ago with the tantalizing and volatile premise that officials of a major pro-Israel lobbying organization were illegally trafficking in sensitive national security information collapsed on Friday as prosecutors asked that all charges be withdrawn."[63] The sad truth is that officials tried to build a preposterous case against the pro-Israel lobby, AIPAC, perhaps as a way of warning them and pro-Israel officials about being too pro-Israel.

The US-Israel relationship has evolved greatly since 1948, from the time when the US helped boycott arms to Israel in 1950 to the time in the 1970s when it became Israel's main arms supplier, even airlifting weapons to Israel in the midst of the 1973 war. Anti-Israel attitudes receded publicly in the 1960s under Presidents John F. Kennedy and Lyndon B. Johnson. Johnson even backed Israel's retention of some of the land it had captured in the 1967 war. Under President Richard Nixon, however, traditional attitudes against Israeli power and "settlements" and in favor of not alienating Arab states resurfaced, as in the case of the Rogers Plan and Henry Kissinger's threatened "re-evaluation" of bilateral ties.

---

61 Norman Kempster, "Espionage Case Not Expected to Disrupt Close U.S.-Egypt Relations," *Los Angeles Times*, June 26, 1988, http://articles.latimes.com/1988-06-26/news/mn-8443_1_espionage-case.

62 "Nation Digest: Sentence Reduced in Pentagon-AIPAC Case," *Washington Post*, June 12, 2009, http://www.washingtonpost.com/wp-dyn/content/article/2009/06/11/AR2009061104280.html.

63 Neil Lewis and David Johnston, "U.S. to Drop Spy Case Against Pro-Israel Lobbyists," *New York Times*, May 1, 2009, A11, http://www.nytimes.com/2009/05/02/us/politics/02aipac.html?_r=0.

This menacing tone was strongly expressed by the Chairman of the Joint Chiefs of Staff, General George Brown, who stated on several occasions in 1974 and 1976 that Israel was a "burden" on the United States, and that Israel and US Jews were siphoning away needed resources.[64] In a major university lecture, he said, "We have the Israelis coming to us for equipment. We say we can't possibly get the Congress to support a program like that. They say, 'Don't worry about the Congress. We'll take care of the Congress.' ... They own, you know, the banks in this country, the newspapers, you just look at where the Jewish money is in this country."[65] Brown charged that during the 1973 Middle East War, the United States resupplied Israel more quickly than its own units. He also complained that American Jews were endangering the United States: "If there is another oil embargo and people in this country are not only inconvenienced and uncomfortable but suffer (they will) get tough minded enough to set down the Jewish influence in this country and break the lobby."[66]

Brown was not the only high-ranking US general to make such comments. "Earlier this year retired general Wesley Clark warned blogger Arianna Huffington that 'New York money people' are pushing America into a war against Iran."[67] General Clark was class valedictorian at the US Military Academy and West Point, as well as a Democratic Party candidate for president in 2004. "The Jewish community is divided," Clark added, "but there is so much pressure being channeled from the New York money people to the office seekers."[68]

An even more malevolent view was held by Admiral Thomas Moorer, chair of the joint chiefs from 1967 to 1970, who believed Israel had deliberately murdered US sailors when attacking the *USS Liberty*. Like General Brown, Moorer felt the Israel lobby controlled America's foreign policy. A baleful and conspiratorial view of Israel and US Jews has also reappeared among US presidents and their top advisors.

President Jimmy Carter's anti-Israel views became apparent after he left office, when he compared Israel to South Africa, saying that Israel had to choose between concessions to make peace or live with a South African-like system of racism.[69] Facing criticism, Carter offered a weak explanation for the title of his best-selling book, *Palestine: Peace not Apartheid*. Later, he also tried to act as an intermediary to and apologist for the terror group Hamas.[70] In truth, Carter's views were not a sur-

---

64 Spencer Rich, "Gen. Brown Again Cites Jews' Influence on Hill," *Washington Post*, June 29, 1976, A2. See also Joseph Alsop, "What General Brown Said," *Washington Post*, November 15, 1974; and Michael Getler, "Ford Scores General on Jewish Remarks," *Washington Post*, November 14, 1974, A1.

65 General George Brown, address at Duke University, October 10, 1974.

66 See "Anti-Semitic Statements by Joint Chiefs of Staff Chairman Provokes Widespread Anger Among Jews," *JTA*, November 14, 1974, http://www.jta.org/1974/11/14/archive/anti-semitic-statements-by-joint-chiefs-of-staff-chairman-provokes-widespread-anger-among-jews-whit.

67 Lenny Ben-David, "Echoing the Moans of Anti-Israel Ghosts," *National Review*, September 4, 2007, http://www.nationalreview.com/articles/222011/echoing-moans-anti-israel-ghosts-lenny-ben-david.

68 Ibid.

69 Jimmy Carter, *Palestine: Peace Not Apartheid* (New York: Simon and Schuster, 2007).

70 The author spoke to Carter in October 2007 aboard a plane returning to the United States after one of his diplomatic junkets.

prise. In 1977, while still in office, Carter planned a US-Soviet summit to impose territorial withdrawal on Israel, but Anwar Sadat and Menachem Begin pre-empted him with their own entente. Privately, Carter was known for his harsh views on Israel and US Jews.[71] Privately, he told Israeli leaders that he would not defend Israel against Arab attacks at the United Nations, even saying he might offer a US resolution of condemnation. In fact, Carter was the president who used the US veto most infrequently to defend Israel at the United Nations (once), and then only to block a resolution critical of the Camp David peace accord with Egypt. As for Carter's book itself, the former president offered a weak apology for some of his anti-Israel remarks, but many Jewish leaders do not regard them as sincere.

Still, Carter was not alone in his often tough sentiments toward Israel and Jews. Even Harry Truman was known to make off-color remarks about Jews and their demands of him, and Richard Nixon's tapes include several Jewish slurs. But neither Truman nor Nixon followed the remarks with actions or public statements that were prejudicial and had little logical or factual underpinning.

Vice President Spiro Agnew apparently harbored strong antisemitic tendencies while serving with President Nixon. After Agnew was forced to resign for corruption, he wrote a novel featuring a vice president who struggled against conspiratorial Jewish forces. Interviewer Barbara Walters asked the ex-vice president, "you have characters in the book talking repeatedly about the Jewish cabal, the Jewish Zionist lobby having too much influence in Congress," Walters asked. "Is this how you see it?" Agnew could not hold back, and he vented his harsh views for several minutes:

> Our policy in the Middle East in my judgment is disastrous, because it's not even-handed. I see no reason why nearly half the foreign aid this nation has to give goes to Israel, except for the influence of this Zionist lobby. I think the power of the news media is in the hands of a few people ... it's not subject to control of the voters, it's subject only to the whim of the board of directors.[72]

Even after being interrupted for a question, Agnew continued, "There is no doubt that there has been a certain amount of Israeli imperialism taking place in the world. There has been an invasion of the West Bank. The Israeli parliament is talking about settling on the Golan Heights, on the Gaza Strip."[73] Referring to an article in the *New York Times* about Israeli settlements, he said, "I feel that because of the Zionist influences in the U.S. these matters of aggression are routinely considered to be permissible." It is clear that Agnew ignores or is not familiar with the basic point that Israel captured the Golan and the West Bank in a war started by Egypt, Syria, and Jordan. Agnew is seemingly oblivious to the fact that the Hashemite Kingdom of Jordan occupied what it called the "West Bank" in 1948-1949, using it as a base to

---

71 Carter was said to hold a grudge against US Jews and evangelical Christians for deserting him in the 1980 elections. Conversation between author and Professor Kenneth W. Stein, a close collaborator with Carter at Emory University.

72 Interview with former Vice President Spiro Agnew by Barbara Walters, *Today Show*, May 10, 1976. See also "Agnew Vents anti-Zionist, anti-Israel Views on 'Today' Show," *JTA*, May 12, 1976, http://www.jta.org/1976/05/12/archive/agnew-vents-anti-zionist-anti-israel-views-on-today-show.

73 Ibid.

attack Israel for nineteen years, and that Syria used the Golan Heights to batter Israeli farms and towns with impunity. This combination of ignorance and/or prejudice is a major block to making sound policy.

Nor was Agnew the only American leader who depicted himself as fighting for all that was good against an implacable monster known as the Jewish lobby. President George H.W. Bush described himself as a lonely warrior against the Israel lobby in 1991-1992, pressing Israel not to respond to Iraqi rocket attacks. Bush reneged on a pledge to give Israel loan support to house a wave of immigrants. Secretary of State James Baker publicly scolded Israel like a child, but his other comments raised the specter of naked Jew-hatred: "Fuck the Jews, they never vote for us anyway," said Baker privately. In public, Baker told Israel to call the White House switchboard: "call us when you're serious about peace."

The United States and Israel have differed on many things, such as war and peace issues, arms sales to Arab countries, negotiating tactics, and other matters, but the two nations have also formed, especially since 1967, a working alliance that strengthened both sides. Still, there have been public and private disagreements in which the specter of antisemitism on the part of certain officials again rose to the surface.

Michael Scheuer was the CIA point-man in the search for Osama bin Laden in the late 1990s. Scheuer wrote several books that were personally approved by CIA director George Tenet, who denied approval to many other agents, several of them decorated veteran field operatives who were critical of CIA policy. The other books were either banned or heavily redacted. Tenet allowed Scheuer to write his books, under the authorship of "Anonymous," and to continue working at the CIA. Scheuer later admitted that his own book was approved because it served Tenet's purposes. In his books, Scheuer contended that Osama bin Laden was attacking the United States because it supported Israel. This is again part of the classic anti-Jewish/anti-Israel line that America's problems end and begin with Israel.

"To understand the perspective of the supporters of bin Laden, we must accept that there are many Muslims in the world who believe that U.S. foreign policy is irretrievably biased in favor of Israel," declares Scheuer.[74] However, this is logically impossible because the ideology of al-Qaeda is based on the ideology of the Muslim Brotherhood, which is directed primarily against corrupt Arab-Islamic regimes. Therefore, Scheuer's theory—"Israel and the Jews are responsible"—is full of holes in its very foundation. After all, the Brotherhood was founded in 1928, Israel in 1948. Israel, which was not yet born, could not have been the cause of Arab-Islamist ennui, though it was later to be used as a frequent excuse. Also, the radicalization of Sayyid Qutb, the main Brotherhood thinker and spiritual guide to other radical groups, came during his time in the United States (1949-1951) and his later years in Egyptian jails. America was not yet deeply involved in Arab affairs, and American policies toward Israel were hardly at their warmest during this period.

So, Scheuer's views had no factual basis. In fact, several researchers, such as Gilles Kepel and Raymond Ibrahim, who researched al-Qaeda's history and documentary record, have conclusively shown that Scheuer's contentions are completely false. After examining al-Qaeda's founding documents, Ibrahim wrote,

---

[74] Michael Scheuer, *Through Our Enemies' Eyes: Osama bin Laden, Radical Islam, and the Future of America*, rev. ed. (Washington, DC: Potomac Press, 2006), 20.

> This volume of translations, taken as a whole, proves once and for all that, despite the propaganda of al-Qaeda and its sympathizers, radical Islam's war with the West is not finite and limited to political grievances—real or imagined—but is existential, transcending time and space and deeply rooted in faith.[75]

Kepel et al., who checked al-Qaeda's on-line messages and pamphlets, wrote:

> These texts are full of references to the epic tales of the Prophet's [Muhammad's] companions and the history of the Arab caliphs.... In this literature, history is simply the infinite repetition of a single narrative: the arrival of the Prophet, the rise of Islam, the struggles to extend its dominion, and its expansion throughout the world. Each generation must apply itself anew to the task of this incomplete proselytism, taking up the original jihad to this end against a multifarious enemy that Al Qaeda's discourse reduces to the characteristics of the initial timeless enemy as stigmatized by the classical authors: the unbeliever, the infidel (*kafr*) the apostate (*murtadd*), and so on.[76]

Al-Qaeda, like the Muslim Brotherhood, began its terror by attacking Arab targets without any ties to Israel. But Scheuer, who knows no Arabic and never served in the field, was also unfamiliar with Arab history. He was familiar with and more interested in conspiracy theories. Somehow, the CIA director and the CIA put their trust in someone displaying such ignorance of the truth, such aversion to common sense, and such hostility to the one US ally with ample experience of Arab terror. This says something about the intelligence community's lack of intelligence and surfeit of prejudice.

Scheuer's wacky views should have gotten him assigned to less sensitive work.

> There is indeed an identifiable fifth column of pro-Israel U.S. citizens—I have described them here and elsewhere as Israel-Firsters—who have consciously made Israel's survival and protection their first priority, and who see worth in America only to the extent that its resources and manpower can be exploited to protect and further the interests of Israel in its religious war-to-the-death with the Arabs. These are disloyal citizens in much the same sense that the Civil War's disloyal northern "Copperheads" sought to help the Confederates destroy the Union. The Israel-Firsters help Israel suborn U.S. citizens to spy for Israel; they use their fortunes and political action organizations to buy U.S. politicians with campaign donations; and most of all they use their ready access to the media to disguise their own disloyalty by denigrating as anti-Semites or appeasers fellow citizens who dare to challenge them. The Israel-Firsters are unquestionably enemies of America's republican experiment and will have to be destroyed as the Copperheads were destroyed—by the people, after a full public debate, at the ballot box.[77]

---

75 Raymond Ibrahim, ed. and trans., *The Al Qaeda Reader: The Essential Texts of Osama bin Laden's Terrorist Organization* (New York: Doubleday, 2007), xii.

76 Gilles Kepel, "General Introduction: Al Qaeda, the Essentials," in *Al Qaeda in Its Own Words*, ed. Gilles Kepel and Jean-Pierre Milelli (Cambridge, MA: Harvard University Press, 2006), 6.

77 See Michael Scheuer, "How to Talk about Israel," *National Journal* blog, March 16, 2009, http://security.nationaljournal.com/2009/03/how-to-talk-about-israel.php (URL no longer valid).

V. Conclusion

America is the strongest democratic country in the world. It has legitimate interests in the Middle East. Making good policy for this region requires good "intelligence" in every sense of the word: knowledge, "street smarts," and data. American educators, journalists, intelligence analysts, and policy-makers need to have the tools to allow them to understand and even help shape events rather than being ambushed by them. Sadly, America's thinking class often appears to be dominated by prejudicial ideas such as Arabism, Islamophilia, and antisemitism.

Free Speech and Antisemitism: Comparative Approaches to Antisemitic Speech in the United States and Europe

Alexander Tsesis*

INTRODUCTION

The US approach to the tolerance of antisemitic propaganda differs significantly from that of many other democracies around the world. These distinct approaches are partly based on distinct comparative histories, with Jews having suffered significantly more intense and sustained discrimination in European and Arab countries than they have in the United States. Even today, the antisemitism emanating from those regions tends to be more menacing than its American counterpart. Despite these different backgrounds, I will seek to demonstrate in this paper that there is as much principled reason to regulate antisemitic speech in the United States as there is abroad.

More specifically, I will focus on the ideologically different approaches to free speech in the United States and abroad. United States politicians and academics primarily take a libertarian attitude toward the protection of speech. Emphasis typically focuses on the self-expressive value of speech. European and Canadian policies, on the other hand, tend to demonstrate greater historical sensitivities to the role of antisemitism in everything from social discrimination, to pogroms, to exterminationism and civic exclusion.

The argument in the United States tends to place great emphasis on the individual interest to make offensive statements and to downplay its potential to harm the targeted audience or society at large. European nations and Canada, on the other hand, are more likely to counterbalance the potential of incitement to negatively impact pluralistic democracy against any personal interest in its expression.

In the United States, public policy also tends to be deferential to speakers who attack Jews, their institutions, practices, or dignity. European and Canadian lawmakers are more careful to guard against the risks that advocacy will turn to action or will result in dignitary harm against the object of ire. Penalizing hate speech, they believe, helps to internalize lessons from the past to set necessary barriers against the aggravation of simmering prejudices. US history is not without its own skeletons, like slavery and Native American relocations, and the potential of destructive

---

* Raymond and Mary Simon Chair in Constitutional Law and Professor of Law, Loyola University, Chicago, School of Law.

statements turning to action against Jews and other minorities should not be taken lightly.

I will first discuss the differing approaches to antisemitic speech in a number of democracies. The comparative discussion will draw out the various rationales that national states have given for restricting hateful groups.

The intellectual sources of international and domestic compacts against hate speech are often premised on the widely accepted historical explanation of how Nazi invocation of antisemitic slogans helped the German leadership recruit, indoctrinate, and energize a broad following. In the United States, unlike other nations around the world, the Supreme Court has clung to an antiquated notion of speech that is more closely aligned with Social Darwinism than it is with historical reality.

I. International Norms

A variety of international compacts prohibit the *instigation* of unlawful conduct, group defamation, and violence against Jews and other minorities. Many, if not most, democracies around the globe recognize that hate propaganda helps perpetuate ethnic strife and poses a threat to the targeted groups. Laws against the dissemination of hate speech have been passed in many countries, including Austria, Belgium, Brazil, Canada, Cyprus, England, France, Germany, India, Israel, Italy, the Netherlands, and Switzerland. European countries are particularly sensitive to the potential for speech to turn into action, having seen the power of propaganda in the European theater of the Second World War.

Three years after the war, the United Nations General Assembly adopted the Convention on the Prevention and Punishment of the Crime of Genocide of 1948.[1] Passage of the provision against incitement to genocide was developed when it was clear that stopping instigation against Jews must be achieved to avert charismatic leaders from channeling popular ethnic hatred into collective discrimination, exclusion, or violence. The Convention was a unified commitment against genocide recurring, and the prevention of incitement was an important part of this pledge.

We know, of course, from events that followed, such as the Khmer Rouge's political atrocities or the Hutu perpetration of genocide in Rwanda, that the international community's commitment often fell woefully short of actual prevention. Among other obligations, signatory states agreed to punish, "[d]irect and public incitement to commit genocide." In the United States, immediate concerns were raised that such a demand would violate the First Amendment. However, despite its initial reservations, the United States ratified the treaty, albeit in 1988, and passed a genocide statute to enforce it that contains a provision against incitement of the crime of genocide.[2]

In 1965, following a series of antisemitic incidents around the world in 1959 and 1960,[3] the United Nations adopted the International Convention on the Elimination

---

1 Convention on the Prevention and Punishment of the Crime of Genocide art. 3, Dec. 9, 1948, 102 Stat. 3045, 78 U.N.T.S. 277.

2 Genocide Convention Implementation Act of 1987, Pub. L. No. 100-606, 102 Stat. 3045 (1988) (codified at 18 U.S.C. § 1091(c) (West 2012)).

3 Natan Lerner, *The UN Convention on the Elimination of All Forms of Racial Discrimination* (Alphen aan den Rijn: Sijthoff & Noordhoff, 1980), 1.

of All Forms of Racial Discrimination. Representatives at the United Nations expressed their concern about the reorganization of antisemitic and neo-Nazi organizations.[4] Although, antisemitism is not specifically mentioned in the Convention, article 4 committed governments to rigorously uprooting hateful messages that threatened fundamental rights and inter-group relations:

> States Parties condemn all propaganda and all organizations which are based on ideas or theories of superiority of one race or group of persons of one colour or ethnic origin, or which attempt to justify or promote racial hatred and discrimination in any form, and undertake to adopt immediate and positive measures designed to eradicate all incitement to, or acts of, such discrimination and, to this end, with due regard to the principles embodied in the Universal Declaration of Human Rights and the rights expressly set forth in article 5 of this Convention, inter alia:
>
> (a) Shall declare an offence punishable by law all dissemination of ideas based on racial superiority or hatred, incitement to racial discrimination, as well as all acts of violence or incitement to such acts against any race or group of persons of another colour or ethnic origin, and also the provision of any assistance to racist activities, including the financing thereof;
>
> (b) Shall declare illegal and prohibit organizations, and also organized and all other propaganda activities, which promote and incite racial discrimination, and shall recognize participation in such organizations or activities as an offence punishable by law;
>
> (c) Shall not permit public authorities or public institutions, national or local, to promote or incite racial discrimination.[5]

Other international agreements, like the International Covenant on Civil and Political Rights, which currently has 168 States Parties, also tied incitement directed against racial and ethnic minorities to hostility and violence.[6]

In a continuing effort to combat antisemitism, xenophobia, and other forms of racism, European nations have increasingly incorporated these international conventions into domestic law. Austria, where hooligans attacked a rabbi in August 2012 with Nazi salutes and calls for Jews to leave the country, enforces § 283 of its Penal Code.[7] That criminal provision establishes a penalty for jeopardizing the public order by inciting hostilities against religious, racial, ethnic, and nationality groups. The underlying purpose of the act is to prevent slanderers attacking "human dignity."

Some countries with a long history of antisemitism have laws against the sale of Nazi paraphernalia. These include France and Germany. In one widely publicized case, a court in France ordered a search engine based in the United States, Yahoo!, to

---

4 Ibid., 10.

5 International Convention on the Elimination of All Forms of Racial Discrimination, art. 4, available at http://www.ohchr.org/EN/ProfessionalInterest/Pages/CERD.aspx.

6 International Covenant on Civil and Political Rights, arts. 18-20, available at http://www.ohchr.org/EN/ProfessionalInterest/Pages/CCPR.aspx.

7 For the text of the provision, see http://www.jusline.at/283_Verhetzung_StGB.html.

block an auction of Nazi memorabilia from reaching browsers in France because such commercial activities were illegal there.[8] A different French court convicted Robert Faurisson, a prominent Holocaust denier.[9] Just as in the *Yahoo!* case, the latter case involved electronic content that had been posted on a US server. Because the antisemitic content could be viewed in France, the country's courts had jurisdiction to hear, adjudicate, and levy fines against the US firms.

Likewise, the Canadian Human Rights Commission ordered the white supremacist and Holocaust denier Ernst Zündel to remove antisemitic statements from his website, even though he operated it from the State of California. The Commission found it enough that Zündel's website was accessible in Canada to justify asserting regulatory authority needed to decide the case under Canadian law.[10]

Like their French and Canadian counterparts, German courts have also recognized democratic society's obligation to hold persons responsible for spreading hateful messages into Germany from outside its borders.[11] In 2009, Germany banned foreign Internet service providers from hosting websites promoting neo-Nazi ideology. Germany's awareness of the risk of inflaming long-established hatreds and adopting them into political rhetoric has translated into policies that counterbalance risks to democracy against the high value of speech. While freedom of speech is guaranteed in the German Basic Law, the right is not absolute.[12] Its criminal code includes a provision for holding anyone accountable for attacking the human dignity of others by (1) inciting hatred against particular segments of the population; (2) advocating violence or discrimination against them; and (3) insulting them, "maliciously exposing them to contempt or slandering them."[13]

The persistence of antisemitism and xenophobia in Germany, despite the horrific lessons of the Holocaust, has also led to the codification of a prohibition against the abuse of free expression, free press, teaching, the right of assembly and association, private correspondence, and telecommunications to "undermine the free democratic basic order."[14] In Germany, as in many other European countries, Arab Muslims have increasingly instigated and participated in antisemitic attacks. That was the

8 The Tribunal's decision in the original French, with an English translation, can be found at Appendix to the Complaint for Declaratory Relief, Yahoo!, Inc. v. La Ligue Contre le Racisme et l'Antisemitisme, 169 F. Supp. 2d 1181 (N.D. Cal. 2001).

9 See Russell L. Weaver et al., "Holocaust Denial and Governmentally Declared 'Truth': French and American Perspectives," *Tex. Tech L. Rev.* 41 (2009): 499.

10 See Georgios I. Zekos, "State Cyberspace Jurisdiction and Personal Cyberspace Jurisdiction," *Int'l J.L. & Info. Tech.* 15 (2007): 36.

11 In one case, the Federal Court of Justice found that Gerald Fredrick Töben, the founder of the Adelaide Institute, could be imprisoned once he arrived in Germany even though his Holocaust denial was posted on a computer outside that country. Bundesgerichtshof [BGH] [Federal Court of Justice] Dec 12, 2000, 1 Str 184/00 (F.R.G.). The content of Töben's website was accessible in Germany. Yulia A. Timofeeva, "Worldwide Prescriptive Jurisdiction in Internet Content Controversies: A Comparative Analysis," *Conn. J. Int'l L.* 20 (2005): 207.

12 Basic Law for the Federal Republic of Germany (Grundgesetz, GG), Art. 5, available at http://www.iuscomp.org/gla/statutes/GG.htm#5.

13 Criminal Code (Strafgesetzbuch, StGB), § 130, available at http://www.iuscomp.org/gla/statutes/StGB.htm#130a.

14 Basic Law for the Federal Republic of Germany (Grundgesetz, GG), Art. 18, available at http://www.iuscomp.org/gla/statutes/GG.htm.

case in August 2012, when several Arab men attacked Rabbi Daniel Alter after recognizing that he was Jewish from his skullcap.

In an attempt to ban Germany's far-right National Democratic Party (NPD), the German Interior Ministry has been gathering information about its speeches and rallies.[15] A committee set up by the Bundestag (German Parliament) in 2009 reported in January 2012 that extremists were increasingly using the Internet to spread Holocaust denial, antisemitism, and radical Islamism in Germany.[16] Following the completion of the Bundestag investigation, members of the NPD may be charged under a criminal statute that prohibits anti-democratic political parties from using "flags, insignia, parts of uniforms, slogans and forms of greeting."[17]

II. The United States' contrarian stance

The United States takes a substantially different approach to incitement than the European countries and Canada, whose laws I reviewed in the previous section. On the whole, the value of speech for robust political debate in the United States is no different than the importance of free expression in France, Germany, Canada, and Austria. What is different is the much more limited regulation of hate speech in the United States than in Europe. The US Supreme Court's jurisprudence has established doctrinal barriers against the creation of robust laws against hateful incitement. The Court's recent decision prohibiting judges from balancing speech against other societal values, such as safety, increases the difficulty of legislators seeking to regulate and provide redress against antisemitic and other ethnocentric incitement.[18] Current First Amendment doctrine denies the constitutionality of any regulations on the content of speech except those that the Court finds to be traditional forms of proscription.[19] In practice, this means that a variety of expressive conducts, such as Holocaust revisionism and outright denial, are protected under current First Amendment doctrine even though other democratic countries outlaw them.

The different approaches to inflammatory speech in the United States and abroad may be attributed to the differing national and cultural experiences. Europe is more aware of the extreme destruction that followed on the heels of overt antisemitism. The United State is of course not immune to antisemitism, as demonstrated, for example, by the quotas on Jewish admission to some Ivy League universities in the early to mid-twentieth century. But the degree of harm against

---

15 Hubert Gude and Holger Stark, "Praise for Hitler: Secret Files Build Case for Banning Far-Right Party," *Spiegel Online International*, Sept. 3, 2012, available at http://www.spiegel.de/international/germany/the-case-for-banning-the-far-right-npd-party-a-853564.html.

16 "German Anti-Semitism 'Deep-rooted' in Society," *BBC News*, Jan. 23, 2012, available at http://www.bbc.co.uk/news/world-europe-16678772.

17 Criminal Code (Strafgesetzbuch, StGB), § 86a, available at http://www.iuscomp.org/gla/statutes/StGB.htm.

18 United States v. Stevens, 130 S. Ct. 1577, 1585 (2010) (holding that "balancing of the value of the speech against its societal costs" is "startling and dangerous").

19 Brown v. Entertainment Merchants Assn., 131 S.Ct. 2729, 2734 (2011) (asserting that a litigant seeking for the Court to announce a new category of unprotected speech must persuade it that the "novel restriction on content is part of a long (if heretofore unrecognized) tradition of proscription").

Jews in Europe, with its centuries of pogroms and attempted genocides, is unknown in the United States.

The case of Canada is different. There too quotas on Jewish admissions existed in some universities, such as McGill. But it would be an unfair stretch to impute to Canada the same cultural antisemitism that instigated the enormous amount of disparagement, discrimination, and violence against European Jews over the centuries. Unlike anti-incitement laws in Europe, therefore, Canada's policy against the dissemination of antisemitic and other hate speech cannot be explained as a response to the shocking extremes of domestic depravity. The Supreme Court of Canada has rather explained that the legal curtailment of ethnic incitement is predicated on the country's commitment to democratic and pluralistic values, including the obligation to foster tolerance and human dignity.[20]

Contrary to the international consensus that hate speech poses a threat, there remains a widely held belief in the United States, which is particularly common among legal academics and members of the media, that the expression of animosity toward specific groups is nothing more than an act of catharsis. Allowing people to express their desire to harm a group, so the argument goes, is just a way of letting off steam that diminishes the risk of action.[21] This mistaken belief is also often coupled with the view that democratic institutions are furthered by leniency toward the expression of group defamation.[22]

While the concern that the regulation of hate speech will inhibit the free exchange of ideas is thought-provoking, its persuasiveness is belied by the accepted regulation of many other forms of self-expression, such as the posting of obscenity on the Internet, which by no means harms democratic values or self-expression.[23] Moreover, the pluralistic values in other democracies that regulate hate speech—such as those of Canada, France, Austria, and Germany—have certainly not been weakened by criminalizing incitement against Jews and other ethnic groups.

---

20 R. v. Keegstra, [1990] 3 S.C.R. 697, 751 (Can.) ("The derision, hostility and abuse encouraged by hate propaganda therefore have a severely negative impact on the individual's sense of self-worth and acceptance. This impact may cause target group members to take drastic measures in reaction, perhaps avoiding activities which bring them into contact with non-group members or adopting attitudes and postures directed towards blending in with the majority. Such consequences bear heavily in a nation that prides itself on tolerance and the fostering of human dignity through, among other things, respect for the many racial, religious and cultural groups in our society.").

21 Stephen G. Gey, "The First Amendment and the Dissemination of Socially Worthless Untruths," *Fla. St. U. L. Rev.* 36 (2008): 5 (asserting that the "safety-valve justification" of free speech is a pragmatic rationale that is predicated on the notion "that the First Amendment allows those who disagree strongly with the political status quo to vent their anger and therefore release pressure that could otherwise potentially build into a revolutionary conflagration").

22 Robert Post has raised the concern that repressing hate speech might "have the counter-intuitive effect of undermining democratic cohesion." Robert Post, "Hate Speech," in *Extreme Speech and Democracy*, ed. Ivan Hare and James Weinstein (New York: Oxford University Press, 2009), 136.

23 Jeremy Waldron, "Dignity and Defamation: The Visibility of Hate," *Harv. L. Rev.* 123 (2010): 1636.

Several legal exceptions that the Supreme Court has carved out to the seemingly categorical US restriction on the content regulation of speech further undermine the safety valve and democratic commitment arguments against the regulation of incitement. While easy access to pornography in residential neighborhoods may be desired by some segments of the population, the Court has held that government can nevertheless zone locations in cities against the introduction of adult movie theaters.[24] Participating in elections is deeply cathartic, political, and self-defining, and yet prohibiting electioneering within 100 feet of a polling place on the day of an election does not violate speakers' First Amendment freedoms.[25] And prohibitions against the deceptive and misleading use of trade names[26] and copyright infringements[27] are treated in the United States as protections for creative self-expression rather than impediments to democracy.

Historically, hate speech has nevertheless enjoyed First Amendment protections in the United States. This doctrinal stand has its origins in a Supreme Court decision, *Brandenburg v. Ohio*, which held that only imminently threatening incitement could be regulated.[28] This granted hate speakers much the same protections as legitimate political actors. Such a legal paradigm ignored historical lessons from around the world about the power of incitement; lessons that European countries internalized in the aftermath of the Holocaust. The evolution of antisemitic propaganda in Germany during the nineteenth century from a vocal political minority headed by Adolf Stoecker, who was the first German politician to successfully exploit anti-Jewish slogans in 1879, and Wilhelm Marr, who coined the term *Antisemitismus* (antisemitism), was not immediate. On the contrary, it took several decades of trial and error to effectively exploit stereotypes about Jews. It was only after slogans such as "Die Juden sind unsere Unglück!" ("The Jews are our misfortune!") and "Judenfreiheit!" ("Freedom from the Jews!") became part of mainstream political discourse that the openly antisemitic Nazis (NSDAP), Catholic Center Party (*Zentrum*), German Nationalist People's Party (*Deutschnationale Volkspartei*, DNVP), and Bavarian People's Party (BVP) were able to win a combined majority of votes in the 1932 election.[29]

The United State might not only have learned from the European experience of the power of repeated destructive slogans, which played such an important role in stereotyping and instigating evil, but from its own experience. In the United States, for example, anti-black stereotypes were essential to the positive representation and perpetuation of slavery, and the savage image of Indians was regularly asserted to justify land misappropriations.[30]

---

24 City of Renton v. Playtime Theatres, Inc., 475 U.S. 41, 54-55 (1986).

25 Burson v. Freeman, 504 U.S. 191, 206, 211 (1992).

26 Friedman v. Rogers, 440 U.S. 1, 15 (1979).

27 Eldred v. Ashcroft, 537 U.S. 186, 219 (2003).

28 395 U.S. 444 (1969).

29 "Result of Elections to the German Reichstag, 1919-1933," available at http://www.yadvashem.org/about_HOLocaust/documents/part1/doc6.html; "Election Results in Germany: 1924-1933," available at https://www.marxists.org/archive/trotsky/germany/elect.htm.

30 Alexander Tsesis, *Destructive Messages: How Hate Speech Paves the Way for Harmful Social Movements* (New York: New York University Press, 2002), ch. 1-4.

In one positive development, a case known as *Virginia v. Black*, the Supreme Court showed an increased recognition that society can legitimately prevent supremacist groups from using their visual symbols to intimidate the public. This was a significant advance away from earlier jurisprudence. From the late 1960s, the governing judicial doctrine was that burning crosses, which are commonly displayed at Ku Klux Klan rallies, are a form of protected speech unless they are likely to cause an imminent threat of harm to the audience.[31] In practical application, this rule from an earlier case, known as *Brandenburg*, made it impossible for law enforcement agents to prevent the gradual cultural infestation of antisemitism, racism, and bigotry of the type that took hold in Germany prior to and during the Nazi period. The hope was simply that more speech would lead to the realization that hate was grounded in false stereotype. But that was based on an aspirational conviction about the power of truth to make itself accepted in the marketplace of ideas, rather than the historic realities of how antisemitism becomes imbedded in cultural and legal norms.

In *Black*, the Supreme Court has shown a significant willingness to expand its understanding of the power of private hate symbols to intimidate audiences. While the Court's decision only directly addressed the constitutionality of laws prohibiting the intentionally intimidating uses of cross burning, there is reason to believe that its rule will extend to other symbols of hatred. I believe the *Black* rationale extends to the banning of other terrorist displays meant to intimidate the public through the display of symbols like the swastika or Hamas and Hezbollah flags. These can be every bit as threatening as the burning cross and should not be protected by the free speech guarantees of the First Amendment.

CONCLUSION

There remains a significant difference between how the United States approaches hate speech regulations as opposed to how European countries and Canada do so. In practice, there is little possibility of reconciliation in the near future. Until the United States becomes an equal party to international agreements prohibiting the disparagement of groups, Holocaust deniers and antisemitic bloggers will continue to exploit US territory to spread stereotypes and propaganda meant to degrade Jews and justify the commission of illegal conduct against them.

Besides the restriction of hate symbols, another approach that courts in the United States might find to be constitutional is the bringing of group defamation law suits. These already exist in Europe, as is clear from the successful prosecution of Holocaust denial actions, which seek to prevent and punish slander. Furthermore, the Supreme Court of the United States has long recognized that it is outside the scope of the First Amendment to "portray depravity, criminality … or lack of virtue of a class of citizens, of any race, color, creed, or religion" and to expose members of those groups to "contempt, derision, or obloquy."[32] This criminal formulation is

---

31 Brandenburg v. Ohio, 395 U.S. 444, 447 (1969) (espousing the principle that "the constitutional guarantees of free speech and free press do not permit a State to forbid or proscribe advocacy of the use of force or of law violation except where such advocacy is directed to inciting or producing imminent lawless action and is likely to incite or produce such action").

32 Beauharnais v. Illinois, 343 U.S. at 251, 266-67 (quoting 38 Ill. Rev. Stat. § 471 (1949)).

similar to that of the 1965 International Convention on the Elimination of All Forms of Racial Discrimination, which requires States Parties to "condemn all propaganda and all organizations" spreading a message of racial and ethnic supremacism.[33] The suggestion to return to group defamation litigation is contrary to the view of many US legal academics, who argue that later judicial developments have rendered the regulation of group defamation to be unconstitutional.[34] I have argued elsewhere[35] that their view is incorrect because the Supreme Court has referred to its group defamation doctrine as recently as cases decided in 2012[36] and 2010.[37]

As things stand, neo-Nazi groups that seek to elude European prosecution rely on US Internet platforms to spread antisemitic slogans.[38] It is high time to look for ways to bring the United States in line with other democracies to diminish the spread and effectiveness of antisemitism.

---

33 International Convention on the Elimination of All Forms of Racial Discrimination, art. 4, available at http://www.ohchr.org/EN/ProfessionalInterest/Pages/CERD.aspx.

34 See, e.g., Erwin Chemerinsky, *Constitutional Law: Principles and Policies*, 2nd ed. (New York: Aspen Law & Business, 2002), 978 (concluding that the statute in Beauharnais "almost certainly would be declared unconstitutional today based on vagueness and overbreadth grounds"); Cedric Merlin Powell, "The Mythological Marketplace of Ideas: *R.A.V.*, *Mitchell*, and Beyond," *Harv. Blackletter L.J.* 12 (1995): 34 (arguing that, after Sullivan, Beauharnais "is no longer persuasive authority").

35 Alexander Tsesis, "Burning Crosses on Campus: University Hate Speech Codes," *Conn. L. Rev.* 43 (2010): 635-43.

36 U.S. v. Alvarez, 132 S.Ct. 2537, 2561 (2012) (stating that "many kinds of false factual statements have long been proscribed without raising any constitutional problem").

37 United States v. Stevens, 130 S. Ct. 1577, 1584 (2010) ("'From 1791 to the present' ... the First Amendment has 'permitted restrictions upon the content of the speech in a few limited areas,' and has never 'include[d] a freedom to disregard these traditional limitations.' These 'historic and traditional categories' ... includ[e] obscenity [and] defamation...").

38 "Eyes on Appleton for Hate Crimes," *The Post-Crescent* (Appleton, WI), Aug. 12, 2009, at A1 ("American neo-Nazi groups, protected by the First Amendment, often publish material and host Internet sites that are aimed at European audiences—materials that would be illegal under European antiracism laws").

Antisemitism, Higher Education, and the Law

Kenneth L. Marcus*

I. Introduction

Ten years ago, while heading the US Department of Education's Office for Civil Rights (OCR), I issued new policy guidance announcing for the first time that OCR would protect the rights of students who were members of groups that bear religious as well as ethnic or ancestral characteristics.[1] This policy, clarifying provisions of Title VI of the Civil Rights Act of 1964 (Title VI),[2] responded to both post-9/11 anti-Sikh discrimination and the nearly simultaneous surge in American campus antisemitism.[3] Previously, OCR had declined to investigate cases involving Jews because the agency lacked jurisdiction over religious discrimination. Under the new policy, OCR would take such cases when ethnic or racial discrimination was involved, because the agency had jurisdiction over discrimination on those bases. This policy has been central to OCR's efforts to address the resurgent antisemitism that has affected many college and university campuses during this period.

Over the ensuing decade, OCR's enforcement of this policy has followed a ragged trajectory, as my successors initially declined to follow it, then formally embraced it, while seldom seeming to fully understand it.[4] Most recently, OCR has fumbled a high-profile trilogy of campus antisemitism cases, dismissing them in

---

* President and General Counsel, Louis D. Brandeis Center for Human Rights Under Law, Washington, DC. Tammi Rossman-Benjamin, Joel Siegal, and Aviva Vogelstein provided helpful comments. Kenneth D. Liebowitz provided excellent research assistance. Nevertheless, all remaining faults remain the responsibility of the author.

[1] Kenneth L. Marcus, Delegated the Authority of Assistant Secretary for Civil Rights, U.S. Department of Education, Dear Colleague Letter, *Title VI and Title IX Religious Discrimination in U.S. Schools and Colleges* (September 13, 2004).

[2] 42 U.S.C. §2000d et seq.

[3] The recent surge in American campus antisemitism is documented in US Commission on Civil Rights, *Campus Anti-Semitism: Briefing Report* (Washington, DC: US Commission on Civil Rights, 2006). See also Eunice G. Pollack, ed., *Antisemitism on the Campus: Past and Present* (Boston: Academic Studies Press, 2011); Richard L. Cravatts, *Genocidal Liberalism: The University's Jihad Against Israel and Jews* (Sherman Oaks, CA: David Horowitz Freedom Center, 2012); Gary A. Tobin, Aryeh K. Weinberg, and Jenna Ferer, *The UnCivil University: Intolerance on College Campuses* (Lanham: Lexington Books, 2009); Manfred Gerstenfeld, ed., *Academics Against Israel and the Jews* (Jerusalem: Jerusalem Center for Public Affairs, 2007).

[4] Kenneth L. Marcus, *Jewish Identity and Civil Rights in America*. (New York: Cambridge University Press, 2010), 33-36.

ways that do not engender public confidence in the agency.[5] These cases raise many issues, including technical issues ranging from statutory time bars to evidentiary requirements. In the end, however, they boil down to two larger questions that are entirely familiar to Jewish studies scholars and the Jewish community: "What is a Jew?" and "What is antisemitism?" During the 2004-2010 period, OCR was paralyzed by its inability to answer the former question, while its failure to resolve the latter has stymied it from 2010 to the present.

The agency's struggles with these two questions can be seen in a quartet of decisions that OCR dismissed on the same day in 2013 in what plaintiffs' counsel characterized as a "Saturday Night Massacre."[6] In these cases, complainants argued that university administrators at three campuses of the University of California (Berkeley, Irvine, and Santa Cruz) had violated the rights of Jewish students by tolerating an environment in which the students were directly harassed or subjected to a hostile environment. In all of them, the agency rejected claims that the university had violated the rights of students under Title VI. Although the agency does not explicitly address either question in its decisions, a close reading reveals that these issues have been at the root of its failure to pursue campus antisemitism cases to their proper conclusions. Readers may disagree on OCR's ultimate decisions in these cases. Regardless of one's view of the disposition of these cases, however, it is difficult to justify the reasoning by which OCR arrived at its dismissals.

II. Background

1. *The University of California at Irvine* (Irvine I)

In 2004, the Zionist Organization of America (ZOA) filed a complaint with OCR alleging that Jewish students at the University of California at Irvine (UCI) faced a hostile environment that the university had failed to address in violation of Title VI. ZOA alleged harassment of particular Jewish students who were targeted with rock-throwing, epithets, and threats. The group also described a general climate that had been poisoned by campus lectures and events, as well as the alleged destruction of a Holocaust memorial.[7] At my direction, OCR's San Francisco regional office opened what would become a lengthy investigation. Regional officials determined that a hostile environment existed for Jewish students, but they believed that Irvine had taken adequate actions to remedy this problem.[8] After my departure from the agency, senior OCR headquarters officials reversed the regional determination, taking the case

5 See Scott Martindale, "U.S. Dismisses UC Irvine Anti-Semitic Claims," *Orange County Register*, August 28, 2013, http://www.ocregister.com/articles/students-523287-irvine-jewish.html (reporting on the dismissals).

6 Joel H. Siegal and Neal M. Sher, appeal letter to Arthur Zeidman, Regional Director, and Zachary Pelchat, Team Leader, US Department of Education, Office for Civil Rights, Region IX, dated September 27, 2013 (emphasis omitted), 5.

7 Kenneth L. Marcus, "A Blind Eye to Campus Anti-Semitism?," *Commentary* (September 2010), http://www.commentarymagazine.com/article/a-blind-eye-to-campus-anti-semitism.

8 The regional director later recanted the latter finding, observing that subsequent events at Irvine demonstrated that the administration's actions had been ineffective. Marcus, *Jewish Identity*, 82-83.

away from OCR's San Francisco (Jewish) regional staff and reassigning it to a new team of (non-Jewish) lawyers with directions to close the case—but then directing the regional officials to sign the documents that the other lawyers had prepared.[9]

The new team drafted a decision closing the case for supposed "insufficient evidence"—despite what one legal scholar has called "an abundance of data" supplied by the complainant.[10] Specifically, OCR dismissed as time-barred ZOA's allegations that anti-Israel activists destroyed a Holocaust memorial and made harassing comments to Jewish students, such as "dirty Jew," "fucking Jew," "go back to Russia," "burn in Hell," "slaughter the Jews," and "take off that pin [bearing flags of Israel and the United States] or we'll beat your ass."[11] OCR conceded, however, that other claims were timely filed, such as intimidation of Jewish students by Arab and Muslim students, defacement of an Israel flag on a student's dormitory room door, and allegations of antisemitic speeches and activities stretching across annual anti-Israel protest events held from May 2001 through at least May 2007. OCR also found that some of these statements were offensive to Jewish students, but nevertheless concluded that they were inactionable because they were based on the students' political views rather than their national origin.

In a workplace discrimination lawsuit later brought by OCR's regional director, OCR leadership admitted under oath that they had been reluctant to enforce the policy that I had issued against antisemitism on the ground that they considered Jewishness to be only a religion and not a race.[12] For this reason, OCR officials were unwilling to move forward against Irvine or indeed against any university that had tolerated a hostile environment for Jewish students. At the same time, they were reluctant to reveal their views publicly, for fear of the public backlash that they might face, especially during the time when I served as Staff Director of the US Commission on Civil Rights and conducted a public education campaign on campus antisemitism.[13]

In a series of publications during and after my tenure at the Commission, I made the case for why Jews must be considered protected by the statute that prohibits discrimination on the basis of race or national origin but not religion.[14] Finally, in 2010, at the behest of a number of Jewish organizations, including my own, the Obama administration's Department of Justice and OCR formally embraced my 2004 policy and agreed to enforce Title VI against antisemitic incidents.[15] Nevertheless, on

---

9 Ibid., 83-87.

10 Kenneth Lasson, "In an Academic Voice: Antisemitism and Academy Bias," *Journal for the Study of Antisemitism* 3, no. 2 (2001): 349, 401.

11 Letter from Charles R. Love, Program Manager, US Department of Education, Office for Civil Rights, Region IX, to Dr. Michael V. Drake, Chancellor, University of California, Irvine, *In re* OCR Case No. 09-05-2013 (November 30, 2007) (hereinafter *In re* University of California at Irvine, OCR Case No. 09-05-2013), available at http://www.ocregister.com/newsimages/news/2007/12/OCR_Report_120507-Z05145157-0001.pdf, p. 2.

12 Marcus, *Jewish Identity*, 23-25.

13 Ibid., 92-95.

14 See ibid.; Kenneth L. Marcus, "Anti-Zionism as Racism: Campus Anti-Semitism and the Civil Rights Act of 1964," *William & Mary Bill of Rights Journal* 15, no. 3 (2007): 837; and Kenneth L. Marcus, "Jurisprudence of the New Anti-Semitism," *Wake Forest Law Review* 44 (2009): 101.

15 Kenneth L. Marcus, "The New OCR Anti-Semitism Policy." *Journal for the Study of Antisemitism* 2 (2011): 9.

August 21, 2013, Deputy Assistant Secretary of Education for Enforcement Sandra Battle affirmed the regional office's dismissal of *Irvine I.* She did so in a short, cursory opinion containing no reasoning or analysis.[16] In the absence of contrary reasoning, Deputy Assistant Secretary Battle's August 2013 ruling appeared to endorse the 2007 regional determination, which we now know was premised on the view that Jewish students should receive not protection under Title VI. This has been a source of some confusion, since it stands in direct conflict with views that Battle's superiors had issued just a few years before.

2. *The University of California at Irvine redux* (Irvine II)

While OCR was investigating *Irvine I,* ZOA provided federal investigators with evidence of continuing problems on the Irvine campus. For arcane administrative reasons, the agencies combined these subsequent allegations into a second case *(Irvine II). Irvine II* contained claims that Jewish students were targeted for adverse treatment, or otherwise subjected to a hostile environment, based on their Jewish identity in nine discrete incidents. Some of them do not amount to much. For example, one Jewish student reports that friendship with Muslim students in her dormitory frayed after they disagreed about a lecture by historian Daniel Pipes. As the argument coarsened, the students exchanged accusations of "racism" and "antisemitism." When the Jewish student stopped speaking to the Muslim students, the Muslims stopped speaking to her. This led to tensions and "unwelcoming looks." The Jewish student asked to be moved to another dormitory, and the university complied. OCR unsurprisingly found the unwelcoming looks to be insufficient basis for a federal lawsuit.

Other incidents were rougher. Muslim students presented an event entitled "Israel: Apartheid Resurrected." Jewish students argued that this spectacle exacerbated the campus's anti-Jewish atmosphere, and they were probably correct. OCR countered that even "rough and discordant expressions" are protected by the First Amendment's guaranty of free speech.[17] This is also correct.[18] But the ugly side of the event came out when a rabbi came to attend and was loudly taunted, "Don't you have somebody's money to steal?"[19] This slur reflects the deeper, age-old anti-Jewish stereotypes underlying much anti-Israel agitation. OCR analyzed this statement, finding it to be "offensive." At the same time, however, the agency found rather that it was not, standing on its own, sufficiently serious to justify the finding of a violation by Irvine.

---

16 Sandra Battle, Deputy Assistant Secretary for Enforcement, US Department of Education, Opinion Letter to Susan B. Tuchman, Zionist Organization of America, dated August 21, 2013 (denying ZOA appeal).

17 *In re* University of California at Irvine, 6.

18 This does not mean, however, that the Muslim students' right to engage in such speech abrogated Irvine's duty to mitigate a hostile environment for Jewish students. That is to say, if the speech contributed to a hostile environment for Jewish students, then the university was obligated to address it in some manner. There are many effective responses that administrators may provide to hurtful and uncivil campus discourse short of punishing speech that is protected under the Constitution. See Kenneth L. Marcus, "Best Practices Guide for Combating Campus Anti-Semitism and Anti-Israelism" (Washington, DC: The Louis D. Brandeis Center for Human Rights Under Law), http://www.brandeiscenter.com/images/uploads/practices/guide_02.pdf.

19 *In re* University of California at Irvine, 4.

This finding was odd, since the allegation unquestionably was not standing on its own. Rather, it was included with a myriad of other troubling allegations not only in *Irvine II* but also in the *Irvine I* complaint from which it had been artificially separated. OCR gave no reason for why the incident should be viewed in isolation when it was alleged to be part of a larger pattern of anti-Jewish incidents.

In other incidents, anti-Israel activists did not resort to explicit anti-Jewish stereotypes, but their actions nevertheless reflected anti-Jewish hostility. For example, several students repeatedly cursed a female Jewish student in obscene terms and called her "whore" and "slut" for wearing a pro-Israel t-shirt to an event sponsored by the Muslim Student Union (MSU) and expressing disagreement with the Union's invited speaker. Similarly, a Muslim student repeatedly pushed a camera in the face of a Jewish Israeli-American student reporter, who wore an "I love Israel" t-shirt, as she tried to interview Ward Churchill. In such cases, questions always arise as to whether the actions are motivated by anti-Jewish or political animus. Here the facts were somewhat murky. The student told OCR that MSU members often placed cameras in the faces of individuals with "pro-Israel or politically conservative views" in order to intimidate them.

During the course of its investigation, OCR found copious evidence of severe problems at Irvine, over a period over several years, that had led some students to transfer to other schools, to avoid certain classes, to curtail involvement with the Jewish community, and to eschew clothing or jewelry that would identify them as Jewish.[20] As with *Irvine I*, most of the incidents involved alleged harm to Jewish students who support the State of Israel by non-Jewish students and non-students who oppose it. Nevertheless, on August 19, 2013, OCR dismissed this case as well. The agency rejected each claim for slightly different reasons, but its predominant rationale was that it had found insufficient evidence to determine that the students were subjected to a hostile environment based on their Jewishness or, in OCR's terminology, their "national origin."[21]

3. *The University of California at Santa Cruz*

In 2009, University of California at Santa Cruz (UCSC) lecturer Tammi Rossman-Benjamin complained to OCR that UCSC had created a hostile environment for Jewish students. Rossman-Benjamin based her complaint on university-sponsored public events at which strongly anti-Israel academic rhetoric had predominated, some of which Rossman-Benjamin argued was both hurtful to Jewish students and "antisemitic" within the meaning of the EUMC Working Definition of Antisemitism. These events included a January 2009 event entitled, "A Pulse on Palestine," featuring a film and panel discussion and a scheduled March 2009 "teach-in," entitled "Understanding Gaza." After a lengthy intake process, OCR opened up an investigation into Rossman-Benjamin's claims.

---

20 Kenneth L. Marcus, "Whitewashing Antisemitism at the University of California Irvine," *Journal for the Study of Antisemitism* 2, no. 1 (2010): 13-48, http://www.jsantisemitism.org/pdf/jsa_2-1.pdf.

21 Zachary Pelchat, Team Leader, US Department of Education, Office for Civil Rights, Region IX, case closure letter to Susan Tuchman, Zionist Organization of America, dated August 19, 2013.

In an irregular move, OCR investigators sent a "survey" to 87 of the 91 students who had signed a petition protesting the "Pulse on Palestine" event. Only four students responded to the survey. Two said that they believe a hostile environment exists for Jewish students at UCSC, and two said that they do not believe a hostile environment exists.[22] OCR also interviewed three students, including two of these respondents, and they provided inconsistent views of the UCSC climate.[23]

The survey was remarkable for many reasons, but especially because it did not address the applicable legal standards for a hostile environment, namely whether severe or pervasive harassment existed for the targeted Jewish students. The appropriate inquiry in such cases is whether the students actually believed they were harassed (the Subjective Test) and whether a reasonable person in their position would consider that a hostile environment had formed (the Objective Test). OCR and the Department of Justice's Civil Rights Division most prominently reiterated these standards in an agreement that they reached on May 9, 2013, with the University of Montana resolving a sexual harassment case that they announced should be a "blueprint" for other institutions.[24]

OCR's survey does not address either question, substituting a Majority Rule test under which the agency apparently substitutes the view of a majority of similarly situated students for the Subjective and Objective Tests that are required by OCR policy. Aside from its disregard for OCR policy, the agency's survey does not seem to justify its conclusions. We cannot draw any inferences about why so few students responded, nor is it clear whether the paltry response was unusual. The results have no statistical significance, so the better practice would be to disregard it altogether. Nevertheless, to the extent that OCR was considering the results of the survey at all, the fact that half of the respondents believe there to be a hostile environment for Jewish students at UCSC surely does not support OCR's final disposition.

OCR dismissed this case on August 19, 2013, finding that the facts did not warrant finding a violation.[25] OCR found that all of the events amounted to "expression on matters of public concern directed to the University community."[26] OCR observed that "exposure to such rough and discordant expressions, even when personally offensive and hurtful, is a circumstance that a reasonable student in higher education may experience."[27] For this reason, the agency found that the

22 Ibid., 2-3.

23 OCR also took note of the mix of campus events relating to Judaism, Israel, Palestine, and/or Islam, and was evidently influenced by the fact that twenty-seven were sponsored or co-sponsored by Jewish student or faculty groups, while fifteen were sponsored or co-sponsored by Muslim groups. The fact that Jewish organizations sponsored many events regarding Israel or Judaism is utterly irrelevant; after all, Rossman-Benjamin has alleged that Jewish academics contributed to the hostile environment for Jewish students, and OCR does not address whether the Jewish-sponsored events had any impact, one way or the other, with respect to the campus climate.

24 DOJ Case No. DJ 169-44-9, OCR Case No. 10126001, 9 (May 9, 2013), http://www.justice.gov/opa/documents/um-ltr-findings.pdf.

25 Zachary Pelchat, Team Leader, US Department of Education, Office for Civil Rights, Region IX, case closure letter to Tammi Rossman-Benjamin, dated August 19, 2013, *In re* OCR Case No. 09-09-2145.

26 Ibid., 3.

27 Ibid.

events "do not constitute actionable harassment."[28] OCR's regional director later affirmed the dismissal of this case as well.

4. *The University of California at Berkeley*

In March 2010, during the so-called "Israel Apartheid Week," Jewish undergraduate student Jessica Felber stood in Sproul Plaza at the University of California at Berkeley holding a sign that read, "Israel wants peace." Provoked by her effrontery, Berkeley Students for Justice in Palestine leader Husam Zakharia allegedly rammed a shopping cart filled with heavy objects into Felber, causing her physical injuries that required medical attention. On another occasion Zakharia had spit at Felber, a pro-Israel activist, and yelled that she was "disgusting." Brian Maissy, a disabled student, was blocked from passage through the Berkeley campus by anti-Israel activists conducting a mock checkpoint protest during the so-called "Israel Apartheid Week."

Felber and Maissy filed a complaint with the US District Court for the Northern District of California, arguing inter alia that Berkeley had tolerated a hostile environment for Jewish students. In addition to their own personal experiences, they cited various other incidents, such as a swastika drawn on a Jewish student's dormitory room door and statements allegedly made against Jews during a student senate debate over a proposed resolution to divest university funds from companies that support certain activities by Israel's military.

The court partially dismissed Felber and Maissey's complaint with leave to amend, holding that much of the protesters' activity was protected under the First Amendment.[29] The court also found that the plaintiffs were not personally harmed by some of the conduct, that they were not denied meaningful educational benefits, and that the university had not acted with "deliberate indifference" to their plight.[30] The students re-filed and then settled their case, as Berkeley adopted a couple of policy changes regulating the place and manner of protest activity, e.g., protesters may not block pedestrian pathways or brandish realistic-looking fake firearms.

The students' lawyers, Neal Sher and Joel Siegal, then filed a substantially similar complaint before OCR, repeating their hostile environment allegations. The assigned OCR team leader dismissed the complaint on August 19, 2013.[31] OCR rejected some claims as untimely and others on the grounds that they had not been properly reported to the university. OCR then held that three of the incidents did not constitute unlawful harassment because they involved "expression on matters of public concern directed to the University community."[32] Sher and Siegal appealed this decision by OCR San Francisco regional director Arthur Zeidman on the ground that OCR had ignored numerous incidents alleged in their complaints, including "six pages of events ... wherein Jewish students and others opposed to the Boycott

---

28 Ibid.

29 Felber v. Regents of the University of California, 851 F.Supp.2d 1182, 1188 (N.D. CA. 2011).

30 Ibid.

31 Zachary Pelchat, Team Leader, US Department of Education, Office for Civil Rights, Region IX ("OCR Investigative Team"), closure letter to Joel H. Siegal and Neal M. Sher, Case No. 09-12-2259, dated August 19, 2013 (the *"Berkeley"* case).

32 Ibid., 3.

Divestment and Sanctions (BDS) movement were threatened with physical violence and intimidation."[33] Moreover, they objected that OCR's treatment of campus antisemitism contrasted sharply with its response to anti-black discrimination, such as the "Compton Cookout," a racist incident at the University of California at San Diego that had drawn a strong response from OCR and the Department of Justice. OCR denied the Berkeley appeal on the same day as the Santa Cruz appeal.

III. JEWISH IDENTITY AND ANTISEMITISM

1. *What is a Jew?*

OCR'S initial challenge was to determine whether Jewish students are ever protected from anti-Jewish harassment by a statutory provision, Title VI, which prohibits certain discrimination on the basis of race, color, or national origin but not on the basis of religion. In other words, the agency had to wrestle with the old and difficult question of Jewish identity: are Jews united by a religion, a race, an ethnicity, a nationality, or something different?

The agency's traditional answer had generally been that Jews are not protected because they form only a religion. The agency's reluctance was due partly to the fact that Congress had omitted the term "religion" from this portion of the Civil Rights Act. It was also due to bureaucratic reluctance to imply that Jews are a "race," given the catastrophic effects of Hitler's prior determination on this matter.[34] This approach belies the fact that modern antisemitism is often based on perceived Jewish ethnic or racial traits. In other words, antisemites have not always focused on Jewish religious beliefs. Rather, they have acted on misperceptions of Jewish ethnic or racial difference. The old OCR approach also misconceives the original intent of Title VI, which was to provide civil rights protections to the kinds of groups that Congress had covered under the Equal Protection Clause of the Fourteenth Amendment to the US Constitution. Jews are unquestionably among these groups.[35]

My 2004 policy should have settled this question. Nevertheless, the agency's senior leadership declined to embrace this position during the period between 2004 and 2010 when *Irvine I* was decided. It is unclear why OCR did not reconsider this decision on appeal, since its final agency decision was issued well after the agency's 2010 commitment to follow the policy that I had announced six years beforehand. On the other hand, OCR seldom reverses its own cases on appeal, so it is unknown how the agency would handle a case similar to *Irvine I* if it were filed today.

2. *What is antisemitism?*

Once the agency determined that Jews are protected from antisemitism, it needed to figure out what counts as antisemitic. The US Department of State has adopted an important, useful, and intelligent definition of antisemitism. It defines antisemitism

---

33 Joel H. Siegal and Neal M. Sher, appeal letter to Arthur Zeidman, Regional Director, and Zachary Pelchat, Team Leader, US Department of Education, Office for Civil Rights, Region IX, Case No. 09-12-2259, dated September 27, 2013 (emphasis omitted).

34 Marcus, *Jewish Identity*, 10.

35 Marcus, "Anti-Zionism as Racism."

as "a certain perception of Jews, which may be expressed as hatred toward Jews. Rhetorical and physical manifestations of anti-Semitism are directed toward Jewish or non-Jewish individuals and/or their property, toward Jewish community institutions and religious facilities." While appropriately cautioning that "criticism of Israel similar to that leveled against any other country cannot be regarded as anti-Semitic," the State Department provides that antisemitism manifests itself with regard to Israel, "taking into account the overall context," when its exhibits any of these characteristics:

Demonize Israel:
- Using the symbols and images associated with classic anti-Semitism to characterize Israel or Israelis
- Drawing comparisons of contemporary Israeli policy to that of the Nazis
- Blaming Israel for all inter-religious or political tensions

Double standard for Israel:
- Applying double standards by requiring of it a behavior not expected or demanded of any other democratic nation
- Multilateral organizations focusing on Israel only for peace or human rights investigations

Delegitimize Israel:
- Denying the Jewish people their right to self-determination, and denying Israel the right to exist[36]

This definition brings an appropriately broad variety of antisemitic acts and words under the concept of "antisemitism," including symbols and images associated with historical antisemitism, demonizing or delegitimizing Israel, drawing comparisons between Jews and Nazis, or condoning or supporting terrorism against Israel or Jews. Unfortunately, OCR has not yet adopted its sister agency's definition. Nor has it adopted any other recognized definition of antisemitism, issued its own guidance on this issue, or given any other public indication of how it would distinguish between genuine and mistaken claims of antisemitism. OCR's failure is especially conspicuous during the current period, when some but not all hostility to Israel involves antisemitism.[37] Without any guidance on the meaning of antisemitism, OCR's staff have understandably floundered when asked to determine whether or not certain incidents are antisemitic.

The State Department definition is based on the older EUMC Working Definition, which had previously been circulated although never formally adopted by the European Union's Monitoring Center on Racism and Xenophobia (EUMC).[38] The Working Definition has been widely applauded and is enormously influential. Shortly after it was issued, the Office for Democratic Institutions and Human Rights (ODHIR) of the Organization for Security and Co-operation in Europe (OSCE) inte-

---

36 US Department of State, Fact Sheet, *Defining Antisemitism* (June 8, 2010), http://www.state.gov/j/drl/rls/fs/2010/122352.htm.

37 This is the topic of my next book, *The Definition of Anti-Semitism* (Oxford University Press, forthcoming).

38 See, generally, Kenneth L. Marcus, "The Definition of Antisemitism," in Charles Asher Small, ed., *Global Antisemitism: A Crisis of Modernity* (Leiden: Brill, 2013): 101-102.

grated the definition into its educational materials.[39] In June 2004, the OSCE prominently referenced the Working Definition at its Cordoba conference.[40] Since then, numerous national and international bodies have used the definition, cited it, or recommended using it, ranging from parliamentary bodies to governmental agencies to nongovernmental organizations to the United Kingdom's National Union of Students and the US Commission on Civil Rights. The EUMC's successor agency, the European Union Fundamental Rights Agency (FRA), no longer includes the Working Definition on its public website.[41] Nevertheless, numerous other bodies continue to embrace it.

For agency officials trying to ascertain whether particular conduct is antisemitic (i.e. whether it is discrimination based on Jewish ethnic or ancestral characteristics), the *Irvine II* case presented difficult challenges. After all, some of the hostility directed at Jewish students appears to be politically motivated, especially as Zionist Jews and conservative speakers were apparently mistreated in a similar manner. Nevertheless, harassment of those who express love for Israel unavoidably creates a hostile environment for Israeli students. Moreover, it may also be viewed as a form of irrational ethnic trait discrimination against Jewish Americans. The harassment was based on the students' sense of connectedness to the State of Israel. This has a political dimension, as the students recognized, but it is also deeply intertwined with age-old elements of Jewish ethnic, cultural, and religious identity.

Investigators should determine whether students are mistreated in ways that meet established standards such as the US Department of State's definition. They would find countless examples. A few months after September 11, 2001, Muhammad al-Asi told students at the University of California at Irvine that, "We have a psychosis in the Jewish community that is unable to co-exist equally and brotherly with other human beings. You can take a Jew out of the ghetto, but you cannot take the ghetto out of the Jew, and this has been demonstrated time and time again."[42] This is the "certain perception of the Jews" to which the State Department and Working Definition refer. Starting around that time, fliers appeared around that campus picturing the Star of David dripping with blood and equating Israeli Jews with Nazis.[43] This is what the State Department definition calls an expression "drawing comparisons of contemporary Israeli policy to that of the Nazis." At another lecture, students were told that Jews use the media to brainwash gentiles, that there is a "psychosis" in the Jewish community, and that Jews must be "reha-

---

39 Office for Democratic Institutions and Human Rights, *Education on the Holocaust and on Anti-Semitism: An Overview and Analysis of Educational Approaches* (Organization for Security and Co-operation in Europe, 2006), 19-20, http://www.osce.org/odihr/18818.

40 Dina Porat, "The International Working Definition of Antisemitism and Its Detractors," *Israel Journal of Foreign Affairs* 5, no. 3 (2011): 6.

41 See, generally, Amy Elman, "The EU's Responses to Contemporary Antisemitism: A Shell Game" (seminar paper delivered at "Deciphering the 'New' Antisemitism," Institute for Contemporary Antisemitism, Indiana University at Bloomington, April 2014), 13.

42 Richard Cravatts, "Antisemitism and the Academic Left," *Journal for the Study of Antisemitism* 3, no. 2 (2011): 435-36.

43 Susan B. Tuchman, "Statement Submitted to the U.S. Commission on Civil Rights Briefing on Campus Anti-Semitism," *Briefing Report on Campus Antisemitism* (Washington, DC: US Commission on Civil Rights, 2006): 13-21.

bilitated." Here we see what the State Department calls "making ... stereotypical allegations about Jews ... especially ... about ... Jews controlling the media...." In March 2004, a Jewish student was called "dirty Jew," reviving yet another old anti-Jewish stereotype.[44] In 2010, during Israel Apartheid Week, Malik Ali publicly told UCI Jewish students that "you Jews are the new Nazis," reinforcing once again the antisemitic practice that State calls "drawing comparisons of contemporary Israeli policy to that of the Nazis."[45]

That same year, 63 UCI faculty members published a letter saying that they "are deeply disturbed about activities on campus that foment hatred against Jews and Israelis," including

> the painting of swastikas on university buildings, the Star of David depicted as akin to a swastika, a statement (by a speaker repeatedly invited by the Muslim Student Union) that the Zionist Jew is a party of Satan, a statement by another MSU speaker that the Holocaust was God's will, the tearing down of posters placed by the student group Anteaters for Israel, and the hacking of their web site.

The professors intimated that some "community members, students, and faculty indeed feel intimidated, and at times, even unsafe."[46] Other faculty disagreed and issued opposing statements, but these incidents nevertheless echo the State Department definition and the Working Definition. Such standards should be applied as rebuttable presumptions rather than bright-line tests, since surrounding contextual information may indicate that some actions are not what they initially seem. While the accused would have a right to be heard, it is difficult to imagine any persuasive defense to the anti-Jewish rhetoric and actions in which anti-Israel activists engaged for several years at Irvine.

3. *Anti-discrimination law and freedom of speech*

We have long maintained that OCR must clarify the extent to which its hostile environment policies must bow to the Speech Clause of the First Amendment. During the Clinton and George W. Bush administrations, OCR provided some guidance on this subject.[47] In recent years, OCR's position on this subject has become somewhat murkier, especially with its controversial *University of Montana* case.[48] While OCR's First Amendment issues are by no means limited to its antisemitism cases, many of these cases require a clear understanding of speech principles.

Even when it finally develops appropriate guidance on the parameters of antisemitism (or embraces the ready-at-hand State Department definition), OCR must still clarify how it will address the speech components in antisemitic campus incidents. This issue has been a problem for both courts and administrative agencies.

---

44 Ibid., 17.

45 Leila Beckwith, "Antisemitism at the University of California," *Journal for the Study of Antisemitism* 3, no. 2 (2011): 451.

46 Ibid., 448.

47 Marcus, "The New OCR Anti-Semitism Policy."

48 DOJ Case No. DJ 169-44-9, OCR Case No. 10126001 (May 9, 2013), http://www.justice.gov/opa/documents/um-ltr-findings.pdf.

In the *Felber* case, for example, Dean Jonathan Poullard allegedly suggested that Felber's assailant had a right to spit *at* her (as opposed to *on* her), since spitting at her may have expressed political convictions. This is a disgraceful suggestion, which ignores that threatening quality that spitting sometimes assumes. Appallingly, the district court sided with the university, suggesting that the perpetrator may indeed have had a constitutional right to spit at Felber.[49] OCR appears to have agreed.

As a preliminary matter, it should be noted that free speech issues cut both ways. Jewish advocates have long observed that campus Israel advocacy is often suppressed or chilled in a variety of ways. This may include, for example, threatening, heckling, disinviting, or intimidating outside speakers; harassing or assaulting activists; or excluding, harassing, and removing pro-Israel students. In some cases, anti-Israel activists explicitly argue that "Zionists" should not be provided the same expressive rights as others for reasons having to do with the oppressive regime that they allegedly sustain. Nevertheless, anti-Israel critics frequently maintain that pro-Israel activists wish to suppress their speech. The issue is not entirely frivolous, as there is a fine line between legitimate enforcement of anti-discrimination law and Speech Clause violations.

Courts have consistently and correctly struck down university efforts to limit speech through speech codes and related restrictions.[50] Despite these clear judicial signals, many universities have long maintained speech codes that are clearly unconstitutional.[51] When responding to claims of sexism or racism, university administrators have frequently overreacted, repeatedly suppressing legitimate expressive conduct in ways that are unquestionably unconstitutional.[52] Worse, their actions have been sporadic, ad hoc, and crisis-driven, leading to charges of selective enforcement and unequal treatment. That is to say, administrators have been much quicker to invoke the First Amendment in response to antisemitism allegations than in response to claims by other groups.[53] Anti-discrimination efforts must be even-handed and consistent with constitutional requirements.

OCR's 2003 "Dear Colleague" letter clarifies that "no OCR regulation should be interpreted to impinge upon rights protected under the First Amendment to the U.S.

49 Felber v. Yudof, 851 F.Supp.2d 1182, 1188 (E.D. Cal. 2011) ("As one example, plaintiffs fault Dean Poullard for asking Felber whether she had been spit on or merely spit at, and for appearing to take the matter less seriously when she acknowledged that she had not been spit on. As offensive as spitting at someone may be, it very well could constitute protected expressive conduct, depending on the precise circumstances, whereas spitting on someone much more likely could rise to an assault or battery, criminally punishable or civilly actionable.").

50 See, e.g., Iota XI Chapter of Sigma Chi Fraternity v. George Mason University, 993 F.2d 386, 393 (4th Cir. 1993); Roberts v. Haragan, 346 F.Supp.2d 853, 867-73 (N.D. Tex. 2004); UWM Post, Inc. v. Board of Regents of the University of Wisconsin, 774 F.Supp. 1163 (E.D. Wis. 1991); Doe v. University of Michigan, 721 F.Supp. 852, 861-67.

51 See Jon B. Gould, "The Precedent That Wasn't: College Hate Speech Codes and the Two Faces of Legal Compliance," *Law and Society Review* 35 (2001).

52 Charles Alan Kors and Harvey A. Silverglate, *The Shadow University: The Betrayal of Liberty on America's Campuses* (New York: The Free Press, 1998); Greg Lukianoff, *Unlearning Liberty: Campus Censorship and the End of American Debate* (New York: Encounter Books, 2012).

53 Kenneth L. Marcus, "Higher Education, Harassment, and First Amendment Opportunism," *William & Mary Bill of Rights Journal* 16 (2008): 1027-1028.

Constitution or to require recipients to enact or enforce codes that punish the exercise of such rights."[54] Specifically, "OCR does not require or prescribe speech, conduct or harassment codes that impair the exercise of rights protected under the First Amendment."[55]

OCR should reiterate that its *Montana* "blueprint" agreement must be read together with OCR's "First Amendment: Dear Colleague Letter," which emphasizes that "no OCR regulation should be interpreted to impinge upon rights protected under the First Amendment to the U.S. Constitution or to require recipients to enact or enforce codes that punish the exercise of such rights."[56] Universities should use their moral suasion to discourage all forms of harassment, including even unwelcome conduct that is neither severe nor pervasive. At the same time, they should avoid taking regulatory conduct with respect to such conduct if it is protected by broadly accepted norms of freedom of expression.

Some commentators argue that antisemitic hate speech on college campuses is not protected by the First Amendment, while others disagree. For example, Alexander Tsesis argues that even public universities may punish students who use university property to spread defamatory and intimidating forms of antisemitism.[57] By contrast, Stephen M. Feldman argues that the question of First Amendment protection is an inherently political discussion, that public universities "may" be unable to prohibit antisemitic hate speech, but that private institutions may do so.[58] Even if there are circumstances in which universities may punish antisemitic hate speech, it is sometimes unwise to do so, since this can suppress the free exchange of ideas or create a public backlash. In some cases, administrators have other alternatives that do not have such problems.

Administrators always have options for active engagement that do not entail suppression or punishment. As a matter of sound policy, universities should take serious and effective measures to address harassing conduct even when it falls short of a legal violation or is protected by the First Amendment. These steps may include raising student awareness through orientation and training, articulating recommended standards of ethical conduct, and speaking out against coarse, degrading, or uncivil behavior even when it takes the form of protected speech. Additionally, universities may take numerous steps that do not raise constitutional concerns, such as:

- non-regulatory responses, such as strong leadership statements;
- regulating non-speech, including responses to the kinds of assault, battery, and vandalism that have been recently alleged to occur on many campuses;
- regulating the time, place, or manner of offensive speech, including insuring effective security to prevent heckling at university lectures;

---

54 Gerald A. Reynolds, Assistant US Secretary of Education for Civil Rights, "First Amendment: Dear Colleague Letter" (July 28, 2003), http://www2.ed.gov/about/offices/list/ocr/firstamend.html.

55 Ibid.

56 Ibid.

57 Alexander Tsesis, "Campus Antisemitic Speech and the First Amendment," in Small, *Global Antisemitism*, 149-58.

58 Stephen M. Feldman, "Great Expectations: Antisemitism and the Politics of Free-Speech Jurisprudence," in Small, *Global Antisemitism*, 291-96.

- regulating non-speech aspects of actions with speech components, such as offensive touching that coincides with offensive speech;
- regulating speech that falls under a specific exception (e.g. threats of imminent violence); and
- providing enhanced discipline for conduct code infractions that are motivated by hate or bias.[59]

These principles are not limited to campus antisemitism but are generally applicable to harassment in higher education. The universities' protocols for addressing incivility should not kick in only when federal law is implicated. Nevertheless, universities—especially if they are public institutions—should exercise great caution in their responses. In particular, they should avoid suppressing or punishing protected speech on the basis of content, but they should not hesitate to respond to this speech with speech of their own.

IV. Conclusion

OCR's disposition of these cases has led some observers to worry that the agency's doors are no longer open to Jewish complainants. In fact, OCR continues to recognize that harassment of Jewish students may violate federal civil rights law, even if this recognition is difficult to discern in recent cases. OCR also acknowledges that certain hostilities toward Israel may violate the rights of Jewish students. This can be seen in a presentation that Deputy Assistant Secretary Seth Galanter prepared for the 2012 annual convention of the American-Arab Anti-Discrimination Committee.[60] Galanter offers the following hypothetical as an example of a case in which OCR would exercise Title VI jurisdiction:

> College students who attend a speech and rally sponsored by a campus group that is known for its support of Israel's policies towards the Palestinians are heckled with shouts of "Zionist" and "Murderer" as they arrive at the rally, are hit by rocks thrown as they enter the rally, and later receive threatening notes under their dorm room doors.
>
> The notes read: "Dear Zionist—For your support of Israel and complicity in its crimes we will hunt you down the way the Nazis hunted your Jewish ancestors."[61]

This is an important presentation, because it demonstrates OCR's recognition that some seemingly political activities directed against Israel's supporters in fact constitute federal civil rights violations.

At first blush, the key to this hypothetical is the reference to "your Jewish ancestors." As the notes to Galanter's presentation indicate, this language suggests "that

59 Marcus, "Best Practices Guide." For further discussion of these alternatives, see William A. Kaplin and Barbara A. Lee, *The Law of Higher Education*, 5th ed. (San Francisco: Jossey-Bass, 2014).

60 US Department of Education, Office for Civil Rights presentation, "Bullying, Peer Harassment, and Civil Rights," 2012 ADC National Convention, June 23, 2012, 25 (PowerPoint slide, "Racial Harassment: Example 4").

61 Ibid.

the students were targeted because of their real or perceived Jewish ancestry."[62] Galanter emphasizes that the fact that "the students may also have been targeted because of their perceived support for Israel (the only evidence thereof being the students' attendance at this event) does not deprive OCR of jurisdiction."[63] In fact, if anything it should reinforce that jurisdiction, insofar as the hypothetical statement exemplifies the State Department's insight that antisemitism includes "accusing Jews ... of being responsible for real or imagined wrongdoing committed by ... the state of Israel...."[64]

OCR needs to be clearer about its standards for identifying antisemitism, as well as its standards for protecting the freedom of speech. The best first step would be to adopt the State Department's official definition of antisemitism. This will ensure consistency between the United States' foreign and domestic policies toward this issue. More specifically, it will ensure that OCR properly distinguishes between those forms of hostility to Israel that should be seen as antisemitic and those that should not. Next, the agency should expand upon Gerald A. Reynolds' 2003 "Dear Colleague" letter on the First Amendment, dispelling any confusion that has subsequently arisen over its *University of Montana* case and its treatment of campus antisemitism allegations. Universities and government officials must both avoid censorship. At the same time, university administrators should never use the First Amendment as an excuse to look the other way when hateful incidents arise, since they always have legally acceptable alternatives that do not raise First Amendment problems.[65]

---

62 Ibid. Galanter acknowledges that the First Amendment may protect some of the hecklers' conduct but that direct physical harassment such as rock-throwing would not be and threats of physical harm are also generally not protected.

63 Ibid.

64 This is not inconsistent with Galanter's subsequent statement, in a letter to the Asian Law Caucus, that "OCR is careful to differentiate between harassment based on an individual's real or perceived national origin, which is prohibited by Title VI, as compared to offensive conduct based on an individual's support for, or opposition to, the policies of a particular nation, which is not."

65 Marcus, "Best Practices Guide."

The Swastika as a Symbol of Happiness: Polish Judges and Prosecutors in Antisemitic and Racist Hate Cases

Aleksandra Gliszczyńska-Grabias*

I. Introduction

It is always extremely difficult to speak critically about one's own country abroad, especially when the topic concerns such a complex and controversial issue as Polish antisemitism. My personal strategy in such situations is to criticize strongly—or even harshly—when talking directly to Polish audiences and to concentrate on the "bright side" of the situation when addressing foreign observers. In this paper, I will try to combine these two approaches, presenting evidence of both the ability and inability of Polish judges, prosecutors, and civil society to successfully fight antisemitism.

But let me start with a brief observation concerning antisemitism in contemporary Poland, which is generally but wrongly perceived as a common and extremely intense phenomenon.[1] It is true that antisemitic attitudes are deeply rooted in Poland's nationalist and Catholic tradition and that antisemitic sentiments come out on many occasions. It is also true that the history of my country and my nation is marked by acts of "blackmail, extortion, denunciation, betrayal, and plunder of the living and the dead"[2] against Jews throughout Poland during the Second World War and its aftermath. But the Poles, especially those of my generation, have made an enormous effort to overcome this hatred and prejudice, and today most statistics indicate that Polish antisemitism is in decline. At the same time, Poland is almost completely free of anti-Israel and anti-Zionist attitudes, which can be credited first and foremost to the absence of an Arab or Muslim minority in Poland but should also be considered in the context of the excellent foreign relations between Poland and Israel. But, as we say in Poland, if it is so good, then why is it so bad? Those of us who are actively engaged in fighting antisemitism in Poland clearly still have a lot to do. The fact that

---

* Research Fellow, ISGAP; Junior Researcher, Poznań Human Rights Centre, Institute of Legal Studies of the Polish Academy of Sciences.

[1] See the country reports prepared by the European Commission against Racism and Intolerance, available at http://www.coe.int/t/dghl/monitoring/ecri/activities/countrybycountry_en.asp. The bi-weekly newsletter of the European Jewish Congress also proves that antisemitism is currently more visible in other European countries than in Poland.

[2] Martin Krygier, "Lifting the Burden of the Past" (keynote address at the symposium *Why Poland? Facing the Demons of Polish-Jewish History*, Melbourne, Australia, November 28, 2012).

antisemitism may be stronger in other places and societies around the world is no reason for Poland and Poles to be satisfied.

The "Open Republic" Association against Anti-Semitism and Xenophobia is one of Poland's oldest and most prominent non-governmental organizations.[3] It was founded by some of the country's most distinguished intellectuals and public figures, and its mission is to make Polish society more sensitive to antisemitism and intolerance, counteract these negative phenomena in public life, and change social attitudes in this regard.

Established in 1999, the association's activities initially focused on writing letters of protest, initiating or signing petitions against antisemitic or racist events, and meeting local government and administration representatives in order to provoke a response to alarming signals and manifestations of racism and xenophobia within their jurisdictions. At this time, Open Republic was confronted with some very problematic attitudes on the part of many officials and representatives of the judiciary and the police, who expressed open hostility, discrimination, and prejudice toward different minority groups—victims of hate speech and hate crimes—in their official correspondence and public statements. Even more alarming was the fact that such statements also appeared in prosecutors' decisions and judges' rulings dismissing charges brought against antisemites and racists. The association therefore decided to launch two legal projects, entitled "Law against Hatred" and "Society against Hatred." In the framework of these projects, it initiated legal actions against persons responsible for circulating antisemitic publications and vandalizing Jewish cemeteries and launched an information campaign to show Poles how to report hate speech and hate crimes to the police and the prosecutor's office. Collecting data and statistics was yet another component of these projects. The association was soon confronted with some troubling cases.

Like the criminal codes of other European countries, the Polish Criminal Code prohibits incitement to racial hatred, offensive speech based on racial, national, ethnic, or religious origin, and public advocacy of Nazi and/or fascist ideology.[4] Those who oppose the penalization of words—including racist and xenophobic words—will most probably not approve of the fact that it is possible to obtain a three-year jail sentence for shouting "Hitler should have finished the job." But the European system of human rights protection to which Poland subscribes, which was founded on the ruins of a continent devastated by the Holocaust and totalitarian regimes, applies legal measures for counteracting antisemitism and racism that limit freedom of speech.[5]

Białystok and Wrocław are big Polish cities where racism, antisemitism, and the activities of extreme right-wing organizations are most visible. In those cities, in the last few years, local prosecutors and judges have made some disquieting and arguably even frightening decisions. In Wrocław, a judge absolved a group of activists from the

---

[3] See http://www.otwarta.org/en.

[4] An English version of the Polish Criminal Code provisions concerning hate speech and hate crimes is available at http://www.ohchr.org/Documents/Issues/Expression/ICCPR/Vienna/Annexes/Poland.pdf.

[5] See Anne Weber, *Manual on Hate Speech* (Strasbourg, Council of Europe Publishing, 2009), http://www.coe.int/t/dghl/standardsetting/hrpolicy/Publications/Hate_Speech_EN.pdf.

National Rebirth of Poland party of blame for causing offense and inciting hatred due to racism, despite the fact that their slogans constituted the purest form of racism one could imagine. The judge's reasoning was shocking. He stated that the opinions of those prosecuted were merely proof of their fascination with the theory of "the preservation of separation in the rich mosaic of races," as developed by Arthur de Gobineau, the author of *An Essay on the Inequality of the Human Races*, whose main ideas were adopted by Hitler and Nazism.[6] If a judge believes that this fact constitutes an excuse for slogans such as "Blacks go back to Africa!," we need to consider the possibility that the judge himself is also "fascinated" by this particular theory.

Not long afterward, a Białystok prosecutor who received notice of a crime committed by unknown perpetrators involving the painting of swastikas on buildings in public spaces decided that the case needed to be dropped because the swastika, despite being a prominent Nazi symbol, is actually regarded as a symbol of happiness and wealth in Asian culture.[7] It is likely that the neo-Nazis who painted those swastikas were outraged by the suggestion that they were propagating Asian culture. Was the prosecutor aware of the scale of the problem of racism in his own city? Did he know about the vandalization of synagogues, the torching of foreigners' homes or neo-Nazi marches? Did his history teachers at school not tell him what the swastika has symbolized in Europe since the Second World War? Had he not heard of the crimes committed by the Nazis in Poland under the banner of this symbol? It is both disappointing and disgraceful that certain representatives of the Polish justice system do not feel the need to pause and think for a moment before referring so blithely to theories of racial inequality or the role of the swastika in Asian culture.

Unfortunately, more decisions and rulings of this kind have been delivered in Poland. A court in Opole dismissed charges against a law school graduate student accused of producing and distributing fascist leaflets on the grounds that the proceedings might harm his future legal career. A prosecutor in the city of Wrocław did not find it necessary to take action against the illegal dissemination of the Polish edition of *Mein Kampf*, accepting the publisher's explanation that the book had been published for "scientific purposes." Another prosecutor did not regard a poster stating "We will expel Jews from Poland" as incitement to hatred based on ethnic or national origin on the vague and legally dubious grounds that in order for the slogan to be antisemitic it would have to be phrased in a different grammatical form: "Let's expel Jews from Poland!"[8]

In the following sections, I will present three cases involving antisemitic hate speech and hate crimes in which Open Republic took legal action.

II. THE *PIETRASIEWICZ* CASE

One of the main problems in the legal discourse on hate speech and hate crimes in Poland concerns the following question: does one need to be a Jew in order to be

---

[6] Aleksandra Gliszczyńska-Grabias and Wojciech Sadurski, "Która zniewaga kary wymaga?" [Which insult demands punishment?], *Gazeta Wyborcza* (Warsaw), December 12, 2012.

[7] Nissan Tzur, "Polish Prosecutor: Swastika a Symbol of Prosperity," *Jewish Post*, June 30, 2013.

[8] All information is available at: http://www.otwarta.org/en.

"entitled" to feel insulted by an antisemitic publication or statement? To foreigners, this question may seem absurd. The reason it matters is that Poland has a very small Jewish community, so antisemitic incidents in Poland are mostly directed against people who are not Jewish in the sense of their ethnic, national, or religious origin or identity. Who then is legally entitled to feel offended? Open Republic has made efforts to introduce legal changes that enable everyone—every citizen—to regard himself or herself as a victim of antisemitism. The association argues that a special provision should be added to the Criminal Code. This provision should establish a legal rule according to which hate speech and hate crimes can be committed against any person, including one who does not belong to a particular group protected under Polish law (e.g. Jews, Muslims, or Roma). Under this rule, it would be sufficient that the hateful act is based on the perpetrator's belief that he or she is attacking a Jew or a Roma person or that the perpetrator associates his or her victim with a group that he or she hates.

The following example illustrates the aim of the proposed legal change. Tomasz Pietrasiewicz, who is the director of the Grodzka Gate Cultural Center in Lublin, is deeply engaged in Polish-Jewish dialogue and the commemoration of Polish Jews who perished during and after the Second World War.[9] For a period of five years, he was the target of numerous antisemitic attacks. In one particular incident in 2010, several bricks painted with swastikas were thrown into his apartment.[10] Questioned by the police, Pietrasiewicz stated, truthfully, that he was not Jewish. The prosecutor consequently did not act on the basis of existing hate crime provisions, instead treating the crime as an "ordinary" act of hooliganism. The hateful and antisemitic motivations of the unknown perpetrator or perpetrators were not taken into account, as Mr. Pietrasiewicz was not of Jewish origin in an ethnic or religious sense. Many other European countries have introduced legal rules addressing the problem raised in the Pietrasiewicz case. In Germany, for example, hateful motivation is regarded as an aggravating circumstance even if the victim of a crime does not actually belong to the "hated group."

Following an intensive media campaign and Open Republic's intervention, the legal characterization of the crime committed against Mr. Pietrasiewicz was changed and its antisemitic character was noted by the prosecutor. Unfortunately, the proceedings were discontinued on the grounds that the perpetrators had not been identified.

III. The Three Holiest Hosts case

In November 2012, Open Republic informed the prosecutor's office about the public dissemination of an antisemitic book by Mieczysław Noskowicz, entitled *The Three Holiest Hosts*. The association claimed that this was in breach of Article 256 of the Polish Criminal Code, which prohibits producing, recording or importing, purchasing, storing, possessing, presenting, transporting or sending (for the purpose of

9 For information concerning Brama Grodzka, see http://teatrnn.pl/node/78/the_grodzka_gate_%E2%80%93_nn_theatre_centre.

10 For information on legal action taken by the Helsinki Foundation for Human Rights, see http://humanrightshouse.org/noop/page.php?p=Articles/18359.html&d=1.

dissemination) printed materials, recordings or other objects with racist (including antisemitic) contents, which incite to hatred and discrimination.

The book, which was published in 2012, was a reprint of a pre-war anti-Jewish work that was used to incite widespread hatred, discrimination, and violence against the Jewish citizens of Poland during that period (particularly in 1926 when it was first published).[11] Open Republic argued that the book contained expressions of deeply-rooted and extreme antisemitic prejudices and stereotypes, which in the past had produced dramatic consequences, including violent pogroms against Polish Jews.

What is of crucial importance here is that the new edition was not accompanied by a contemporary critical commentary. Thus, readers were not made aware of the historical context of the original edition. It should also be emphasized that the public dissemination of materials that directly promote "classic" antisemitic prejudices (e.g. accusing Jews of killing Christ, ritually murdering Christian children, or poisoning wells) was considered a form of antisemitism under the EU Monitoring Centre on Racism and Xenophobia's working definition of antisemitism of 2005 (which was later dropped by its successor—the EU Fundamental Rights Agency).

In its official letter to the prosecutor, Open Republic noted that the book constituted an incitement to antisemitic hatred both as a whole and in part. To quote just one passage from the book: "It is known to everyone who is even minimally familiar with world history that from the time immemorial, from the moment Christianity was born, there existed an enormous hatred of Jews toward Christians. After two thousand years they have not stopped hating us for one moment."

Open Republic reminded the authorities that the Polish state has an international and legally binding obligation to effectively counteract racist, antisemitic, and other xenophobic acts using the instruments of law. This obligation arises from such international agreements as the International Covenant on Civil and Political Rights, the International Convention on the Elimination of All Forms of Racial Discrimination, and European Council Framework Decision 2008/913/JHA of 28 November 2008 on combating certain forms and expressions of racism and xenophobia by means of criminal law. Furthermore, Open Republic cited several key decisions of the European Court of Human Rights and the UN Human Rights Committee confirming that the public dissemination of antisemitic publications does not amount to a legitimate exercise of freedom of speech and should be treated as incitement to hatred, discrimination, or violence, which is strictly prohibited under international human rights law. It is important to remember—and Polish prosecutors should take particular note—that the general primacy of counteracting racism over freedom of speech or association has been established in the case law of the international human rights protection bodies.

Despite Open Republic's intervention and the strong reaction of the Polish media, the proceedings in *The Three Holiest Hosts* case were discontinued because the prosecutor did not find sufficient legal reasons to press for an indictment against the publisher. As a result, this antisemitic book is still freely available.

---

11 For press information concerning this case, see http://poznan.naszemiasto.pl/artykul/1278177,antysemicka-ksiazka-najswietsze-trzy-hostie-mieczyslawa,id,t.html (in Polish).

IV. The *Michnik* case

The third case concerns a person who was one of the leaders and symbols of the Solidarity movement, which brought about the establishment of a free, democratic Poland after years of Communist rule. This person is Adam Michnik, a leading Polish intellectual and editor-in-chief of Poland's largest serious newspaper, *Gazeta Wyborcza*.[12] Before discussing the details of the legal case, some explanations are needed. Adam Michnik is a Polish Jew who has never denied or concealed his Jewish origins. Because he is a public figure and because his newspaper, which is known for its left-liberal stance, often discusses the sensitive topic of Polish antisemitism, Michnik is regarded as the epitome of Jewish influence over Polish affairs in the country's far-right and ultra-Catholic circles. For the past twenty-five years, he has therefore repeatedly suffered antisemitic attacks.

In March 2012, the grave of Michnik's parents, Helena Michnik and Ozjasz Szechter, was vandalized for the third time in the space of a few years.[13] Open Republic informed the prosecutor that the crimes of vandalism and desecration were aggravated by the crime of spreading antisemitic hatred, as the grave was spray-painted with a Star of David hanging from a gallows. Open Republic claimed that the antisemitic and hateful character of this act left no doubt as to its motivation. Through their act, the perpetrators sought not only to vandalize and desecrate the grave but also to express their hatred toward Jews and to incite others to such hatred. A Star of David hanging from a gallows should also be seen as a manifestation of hatred and contempt toward Adam Michnik, given his Jewish origins.

The response of the prosecutor's office indicated a complete lack of understanding of the nature of hate crimes and the context of the case. But what is perhaps even more disturbing is the prosecutor's erroneous interpretation of the relevant legal provisions. In his reasoning for dropping the proceedings in the Michnik case, the prosecutor from one of Warsaw's district courts offered a vague and absurd interpretation. In order to characterize the depiction of a Star of David hanging from a gallows as an act of antisemitic hatred, the act would have to demonstrate "the superiority of one's own [i.e. Polish] nation over another nation." According to the prosecutor, the vandalization and desecration of the grave was only an act of hooliganism that deserved condemnation but could not be legally qualified as a hate crime.

It is worth quoting Open Republic's official position regarding the prosecutor's decision to discontinue the proceedings:

> The fact that the Polish state is unable to identify, judge, and punish those responsible for the third antisemitic destruction of the Michnik family grave is a disgrace for the Polish police, prosecutor's office, and judiciary. Thus we are unable to accept the decision of the prosecutor in the present case. It is fundamentally important to continue the proceedings and bring them to a successful conclusion. Polish society must be convinced by the prosecutor's actions and firm position that all cases of racist or antisemitic hate speech and hate crime will be handled with the highest urgency.

---

12 For more information on *Gazeta Wyborcza*, see http://www.agora.pl/agora_english/0,0.html.

13 Images depicting an earlier act of vandalism can be seen at http://info.wyborcza.pl/temat/wyborcza/nagrobek+rodzic%C3%B3w.

The association also stated that

> The prosecutor's legal opinion, according to which there is no basis for invoking hate crime provisions because the depiction of a Star of David hanging from a gallows on a Jewish grave allegedly does not express the superiority of one nation over another, shows not only a complete lack of understanding of the nature of antisemitism in Poland but also constitutes an incorrect interpretation of the Polish Criminal Code. It is common knowledge that Polish far-right and nationalist circles regard the symbol of the Star of David as a direct synonym for Jews as a national, ethnic, and religious group. Thus, the depiction of a Star of David hanging from a gallows on a Jewish grave represents nothing less than a Jew hanging from a gallows. It is hard to imagine a more explicit example of incitement to antisemitic hatred.

Just recently, the Prosecutor General has decided to re-examine the case.

V. Comments

It seems obvious that the cause of such insensitive and sometimes outrageous decisions by prosecutors and judges lies in a lack of awareness and knowledge, which in turn are shaped mostly by their social environment and education. As a result, legal provisions are being ignored or misinterpreted, and prosecutors and judges are able to avoid taking action. In this context, it is worth quoting one of Poland's most distinguished legal scholars and a former judge of the Polish Constitutional Tribunal, Professor Ewa Łętowska, on the subject of hate speech and problems relating to the prosecution of hate crimes:

> It is not about changing the law (which I do not consider necessary) but about changing the practice (from a convenient one to an inconvenient one for the prosecutors), or even about making prosecutors acknowledge the things they pretend not to notice. … The truth is simple and clear: prosecutors do not bother, because it is more convenient not to act.[14]

Positive changes arrive slowly, and the usual reaction is to deny and reject the accusations instead of seizing the opportunity to improve the situation. Some time ago, BBC journalists produced a TV documentary in which they revealed the most extreme forms of racism and antisemitism in Polish football to a British audience. Almost all Polish politicians—and a large part of Polish society—protested fiercely, arguing that the situation was not as bad as shown, that the BBC had insulted them, that things were much worse in other countries, and so forth. This may all be true, but this type of reaction is also indicative of an inability to engage in self-criticism and reflection—an inability shared by many prosecutors and judges.

It is high time for the Polish people to ask themselves what other people see when they visit Poland. When they walk the streets they come across antisemitic images and slogans on the walls of buildings that have not been washed off by anyone. When they visit the museum at Treblinka concentration camp they read in

---

[14] Ewa Siedlecka, "Co zrobić z mową nienawiści?" [What to do with hate speech?], *Gazeta Wyborcza*, August 5, 2012.

the visitors' memorial book that "Hitler should have finished the job." When they go to old Jewish cemeteries they are shocked by the antisemitic destruction of gravestones. They do not hear Poles opposing this hatred, so how can they know that not all Polish people are full of hate? Society itself undoubtedly bears responsibility for this image and for not rising up in protest against all manifestations of hate and prejudice.

Speaking as a lawyer, I regard the law as a key element in shaping social attitudes and as a kind of testimony. When the state uses its authority to punish hate speech and hate crimes, it sends a clear signal as to what it considers an unacceptable abuse of rights and freedoms. However, three conditions must be fulfilled simultaneously. First, the law must be implemented in an effective way and without any exceptions. Second, public authorities and officials must openly speak out against racist and xenophobic hatred every time it appears in the public sphere. Finally, legal actions must be accompanied by responsible and honest efforts to educate. For example, teachers at Polish schools must teach about the pogroms, the Jedwabne massacre, and the antisemitic campaign of March 1968 in Communist Poland.

VI. Conclusions

As I noted at the beginning of this paper, there are also numerous positive examples of attitudes and actions opposing antisemitism and racism in Poland. It happens more and more frequently, although still not frequently enough, that responsible and reasonable judges and prosecutors openly call racism and antisemitism by their true names. It is especially important to single out and praise those prosecutors and judges who are not hesitant to break this disgraceful pattern of discontinued proceedings and court acquittals, which is typical of cases brought against football hooligans who parade their antisemitic and racist attitudes at football matches.

Poland has waited a long time for a judgment of the kind that was recently handed down by a district court in Warsaw.[15] The court sentenced seventeen football hooligans to perform community service, pay financial compensation to the Union of Jewish Religious Communities in Poland, and watch Izabella Cywińska's movie *The Purim Miracle*. After an investigation lasting almost a year, the prosecutors charged the aforementioned hooligans with publicly inciting others to racial and religious hatred. Initially, the court discontinued the case and stated that chanting such slogans could not be characterized as hate speech. The prosecutors did not agree with the verdict, and the case was subsequently re-examined by the court. This time, a judge determined that the phrase "Juden auf den Gas" (Jews to the gas) was synonymous with incitement to hatred against Jews.

The court's verdict in this case constitutes a success of the justice system, but ordering the accused to watch *The Purim Miracle* sets a legal precedent. This movie tells the story of an ordinary Polish worker, Jan Kochanowski—it is difficult to imagine a "purer" Polish surname—who lives an ordinary life in a flat in Łódź with his wife and son, who is an antisemitic football fan. When Kochanowski loses his job,

---

15 Aleksandra Gliszczyńska-Grabias, "The Purim Miracle in a Courtroom," *Louis D. Brandeis Center Blog*, January 8, 2014, http://brandeiscenter.com/blog/the-purim-miracle-in-a-courtroom.

he blames all his misfortunes on Western capitalists and Jews. One day, he is shocked to receive a telephone call from an American lawyer telling him that he has inherited an estate from an unknown relative. The only condition he must meet in order to receive the estate is to convert to Judaism. At the same time, Kochanowski learns that he has Jewish roots and that his family name was originally Cohen. He then receives yet another "blow" when his wife admits to her own Jewish ancestry. The movie shows how the family members, including the son, an ardent football fan known for chanting antisemitic slogans, discover the Jewish faith and its traditions and undergo a true transformation that ultimately has nothing to do with the inheritance. The stupidity and harmfulness of antisemitic prejudices are mercilessly exposed in this movie, as anyone who watches it will understand.

It is doubtful that the aforementioned football fans will undergo a similar transformation after watching the movie. But perhaps one or two of them will think twice before shouting antisemitic slogans, having realized that their hateful, brutal words hurt others—and that those others are not the fans of the opposing football team. It would appear that judgments of this kind are the only reasonable and effective solution to the problem of penalizing hate speech. They belong to the category of retributive justice, which focuses on reversing the harm and damage done, including at the wider social level, and on effecting authentic change in the attitudes of perpetrators. It is more about teaching perpetrators how to deal with the causes of their anger or hatred than punishing them. This practice is still almost unprecedented in Polish case law, and one can only wish that such "miracles of Purim" as the one that took place in a Warsaw courtroom happen more often.

Other positive and hopeful signals include the launch of a series of training courses on hate speech and hate crimes for police officers, prosecutors, and judges by the Polish ombudsman and the prosecutor general, as well as the firm statements of the new Minister of the Interior, who publicly declared war on antisemites and racists during a prime-time TV interview. Other important events include an official Hanukkah celebration in the palace of Polish President Bronisław Komorowski and the opening of the Museum of the History of Polish Jews in Warsaw, where many of the exhibits present the problem of Polish antisemitism in a courageous and unambiguous way. Interestingly, it appears that schools from all over Poland intend to organize visits to the museum for their students.

I am aware of the fact that Poland and the Poles are perceived by many as being indelibly marked by antisemitism. But as a Pole who is deeply engaged in fighting antisemitism I believe that Polish society is changing. It is learning about its history and its murkier moments; it is rediscovering and celebrating Poland's Jewish heritage; and it is becoming more human rights oriented. These changes are neither rapid nor spectacular but are nonetheless already noticeable. Obviously, this does not constitute an excuse for Polish police officers, prosecutors, and judges—or Polish society as a whole—to do nothing when antisemitism occurs. But my impression is that more and more Poles are aware of their responsibility to fight antisemitism. I hope that the years ahead will prove that I am right.

The Forgotten Nuremberg Hate Speech Case: Otto Dietrich and the Future of Persecution Law*

Gregory S. Gordon**

I. INTRODUCTION

Among international jurists, the conventional wisdom is that atrocity speech law sprang fully formed from two judgments issued by the International Military Tribunal (IMT) at Nuremberg: those of Julius Streicher,[1] editor-in-chief of the virulently antisemitic newspaper *Der Stürmer*, and Hans Fritzsche,[2] Head of the Radio Division of the Third Reich's Propaganda Ministry.[3] Streicher was convicted of persecution as a crime against humanity for his genocidal propaganda.[4] Fritzsche was acquitted of the same charge.[5] And so the two cases have often been cited to support antithetical positions among jurists and scholars—*Streicher* for the proposition that international

---

* This article was previously published in the *Ohio State Law Journal* and is properly cited as Gregory S. Gordon, "The Forgotten Nuremberg Hate Speech Case: Otto Dietrich and the Future of Persecution Law," *Ohio St. L.J.* 75 (2014): 571. It is reprinted with permission.

** Associate Professor of Law, University of North Dakota School of Law, and Director, UND Center for Human Rights and Genocide Studies; former Prosecutor, International Criminal Tribunal for Rwanda and United States Department of Justice; J.D., U.C. Berkeley School of Law. This piece was originally presented at Harvard Law School (HLS) as part of a seminar sponsored by the Institute for the Study of Global Antisemitism and Policy (ISGAP). I would like to thank HLS and ISGAP, especially Director Charles Asher Small, for providing a superb forum and excellent feedback. I am also grateful for the outstanding work of our law library's Head of Faculty Services, Jan Stone. Jim Saywell, Dave Twombly, Matt Borden and the other editors of the *Ohio State Law Journal* have been such a pleasure to work with in preparing this article for publication—I would like to acknowledge their able assistance. And thanks, as always, to my amazing wife, whose support made this article possible.

1 See The Nurnberg Trial, 6 F.R.D. 69, 161-63 (Int'l Mil. Trib. 1946).

2 See id. at 186-87.

3 See, e.g., Prosecutor v. Nahimana, Barayagwiza & Ngeze, Case No. ICTR 99-52-T, Judgment and Sentence, ¶¶980-82 (Dec. 3, 2003), http://www.refworld.org/pdfid/404468bc2.pdf (beginning "review of international law and jurisprudence on incitement to discrimination and violence" with exclusive exposition of IMT *Streicher* and *Fritzsche* judgments); see also Prosecutor v. Ruggiu, Case No. ICTR 97-32-I, Judgment and Sentence, ¶19 (June 1, 2000), http://www.unictr.org/Portals/0/Case/English/Ruggiu/judgement/rug010600.pdf (examining "significant legal precedents related to the crime of persecution" and then uniquely citing *Streicher*); Prosecutor v. Jean-Paul Akayesu, Case No. ICTR 96-4-T, Judgment, ¶550 (Sept. 2, 1998), http://www.unictr.org/Portals/0/Case/English/Akayesu/judgement/akay001.pdf (citing *Streicher* as the "most famous conviction for incitement").

4 The Nurnberg Trial, 6 F.R.D. at 161-63.

5 Id. at 186-87.

criminal charges against propagandists are viable and can target a wide range of speech;[6] *Fritzsche* to back the contention that such charges have their limits and must be directed at only a narrow category of expression.[7] And even without *Fritzsche*, the *Streicher* judgment is somewhat equivocal in its holding.[8] In particular, parts of it suggest that persecution can be proved by speech not amounting to direct calls for violence.[9] Other portions suggest otherwise.[10]

But exclusive reference to the IMT judgments as the founding texts of atrocity speech law is misplaced. Not long after *Streicher* and *Fritzsche*, and in the same courtroom, the United States Nuremberg Military Tribunal (NMT) in the *Ministries Case* issued an equally significant crimes against humanity judgment against a Nazi propaganda defendant—Reich Press Chief Otto Dietrich.[11] To the extent *Streicher* and *Fritzsche* arrived at different results, *Dietrich* broke the tie. For his inflammatory language in service of the Hitler regime, the NMT found the Press Chief guilty of persecution as a crime against humanity.[12] And it did so despite the fact that the language at issue in that case did not directly call for violence.[13]

So why is the *Dietrich* judgment, a relatively obscure holding, issued sixty-five years ago, so significant today, after the development of a substantial body of ad hoc tribunal jurisprudence on atrocity speech?[14] It is because the seemingly antithetical

---

6 See, e.g., *Nahimana*, Case No. ICTR 99-52-T, Judgment and Sentence, ¶¶980-82 (finding that hate-speech radio broadcasts not necessarily calling for action blatantly deprived the target ethnic group of fundamental rights and thus, even without proof of causally related violence, could be the basis for charging persecution as a crime against humanity); *Ruggiu*, Case No. ICTR 97-32-I, Judgment and Sentence, ¶21 (taking a similarly expansive view of hate speech and persecution); Gregory S. Gordon, "From Incitement to Indictment? Prosecuting Iran's President for Advocating Israel's Destruction and Piecing Together Incitement Law's Emerging Analytical Framework," 98 *J. Crim. L. & Criminology* 853, 886-90 (2008) (finding that Iran's president could be liable for persecution based on hate speech directed at Israel).

7 See, e.g., Prosecutor v. Kordic & Cerkez, Case No. IT-95-14/2-T, Judgment, j 209 (Int'l Crim. Trib. for the Former Yugoslavia Feb. 26, 2001), http://www.icty.org/x/cases/kordic_cerkez/tjug/en/kor-tj010226e.pdf (finding that the hate speech alleged in the indictment did not constitute persecution because it did not directly call for violence and thus failed to rise to the same level of gravity as the other enumerated CAH acts, such as murder and rape); Diane F. Orentlicher, "Criminalizing Hate Speech in the Crucible of Trial: *Prosecutor v. Nahimana*," 12 *New Eng. Int'l & Comp. L. Ann.* 17, 39-40 (2005) (suggesting that, in light of freedom of expression concerns, hate speech not directly calling for violence should not be the basis for crimes against humanity (persecution) charges).

8 See *infra* notes 28-38 and accompanying text.

9 See *infra* notes 28-38 and accompanying text.

10 See *infra* notes 28-38 and accompanying text.

11 See United States v. Ernst von Weizsaecker, et al. (*Ministries Case*), Judgment, in XIV *Trials of War Criminals before the Nuernberg Military Tribunals under Control Council Law No. 10: "The Ministries Case"* [hereinafter *Trials of War Criminals*] 575-76 (1949-1953).

12 See id.

13 See id.

14 See *supra* notes 6-7; see also Prosecutor v. Niyitegeka, Case No. ICTR 96-14-T, Judgment and Sentence, ¶142 (May 16, 2003), http://www.unictr.org/Portals/07Case/English/Niyitegeka/judgement/index.pdf (incitement charge against Minister of Information of rump genocide regime); Prosecutor v. Kambanda, Case No. ICTR 97-23-S, Judgment and Sentence, ¶44 (Sept. 4, 1998), http://www.unictr.org/Portals/0/Case/English/Kambanda/decisions/kambanda.pdf (incitement charge against Prime Minister of rump genocide regime).

holdings in *Streicher* and *Fritzsche* are more than just the subject of academic discourse. The next generation of atrocity speech decisions, it turns out, is at loggerheads about the relationship between hate speech and persecution as a crime against humanity.[15] Trial chambers for the International Criminal Tribunal for Rwanda (ICTR) have found that hate speech, standing alone, can be the basis for crimes against humanity (persecution) charges.[16] A trial chamber for the International Criminal Tribunal for the former Yugoslavia (ICTY) has reached the opposite conclusion.[17] And an appeals chamber for the ICTR, which could have resolved the split between the two Tribunals, refused to do so.[18]

Surprisingly, these judicial decisions, like the academic commentary, have completely ignored the *Dietrich* judgment.[19] This article fills in the significant lacunae in the judicial and academic literature regarding *Dietrich* by elucidating its holding, showing its relationship to the IMT and ad hoc tribunal decisions, explaining its significance for future hate speech cases and offering an explanation for why it has lain in obscurity for over six decades. In the end, it concludes that the proper consideration of this overlooked decision could lend normative sanction to charging persecution for less direct forms of hate speech that nonetheless dehumanize the victim population and condition the perpetrator population to commit mass atrocity—all in service of a widespread or systematic attack against a civilian population. In such situations, concerns about protecting free speech abate and the proper emphasis on protecting the persecuted holds sway.

The article is divided into four sections. Part Two provides background regarding the Nuremberg Nazi propaganda defendants with a particular focus on Otto Dietrich. More specifically, it provides an overview of the *Ministries* trial proceedings against him and an analysis of the NMT's judgment. Despite some ambiguities in the record, it shows that Dietrich was convicted of persecution as a crime against humanity on the basis of his speech-related activity on behalf of the Third Reich. Part Three will examine the ad hoc tribunal cases regarding persecution as a crime against humanity, including the split between the ICTR and ICTY, the refusal of the ICTR Appeals Chamber to resolve the split, and the academic commentary surrounding the split. Finally, Part Four will explain *Dietrich's* significance in resolving

---

15 Gregory S. Gordon, "Hate Speech and Persecution: A Contextual Approach," 46 *Vand. J. Transnat'l L.* 303, 305-6 (2013). This article is a follow-up to "Hate Speech and Persecution," which considered the *Dietrich* case more parenthetically. The analysis herein fleshes out that article's collateral implications regarding *Dietrich* and provides an essential historical account of what ought to be a cornerstone judgment in the development of atrocity speech law.

16 See Prosecutor v. Nahimana, Barayagwiza & Ngeze, Case No. ICTR 99-52-T, Judgment and Sentence, ¶¶980-82 (Dec. 3, 2003), http://www.refworld.org/pdfid/404468bc2.pdf; Prosecutor v. Ruggiu, Case No. ICTR 97-32-I, Judgment and Sentence, ¶19 (June 1, 2000), http://www.unictr.org/Portals/0/Case/English/Ruggiu/judgement/rug010600.pdf.

17 See Prosecutor v. Kordic & Cerkez, Case No. IT-95-14/2-T, Judgment, ¶209 (Int'l Crim. Trib. for the Former Yugoslavia Feb. 26, 2001), http://www.icty.org/x/cases/kordic_cerkez/tjug/en/kor-tj010226e.pdf.

18 Nahimana, Barayagwiza & Ngeze v. Prosecutor, Case No. ICTR 99-52-A, Judgment, ¶987 (Nov. 28, 2007), http://www.refworld.org/pdfid/404468bc2.pdf.

19 See Gordon, *supra* note 15, at 359 (referring to *Dietrich* and noting that "commentators and scholars have overlooked an extremely important piece of Nuremberg' s jurisprudential mosaic").

the dispute. Given ongoing or recent instances of hate speech connected to atrocity in different parts of the world, including such place s as Burma, Iran, Kenya, the Ivory Coast, and Sudan, the issue of whether hate speech standing alone may support a charge of persecution as a crime against humanity takes on significant relevance going forward.

Forums such as the International Criminal Court, dealing with both current and future cases, as well as domestic or ad hoc tribunals established to try recent and ongoing crimes, including those connected with the recent bloodshed in Egypt, may be called on to resolve the split between the ICTR and ICTY. And the judgment against Otto Dietrich may well resolve it in favor of finding that hate speech not explicitly calling for action, and standing on its own, may be the basis of a charge of persecution as a crime against humanity.

II. The Nuremberg Propaganda Cases

A. Overview

On achieving victory over Axis forces in World War II, the Allies established the International Military Tribunal at Nuremberg (IMT) to bring major Nazi perpetrators to justice.[20] Among the accused were two Third Reich media figures: Julius Streicher and Hans Fritzsche.[21] The IMT convicted Streicher for crimes against humanity based on the virulently antisemitic pieces in his weekly tabloid, *Der Stürmer*, published from 1923 through 1945.[22] Fritzsche was similarly charged owing to his work as head of the Radio Division of Nazi Germany's "Ministry of Public Enlightenment and Propaganda" (Propaganda Ministry).[23]

Following the IMT proceeding, the United States instituted twelve trials of lower-ranking Nazi officials in the so-called subsequent Nuremberg proceedings, pursuant to Control Council Law Number 10.[24] The penultimate proceeding is referred to as the *Ministries Case*, which tried defendants in important posts in the Nazi ministries in the center of Berlin.[25] Among those defendants was the Propaganda Ministry's Press Chief, Otto Dietrich, whose job was to control the content of the Third Reich's newspapers and inform Adolf Hitler of newspaper content domestically and internationally.[26] Dietrich was convicted of crimes against humanity.[27]

---

20 Charter of the International Military Tribunal, Aug. 8, 1945, 59 Stat. 1544, 82 U.N.T.S. 279 [hereinafter Nuremberg Charter], reprinted in *Report of Robert H. Jackson, United States Representative to the International Conference on Military Trials* 420-28 (1949).

21 J. Benton Heath, "Human Dignity at Trial: Hard Cases and Broad Concepts in International Criminal Law," 44 *Geo. Wash. Int'l L. Rev.* 317, 363 (2012).

22 See Antonio Cassese, Guido Acquaviva, Mary Fan and Alex Whiting, *International Criminal Law: Cases and Commentary* 156 (2011).

23 Michael G. Kearney, *The Prohibition of Propaganda for War in International Law* 42 (2007).

24 Steven Fogelson, "The Nuremberg Legacy: An Unfulfilled Promise," 63 *S. Cal. L. Rev.* 833, 859 n. 198 (1990).

25 Larry May, *Aggression and Crimes Against Peace* 171-72 (2008).

26 Lyn Gorman and David McLean, *Media and Society into the 21st Century: A Historical Introduction* 93-94 (2d ed. 2009).

27 Sarabeth A. Smith, Note, "What's Old Is New Again: Terrorism and the Growing Need To Revisit the Prohibition on Propaganda," 37 *Syracuse J. Int'l. L. & Com.* 299, 319 (2010).

Each of these cases shall be considered in turn.

B. Julius Streicher

Julius Streicher was born on February 12, 1885, in the Upper Bavarian village of Fleinhausen.[28] He began his career as a teacher and then enlisted in the German Army during World War I. He served with distinction, earning, among other medals, the Iron Cross, First Class.[29] After World War I, Julius Streicher became the leader of the "German Socialist Party" and was initially a rival of Hitler.[30] But given their ideological affinities, they joined forces and Streicher became a loyal Hitler lieutenant. Streicher soon amassed much power, becoming, in rapid succession, a general in the SA Storm Troopers, the Gauleiter (district leader) of Franconia, and a member of the Reichstag.[31] On his own initiative, he also founded a viciously anti-Jewish newspaper in 1923 called *Der Stürmer*.[32] Read by 600,000 subscribers at its peak, this crude rag published a constant stream of hate screeds and grotesque caricatures meant to vilify and dehumanize Jews.[33] Displayed on public bulletin boards in glass-covered cases, the publication exerted a significant influence on German attitudes toward the Jewish community. As Nuremberg prosecutor Alexander Hardy noted:

> The full force and effect of [Streicher's] press propaganda on the masses is contained in an episode relating to the time when Streicher, as a Gauleiter, delivered a Christmas story to the children of Nuremberg. Reaching the climax of his Yuletide tale, which concerned a "little Aryan boy and girl," Streicher suddenly asked the children, "do you know who the devil is?" And the little ones shrieked in chorus, "The Jew, the Jew."[34]

The IMT judgment against Streicher started with an observation regarding his antisemitic rhetoric and reputation: "For his twenty-five years of speaking, writing, and preaching hatred of the Jews, Streicher was widely known as 'Jew-Baiter Number One.'"[35] The judgment reviewed a skein of pre- and post-war pieces Streicher penned himself calling for the annihilation, "root and branch," of the Jewish people.[36] It wrote that "[i]n his speeches and articles week after week, month after month, he infected the German mind with the virus of anti-Semitism, and incited the German people to active persecution."[37] The judgment further specified that Streicher wrote a good portion of these genocidal texts contemporaneous with Jews being liquidated in Eastern Europe. And Streicher, the Tribunal concluded,

---

28 Randall L. Bytwerk, *Julius Streicher: Nazi Editor of the Notorious Antisemitic Newspaper* Der Stürmer 2 (2001).

29 Id. at 5-6.

30 Alexander G. Hardy, *Hitler's Secret Weapon: The "Managed Press" and Propaganda Machine of Nazi Germany* 82 (1967).

31 Id.

32 Ann Tusa and John Tusa, *The Nuremberg Trial* 503 (1984).

33 Hardy, *supra* note 30, at 82.

34 Id. at 83.

35 See, e.g., The Nurnberg Trial, 6 F.R.D. 69, 162 (Int'l Mil. Trib. 1946).

36 Id. at 161-63.

37 Id. at 162.

knew about Nazi atrocities to the east when he published these articles. The judgment concluded: "Streicher's incitement to murder and extermination at the time when Jews in the East were being killed under the most horrible conditions clearly constitutes persecution on political and racial grounds in connection with war crimes, as defined by the Charter, and constitutes a crime against humanity."[38]

C. Hans Fritzsche

The son of a civil servant,[39] Hans Fritzsche was born in Bochum, in the Ruhr area of the western part of Germany, in 1900.[40] After serving as a private in the infantry of the German Army at the end of World War I, Fritzsche studied modern languages, history, and philosophy at Griefswald and Berlin without passing his examinations.[41] From there he transitioned into journalism, working as a correspondent for the *Hamburg Press*[42] and as an editor for the *Telegraphen Union* news agency and the International News Service. He then gained expertise in a new medium, radio, ultimately becoming the head of the *Drahtloser Dienst* (Wireless News Service) in 1932.[43]

In May 1933, Fritzsche joined the staff of the Nazi Propaganda Ministry and by 1938 had risen to the level of Chief of the German Press Division.[44] In this capacity, he issued Nazi propaganda "press directives" to newspaper editors on a daily basis.[45] These were essentially orders issued at a daily press conference for what the press should publish.[46] The IMT described these as "instructions [directing] the press to present to the people certain themes, such as the leadership principle, the Jewish problem, the problem of living space, or other standard Nazi ideas."[47] In 1942, Fritzsche became head of the Radio Division of the Propaganda Ministry and hosted a daily radio program "*Hans Fritzsche Speaks*."[48]

These broadcasts were the basis of the crimes against humanity charges against Fritzsche. The evidence presented against him at trial demonstrated that such radio emissions espoused the general policies of the Nazi regime, which "arouse[d] in the German people those passions which led them to the commission of atrocities."[49] The Tribunal did not find Fritzsche guilty, though, because it concluded his Jeremiads against the Jews did not directly urge their persecution and "[h]is position and official duties were not sufficiently important ... to infer that he took part in originating or formulating propaganda campaigns."[50]

---

38 Id. at 163.

39 Robert S. Wistrich, *Who's Who in Nazi Germany* 68 (2002).

40 Leslie Alan Horvitz and Christopher Catherwood, *Encyclopedia of War Crimes and Genocide* 159 (2006).

41 Wistrich, *supra* note 39, at 68.

42 Horvitz and Catherwood, *supra* note 40, at 159.

43 Hardy, *supra* note 30, at 87.

44 Id.

45 Id.

46 Wistrich, *supra* note 39, at 68.

47 See The Nurnberg Trial, Judgment, Fritzsche (Int'l Mil. Trib. Sept. 30, 1946), reprinted in 6 F.R.D. 69, 186 (1946).

48 Hardy, *supra* note 30, at 87.

49 The Nurnberg Trial, 6 F.R.D at 186-87.

50 Id.

Nuremberg prosecutor Alexander Hardy later observed that evidence not available by the time of the earlier IMT proceeding certainly would have resulted in a guilty conviction for Fritzsche:

> [His work as Chief of the German Press Division] was far more important than the task of venting his golden voice.... [Later found press directives] brought the lie to Fritzsche's denials, during his trial before the IMT, of knowledge of such crimes as the extermination of the Jews and atrocities in concentration camps. He not only knew of them but played an important part in bringing them about.[51]

In fact, Fritzsche later faced justice before a German *Spruchkammer*, or Denazification Court, and was sentenced to eight years, the maximum punishment such courts could mete out.[52]

D. Otto Dietrich

1. Background

Otto Dietrich was born in the western German city of Essen, also in the Ruhr, in 1897.[53] Described by one expert as "resolutely middle-class," he attended a local grammar school before volunteering to serve in the German Army with the outbreak of World War I.[54] He was assigned to the western front and was ultimately awarded the Iron Cross, First Class.[55] He then studied at the Universities of Munich, Frankfurt am Main, and Freiburg, earning a doctorate in political science in 1921.[56] He began his career as a research assistant for the Essen Chamber of Commerce and then transitioned into the newspaper business. He started as a deputy editor of the Essen *Nationalzeitung*.[57] Then, in 1928, he became business manager for the *Augsburger Zeitung*, a German-national evening paper.[58]

He then married into a newspaper family. As the son-in-law of the influential owner of the *Rheinisch-Westfalische Zeitung*, he forged important links with Rhineland heavy industry and became himself an adviser of a big steel trust.[59] In 1929 he joined the Nazi Party and began working for Adolf Hitler as the Nazi leader's "Press Referent." He then used his industrial connections to introduce Hitler to Westphalian coal and iron magnates.[60] Owing to his vital role in Nazi fundraising efforts, he was able to forge a close relationship with Hitler.[61]

Dietrich also became an active publicist and prolific writer for the Nazi Party.[62] Throughout the 1930s, he published a number of texts that "recalled the 'heroic'

---

51 Hardy, *supra* note 30, at 87.

52 Id. at 85.

53 Roger Moorhouse, *Introduction to Otto Dietrich, The Hitler I Knew: Memoirs of the Third Reich's Press Chief*, at ix (2010).

54 Id.

55 Wistrich, *supra* note 39, at 39.

56 Id.

57 Id.

58 Id.

59 Id.

60 Hardy, *supra* note 30, at 50; Moorhouse, *supra* note 53, at ix.

61 Hardy, *supra* note 30, at 50.

62 Moorhouse, *supra* note 53, at ix.

phase of the Party struggle, outlined Nazism's philosophical underpinning or contributed to the growing deification of Hitler."[63] These works included *Mit Hitler an die Macht* (With Hitler on the Road to Power) (1933), *Die philosophischen Grundlagen des Nationalsozialismus* (The Philosophical Foundations of Nazism) (1935), and *Der Führer und das deutsche Volk* (The Führer and the German People) (1936).[64]

2. Dietrich and the press

Roger Moorhouse notes that "for all his publications, Dietrich's main responsibility was as a controller of his fellow journalists."[65] In 1931, Hitler made Dietrich Director of the Nazi Party's Reich Press Office.[66] In that position, he further impressed the future Führer by closely managing all press details of Hitler's 1931 "aerial" election campaign, which involved flying 30,000 miles and addressing 10,000,000 Germans at 200 meetings.[67] On February 28, 1934, soon after becoming Reich Chancellor, Hitler named Dietrich the Nazi party "Reich Press Chief."[68] In his decree doing so, Hitler wrote: "He (Dietrich) directs in my name the guiding principles for the entire editorial work of the Party Press. In addition, as my Press Chief he is the highest authority for all press publications of the Party and all its agencies."[69]

Dietrich's authority over the press soon extended beyond the party and into the government with his appointment as Reich Press Chief of the Government in November 1937. In that position, he exerted control over the policy and content of print media in the Third Reich. This included the German Press, Foreign Press, and Periodical Press in the umbrella "Press Division" of the Propaganda Ministry.[70]

His control was exerted in two primary ways. First, he or one of his subordinates held daily "press conferences" with representatives of all German newspapers, orally giving them the "*Tagesparolen*" or daily press directives.[71] The significance of the *Tagesparolen* was described by the IMT in the Fritzsche trial: "[The *Tagesparolen*], as these instructions were labeled, directed the press to present certain themes, such as the leadership principle, the Jewish problem, the problem of living space, or other standard Nazi ideas."[72]

---

63 Id.

64 Id. at ix n. 1.

65 Id. at ix-x.

66 Hardy, *supra* note 30, at 50.

67 Id.

68 Id.

69 Id. at 50-51.

70 Id. at 52.

71 Id. at 40-44.

72 The Nurnberg Trial, 6 F.R.D. 69, 186 (Int'l Mil. Trib. 1946). According to Alexander Hardy, Fritzsche was acquitted mainly because the evidence before the IMT contained only isolated copies of the *Tagesparolen*—"and none replete with criminal overtone such as those received as evidence in the Dietrich case." Hardy, *supra* note 30, at 41. Dietrich ordered all written copies of the *Tagesparolen* destroyed by the editors who received them. By the time of Dietrich's trial, prosecutors had found two editors who had not destroyed their copies. Those had not been discovered by the time of the IMT's judgment. Id. at 40-41.

Second, Dietrich exercised control through the "Editorial Control Law," which he helped formulate.[73] The law obligated all newspaper and periodical editors to be members of the "Reich League of the German Press."[74] Dietrich, as Chairman of the Reich League, operated courts that disciplined and removed editors who did not toe Nazism's ideological line.[75] As one historian has noted:

> Dietrich cooked the German news to Hitler's prescriptions [and ensured] complete regimentation of editors and journalists.... On 22 February 1942 Hitler expressed his admiration for Dietrich's resourcefulness in one of his rambling table talks: "Dr. Dietrich may be physically small, but he is exceptionally gifted at his job.... I am proud of the fact that with his handful of men I can at once throw the rudder of the press through 180 degrees—as happened on 22 June 1941 [the day Germany invaded Russia]. There is no other country which can copy us in that."[76]

At the same time, Dietrich also served a special personal function for Hitler—his daily presentation of the so-called "Führer Material." This was a compilation of news material from domestic and foreign press news sources and it "gave Dietrich added exposure to Hitler and gained him tremendous influence, as he virtually determined what he wanted Hitler to read.... Hitler's political decisions were influenced by the perusal of this material."[77]

3. Dietrich in the Nazi power hierarchy

Consistent with this influence, Dietrich's growing stature in the party was marked by promotion in other branches of the Nazi power structure. In 1933, Hitler had selected Dietrich for membership in the exclusive "Party Cabinet Members," a group which included the highest strata of Nazi leaders such as Deputy Führer Rudolf Hess, Stürmabteilung (SA) Chief Ernst Röhm, Schutzstaffel (SS) Chief Heinrich Himmler, German Labor Front Leader Robert Ley, Minister of Food and Agriculture Walther Darré, Propaganda Minister Josef Goebbels, Governor General Hans Frank, and Foreign Policy Office Leader and Party Philosopher Alfred Rosenberg.[78]

Dietrich also became a powerful leader within the SS. On December 24, 1932, shortly before Hitler's accession to the chancellorship, Dietrich joined the organization with the rank of SS Oberführer.[79] From there, he advanced rapidly, becoming an SS Brigadeführer a little over a year later, and within three weeks of that an SS Gruppenführer. He was attached to Heinrich Himmler's staff in April 1936, and by 1941 he had attained the rank of SS Obergruppenführer. Within this rank was an exclusive list of elite SS leaders at the top of which was Himmler himself, at No. 1. Dietrich was No. 21.[80]

---

[73] Jeffrey Herf, *The Jewish Enemy: Nazi Propaganda During World War II and the Holocaust* 18 (2006).

[74] Id.

[75] Id.

[76] Wistrich, *supra* note 39, at 40.

[77] Hardy, *supra* note 30, at 65-66.

[78] Id. at 51.

[79] Id.

[80] Id.

4. Dietrich and the persecution of the Jews

In 1937, Dietrich was appointed to the position of State Secretary (for the German Press, Foreign Press and Periodicals Divisions) in the Propaganda Ministry, a post at which he remained until the end of the war.[81] Although formally subordinate to Goebbels, Dietrich's close relationship with Hitler permitted him to go over Goebbels's head whenever he wanted. In the words of Nuremberg prosecutor Alexander Hardy: "Dietrich exploited [his various positions of power] and his constant intimacy with the Fuehrer to disseminate the principal doctrines of the Nazi conspirators."[82]

Hardy goes on to specify Dietrich's significant role in the conditioning of the German people for persecution of the Jews:

> It was Dietrich, the *Poisoned Pen*, who led the press propaganda phases of the program which incited hatred and conditioned public opinion for mass persecutions on political, racial, and religious grounds. Heretofore, Dietrich's role has been ignored by historians, but actually he, more than anyone else, was responsible for presenting to the German people the justification for liquidating the Jews.... Dietrich had at his disposal not only Streicher's paper, but more than 3,000 other publications in the newspaper field and 4,000 publications in the periodical field with a circulation of better than 30,000,000 to disseminate anti-Semitism in a vastly more comprehensive manner. And, he did just that![83]

5. The trial and conviction of Otto Dietrich

i. Background

A die-hard Nazi until the final days of the war, Dietrich finally fell afoul of Hitler only a month before the Führer's suicide.[84] On March 30, 1945, Hitler accused Dietrich of defeatism in a heated exchange over propaganda tactics.[85] Hitler then placed him on indefinite leave.[86] He eventually resurfaced in the post-war chaos and was arrested by the British.[87]

Given the timing of his arrest and his being technically subordinate to Goebbels, Dietrich was not tried in the IMT proceeding of the major war criminals.[88] Rather, he was prosecuted by the Americans in their occupation zone as part of one in a series

---

81 Id.

82 Id.

83 Hardy, *supra* note 30, at 188-89.

84 Moorhouse, *supra* note 53, at x.

85 Id.

86 Id.

87 Id.

88 Of course, Fritzsche, an IMT defendant, was also subordinate to Goebbels. But Fritzsche was put in the dock at the IMT at the insistence of the Soviet Union, which had in its custody significantly fewer IMT defendants than the other allies, especially the Americans. See "How Did Hans Fritzsche Avoid the Noose?," *Propagander FAQ*, http://grwa.tripod.com/050.html (last visited Mar. 23, 2013). Fritzsche was one of only two high-ranking Nazis captured by the Soviets (the other being Raeder). Id. They felt Fritzsche's inclusion would help balance the inequality regarding IMT defendants vis-à-vis the other allies. Id. So his prosecution before the IMT, as opposed to a subsequent trial in the Russian zone, was motivated largely by incipient Cold War political considerations. Id.

of twelve trials of lesser-ranking officials that followed the IMT.[89] The trials were conducted pursuant to Allied Control Council Law No. 10 (CCL No. 10) before the Nuremberg Military Tribunals (NMTs). Pursuant to Article II(a) of CCL No. 10, "Crimes against Humanity" are defined as "atrocities and offenses, including but not limited to murder, extermination, enslavement, deportation, imprisonment, torture, rape, or other inhumane acts committed against any civilian population, *or persecutions on political, racial or religious grounds* whether or not in violation of the domestic laws of the country where perpetrated."[90]

Of these subsequent trials, Dietrich was a defendant in the so-called *Ministries Case*, also known as the *Wilhelmstrasse Case* or *United States v. Ernst von Weizsaecker, et al.*[91] The eleventh of the twelve trials, the twenty-one defendants in the case were officials of various Reich ministries and other prominent government members, bankers, and armaments officials.[92]

ii. The indictment

The Ministries indictment was filed on November 18, 1947, and the defendants were arraigned two days later.[93] The indictment listed eight counts: *Count 1*—Crimes against Peace (styled "Planning, Preparation, Initiation, and Waging of Wars of Aggression and Invasions of Other Countries"); *Count 2*—Conspiracy to Commit Crimes against Peace (styled "Common Plan and Conspiracy"); *Count 3*—War Crimes (styled "War Crimes: Murder and Ill-Treatment of Belligerents and Prisoners of War"); *Count 4*—Crimes against Humanity (styled "Crimes against Humanity: Atrocities and Offenses Committed against German Nationals on Political, Racial and Religious Grounds from 1933 to 1939"); *Count 5*—War Crimes and Crimes against Humanity (styled "War Crimes and Crimes against Humanity: Atrocities and Offenses Committed against Civilian Populations"); *Count 6*—War Crimes and Crimes against Humanity (styled "War Crimes and Crimes against Humanity: Plunder and Spoliation"); *Count 7*—War Crimes and Crimes against Humanity (styled "War Crimes and Crimes against Humanity: Slave Labor"); and *Count 8*—Membership in Criminal Organizations.[94]

---

89 "Subsequent Nuremberg Proceedings, Case #11, The Ministries Case," *U.S. Holocaust Memorial Museum*, http://www.ushmm.org/wlc/en/article.php?ModuleId=10007082 (last updated June 10, 2013) [hereinafter *Holocaust Encyclopedia*].

90 Allied Control Council Law No. 10, Punishment of Persons Guilty of War Crimes, Crimes Against Peace and Against Humanity, art. III(c) (Dec. 20, 1945) (emphasis added), reprinted in Telford Taylor, *Final Report to the Secretary of the Army on the Nuernberg War Crimes Trials Under Control Council Law No. 10*, at 250 (1949) [hereinafter CCL No. 10].

91 United States v. Ernst von Weizsaecker, et al. (*Ministries Case*), Opening Statements, in XII *Trials of War Criminals*, *supra* note 11, at 350. It is also known as the "Wilhelmstrasse Trial" because the German Foreign Office, where a number of the defendants worked, was located on the Wilhelmstrasse in Berlin. *The Nuremberg Trial and International Law* 268 (George Ginsburgs and V.N. Kudriavtsev eds., 1990).

92 *Holocaust Encyclopedia*, *supra* note 89.

93 Id.

94 United States v. Ernst von Weizsaecker, et al. (*Ministries Case*), Indictment, in XII *Trials of War Criminals*, *supra* note 11, at 13-63.

Not every defendant was indicted on every count of the indictment. Dietrich himself was indicted only with respect to Counts 1 (Crimes against Peace), 3 (War Crimes), 4 (Crimes against Humanity: Persecution of German Nationals), 5 (Crimes against Humanity: Atrocities and Offenses Committed against Civilian Populations), and 8 (Membership in Criminal Organizations).[95]

iii. The conviction

At trial's end, Dietrich was convicted on only Counts 5 and 8.[96] Count 4, whose title in the indictment was "Crimes against Humanity: Atrocities and Offenses Committed against German Nationals on Political, Racial and Religious Grounds from 1933 to 1939," was dismissed by the Tribunal prior to the judgment (given its unique focus on pre-war conduct).[97] Count 4's title, in relation to the definition of "persecution" in CCL No. 10, Art. III(a), indicates explicitly that it charged the named defendants with persecution.[98]

That is not true of Count 5, the charge on which Dietrich was convicted in relation to his media activity and hate speech. Styled "War Crimes and Crimes against Humanity: Atrocities and Offenses Committed against Civilian Populations," Count 5 certainly encompasses different categories of criminal conduct.[99] But that conduct includes persecution based on speech activity. In particular, paragraph 38 of the indictment (the first paragraph under Count 5) states that the defendants committed "crimes against humanity, as defined by Article II of Control Council Law No. 10, in that they participated in atrocities and offenses, including ... persecutions on political, racial, and religious grounds."[100] Paragraph 39 specifies that "[t]he defendants created, formulated and disseminated inflammatory teachings which incited the Germans to the active persecution of 'political and racial undesirables.'"[101] Paragraph 46 centers this specifically on Dietrich's hate speech, noting that, in relation to the program to exterminate the Jews, Dietrich and the other specified defendants "presented to the German people" "the rationale and justification for, and the impetus to, mass slaughter."[102] Paragraph 48 goes on to declare that, in execution of this program "the defendant Dietrich conditioned public opinion to accept this program."[103]

The prosecution's opening statement makes the point explicitly:

---

95 Kevin Jon Heller, *The Nuremberg Military Tribunals and the Origins of International Criminal Law* 457 (2011). Dietrich's conviction on Count 8 meant the Tribunal found him to be a member of the SS and Leadership Corps of the Nazi party. Id. at 290-91. The conviction on that count did not implicate Dietrich's hate speech or media conduct. Id.

96 Id. at 457.

97 Id.

98 Id. at 473-74.

99 United States v. Ernst von Weizsaecker, et al. (*Ministries Case*), Indictment, in XII *Trials of War Criminals*, *supra* note 11, at 43.

100 Id. at 43-44.

101 Id. at 44. The paragraph concludes: "In speeches, articles, news releases, and other publications, it was constantly reiterated that those groups were germs, pests, and subhumans who must be destroyed." Id.

102 Id. at 47.

103 Id. at 48.

> The war crimes and crimes against humanity charged in the indictment fall into three broad categories. First, there are war crimes committed in the actual course of hostilities or against members of the armed forces of countries at war with Germany. These are set forth in count three of the indictment. Second, there are crimes committed, chiefly against civilians, in the course of and as part of the German occupation of countries overrun by the Wehrmacht. These include various crimes set forth in count five of the indictment, the charges of plunder and spoliation in count six, and the charges pertaining to slave labor in count seven. Many of the crimes in this second category constitute, at one and the same time, war crimes as defined in paragraph 1*(b)* and crimes against humanity as defined in paragraph 1*(c)* of Article II of Law No. 10. *Third, there are crimes committed against civilian populations in the course of persecution on political, racial, and religious grounds. Such crimes, when committed prior to the actual initiation of Germany's invasions and aggressive wars, are set forth in count four of the indictment; when committed thereafter, they are charged in count five.* The crimes described in count four accordingly, are charged only as crimes against humanity; those charged in count five, for the most part, constitute at one and the same time war crimes and crimes against humanity.[104]

In its closing statement concerning Dietrich, with respect to persecution, the prosecution stressed that Dietrich's criminal responsibility arose from his conditioning the German people to embrace persecution of the Jews. Noting that, like Streicher, Dietrich "infected the German mind with the virus of anti-Semitism, and incited the German people to active persecution," the prosecution pointed out that Dietrich's influence was even further-reaching.[105] Streicher's paper, *Der Stürmer*, at its peak, boasted a circulation of only 600,000.[106] But, the prosecution stressed, "Dietrich had at his disposal not only Streicher's paper, but more than 3,000 other publications with a circulation of better than 3,000,000."[107] The prosecution went on: "The evidence shows the character and intensity of the anti-Semitic directives released by the defendant Dietrich during the period to which the IMT referred in passing judgment on Streicher."[108] The prosecution then concluded that Dietrich "directed the press to present to the people certain themes, such as the leadership principle, the Jewish problem, the problem of living space, or other standard Nazi ideas which served as a condition precedent in tempering the masses of German people to each aggression."[109]

iv. A finding of persecution in the judgment

Most significantly, in its judgment, the NMT found Dietrich guilty on Count 5 based on his conditioning of the German people for the Final Solution:

---

104 United States v. Ernst von Weizsaecker, et al. (*Ministries Case*), Opening Statements, in XII *Trials of War Criminals*, *supra* note 11, at 167-68 (emphasis added).

105 United States v. Ernst von Weizsaecker (*Ministries Case*), Closing Statements, in XIV *Trials of War Criminals*, *supra* note 11, at 39-40.

106 Id. at 40.

107 Id.

108 Id.

109 Id.

> It is thus clear that a well thought-out, oft-repeated, persistent campaign to *arouse the hatred* of the German people against Jews was fostered and directed by the press department and its press chief, Dietrich. That part or much of this may have been inspired by Goebbels is undoubtedly true, but Dietrich approved and authorized every release....
>
> The only reason for this campaign was to blunt the sensibilities of the people regarding the campaign of persecution and murder which was being carried out.
>
> ...
>
> These press and periodical directives were not mere political polemics, they were not aimless expressions of anti-Semitism, and they were not designed only to unite the German people in the war effort.
>
> Their clear and expressed purpose was to enrage the German people against the Jews, to justify the measures taken and to be taken against them, and to subdue any doubts which might arise as to the justice of measures of racial persecution to which Jews were to be subjected.
>
> By them Dietrich consciously implemented, and by furnishing the excuses and justifications, participated in, the crimes against humanity regarding Jews.[110]

Although the Tribunal does not use the word "persecution" in the last sentence, it is clear that Dietrich's crimes against humanity conviction is based on persecution. Most significantly, the Tribunal referred to "persecution" in the sentence immediately preceding it (i.e., the purpose of Dietrich's press directives was to "subdue any doubts" regarding measures of "racial persecution" against the Jews).[111] Similarly, two paragraphs previously, the Tribunal opined that the only reason for Dietrich's campaign was to blunt the sensibilities of the people regarding the campaign of persecution.[112] Consistent with this, as revealed by the prosecution's opening statement, Count 5 of the indictment clearly includes persecution within its ambit.[113] And in its closing statement, in analogizing Dietrich with Streicher, the prosecution quoted that part of the IMT judgment against Streicher that referred to Streicher's "infecting the German mind with the virus of anti-Semitism" and thereby inciting the German people to "active persecution."[114] Streicher, as demonstrated previously, was convicted of persecution as a crime against humanity based on his hate speech.[115]

The final sentence also stands out for what it says about the basis for the persecution conviction. It was not specific calls or incitements to engage in particular action. Rather, to quote the judges, it was a "furnishing" of "excuses and justifications" to "subdue any doubts which might arise as to the justice of measures of racial persecution to which Jews were to be subjected."[116]

---

110 United States v. Ernst von Weizsaecker, et al. (*Ministries Case*), Judgment, in XIV *Trials of War Criminals, supra* note 11, at 575-76.

111 Id. at 576.

112 Id.

113 See *supra* notes 93-94 and accompanying text.

114 See *supra* note 104 and accompanying text.

115 See *supra* notes 35-38 and accompanying text.

116 United States v. Ernst von Weizsaecker, et al. (*Ministries Case*), Judgment, in XIV *Trials of War Criminals, supra* note 11, at 575-76.

III. HATE SPEECH AND PERSECUTION IN THE MODERN CASES AND COMMENTARY

A. Hate speech and persecution in the Rwandan Genocide cases

1. Georges Ruggiu

Over fifty years after the judgment at Nuremberg against Otto Dietrich, the International Criminal Tribunal for Rwanda charged Belgian national Georges Ruggiu with persecution as a crime against humanity for his incendiary radio broadcasts during the Rwandan Genocide.[117] Ruggiu was an announcer for Radio Télévision des Milles Collines (RTLM), an extremist Hutu radio outlet that urged the Rwandan majority group to slaughter Tutsis.[118] Ruggiu pled guilty to one count of crimes against humanity (persecution) in connection with his RTLM broadcasts. In sentencing him, the Tribunal summarized the elements that comprise the crime against humanity of persecution as follows: (1) "those elements required for all crimes against humanity under the Statute"—i.e., certain acts (such as persecution) when committed as part of a widespread or systematic attack directed against any civilian population, with knowledge of the attack; (2) "a gross or blatant denial of a fundamental right reaching the same level of gravity as the other acts prohibited under Article 5"; and (3) "discriminatory grounds."[119]

With respect to the mens rea required for the crime, the Tribunal held:

> The perpetrator must knowingly commit crimes against humanity in the sense that he must understand the overall context of his act.... Part of what transforms an individual's act(s) into a crime against humanity is the inclusion of the act within a greater dimension of criminal conduct. Therefore an accused should be aware of this greater dimension in order to be culpable thereof. Accordingly, actual or constructive knowledge of the broader context of the attack, meaning that the accused must know that his act(s) is part of a widespread or systematic attack on a civilian population and pursuant to some kind of policy or plan, is necessary to satisfy the requisite *mens rea* element of the accused.[120]

The Tribunal then found that Ruggiu's broadcast satisfied these elements:

> [W]hen examining the [admitted] acts of persecution ... it is possible to discern a common element. Those acts were direct and public radio broadcasts all aimed at singling out and attacking the Tutsi ethnic group ... on discriminatory grounds, by depriving them of the fundamental rights to life, liberty and basic humanity enjoyed by members of wider society. The deprivation of these rights can be said to have as its aim the death and removal of those persons from the society in which they live alongside the perpetrators, or eventually even from humanity itself.[121]

---

117 Gordon, *supra* note 15, at 320-21.

118 Id.

119 Prosecutor v. Ruggiu, Case No. ICTR 97-32-I, Judgment and Sentence, ¶21 (June 1, 2000) (citing Prosecutor v. Kupreskic, Case No. IT-95-16, Judgment (Int'l Crim. Trib. for the Former Yugoslavia Jan. 14, 2000)).

120 Id. ¶20 (citing Prosecutor v. Kayishema, Case No. ICTR 95-1-T, Judgment (May 21, 1999)).

121 Id. ¶22.

Significantly, the Tribunal noted the *Streicher* judgment was particularly relevant since Ruggiu, like Streicher, "infected peoples' [sic] minds with ethnic hatred and persecution."[122]

2. The ICTR *Media Case*

The ICTR then analyzed crimes against humanity (persecution) in the speech context as part of the famous *Media Case* judgment concerning media executives Ferdinand Nahimana, Jean-Bosco Barayagwiza, and Hassan Ngeze.[123] Nahimana and Barayagwiza were founders of RTLM and Ngeze was founder and editor-in-chief of the extremist Hutu newspaper *Kangura*.[124] All three defendants were convicted of crimes against humanity (persecution) charges.[125]

In finding the defendants guilty of these charges, the trial chamber reaffirmed that hate speech targeting a population on discriminatory group identity grounds constitutes the crime against humanity of persecution:

> Hate speech is a discriminatory form of aggression that destroys the dignity of those in the group under attack. It creates a lesser status not only in the eyes of the group members themselves but also in the eyes of others who perceive and treat them as less than human. The denigration of persons on the basis of their ethnic identity or other group membership in and of itself, as well as in its other consequences, can be an irreversible harm.[126]

The Tribunal pointed out that persecution is not a provocation to cause harm—it is the harm itself:

> Accordingly, there need not be a call to action in communications that constitute persecution. For the same reason, there need be no link between persecution and acts of violence. The Chamber notes that Julius Streicher was convicted by the International Military Tribunal at Nuremberg of persecution as a crime against humanity for anti-Semitic writings that significantly predated the extermination of Jews in the 1940s. Yet they were understood to be like a poison that infected the minds of the German people and conditioned them to follow the lead of the National Socialists in persecuting the Jewish people. In Rwanda, the virulent writings of *Kangura* and the incendiary broadcasts of RTLM functioned in the same way, conditioning the Hutu population and creating a climate of harm, as evidenced in part by the extermination and genocide that followed.[127]

3. The *Mugesera Case*

Another Rwandan Genocide case implicating hate speech as a crime against humanity was adjudicated by the Supreme Court of Canada. In November 1992, not long before the Rwandan Genocide, Léon Mugesera delivered a venomous anti-Tutsi

---

122 Id. ¶19.

123 Gordon, *supra* note 15, at 323.

124 Id.

125 Id. at 324-25.

126 Prosecutor v. Nahimana, Barayagwiza & Ngeze, Case No. ICTR 99-52-T, Judgment and Sentence, ¶1072 (Dec. 3, 2003), http://www.refworld.org/pdfid/404468bc2.pdf.

127 Id. ¶1073.

speech to Hutu extremist supporters in Kabaya, Gisenyi province.[128] In the speech, Mugesera dehumanized the Tutsis, referring to them as cockroaches and snakes that should be expelled from Rwanda.[129] Based on the speech, Rwandan authorities indicted Mugesera, who fled to Canada and became the object of a Canadian deportation case.[130] Mugesera appealed adverse rulings all the way up to the Canadian Supreme Court, which confronted the issue of whether Mugesera was liable for persecution as a crime against humanity and was therefore, pursuant to immigration law, ineligible to enter Canada.[131]

As part of its opinion, the Court specifically grappled with the issue of whether "a speech that incites hatred, which as we have seen Mr. Mugesera's speech did, [can] meet the initial criminal act requirement for persecution as a crime against humanity."[132] The Canadian Supreme Court then decided that it could. It started its analysis by examining the link between Mugesera's toxic oratory and the widespread and systematic attack against the civilian population:

> [The] attack must be directed against a relatively large group of people, mostly civilians, who share distinctive features which identify them as targets of the attack. A link must be demonstrated between the act and the attack. In essence, the act must further the attack or clearly fit the pattern of the attack, but it need not comprise an essential or officially sanctioned part of it. A persecutory speech which encourages hatred and violence against a targeted group furthers an attack against that group. In this case, in view of the [lower court's] findings, [Mugesera's] speech was a part of a systematic attack that was occurring in Rwanda at the time and was directed against Tutsi and moderate Hutu....[133]

In light of these considerations, the Court determined that "the harm in hate speech lies not only in the injury to the self-dignity of target group members but also in the credence that may be given to the speech, which may promote discrimination and even violence."[134] As a result, the Court concluded that Mugesera's speech constituted persecution as a crime against humanity.[135]

B. Hate speech and persecution at the ICTY

In its only case to deal with hate speech and persecution as a crime against humanity, the ICTY has taken a different approach. In *Prosecutor v. Kordic & Cerkez*, an ICTY trial chamber found, without exception, that hate speech not calling for action, and on its own, could not be the basis for a crimes against humanity (persecution) charge.[136] The indictment in that case alleged that defendant Dario Kordic, along

---

128 Mugesera v. Canada, [2005] 2 S.C.R. 100, ¶¶4-6 (Can.).

129 See Gordon, *supra* note 15, at 331-32.

130 Id.

131 Id. at 332.

132 *Mugesera*, 2 S.C.R. 100, ¶137.

133 Id. at 10 (Case Synopsis—"Crimes against Humanity").

134 Id. ¶147. But the Court also emphasized that "hate speech always denies fundamental rights. The equality and the life, liberty and security of the person of target-group members cannot but be affected." Id.

135 Id. ¶148.

136 Prosecutor v. Kordic & Cerkez, Case No. IT-95-14/2-T, Judgment, ¶209 (Int'l Crim. Trib. for the Former Yugoslavia Feb. 26, 2001).

with other persons, carried out an ethnic cleansing campaign by, inter alia, "encouraging, instigating and promoting hatred, distrust, and strife on political, racial, ethnic or religious grounds, by propaganda, speeches and otherwise."[137]

In its decision, the trial chamber found that the speech at issue could not amount to persecution. It held that "criminal prosecution of speech acts falling short of incitement finds *scant* support in international case law."[138] To back that statement, it cited *Streicher* and observed that "the International Military Tribunal convicted the accused of persecution because he 'incited the German people to active persecution,'" which amounted to "*incitement* to murder and extermination."[139]

C. *The* Media Case *appeals chamber decision*

In the meantime, the *Media Case* trial judgment had been appealed.[140] By this time, the parties could look to a burgeoning body of jurisprudence regarding the issue of hate speech and persecution. And the defendants relied on the ICTY trial chamber's judgment in *Kordic* to argue that mere hate speech could not be the basis of a crimes against humanity (persecution) conviction.[141] This argument was bolstered by an amicus curiae brief from the Open Society Institute (OSI), an American nongovernmental organization (NGO). In contending that the defendant's persecution convictions should be overturned, the brief emphasized that Streicher's persecution conviction was entirely grounded in his "prompting 'to murder and extermination at the time when Jews in the East were being killed under the most horrible conditions.'"[142] OSI further supported this argument by referencing the IMT's acquittal of Hans Fritzsche "on grounds that his hate speeches did not seek 'to incite the Germans to commit atrocities against the conquered people.'"[143]

In upholding the convictions, the appeals chamber ruled that hate speech, in the context of other acts constituting a persecutory campaign against a victim population, could be the basis for a crimes against humanity (persecution) conviction.[144] But it refused to decide whether hate speech, on its own and not directly calling for violence, could be the predicate for a charge of persecution as a crime against humanity: "The Appeals Chamber is of the view that it is not necessary to decide here whether, in themselves, mere hate speeches not inciting violence against the members of the group are of a level of gravity equivalent to that for other crimes against humanity."[145]

---

137 Id. ¶37.

138 Id. at 59 n. 272 (emphasis added).

139 Id. As will be discussed in greater depth *infra*, the *Kordic* chamber omitted, inter alia, the following language in Streicher: "In his speeches and articles, week after week, month after month, he infected the German mind with the virus of anti-Semitism, and incited the German people to active persecution." The Nurnberg Trial, Streicher Judgment, 6 F.R.D. 69, 162 (Int'l Mil. Trib. 1946) (emphasis added).

140 Nahimana v. Prosecutor, Case No. ICTR 99-52-A, Judgment (Nov. 28, 2007).

141 Id. ¶972.

142 Id. ¶979.

143 Id. The brief also criticized the *Media Case* trial chamber for failing to follow the *Kordic* judgment, which had found that mere hate speech could not constitute persecution. Id.

144 Id. ¶¶985-86.

145 Id. ¶987.

Individual judges submitted partly dissenting opinions that tackled the issue of persecution. Of these, the partial dissent of American Judge Theodor Meron rejected the majority approach as *too* permissive regarding hate speech as the basis for a persecution conviction.[146] According to Judge Meron, in every case, "mere hate speech may not be the basis of a criminal conviction."[147] Instead, echoing the arguments of the Open Society Institute amicus brief citing *Streicher*, hate speech should constitute a criminal offense, he opined, only when it "rises to the level of inciting violence or other imminent lawless action."[148]

Also of note was the partially dissenting opinion of Judge Mohamed Shahabuddeen, who took the opposite position of Judge Meron—he thought the majority decision's approach to hate speech and persecution was too limited.[149] In other words, he believed (in accord with Judge Fausto Pocar's partially dissenting opinion) that the Tribunal should have held that hate speech can per se constitute an underlying act of persecution.[150] In so holding, Judge Shahabuddeen explained that his position was not contradicted by the IMT's *Fritzsche* judgment. Fritzsche's acquittal, according to Judge Shahabuddeen, owed to the fact that "he did not take part 'in originating or formulating propaganda campaigns.'"[151] In addition, even though the IMT happened to observe that Fritzsche did not evidently aim "to incite the German people to commit atrocities on conquered people," this does not evidence an intention to make advocacy to genocide or extermination an essential element "to the success of a charge for persecution (by making public statements) as a crime against humanity."[152]

D. Scholarly and expert commentary

Scholarly and expert commentary regarding the issue of hate speech and persecution has similarly split into camps that, respectively, favor limiting the crime to speech explicitly advocating violence and those believing that noxious rhetoric uttered as part of a widespread or systematic attack against a civilian population should qualify. And perceptions of the IMT propaganda precedents factor into that split. For example, Professor Diane Orentlicher, in her article "Criminalizing Hate Speech in the Crucible of Trial: *Prosecutor v. Nahimana*," calls for limiting the scope of crimes against humanity (persecution) in relation to speech.[153] In doing so, she relies explicitly on *Streicher* and *Fritzsche*:

> Yet, it is difficult to see how the *Streicher* verdict could support a conclusion to the effect that "communications that constitute persecution" need not include a call to action, let alone a call to violence. Although the IMT did not clearly enunciate the elements of persecution as a crime against humanity, its conviction of Streicher and acquittal of Fritzsche strongly suggest that the Tribunal was prepared to

146 *Nahimana*, Case No. ICTR-99-52-A, ¶13 (Meron, J., partially dissenting).
147 Id. ¶¶12-13.
148 Id. ¶12.
149 See id. ¶7 (Shahabuddeen, J., partially dissenting).
150 See id. ¶¶7-9.
151 Id. ¶10.
152 *Nahimana*, Case No. ICTR-99-52-A, ¶¶10-11.
153 See Orentlicher, *supra* note 7, at 18-19.

judge a defendant guilty of persecution as a crime against humanity based upon his expressive activity only when he intentionally urged listeners to commit atrocities.[154]

Orentlicher even goes on to criticize the *Media Case* trial judgment for "incorrectly impl[ying] that the IMT convicted Streicher for speech that did not call for extermination of Jews."[155]

Similarly, First Amendment expert Kevin Goering has criticized the *Media Case* judgment's treatment of hate speech and persecution for "[a]llowing discriminatory advocacy" in cases when "there was no call to arms."[156] Goering's conclusion rests in part on an assumption that the *Streicher* persecution holding was based on "inciting speech."[157]

In contrast, experts such as Fausto Pocar, based on his partial dissent in the *Media Case* appeals judgment and his article "Persecution as a Crime Under International Criminal Law,"[158] as well as this author,[159] believe that the ICTR's interpretation of *Streicher* can be supported—i.e., that the defendant was convicted of CAH-persecution: (1) "for anti-[S]emitic writings that significantly predated the extermination of Jews in the 1940s";[160] and (2) based, at least in substantial part, on Streicher's injecting a poison "into the minds of the Germans which caused them to follow the National Socialists' policy of Jewish persecution."[161] Similarly, with regard to *Fritzsche*, "language in the Fritzsche judgment also permits the inference that speech not calling for violence could constitute persecution."[162]

---

154 Id. at 38-39.

155 Id. at 39-40; see also Diane F. Orentlicher, "Criminalizing Hate Speech in the Crucible of Trial: Prosecutor v. Nahimana," 21 *Am. U. Int'l L. Rev.* 557 (2006) (reprising the same arguments).

156 Kevin W. Goering et al., "Why U.S. Law Should Have Been Considered in the Rwanda Media Convictions," 22 *Comm. Law.*, Spring 2004, at 10, 10-12 ("However, the charges for persecution would be considered attacking mere advocacy, and would not have been sustained in the United States.").

157 Id. at 10. This would appear to be based on a flawed understanding of the term "incitement." Elsewhere in the article, Goering states that:

[A]lthough the judgment against Streicher did not "explicitly note a direct causal link" between his publication and "specific acts of murder," the judgment did find the publication "was a poison injected into the minds of Germans which caused them to follow the National Socialists' policy of Jewish persecution and extermination," and this sustained a conviction of incitement.

Id. In fact, Streicher was convicted of persecution as a crime against humanity, not incitement. Moreover, if Streicher's speech was a "poison injected into the minds of Germans" which conditioned them for accepting the Final Solution, that would not amount to "incitement" in the non-legal sense either because the speech was not directly calling for action. Id. at 10.

158 Fausto Pocar, "Persecution as a Crime Under International Criminal Law," 2 *J. Nat'l Security L. & Pol'y* 355, 359 (2008).

159 See Gordon, *supra* note 15, at 356-58.

160 Prosecutor v. Nahimana, Barayagwiza & Ngeze, Case No. ICTR 99-52-T, Judgment and Sentence, ¶1073 (Dec. 3, 2003), http://www.refworld.org/pdfid/404468bc2.pdf.

161 Goering et al., *supra* note 156, at 10.

162 Gordon, *supra* note 15, at 358.

IV. THE SIGNIFICANCE OF THE *DIETRICH* CASE GOING FORWARD

A. *The importance of criminalizing hate speech not explicitly calling for violence for persecution offenses*

Hate speech and mass atrocity have consistently gone hand in hand[163]—empirically, the latter has not been possible without the former.[164] This is certainly true for crimes against humanity.[165] Zealous free speech advocates are opposed to criminalizing hate speech not explicitly calling for violence as persecution because they believe it will stifle legitimate, if repugnant, expression.[166]

However, in accord with the modern jurisprudence, speech may be prosecuted as a crime against humanity (persecution) only if uttered as part of a widespread or systematic attack against a civilian population (with the defendant having knowledge of his speech being part of the attack).[167] Such speech, used specifically in service of the attack, is not the sort of expression the First Amendment seeks to protect.[168] First of all, if such an attack is taking place, the marketplace-of-ideas rationale no longer applies as the government sponsoring the attack has likely shut down the marketplace.[169] Thus, such speech does not promote collective democracy or individual self-actualization.[170] It is merely meant to spur or justify violence.

If the crimes against humanity (persecution) incitement versus non-incitement gridlock promoted by the ambiguities of *Streicher* and *Fritzsche* is allowed to persist, then certain significant criminal speech may go unpunished. *Dietrich*'s persecution holding with respect to hate speech not directly calling for violence has the potential to break the gridlock and allow for punishment of what is truly criminal speech.

B. *Moving beyond the strict confines of incitement to genocide*

Moreover, even were such speech prosecuted as incitement to genocide, it could still go unpunished. Unfortunately, the mens rea for incitement is directly linked to that of genocide. It consists of a dual intent: (1) to provoke another to commit genocide;

---

163 See David Livingstone Smith, "Dehumanization, Genocide, and the Psychology of Indifference," *Psychol. Today* (Dec. 2, 2011), http://www.psychologytoday.com/blog/philosophy-dispatches/201112/dehumanization-genocide-and-the-psychology-indifference-0 ("There is no disputing the fact that dehumanization and atrocity often go hand in hand.").

164 See Alexander Tsesis, "Inflammatory Speech: Offense Versus Incitement," 97 *Minn. L. Rev.* 1145, 1171 n. 148 (2013) (providing a list of historical examples of this phenomenon including the Turkish atrocities against Armenians, Nazi slaughter of the Jews, mass murder in Rwanda and Darfur, and the 2007-2008 post-election violence in Kenya).

165 Id.

166 See Gordon, *supra* note 15, at 348-50 (discussing the concerns of the staunchest defenders of free expression).

167 Id. at 347-48 (referring to the chapeau of Article 7 of the Rome Statute of the International Criminal Court, which also requires that the broader attack be pursuant to or in furtherance of a state or organizational policy involving the multiple commission of enumerated crimes against humanity acts).

168 Id. at 349.

169 Id. at 348-49.

170 Id.

and (2) to commit the underlying genocide itself.[171] And the intent necessary to prove genocide consists of a desire to destroy, in whole or in part, a national, ethnical, racial, or religious group, as such.[172]

But proving genocidal intent is notoriously difficult, with its heightened intent requirement (known as *dolus specialis*) and its singular focus on destruction. As William Schabas notes: "The specific intent necessary for a conviction of genocide is even more demanding than that required for murder. The crime must be committed with intent to destroy, in whole or in part, a protected group [of people], as such."[173] Similarly, Stuart Ford observes that "genocide is exceptionally difficult to prove because of the specific intent requirement and genocide convictions are relatively rare."[174]

On the other hand, as noted previously, the mens rea for crimes against humanity is the defendant's *knowledge* that his acts are part of a widespread or systematic attack against a civilian population. When compared to proving the mens rea for genocide, the burden of proving the same for crimes against humanity is much lower. Criminal law expert Wayne LaFave explains that "specific intent" involves the actor consciously desiring "to cause some definite result."[175] He goes on to explain that specific intent is the highest degree of mens rea and that "knowledge" is lower in the mens rea hierarchy.[176] One court has written:

> "[K]nowledge" as contrasted with "intention" signif[ies] a state of mental realisation with the bare state of conscious awareness of certain facts in which [the] human mind remains [simple] or inactive. On the other hand, "intention" is a conscious state in which mental faculties are aroused into activity and summoned into action for the purpose of achieving a conceived end. It means shaping of one's conduct so as to bring about a certain event.[177]

Of course, in addition to the awareness of the existence of a widespread or systematic attack on the civilian population (as required for all crimes against humanity), persecution also requires discriminatory intent.[178] Thus, "the mens rea element of the crime of persecution is higher than the one required for ordinary crimes against humanity, although lower than the one required for genocide."[179] Thus, with respect to the mental element alone, crimes against humanity (persecution) charges carry an easier burden for conviction than incitement to genocide charges.

---

171 Prosecutor v. Akayesu, Case No. ICTR 96-4-T, Judgment, 1 544 (Sept. 2, 1998), http://www.unictr.org/Portals/0/Case/English/Akayesu/judgement/akay001.pdf.

172 Id. ¶731.

173 William A. Schabas, *Genocide in International Law: The Crime of Crimes* 265 (2d ed. 2009).

174 Stuart Ford, "Is the Failure To Respond Appropriately to a Natural Disaster a Crime Against Humanity? The Responsibility To Protect and Individual Criminal Responsibility in the Aftermath of Cyclone Nargis," 38 *Denv. J. Int'l L. & Pol'y* 227, 275 (2010).

175 See Wayne R. LaFave, *Handbook on Criminal Law* § 3.5(e) (3d ed. 2000).

176 See id. § 3.4(a).

177 Prakash v. State (1991) 1 S.C.R. 2012, 212 (India).

178 David L. Nersessian, "Comparative Approaches to Punishing Hate: The Intersection of Genocide and Crimes Against Humanity," 43 *Stan. J. Int'l L.* 221, 243 (2007).

179 Yaron Gottlieb, "Criminalizing Destruction of Cultural Property: A Proposal for Defining New Crimes Under the Rome Statute of the ICC," 23 *Penn St. Int'l L. Rev.* 857, 876 (2005).

Once again, though, it is not clear that speech-related charges for persecution minus evidence of explicit calls for violence would be viable if supported merely by the IMT precedents, in particular *Streicher*. As Professor Orentlicher points out:

> Why does this matter? For present purposes the key point is that if Streicher had been convicted of pre-war conduct, Nuremberg could more readily be interpreted as precedent for convicting a defendant of persecution as a crime against humanity by virtue of speech that does not include a call to violence but that nonetheless helps condition a society to engage in persecution.[180]

Of course, Professor Orentlicher's argument assumes that, with respect to persecution cases, "Nuremberg" is limited to the *Streicher* and *Fritzsche* judgments. And therein, once more, lies the significance of the *Dietrich* decision. While *Streicher* and *Fritzsche* alone may leave ambiguity regarding the required scope of hate speech vis-à-vis a persecution charge (even after the ICTR *Media Case* appeals judgment), *Dietrich* does not. It clearly stands for the proposition that, on its own, speech short of explicit calls for violence may be the basis for charging crimes against humanity (persecution).

This is especially crucial as the International Criminal Court has yet to interpret persecution as a crime against humanity. Article 7 of the Rome Statute reads, in relevant part, as follows:

> 1. For the purpose of this Statute, "crime against humanity" means any of the following acts when committed as part of a widespread or systematic attack directed against any civilian population, with knowledge of the attack: [a list of enumerated acts follows—murder, extermination, enslavement, deportation, imprisonment, torture, rape/sexual slavery] ...
>
> (h) Persecution against any identifiable group or collectivity on political, racial, national, ethnic, cultural, religious, gender as defined in paragraph 3, or other grounds that are universally recognized as impermissible under international law, in connection with any act referred to in this paragraph or any crime within the jurisdiction of the Court.[181]

This formulation is largely consistent with the formulations of crimes against humanity (persecution) in the respective statutes of the ICTR and ICTY. Thus, the ICC will very likely be in a position to choose between the positions taken by one or the other ad hoc tribunal with respect to the scope of persecution in reference to non-direct advocacy hate speech. *Dietrich* may very well tilt the balance in favor of a finding that hate speech not explicitly calling for violence may be charged as crimes against humanity (persecution).

And, to vary Professor Orentlicher's question somewhat, why does that matter in reference to specific cases at issue today? A review of current hate speech cases with atrocity implications is instructive in this regard.

---

180 Orentlicher, *supra* note 7, at 41.

181 Rome Statute of the International Criminal Court, art. 7(1)(a-h), opened for signature July 17, 1998, 2178 U.N.T.S. 3 (entered into force July 1, 2002) [hereinafter Rome Statute].

C. Specific cases

1. The case of Myanmar and the Muslims

In Myanmar (formerly Burma), as the country transitions from a long military dictatorship to a semblance of civilian rule, the Muslim minority has been subject to religiously motivated violence by organized bands of Buddhist attackers. According to Human Rights Watch, in June 2012, dozens of Rohingya Muslims were killed and approximately 100,000 displaced after an attack by Arakan Buddhists.[182] Human Rights Watch reported that "[t]he hostilities were fanned by anti-Muslim media accounts and local propaganda."[183] It also detailed collusion between Arakan Buddhists and local government security forces. Two days later, in related follow-on attacks, government forces directly participated in the violence:

> At this point, a wave of concerted violence by various state security forces against Rohingya communities began. For example, Rohingya in Narzi quarter—the largest Muslim area in Sittwe, home to 10,000 Muslims—described how Arakan mobs burned down their homes on June 12 while the police and paramilitary Lon Thein forces opened fire on them with live ammunition.[184]

More recently, in a flare-up of violence at the end of March 2013 in the central part of the country, Buddhist mobs murdered forty Muslims and displaced thousands more. Shortly thereafter, an op-ed in the *New York Times* titled "Kristallnacht in Myanmar," reported that the country's Islam Council "has issued a statement saying the violence had been premeditated."[185] The op-ed went on to suggest that the Burmese government has been supporting the violence.[186] At about the same time, the UN special rapporteur on Myanmar human rights, Tomas Ojea Quintana, issued a statement saying, "I have received reports of State involvement in some of the acts of violence."[187]

In an early April 2013 speech, former US President Jimmy Carter expressed "'deep concern' over the recent inter-communal violence between Buddhists and Muslims, and the use of 'hate speech' by some leaders."[188] The BBC News featured a sample of some of that hate speech, much of which allegedly emanates from a

---

182 Human Rights Watch, *"The Government Could Have Stopped This": Sectarian Violence and Ensuing Abuses in Burma's Arakan State* 1 (2012), available at http://www.hrw.org/sites/default/files/reports/burma0812webwcover_0.pdf.

183 Id.

184 Id. at 1-2.

185 Swe Win, "Kristallnacht in Myanmar," *N.Y. Times Latitude Blog* (Mar. 29, 2013, 10:23 AM), http://latitude.blogs.nytimes.com/2013/03/29/violence-against-muslims-in-meiktila-myanmar/?ref=myanmar.

186 Id.

187 "UN: Reports Show Myanmar Govt. Involved in Violence Against Rohingya Muslims," *Stateless Rohingya* (Mar. 29, 2013), http://www.thestateless.com/2013/03/un-reports-show-myanmar-govt-involved.html.

188 Paul Vrieze, "Jimmy Carter 'Deeply Concerned' by Sectarian Violence and 'Hate Speech,'" *Irrawaddy* (Apr. 6, 2013), http://www.irrawaddy.org/us/jimmy-carter-deeply-concerned-by-sectarian-violence-and-hate-speech.html.

prominent Buddhist monk.[189] The monk is quoted as accusing "Muslim men of repeatedly raping Buddhist women, of using their wealth to lure Buddhist women into marriage, then imprisoning them [at] home."[190]

This type of speech does not represent direct calls for action. And yet it was seemingly sponsored or sanctioned by the government and was uttered in service of a widespread or systematic attack against a civilian population (and patently motivated by religious animus). With support of the *Dietrich* precedent, validating the ICTR jurisprudence, such hate speech should be chargeable as crimes against humanity (persecution).

2. The case of Iran and the Israelis

Much of the spotlight on Iran's hate speech relates to statements issued by former President Mahmoud Ahmadinejad directly calling for Israel's destruction. He infamously called for Israel to be "wiped off the map."[191] And he has less directly called for Israel's destruction in other instances, stating on one occasion that the country is "heading toward annihilation."[192] On another occasion, he declared that Israelis "should know they are nearing the last days of their lives."[193] And on yet still another, he announced that "Israel is destined for destruction and will soon disappear."[194] However, Ahmadinejad was not eligible to run for re-election in 2013, given that he had already served two terms.[195] In June of last year, Iranians elected Hassan Rouhani president, a cleric and self-professed moderate[196] with "a long record as a regime insider with a record that is scarcely liberal."[197] And yet, even with Ahmadinejad out of office, and a comparative moderate in his place, one cannot dismiss the threat posed by noxious Iranian rhetoric. As Michael Gerson wrote last year: "It is easy to dismiss this rhetoric as being designed for domestic consumption.... But the problem is this: Ahmadinejad's language is not exceptional within the Iranian regime."[198]

In particular, the country's supreme leader, Ayatollah Ali Khamenei, as well as other senior Iranian leaders, have also recently spewed hate speech directed at the people of Israel. Gerson continues:

---

189 Jonathan Head, "What Is Behind Burma's Wave of Religious Violence?," *BBC News* (Apr. 4, 2013, 5:41 PM), http://www.bbc.co.uk/news/world-asia-22023830.

190 Id.

191 See Nazila Fathi, "Iran's President Says Israel Must Be 'Wiped Off the Map,'" *N.Y. Times*, Oct. 26, 2005, at A8.

192 See Michael Gerson, "Iran's Incitement to Genocide," *Wash. Post*, Apr. 4, 2013, http://www.washingtonpost.com/opinions/michael-gerson-irans-hate-speech-is-an-incitement-to-genocide/2013/04/04/2686e7a8-9ca1-11e2-9a79-eb5280c81c63_story.html.

193 Id.

194 Id.

195 See Ladane Nasseri, "Velayati May Run for Iran President as Calm to Ahmadinejad Storm," *Bloomberg* (Mar. 26, 2013), http://www.bloomberg.com/news/2013-03-26/velayati-may-run-for-iran-president-as-calm-to-ahmadinejad-storm.html.

196 Thomas Erdbrink, "Next Iran Leader Pledges Freedoms," *N.Y. Times*, June 30, 2013, at A18.

197 Joshua Muravchik, "Iran's Hassan Rouhani Stands Out as a 'Moderate' Among Reactionaries," *Forbes* (June 20, 2013, 8:00 AM), http://www.forbes.com/sites/realspin/2013/06/20/irans-hassan-rouhani-stands-out-as-a-moderate-among-reactionaries.

198 Gerson, *supra* note 192.

> Iran's supreme leader, Ayatollah Ali Khamenei, also has referred to Israel as a "cancerous tumor." … Senior Iranian military leaders, presidential advisers and religious authorities can be quoted endlessly in a similar vein. Zionists are "microbes" and "bacteria" and a "cancerous growth." "Jews are very filthy people," who are responsible for spreading disease and drug abuse.[199]

This dehumanizing hate speech does not amount to direct calls for violence against the Israeli people.[200] However, in connection with Hamas's Iranian-sponsored rocket launches at Israeli civilians from Gaza, such speech is arguably uttered as part of a widespread or systematic attack against Israeli civilians. In November 2012, Hamas fired over a thousand of these rockets into Israeli "neighborhoods, striking schools and homes" and killing innocent Israeli civilians.[201] On April 3, 2013, Hamas fired more rockets into southern Israel, the third time it had done so since a November ceasefire.[202] Significantly, these attacks were sponsored and financed by Iran.[203] After the November ceasefire, Hamas leader Ismail Haniyeh thanked Iran for providing Hamas with "arms and money" for the attack.[204]

To the extent Hamas can be considered a proxy for Iran in the rocket attacks against Israeli civilians, the Iranian leaders' hate speech, even though not calling directly for violence, might be prosecutable as crimes against humanity (persecution).[205] Once again, the *Dietrich* decision would exponentially strengthen the doctrinal underpinnings of any such prosecution.[206]

3. Other cases

i. Kenya

A myriad of other potential persecution cases could be affected by including consideration of the *Dietrich* precedent. Kenya is a prominent example. In the country's

---

199 Id.

200 Nevertheless, those are also arguably implicated. Gerson points to Khamenei's statement that "'[t]he perpetual subject of Iran' … 'is the elimination of Israel from the region.'" Id. Gerson provides another seemingly direct call from Khamenei: "There is only one solution to the Middle East problem, namely the annihilation and destruction of the Jewish state." Id. In early 2013, Khamenei promised that, if the Iranian nuclear program is attacked, he would "level down Tel Aviv and Haifa." Id. Other senior Iranian officials have stated, according to Gerson, that there is a religious duty to "fight the Jews and vanquish them so that the conditions for the advent of the Hidden Imam will be met." Id.

201 Michele Chabin, "Israeli-Hamas Cease-Fire May Be in Jeopardy," *USA Today*, Apr. 4, 2013, http://www.usatoday.com/story/news/world/2013/04/03/israel-gaza-strikes/2048805.

202 See id.

203 See "Hamas Acknowledges Iran's Support," *Global Res. News* (Nov. 24, 2012), http://www.globalresearch.ca/hamas-acknowledges-irans-support/5312719.

204 Id.

205 See Gordon, *supra* note 6, at 907-8 (suggesting that terrorist attacks against Israelis sponsored and financed by Iran could, in the context of Ahmadinejad's hate speech against Israel, qualify as a widespread or systematic attack against a civilian population for purposes of charging Ahmadinejad with crimes against humanity (persecution)).

206 Of course, the Iranian leaders might also be liable for the crime of direct and public incitement to commit genocide. See id. at 857 (evaluating prospects for charging direct and public incitement to commit genocide).

2007-2008 post-election violence, for example, hate speech predominated on the air waves and through other media.[207] One expert has noted that "Kenyan hate radio programs helped instigate violence between the Kikuyu and Luo peoples."[208] Much of this discourse did not, it would appear, involve direct calls for violence. In particular, following the December 30 declared presidential election win of incumbent candidate Mwai Kibaki, supporters of his opponent, Raila Odinga, declared fraud and began disseminating rancorous invective against Kibaki's backers.[209] This hate speech had an ethnic component as Kibaki, as well as most of his advocates, were of the Kikuyu tribe. Odinga's backers were largely Luo and Kalenjin.[210] Much of this vituperation, originating from FM radio stations, did not, it would appear, involve direct calls for violence.[211] As the Kenyan Commission of Inquiry into Post-Election Violence found: "Witnesses made specific reference to KASS FM. They claimed KASS FM in conjunction with politicians used derogatory language against Kikuyus, mouthed hate speech, and routinely called for their eviction, thereby helping to build up tensions that eventually exploded in violence."[212]

Kalenjin radio announcer Joshua arap Sang, who broadcast for KASS FM, has been indicted by the ICC in connection with his broadcasts dehumanizing political opponents.[213] He has been accused of "whipping up ethnic hatred on the airwaves" that led to mass violence, including "the burning of a church near Eldoret where [ethnic Kikuyus] were sheltering."[214] Arap Sang has been charged with crimes against humanity but not persecution based on the hate speech.[215] Perhaps if the prosecutor had taken the *Dietrich* precedent into account, arap Sang might have been charged with persecution.

ii. Côte d'Ivoire

In Côte d'Ivoire, in the spring of 2011, while President Laurent Gbagbo insisted on maintaining power despite losing the presidency in a November 2010 election, radio broadcasters supporting him exploited the airwaves to demonize the supporters of Gbagbo's victorious opponent, Alassane Ouattara.[216] Partly owing to such hate speech, Gbagbo loyalists attacked pro-Ouattara civilians.[217] None of these supporters,

---

207 See "Kenya: Spreading the Word of Hate," *IRIN News* (Jan. 22, 2008), http://www.irinnews.org/report/76346/kenya-spreading-the-word-of-hate.

208 Tsesis, *supra* note 164, at 1172 n. 148.

209 "Kenya's 2013 Election: Will History Repeat Itself?," *Think Afr. Press* (Nov. 8, 2012, 4:53 PM), http://thinkafricapress.com/kenya/projections-upcoming-2013-elections.

210 Id.

211 Kenya Comm'n of Inquiry into Post-election Violence, *Final Report* 301-2 (2008), available at http://reliefweb.int/sites/reliefweb.int/files/resources/15A00F569813F4D549257607001F459D-Full_Report.pdf.

212 Id. at 298-99.

213 See Gregory S. Gordon, "Setting the Record Straight on International Speech Crime Law," *Jurist* (May 24, 2011), http://www.jurist.org/forum/2011/05/gregory-gordon-arap-sang.php.

214 "At a Glance: Kenya Poll Violence Suspects," *BBC News* (Sept. 6, 2013, 4:52 PM), http://www.bbc.co.uk/news/world-africa-12001281.

215 Gordon, *supra* note 213.

216 See "Ivory Coast in Speech-Fueled Catastrophe," *Voices that Poison* (Apr. 2, 2011), http://voicesthatpoison.wordpress.com/2011/04/02/ivory-coast-in-speech-fueled-catastrophe.

217 Id.

or Gbagbo himself, has been charged with persecution as a crime against humanity specifically in connection with hate speech.[218] This may very well be attributable to prosecutors' ignoring the obvious implications of the *Dietrich* judgment.

iii. Sudan

In addition to the ongoing genocide in Darfur,[219] the government of Sudan has also recently inflicted violence against the same victim group in a different region—Christians and black African Muslims on its border with South Sudan.[220] After decades of civil war, and owing to border disputes related to the recent division of the two countries pursuant to the Comprehensive Peace Agreement, Sudan has subjected citizens on the frontier with South Sudan to aerial attacks resulting in the death of thousands of innocent civilians in the South Kordofan and Blue Nile States.[221] The violence has been especially egregious in South Kordofan's Nuba Mountain region, where hundreds of thousands of Nuba indigenous people have been displaced or murdered by Sudanese military personnel.[222] This violence has been fueled and accompanied by hate speech coming from the highest levels of the Sudanese government. Last year, in an address to his supporters, Sudanese president Omar al-Bashir referred to southerners as "insects" and a "disease."[223]

Such speech, although not explicitly calling for violence, is arguably part of a campaign targeting the Nuba Mountains/Blue Nile regions "to establish an Arab Islamic hegemony by eradicating both the Sudanese Christians and the indigenous black, African Muslims."[224] Although Bashir and other members of his regime are under indictment for atrocities committed in Darfur, the regime's murderous conduct

---

218 See, e.g., Prosecutor v. Laurent Gbagbo, Case No. ICC-02/11, Warrant of Arrest, ¶3 (Nov. 23, 2011), http://www.icc-cpi.int/iccdocs/doc/doc1276751.pdf (significantly, the arrest warrant does not specifically indicate that hate speech is a specific ground for the persecution charge against Gbagbo).

219 See Nicholas D. Kristof, "A Policy of Rape Continues," *N.Y. Times*, July 25, 2013, at A27 ("The Sudanese government, which tends to calibrate its brutality to the degree of attention it receives, is taking advantage of the lack of scrutiny by stepping up its decade-long campaign in Darfur of mass murder, burned villages and sexual violence.").

220 See "Sudan's South Kordofan: 'Huge Suffering from Bombs,'" *BBC News* (June 14, 2011, 11:12 PM), http://www.bbc.co.uk/news/world-africa-13767146; see also Samuel Totten, *Genocide by Attrition: The Nuba Mountains of Sudan* 119 (2012).

221 Totten, *supra* note 220, at 103-4.

222 Id. at 103.

223 Imran Khan, "Bashir Calls South Sudan Leaders 'Insects,'" *Sudan Trib.* (Apr. 19, 2012), http://www.sudantribune.com/spip.php7mot422; "Sudan President Seeks To 'Liberate' South Sudan," *BBC News* (Apr. 18, 2012, 8:03 PM), http://www.bbc.co.uk/news/world-africa-17761949. Bashir's comments were nominally directed at "South Sudan," and South Kordofan and Blue Nile are technically in Sudan, not South Sudan. See Johan Brosché and Daniel Rothbart, *Violent Conflict and Peacebuilding: The Continuing Crisis in Darfur* 101 (2013) (noting that the South Kordofan and Blue Nile States are officially part of Sudan). But both states are on the border of South Sudan, and are populated by numerous pro-South Sudan communities, especially in the Nuba Mountains, many of which fought with southern rebels during the 1983-2005 north-south civil war. Id.

224 Faith J.H. McDonnell, "Sudan and Obama's Legacy of Death," *Frontpage Mag.* (Aug. 15, 2013, 12:12 AM), http://frontpagemag.com/2013/faith-j-h-mcdonnell/sudan-obamas-legacy-of-death.

on the southern border has thus far been immune from law enforcement measures.[225] Certainly, the dehumanizing speech that helps justify and fuel al-Bashir's murder campaign in South Kordofan and the Blue Nile has completely eluded judicial scrutiny.

In Darfur itself, as in South Kordofan and the Blue Nile, atrocities have been "fueled by hate speech"—with the government using it to dehumanize blacks and spur the Janjaweed's ethnic violence against them.[226] As one expert has noted:

> The violence is not restricted to Darfur, where between two and four hundred thousand people have already been murdered. It has spread to Abyei, the Blue Nile State, the Nuba mountains, and possibly elsewhere. It's clear from the rhetoric of the Janjaweed militias that dehumanization lubricates the machinery of slaughter in Sudan.
>
> "Dog, son of dogs, we came to kill you and your kids."
> "Kill the black donkeys! Kill the black dogs! Kill the black monkeys!"
> "You blacks are not human. We can do anything we want to you."
> "We kill our cows when they have black calves. We will kill you too."
> "You make this area dirty; we are here to clean the area."
> "You blacks are like monkeys. You are not human."[227]

Unfortunately, despite the central role such speech has played in the atrocities committed against innocent civilian victims in Darfur, none of the Sudanese defendants indicted by the International Criminal Court has been charged with crimes against humanity (persecution) to date.[228] A healthy appreciation for *Dietrich*

---

225 See, e.g., "Omar Hassan Ahmad al-Bashir," *Hague Just. Portal*, http://www.haguejusticeportal.net/index.php?id=9502 (last visited Mar. 12, 2014) (noting the Security Council's referral of the situation in Darfur by Resolution 1593 and its indictment of al-Bashir and current Sudanese minister Ahmad Muhammad Harun ("Ali Kushayb")).

226 Tsesis, *supra* note 164.

227 Smith, *supra* note 163.

228 See Prosecutor v. Omar Hassan Ahmad Al Bashir, Int'l Crim. Ct., http://www.icc-cpi.int/en_menus/icc/situations%20and%20cases/situations/situation%20icc%200205/related%20cases/icc02050109/Pages/icc02050109.aspx (last visited Feb. 26, 2014) (indicating that Bashir has been charged with five counts of crimes against humanity—but not persecution—two counts of war crimes, and three counts of genocide); Prosecutor v. Abdel Raheem Muhammad Hussein, Int'l Crim. Ct., http://www.icc-cpi.int/en_menus/icc/situations%20and%20cases/situations/situation%20icc%200205/related%20cases/icc02050112/Pages/icc02050112.aspx (last visited Feb. 26, 2014) (showing that Hussein has been charged with seven counts of crimes against humanity, including persecution, and six counts of war crimes). Although Hussein, the current Minister of National Defense, former Minister of the Interior, and former Sudanese President's Special Representative in Darfur, has been charged with crimes against humanity (persecution), his arrest warrant does not specifically indicate that hate speech is a basis for the persecution charge. See Prosecutor v. Abdel Raheem Muhammad Hussein, Case No. ICC-02/05-01/12, Warrant of Arrest (Mar. 1, 2012), http://www.worldcourts.com/icc/eng/decisions/2012.03.01_Prosecutor_v_Hussein2.pdf#search="hussein"; see also Prosecutor v. Ahmad Harun and Ali Kushayb, Int'l Crim. Ct., http://www.icc-cpi.int/en_menus/icc/situations%20and%20cases/situations/situation%20icc%200205/related%20cases/icc%200205%200107/Pages/darfur_%20sudan.aspx (last visited Feb. 26, 2014) (demonstrating that Harun and Kushayb have been charged with various counts of war crimes and crimes against humanity, including persecution). Once again, the arrest warrants for Harun and Kushayb do not specifically indicate that

would help raise judicial awareness and perhaps contribute to prosecutorial initiative with respect to charging persecution against these defendants in relation to their use of hate speech.

V. CONCLUSION

At the end of June 2013, four Shia Muslims were lynched by a mob outside of Cairo after months of virulent anti-Shia hate speech, "which the Muslim Brotherhood [Egypt's ruling party at the time], condoned and at times participated in."[229] The speech denigrated the victims but did not directly implore the majority group to commit violence against them.[230] According to Human Rights Watch, "from the outset three vans of riot police who had been dispatched were stationed nearby but ... they failed to intervene to disperse the mob."[231] These lynchings appear to have been part of a broader campaign by the Muslim Brotherhood to inflict violence on religious minorities—one source reports that the Brotherhood has also "engaged in a full-scale campaign of terror against Egypt's Christian minority."[232] If the crimes of the Muslim Brotherhood were to be prosecuted by an international tribunal, either through self—or Security Council—referral to the ICC[233] or through establishment of

---

hate speech is a specific ground for the persecution charge. See Prosecutor v. Ahmad Harun & Ali Kushayb, Case No. ICC-02/05-01/07, Warrant of Arrest for Ali Kushayb (Apr. 27, 2007), http://www.icc-cpi.int/iccdocs/doc/doc279860.pdf; Prosecutor v. Ahmad Harun and Ali Kushayb, Case No. ICC-02/05-01/07, Warrant of Arrest for Ahmad Harun (Apr. 27, 2007), http://www.icc-cpi.int/iccdocs/doc/doc279813.pdf. It should be noted that the charges against Harun include liability pursuant to Article 25(3)(b), which ascribes criminal responsibility for a person who "[o]rders, solicits or induces the commission of ... a crime which in fact occurs or is attempted." Rome Statute, *supra* note 181, art. 25(3)(b). While this is speech related, it is different from crimes against humanity (persecution). Article 25(3)(b) of the Rome Statute implicates speech that results in the commission of other enumerated crimes under the Rome Statute. See id. In the case of persecution as a crime against humanity, the speech itself is the crime, regardless of any subsequent action taken pursuant to or in consideration of the speech. Id.; see also Gordon, *supra* note 15, at 324 (noting that hate speech as persecution "is not a provocation to cause harm. It is itself the harm.").

229 "Egypt: Lynching of Shia Follows Months of Hate Speech," *Hum. Rts. Watch* (June 27, 2013), http://www.hrw.org/news/2013/06/27/egypt-lynching-shia-follows-months-hate-speech. In June 2012, the Muslim Brotherhood came to power in Egypt with the election of its leader, Mohamed Morsi, as President. See "Muslim Brotherhood-Backed Candidate Morsi Wins Egyptian Presidential Election," *Fox News* (June 24, 2012), http://www.foxnews.com/world/2012/06/24/egypt-braces-for-announcement-president. Morsi and the Muslim Brotherhood were removed from power by the Egyptian military in July 2013. See David D. Kirkpatrick and Mayy El Sheikh, "An Egypt Arrest, and a Brotherhood on the Run," *N.Y. Times*, Aug. 20, 2013, at A1 (describing arrests of key Brotherhood leaders and arrogation of power by the Egyptian military).

230 *Hum. Rts. Watch*, *supra* note 229.

231 Id.

232 Kirsten Powers, "The Muslim Brotherhood's War on Coptic Christians," *Daily Beast* (Aug. 22, 2013), http://www.thedailybeast.com/articles/2013/08/22/the-muslim-brotherhood-s-war-on-coptic-christians.html.

233 Egypt is not a state party to the International Criminal Court. See "The State Parties to the Rome Statute", *Int'l Crim. Ct.*, http://www.icc-cpi.int/en_menus/asp/states%20parties/Pages/the%20states%20parties%20to%20the%20rome%20statute.aspx (last visited Aug. 27, 2014). Even

an ad hoc tribunal, would the purveyors of the hate speech connected to the murder of the Shia Muslims be charged with crimes against humanity (persecution)?

Assuming the charges were based on the speech itself and the chapeau were satisfied, given the split in jurisprudence between the ICTR and ICTY, the answer is not clear. And reference to the IMT's decisions on hate speech at Nuremberg—*Streicher* and *Fritzsche*—fails to clarify matters either. Jurists and scholars have traditionally cited to those opinions but they are altogether too sparse and equivocal. However, as this article has demonstrated, the subsequent decision of the NMT with respect to Reich Press Chief Otto Dietrich has the effect of cutting through this doctrinal morass. The tribunal found Dietrich guilty of crimes against humanity (persecution) for his steady stream of media invective against the Jewish people that helped lay the groundwork for the Holocaust. Dietrich's toxic rhetoric did not directly urge Germans to commit acts of violence against Jews. But liability for the crime of persecution attached nonetheless.

So why have jurists and scholars largely ignored it in the decades since? Perhaps it is because the decision never explicitly found Dietrich guilty of persecution for his speech activities. It only alluded to liability for crimes against humanity and Dietrich was convicted of Count 5 of the *Ministries* indictment, whose title lumps together war crimes and crimes against humanity—without mentioning persecution or associated language. Perhaps this reticence to cite *Dietrich* as a persecution case is compounded by the fact that Count 4 of the same indictment did specifically refer to the operative language of persecution but that count was dismissed prior to trial.

This article, however, has demonstrated through reference to the subsequent specific language of the indictment, as well as to the prosecution's arguments and to the totality of the NMT's decision, that Dietrich was indeed convicted of persecution in connection with his hate-media activities. And that revelation should not be ignored. As multitudes of innocent people are being set up for murder through broadcast and publication of incendiary discourse, it is time to dust off this valuable precedent and employ it to uphold essential human rights protections. Hate speech not explicitly calling for action but in service of a widespread or systematic attack against a civilian population should be criminalized. The would-be targets of such hate are entitled to the law's protection; its actual victims and their families are entitled to justice. The judgment against Otto Dietrich may go a long way toward finally assuring them of attaining those goals.

---

though Egypt is not a party to the Rome Statute, the new government may, on an ad hoc basis, refer to the ICC alleged crimes of the Muslim Brotherhood. See Rome Statute, *supra* note 181, art. 12(3) ("If the acceptance of a State which is not a Party to this Statute is required under paragraph 2, that State may, by declaration lodged with the Registrar, accept the exercise of jurisdiction by the Court with respect to the crime in question."). Alternatively, the Security Council could refer the case to the ICC. See id. art. 13(b).

Misunderstanding of the Phenomenon of Antisemitism in Some Recent Influential Studies on the Holocaust

Dan Michman*

INTRODUCTION

As is well-known, certainly by scholars involved in research on antisemitism, the term "antisemitism" emerged in the late 1870s. Its introduction into the political arena is usually attributed to the German journalist Wilhelm Marr,[1] although it was already in use before then, For example, it can be found in Moritz Steinschneider's writings in response to Ernest Renan's linguistic-historical-biologistic theories.[2] It was a new term that was coined in the context of mid-nineteenth century scholarly research on race, whose scientific and pseudo-scientific findings were understood as being objective and true and, as such, having important social and political implications. The inventor(s) of the term antisemitism therefore viewed it as being different from the existing term *Judenhaß* (Jew-hatred), which was understood to express feelings. In his earlier writings, Marr emphasized that Jews and non-Jews could not really live together:

> [T]he reason is not religious Jew-hatred from one side [the non-Jews], such hatred does not exist in well-educated people; it is *the different nature of the essence itself* which is "chemically" unbearable, if one can call it that way, and which causes it to be knocked off in an "anorganic" process, if we may call it so.[3]

Within a very short time—less than two years after the term made its appearance in the German political discourse—the term was already widely used in Germany.[4] It later caught on in France and elsewhere, as a result of the flourishing of political antisemitism within the context of the political game of parties competing for electoral

* Head of the International Institute for Holocaust Research and Incumbent of the John Najmann Chair of Holocaust Studies, Yad Vashem; Professor of Modern Jewish History and Chair of the Arnold and Leona Finkler Institute of Holocaust Research, Bar-Ilan University.

[1] On Marr, see Moshe Zimmermann, *Wilhelm Marr: The Patriarch of Anti-Semitism* (New York: Oxford University Press, 1987).

[2] Alex Bein, *Die Judenfrage. Biographie eines Weltproblems*, 2 vols. (Stuttgart: Deutsche Verlags-Anstalt, 1980), 1: 217-18, 2: 163-68.

[3] Wilhelm Marr, *Der Judenspiegel* (Hamburg, 1862), 40.

[4] For a recent study on the German context, see Götz Aly, *Warum die Deutsche? Warum die Juden? Gleichheit, Neid und Rassenhass* (Frankfurt a.M.: S. Fischer, 2011), 73-143.

success in the newly developing democratic systems. In German, the term replaced the older term *Judenhaß*. In other linguistic contexts, it was embraced as the proper term for an existing but as yet unnamed phenomenon. Antisemitism—which should be treated as a single word like the German *Antisemitismus*—thus became a general name for a broad variety of anti-Jewish and anti-Judaistic attitudes. It is important to realize that it was precisely this combination of existing anti-Jewish sentiments and stereotypes with new trends, ideologies, ideas (whether pseudo-scientific, political, or otherwise), and certain political conditions that turned this age-old, disturbing, discriminating, occasionally lethal but ultimately survivable phenomenon into an apocalyptic ideology that envisioned the total and immediate annihilation of the Jews. However, sound scholarly research on the fate of the Jews under the Nazis cannot explain the wholesale murder of the Jews (and a whole range of other anti-Jewish measures) by simply stating that the Nazis were "antisemitic." This is especially true because, in the 1930s, the Jews of Europe (and North Africa) were not concentrated in one territory and were not a coherent collective with a clear identity. On the contrary, they were scattered all over the place, had multiple identities, underwent assimilation and conversion, and in no way posed a real threat. And yet, in some recent influential studies on the Holocaust, one encounters a shocking misunderstanding of the nature of antisemitism during the Nazi era.

I. Origins of the Terms "Genocide" and "Holocaust"

The term "genocide" was coined by Raphael Lemkin in 1943 to describe the Nazi's murderous activities of the time, but also with the massacre of the Armenians by the Turks in 1915 in mind. Lemkin invented the term with the purpose of developing a concept that could be used to prevent similar events in the future. It therefore needed to be defined clearly, which is precisely what Lemkin did. His definition, as formulated in his 1944 book, reads as follows:

> I. GENOCIDE—A NEW TERM AND NEW CONCEPTION FOR DESTRUCTION OF NATIONS
>
> New conceptions require new terms. By "genocide" we mean the destruction of a nation or of an ethnic group. This new word, coined by the author to denote an old practice in its modern development, is made from the ancient Greek word *genos* (race, tribe) and the Latin *cide* (killing), thus corresponding in its formation to such words as tyrannicide, homocide, infanticide, etc. Generally speaking, genocide does not necessarily mean the immediate destruction of a nation, except when accomplished by mass killings of all members of a nation. It is intended rather to signify a coordinated plan of different actions aiming at the destruction of essential foundations of the life of national groups, with the aim of annihilating the groups themselves. The objectives of such a plan would be disintegration of the political and social institutions, of culture, language, national feelings, religion, and the economic existence of national groups, and the destruction of the personal security, liberty, health, dignity, and even the lives of the individuals belonging to such groups. Genocide is directed against the national group as an entity, and the actions involved are directed against individuals, not in their individual capacity, but as members of the national group....

> Genocide has two phases: one, destruction of the national pattern of the oppressed group; the other, the imposition of the national pattern of the oppressor. This imposition, in turn, may be made upon the oppressed population which is allowed to remain, or upon the territory alone, after removal of the population and the colonization by the oppressor's own nationals.[5]

The term caught on immediately. It was used in international legal discourse after the end of World War II and featured in the Nuremberg trials. In December 1948, a Convention for the Prevention of Genocide was approved by the United Nations.[6] Although the formulation was less comprehensive (due to pressure from the Soviet Union political genocide was not included), the definition still set a pattern. In later genocide research, which has developed enormously since the beginning of the 1980s and peaked during the past decade, many scholars proposed differing definitions. However, the need for a clear set of basic characteristics for defining a murderous event as "genocide" has kept the concept within the realm of the social sciences, although the term is widely used (and misused) in present-day lay and scholarly discourse. British genocide sociologist Martin Shaw has even tried to make the case for defining the concept and understanding the phenomenon of genocide based on the "structure of the conflict" rather than the intentions of the perpetrators.[7] For an historian this is a very questionable—not to say absurd—approach, because it downplays intentions as a major component of the human motivation for action.

In contrast, the term "Holocaust" and its equivalents (like *Shoah*, *Churbn*, and others) emerged in an entirely different way. They were all pre-existing words that were gradually embraced in popular discourse to designate the events that befell the Jews between 1933 and 1945. They were somewhat vague insofar as what they were meant to designate, but they had in common that their scope was limited to the fate of the Jews. In the beginning, some of them had a strong emotional component, but they were gradually accepted by scholars in the wake of their use in popular discourse.[8]

The terms genocide and Holocaust thus have very different origins and connotations, giving rise to important methodological questions regarding their use and the relationship between them. This in turn has repercussions for the study and understanding of antisemitism.

II. The Holocaust: Scope and Motivations

Attempts to properly understand the Holocaust have given rise to decades of research. Explanations have focused on a variety of issues, but it is commonly accepted that its ultimate purpose was to wipe out the Jewish people. It is also widely agreed that the

---

5 Rapahel Lemkin, *Axis Rule in Occupied Europe: Laws of Occupation—Analysis of Government—Proposals for Redress* (Washington, D.C.: Carnegie Endowment for International Peace, 1944).

6 UN General Assembly Resolution 260 (III) of 9 December 1948 (Prevention and Punishment of the Crime of Genocide).

7 Martin Shaw, *What is Genocide?* (Cambridge: Polity Press, 2007), 4.

8 For a short analysis of the use of terminology, see Dan Michman, "The Jewish Dimension of the Holocaust in Dire Straits? Current Challenges of Interpretation and Scope," in *Jewish Histories of the Holocaust: New Transnational Approaches*, ed. Norman Goda (New York: Berghahn, 2014), 17-38.

Holocaust includes the non-lethal anti-Jewish policies of the 1930s in Germany (which are usually perceived as paving the way for the campaign of extermination), that it was an enterprise encompassing the whole of Europe and even some areas beyond it, that its anti-Jewish drive was an essential feature that had its roots in European traditions, and that it is central to understanding the entire Nazi project.[9]

However, the "genocide angle," if we may call it that, has had an impact on the way some scholars have reinterpreted and recontextualized the Holocaust, as in the case of the following three influential studies: Donald Bloxham's *The Final Solution: A Genocide*, Mark Mazower's *Hitler's Empire*, and Timothy Snyder's *Bloodlands*. This paper does not analyze these books in detail—as this has already been done elsewhere—but focuses on those points that are essential to this particular discussion.

In the opening sentences of his book, Bloxham states that

> between 5,100,000 and 6,200,000 Jews were murdered during the Second World War, an episode the Nazis called the "final solution of the Jewish question." The world today knows it as the Holocaust. The subtitle I have chosen for this book—*A* Genocide—uses the indefinite article not to diminish the magnitude of the Holocaust but to encourage the reader to think of it as a particular example of a broader phenomenon.[10]

Bloxham, in short, says that the Holocaust is synonymous with the Final Solution, which is synonymous with the murder of about six million Jews. In other words, these are all different names for the same thing/event. The Holocaust is therefore just one example of a broader phenomenon known as genocide. Moreover, although the book deals with the historical development of the fate of the Jews, Bloxham ultimately regards the drive behind the Nazi project as being of an ethnic nature.

According to Mazower, the Nazis' main goal was to control Europe, and Hitler was nothing more than "a Greater German nationalist" whose aspirations should be seen within the context of European nationalist antagonisms after 1848. Nazi empire-building was a form of colonialism resulting from earlier examples of European imperial enterprises and had at its heart the quest for *Lebensraum*. As this *Lebensraum* lay to the east, Eastern Europe "must lie at the heart of any account of the Nazi empire." Hitler's imperial fantasy caused, *as a by-product*, the deaths of "millions of Russians, Poles, Jews and Belorussians"—in the "War of Annihilation" conducted against the Soviet Union (ch. 6). "The Final Solution: The Jewish Question" gets a separate chapter (ch. 12), but only in the context of the aforementioned war. The topic is dealt with as distinct from the enormous anti-Jewish enterprise of the 1930s (an issue described in two short and entirely insufficient paragraphs in an earlier chapter). "The Jews certainly occupied a special place in the political demonology of the Third Reich," according to Mazower. In his eyes, this statement, which does not describe what that "special place" was, suffices to explain why they were targeted. Moreover, he disregards ample research on the Nazis' views on Eastern Europe and Nazi "academic" research on Eastern European Jewry when he claims that the Germans had not

---

9 For an analysis of a series of these attempts, see Dan Michman, *Holocaust Historiography: A Jewish Perspective: Conceptualizations, Terminology, Approaches and Fundamental Issues* (London: Vallentine Mitchell, 2003), 9-58.

10 Donald Bloxham, *The Final Solution: A Genocide* (Oxford: Oxford University Press, 2008), 1.

foreseen (!) the consequences of their actions and that they "had somehow stumbled into the great centers of east European Jewry." Finally, he reiterates that the Jews "constituted only ... one of the regime's *ethnic* targets" (emphasis added) without explaining why non-Jewish Jews and unidentifiable Jews were also eagerly persecuted throughout Europe and even in North Africa. Indeed, he ignores the distinct nature of Nazi antisemitism and provides no framework for understanding the obsessiveness and intensity of the persecution of Jews and Judaism under the Nazi regime and by so many people—both German and non-German. In this context, it is quite interesting to note that, in this book, Mazower ignores his own detailed study on Greece,[11] in which he devotes much attention to the persecution and murder of the Greek Jews. To all this, Mazower adds that "it was thanks to Nazism that German soldiers and civilians ended up dying in numbers that were probably not far short of the toll of the Final Solution itself."[12] This twisted formulation, which leaves a bitter taste in the mouth, might have better been omitted.

Last but not least is Snyder's best-selling and award-winning book. *Bloodlands* is not just the title of the book but is presented as a historical concept describing a specific area of mass killings carried out between 1933 and 1948, even though they were carried out by different regimes, on the basis of different motives, and during different—though largely proximate—periods. In a lecture at Yad Vashem in 2011, Snyder summarized his argument as follows:

> the territories where the Holocaust took place ... where the Jews were killed ... overlap almost perfectly with a couple of other maps, one of these is where most of the victims of the Germans and Soviets [were] killed. ... Out of that 17 million people [who were killed by the Nazi and Soviet regimes throughout the territories they dominated], 14 million, including of course 5.5 million Jews ... were killed on those *bloodlands,* which is a very small part of that territory. ... If 14 million people are killed in a certain time and place we should take that seriously ... it seems rather interesting and perhaps of *fundamental importance that the killings of the two regimes were concentrated on this place and not elsewhere.* ... What I am describing is—*in simple numerical and geographical terms* [emphasis added]—the single worst bloodying in the history of the modern West. Nothing like this happened before and nothing like this has happened since.[13]

In his book Snyder, summarizes the argument as follows:

> the Germans and the Soviets ... [provoked] one another to ever greater crimes.... These atrocities shared a place, and they shared a time: the bloodlands between 1933 and 1945. To describe their course has been to introduce to European history its *central event* [emphasis added].[14]

---

11 Mark Mazower, *Inside Hitler's Greece: The Experience of Occupation, 1941-1944* (Yale: Yale University Press, 1993).

12 Mark Mazower, *Hitler's Empire: How the Nazis Ruled Europe* (New York, 2008). The quotes are from pp. 5, 4, 414, 12.

13 Transcript of Timothy Snyder's lecture at the Yad Vashem scholarly seminar, June 21, 2011, kept by this author. On the issue of numbers and terms, see also Timothy Snyder, *Bloodlands: Europe Between Hitler and Stalin* (New York: Basic Books, 2010), 409-14.

14 Snyder, *Bloodlands,* 380-81.

In short, the Holocaust describes the murder of the Jews, but it was part and parcel of a larger, bloodier event conducted by Hitler and Stalin. The act of murder stands central. "This is a study of the dying,"[15] says Snyder, which seems to imply that it emphasizes a particular moment—the final moment, to be clear—over causality and historical context. The reason why the sheer number of individual victims and the almost obsessive calculation of this figure are so important in his book is that they glue all the atrocities together.[16]

What do the three studies have in common? They reduce the Holocaust to a simple murder campaign by claiming that it had no special or extraordinary characteristics or dimensions. In doing so, they blur the Holocaust's unique nature and fold into larger murder campaigns. As a result, the nature of antisemitism in general and Nazi antisemitism in particular becomes unimportant. It is just another ethnic or social hatred like so many others that have caused mass violence and mass murder/ genocide at some point in history. In the words of a close colleague of Bloxham, Dirk Moses:

> Whether similarities [between the Holocaust and other genocides] are more significant than the differences is ultimately a political and philosophical, rather than a historical question.... Uniqueness is not a category for historical research; it is a religious or metaphysical category.[17]

III. Understanding the Holocaust as a product of Nazi antisemitism

I have previously analyzed the core characteristics of the Holocaust in great depth.[18] In the following, I will focus on the key factors that are essential to our discussion.

The vision that stood at the heart of the entire Nazi anti-Jewish enterprise was that the world—the universe—should be entirely cleansed of the "Jewish idea" of human equality—an idea that polluted, haunted, and undermined the world because it ran counter to the "natural" principle of hierarchy. In a revealing piece of testimony provided in 1946, SS-man Dieter Wisliceny, one of Adolf Eichmann's aides, explained that in Nazism's view

> the world is directed by forces of good and evil. According to this view, the principle of evil was *embodied* in the Jews [emphasis added]. ... This world of images is totally incomprehensible in logical or rational terms. ... Millions of people believed these things ... something that can be compared only to similar phenomena from the Middle Ages, such as the mania of witches (*Hexenwahn*).[19]

---

15 Ibid., 410.

16 The calculation of victim numbers also plays an important role in Mazower's book. See Mazower, introduction to *Hitler's Empire*, especially pp. 4 and 12.

17 A. Dirk Moses, "Conceptual Blockages and Definitional Dilemmas in the 'Racial Century': Genocides of Indigenous Peoples and the Holocaust," *Patterns of Prejudice* 36, no. 4 (2002): 7-36. The quote is from p. 1.

18 See, e.g., Dan Michman, *Holocaust Historiography*.

19 Dieter Wisliceny, "Bericht," Bratislava, November 18, 1946, Yad Vashem Archives, M-5/162, p. 8ff. See Dan Michman, "Täteraussagen und Geschichtswissenschaft: Der Fall Dieter Wisliceny und der Entscheidungsprozess zur 'Endlösung,'" in *Deutsche, Juden, Völkermord. Der Holocaust als Geschichte und Gegenwart*, ed. Jürgen Matthäus and Klaus-Michael Mallmann

In other words, the Jewish spirit had to be exorcised, and one of the most effective ways to achieve that goal was through the removal of its human-like carriers—the Jews—as well as through a Sisyphean *Kampf* (struggle) against all expressions of "Jewishness." Yet, Jewishness was not what Jews perceive as such—Jewish religious life, tradition, community, and language—but all kinds of ideas and political systems that are based on and/or promote equality. The *jüdischen Geist* had polluted the universe. It had penetrated into political systems, legal thinking, and daily life, and it had done so though a variety of channels, such as academia, books, theater, music, and art.

This idea had earlier origins. There was a long-standing European (or Western) tradition of casting "Judaism" as the enemy of "life."[20] Jews could be healed up to a certain point, but Judaism remained evil. This changed during the second half of the nineteenth century, which saw enormous political, economic, and social upheaval, as well as scientific racism. According to the modern antisemitism that developed during this period, the Jews could no longer be healed. On the contrary, they came to be viewed as the carriers of the virus-like "Jewish spirit."

Hitler's world view developed in this context. Within his grand vision to restructure the world on the basis of the racial principle, the war against the Jews became a central obsession that dominated his entire political career. In September 1919, in his first political writings, he differentiated between emotional antisemitism, which gave rise to pogroms every now and then but then retreated, allowing people to interact with Jews again, and *Antisemitismus der Vernunft* (rational antisemitism), which was more systematic. The goal of rational antisemitism was "die Entfernung der Juden überhaupt" (the total removal of the Jews),[21] and this would remain the guiding principle of Hitler's entire enterprise.

Hitler proved to be successful transformational leader, that is to say, a leader who has the ability to activate people to such a degree that society is changed. He was able to recruit people from all levels of German society to his anti-Jewish enterprise because the ingredients were not entirely new and well suited to the post-World War I economic, social, and psychological crisis gripping German and European society.

Hitler's extreme vision was shared by intellectuals as well as by low-level functionaries "working toward the *Führer*." As early as 1929, the leading philosopher of the period, Martin Heidegger, wrote in a personal letter that Germany faced a choice

---

(Darmstadt: Wissenschaftliche Buchgemeinschaft, 2006), 209-10. On the identification of Jews with the devil in Christian tradition, see the still valuable study by Joshua Trachtenberg, *The Devil and the Jews: The Medieval Conception of the Jew and Its Relation to Modern Antisemitism* (New Haven, CT: Yale University Press, 1943). On the historical alleged connection between Jews and witchcraft in medieval and early modern Europe, see Ronnie Po-Chia Hsia, "Witchcraft, Magic and the Jews in Late Medieval and Early Modern Germany," in *From Witness to Witchcraft: Jews and Judaism in Medieval Christian Thought*, ed. Jeremy Cohen (Wiesbaden: Harrassowitz Verlag, 1996), 419-33.

20 See David Nirenberg, *Anti-Judaism: The Western Tradition* (New York: W.W. Norton, 2013); and Michael Walzer, "Imaginary Jews," review of *Anti-Judaism: The Western Tradition*, by David Nirenberg, *New York Review of Books*, March 20, 2014.

21 Eberhard Jäckel, *Hitler. Sämtliche Aufzeichnungen 1905-1924* (Stuttgart: Deutsche Verlags-Anstalt, 1980), 88-90.

between strengthening German spiritual life through its reconnection to the soil and the "growing Judaization in both the broader and restricted meaning."[22] On April 6, 1933, only two months after Hitler's ascent to power, a draft law "to regulate the status of the Jews" prepared by an inter-ministerial committee stated that the goal of anti-Jewish policies should be "to use this unique moment to purify the German people and liberate it from the alien power which had been controlling it hitherto in its own home, in overt and covert ways which were an existential danger." All efforts had to be combined to create the tools to enable the immediate eradication of this "overt and covert" Jewry from all leading positions in all spheres of German life.[23] Five years later, on April 9, 1938, the Jewish Department (II 112) of the SS's *Sicherheitsdienst* (SD) security service formulated the framework for action as follows: "the task when carrying out the solution of the Jewish question remains *as before*—their removal from the national body in both the *practical and spiritual meaning* [emphasis added]."[24]

Many more examples of this attitude can be found in letters of soldiers, pamphlets, academic conferences, and so forth. Among the many enemies of Nazi Germany, the Jews were the only group to which the terms "world" or "international" were attributed (e.g. *Weltjudentum* or *internationales Judentum*). Jews were described as being everywhere in the world. Moreover, as SD expert Paul Zapp wrote in 1943, they were the "binding element of the obstacle front of all adversaries of National-Socialism."[25] The all-embracing campaign against the Jewish spirit also included acts of self-purification, the battle for the de-Judaization (*Entjudungskampf*) of the German language.[26] Similarly, in 1936, the well-known philosopher and jurist Carl Schmitt called upon the German legal profession to fight against the "Jewish spirit" that had penetrated into and polluted German legal thought.[27]

---

22 Letter quoted in extenso in Ulrich Sieg, "Die Verjudung des deutschen Geistes," *Die Zeit*, December 22, 1989. See also Timothy O'Hagan, "Philosophy in a Dark Time: Martin Heidegger and the Third Reich," in *Liber Amicorum Pascal Engel*, ed. Julien Durlant, David Fassio and Anne Meylan (Université de Genève, Faculté des lettres, Département de philosophie, 2014), 944-60, available at http://www.unige.ch/lettres/philo/publications/engel/liberamicorum.

23 See "Der nicht realisierte Entwurf eines Gesetzes 'zur Regelung der Stellung der Juden,' vom 6. April 1933," *Verfolgung und Ermordung der europäischen Juden durch das nationalsozialistische Deutschland 1933-1945*, vol. 1, *Deutsches Reich 1933-1937*, ed. Wolf Gruner (Munich: Oldenbourg, 2008), 122.

24 "SD-Hauptamt/Sonderkommando II 112 Wien, an II 1, Betr. Unterabschnittstagung am 11.4.38," Bundesarchiv Berlin, R58/982.

25 This is a quote from SD expert Paul Zapp's educational essay "Das Judentum als tragendes Element der weltanschaulichen Gegnerfront," as quoted in Konrad Kwiet, "Paul Zapp—Vordenker und Vollstrecker der Judenvernichtung," in *Karrieren der Gewalt. Nationalsozialistische Täterbiographien*, ed. Klaus-Michael Mallmann and Gerhard Paul (Darmstadt: Deutsche Buchgesellschaft, 2005), 254-55.

26 Thomas Pegelow Kaplan, "Rethinking Nazi Violence: Linguistic Injuries, Physical Brutalities, and Dictatorship Building" (paper presented at an international conference on "Violence and Politics in Germany: Origins and Consequences of Nazism," Bar-Ilan University and Tel Aviv University, January 13-14, 2013).

27 "Schlußwort des Reichsgruppenwalters Prof. Dr. Carl Schmitt," in Carl Schmitt, "Die deutsche Rechtswissenschaft im Kampf gegen den jüdischen Geist: Schlußwort auf der Tagung der Reichsgruppe Hochschullehrer des NSRB vom 3. und 4. Oktober 1936," *Deutsche Juristen-Zeitung* 41 (1936), columns 1193-99.

Thus, from the moment of Hitler's ascent to power, we can observe an explosion of attempts to achieve the goal of the "total removal" of the Jews. What exactly did "total removal" mean? That was not clear, not even to Hitler, which explains why this enterprise took many different forms that were neither complementary nor contradictory. They included attempts by many actors and ideologues to translate this goal into actions—whether political, economic, intellectual, legal, linguistic or otherwise—that they believed would bring about its achievement. It was a trial-and-error process, and the evolving historical realities allowed for the adoption of ever more extreme methods. This explains the planned, bureaucratic measures as well as the improvised, chaotic popular actions that took place side by side. The comprehensive murder campaign started in the context of the invasion of the Soviet Union in June 1941 but subsequently crystallized and engulfed all parts of the European continent controlled or influenced by the Nazis (and was about to spill over to other parts of the world). The murder of more than 300,000 Jews by the Romanian regime, the eagerness of the Slovak authorities to deport the country's Jews, and the collaboration of many local populations throughout Europe (e.g. in Vichy France, Bulgaria, Hungary, Norway, the Netherlands, and elsewhere) show that the Nazi's campaign to eradicate the Jews had a strong European dimension. This is not surprising given that it had its roots in Europe's anti-Jewish tradition.

The Holocaust-era anti-Jewish campaign was an attempt to eradicate Jews *and* Jewry. This was not a simple process given the realities of the Jewish world and individual Jews, who in many cases were integrated in society, widely scattered, and often unidentifiable. The campaign to eradicate the Jews relied on various means of identification, including legal definitions, visual markings, and so forth. Hitler was central to the Holocaust: he came up with the goal of "total removal," and his ascent to power initiated the anti-Jewish campaign. However, the implementation of this goal was not a simple top-down process and was not implemented solely by German Nazis. In fact—and this is one of the key conclusions of this paper—Nazi antisemitism activated and radicalized other types of antisemitism that were part of the Christian-European anti-Jewish tradition. These antisemitisms—plural!—contributed enormously to the success of the whole enterprise.

When the option of mass murder arose, it played a decisive role in the adoption of the goal of getting rid of all Jews everywhere, but it did not turn it into the Nazi's *exclusive goal*. The murder of close to six million Jews was only one of several goals of the Final Solution, which in turn was only one, albeit extreme and irreversible, chapter of the Holocaust. The main goal of the Holocaust—the Nazi's anti-Jewish and anti-Jewishness enterprise—went beyond the physical extermination of the Jews: its aim—"die Entfernung der Juden überhaupt"—was to rid the world of the "Jewish spirit" and its carriers, the Jews.

CONCLUSION

So what are the reasons for this failure to understand or acknowledge the unique scope and nature of the Holocaust in the aforementioned studies, as well as other, more recent ones. Does this "misunderstanding" merely result from a lack of knowledge of the specific characteristics of Nazi antisemitism, or are there other factors at play? Sometimes it is indeed the result of insufficient familiarity with the relevant sources. In other cases, however, efforts to downplay the true motivations behind the Holocaust result from non-scholarly considerations, such as competing victimhoods, political correctness, anti-Israelism, and perhaps even a covert form of new antisemitism. A detailed analysis of the reasons for this omission does not fall within the scope of this paper, but the issue is undoubtedly deserving of further study.